VISUAL QUICKSTART GUIDE

JOOMLA!

Marni Derr and Tanya Symes

Peachpit Press

Visual QuickStart Guide
Joomla!
Marni Derr and Tanya Symes

Peachpit Press
1249 Eighth Street
Berkeley, CA 94710
510/524-2178
510/524-2221 (fax)

Find us on the Web at: www.peachpit.com
To report errors, please send a note to errata@peachpit.com

Peachpit is a division of Pearson Education

Project Editor: Nancy Peterson
Development Editor: Linda Laflamme
Production Editor: Rebecca Winter
Copyeditor: Darren Meiss
Compositor: WolfsonDesign
Indexer: Jack Lewis
Cover Design: Peachpit Press

ISBN-13 978-0-321-59058-9
ISBN-10 0-321-59058-9

9 8 7 6 5 4 3 2 1

Printed and bound in the United States of America

This book is dedicated to open source developers and the Joomla community. Without you this book would not be possible.

Acknowledgements

When we first conceived of this book, we knew it would be a challenge to cover everything we wanted to cover yet keep the book from becoming too technical or overwhelming. As always it took many people to get this book into your hands, and we would like to extend our thanks to all.

First, thanks to our editors, Nancy, Linda, and Darren. Nancy who patiently pushed us to stay on schedule. To Linda for helping us to better explain the more obscure and vague concepts, and to Darren for having such a keen eye. To Rebecca and Owen for laying out the book so splendidly and putting up with our constant changes.

We would like to extend a very special thank you to our friend and instructor David McFarland for those simple words that started it all, "You should look into Joomla!"

And finally to all of our friends and family who always believed we could do it.

TABLE OF CONTENTS

INTRODUCTION

In the world of the web today, users are drawn to dynamic web sites. The more interactive the site, the more people feel engaged, as if they are an integral part of the site themselves. Not only do users expect to see a site constantly evolve and provide easily identifiable information, so do today's search engines. If you want to land high in the search engine rankings, you need to live up to these expectations.

The challenge of today's web sites is handling the amount of maintenance required to create and sustain a dynamic site, while ensuring the site responds quickly. Meeting this challenge may require knowledge in scripting languages, such as PHP, ASP, or ColdFusion; the ability to create the database, such as MySQL or Microsoft SQL; and the skill to add the interactive elements using Adobe Flash, JavaScript, or Ajax. Building and maintaining these features can be a daunting, if not difficult task, even with a full staff.

So what is the solution if your staff is overallocated? Or if you're a designer who's been asked to not only design a site but code it as well? Or if you're a small business owner who doesn't have a staff? Maybe you just have a great idea but don't know how you're going to create an entire site yourself. The solution is a web content management system. The solution is Joomla.

What is a Web Content Management System?

A *content management system* (CMS) creates a database repository for all your content, menus, dynamic elements, and text, using a graphical user interface. It then uses a template to display all your data as a web site. A content management system works like any software application: You input information and save it. The content management system writes the code that transforms the data into a web page.

Before content management systems and the popularity of Web 2.0, smaller web sites, and even some large ones, were commonly a series of static pages. A developer created *x* number of pages, placed content directly into individual HTML pages, and then placed *x* number of links so users could navigate to the content they needed. Even large dynamic sites, requiring a web team with coding and database skills, can have a heavy maintenance overhead. Now, with content management systems, a dynamic, data-driven site is accessible to everyone.

Why Use Joomla 1.5.x?

So why choose Joomla 1.5.x over other content management systems? The advantages are many:

- Joomla is easy to update.
- Joomla is easy to maintain.
- Setup and configuration are quick.
- Joomla is customizable.
- There are thousands of third-party developers and extensions to help customize your site.
- Creating custom templates is easy.
- Joomla is free.

For designers, Joomla offers added benefits:

- You don't have to have any coding experience.
- Presentation and content are completely separated by the CMS.
- Implementing a template is as quick as installing.

Who This Book Is For

This book is for creative professionals, covering the spectrum from web designers and developers to small and medium businesses and sole proprietorships. Even large corporations have implemented Joomla web sites. See Appendix B, "Resources" for some examples.

It is not necessary to know HTML, CSS, PHP, or JavaScript, or to understand databases, to create a complete Joomla web site. You can complete this book and have a fully functional web site at the end. If you are a web developer with coding skills, however, this book walks you through using all of the features Joomla has to offer, including creating custom templates with HTML and CSS. As always, a good understanding of web site usability and design is extremely helpful.

If you want to learn more about HTML/CSS, JavaScript, or PHP and MySQL, check out these Peachpit titles:

- *PHP and MySQL for Dynamic Web Sites: Visual QuickPro Guide*
- *JavaScript and Ajax for the Web: Visual QuickStart Guide, Seventh Edition*
- *HTML, XHTML, and CSS: Visual QuickStart Guide, Sixth Edition*

Joomla Requirements

Joomla has few requirements and will run on any Linux- or Windows-based web server with PHP and MySQL installed. Whether you are using a local or hosted server, Joomla requires the following to operate properly:

- A local web server and/or remote web server
- A MySQL database version 3.23 or greater
- PHP 4.2 or greater (5.1 recommended)
- A standards-compliant web browser, such as Firefox, Safari, or Internet Explorer

If you have not used or installed a local server before, we recommend installing a server package such as MAMP or XAMPP. For more information about installing MAMP or XAMPP, see Appendix A, "Local and Remote Servers."

About This Book

This book walks you through each feature and function of Joomla 1.5.x, such as installing and configuring; creating content; using components, modules, and plugins; managing links; and installing extensions.

- Chapter 1, "Installing Joomla"
  Here's where you begin. You'll learn to install Joomla on a local server.
- Chapter 2, "Getting Started"
  You'll get oriented in Joomla by taking an investigative tour of the administrative back end, navigation, and key features.
- Chapter 3, "Adding Your Content"
  Content is the heart of any web site. Here's where you'll learn how to develop all of your content using articles and then organize the content by creating sections and categories.
- Chapter 4, "Making Your Site Dynamic with Menus"
  Here's where you'll learn about all of the different menu types to create all the navigation for your site.
- Chapter 5, "Working with Modules"
  You'll learn to add flair and interactive elements to your site with Joomla's modules and components.
- Chapter 6, "Extending Your Site"
  Learn to extend your site further with advanced components and modules, third-party extensions, and plugins.
- Chapter 7, "Modifying Global Settings"
  Learn how to customize your global Joomla settings and how these global settings impact your web site.
- Chapter 8, "Engaging Your Users"
  Learn how to get your users involved in your site by adding content through the web site front end.
- Chapter 9, "Creating Joomla Templates"
  Here's where you'll learn to take any HMTL/CSS design and turn it into a Joomla template.
- Appendix A, "Local and Remote Servers"
  Covers installing a local server, uploading your site to a remote server, and creating backups.
- Appendix B, "Resources"
  Here you'll find a list of all the Joomla CSS classes and details of the configuration.php file, as well as some sample Joomla web sites.

Companion Web Site

You will find a companion web site for this book at www.writingyourdreams.com. From here you can provide feedback and also download all the files used throughout the book, errata sheets, and information and links on Joomla resources.

Installing Joomla

Installing Joomla is quick, simple, and takes about five minutes. Simply download the Joomla installation package and follow the installation wizard. Before running the installation make sure

- You have access to the Internet.
- Your local server is running.
- You know the location of your web server's root folder.

This chapter covers installing Joomla on a local server. For instructions on installing a local server, see Appendix A, "Local and Remote Servers."

✔ Tip

- We strongly recommend that you use a local server running on your computer when first creating and testing a web site. Running a local server gives you the opportunity to test all of your changes locally before deploying to a live web site.

Downloading Joomla

The Joomla installation files are in a single compressed file.

To download Joomla:

1. Open a web browser and go to www.joomla.org.
2. Click Download Latest.
3. Download Joomla 1.5.x, and then save this file to your desktop.

   There are three file types: .zip, .tar.gz, and .tar.bz2. Each one contains the same set of files. Because Windows and Macintosh operating systems can both extract a .zip file, this is the one we are going to use here.

✔ Tip

- Do not download any file that includes the word "patch." These files are for upgrading existing Joomla web sites and do not contain the full Joomla installation package.

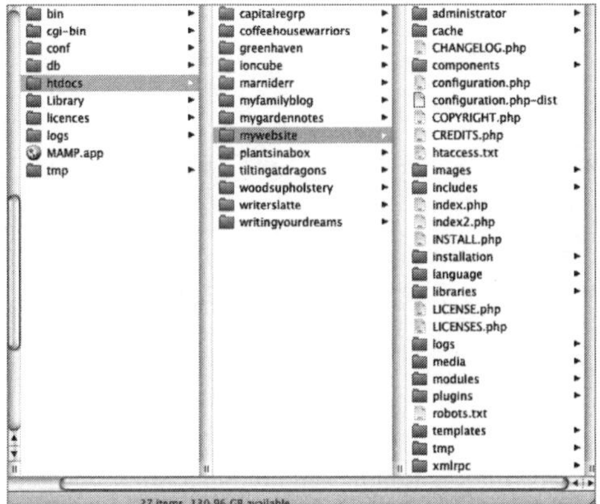

Figure 1.1 Root folder structure for Joomla

To extract the Joomla files:

1. Locate and open your web server's root folder.

   The name of the web server's root folder depends on the server type you are using. For example on a

   ▲ Local Apache web server, the folder is generally named *htdocs*.

   ▲ Local Windows IIS web server, the folder is generally named *www* or *webroot*.

   ▲ Hosted server, you will need to check with your service provider.

2. Copy the Joomla_1.5.x Full_Package.zip into the root folder.

3. Double-click, or use an extraction utility, to unzip the Joomla files.

   You now have a folder containing all the Joomla core files.

4. Rename this folder to `mywebsite`.

   We will refer to mywebsite throughout the book, feel free to replace this name with your domain name. Your file structure should now look like **Figure 1.1**.

Running the Joomla Installation

The Joomla installation wizard guides you through entering the information Joomla requires to run your web site.

You will need the following information during the installation process:

- Your MySQL database user name and password (generally *root* / *root*)
- A name for your database
- A valid email address for users to contact you
- An administrative password

To launch the Joomla installation wizard:

- In your web browser's address field, type `http://localhost/mywebsite`, and then press Enter.

  The installation wizard starts.

To select a language:

1. Select your language from the list.
2. Click Next to continue (**Figure 1.2**).

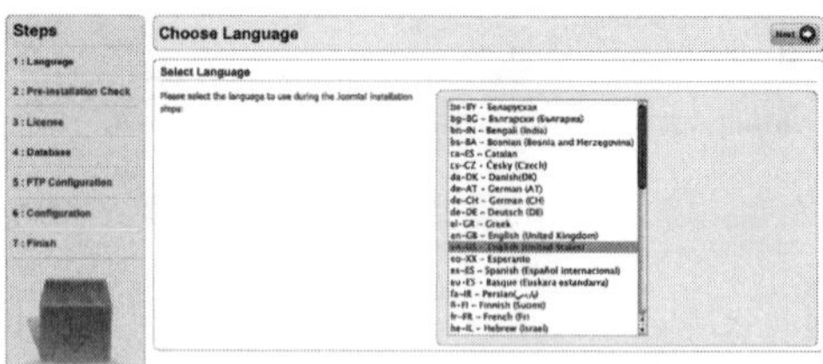

Figure 1.2 Step 1: Selecting your language

✔ Tips

- Joomla is UTF-8 compliant and supports many languages. After you select a language, the rest of the installation appears in the chosen language.
- On the Joomla.org web site, you can download language packages that run the administrative interface in the user's native language.

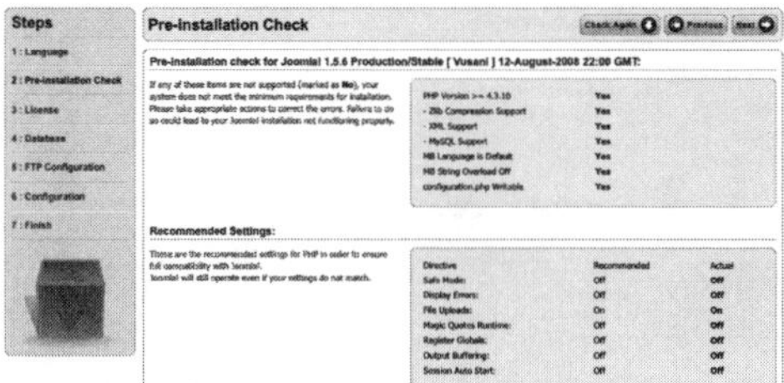

Figure 1.3 Step 2: Pre-installation check

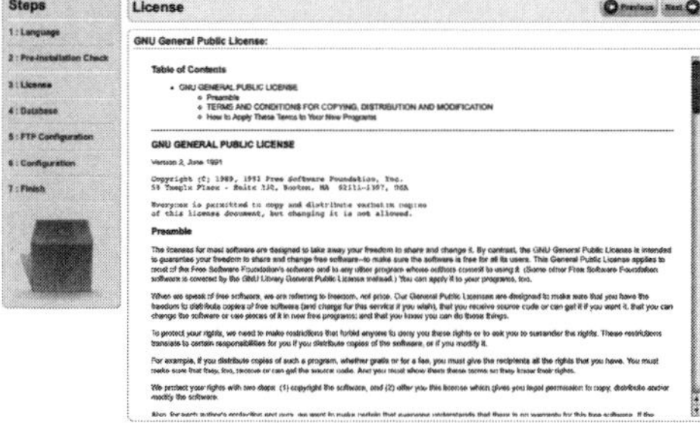

Figure 1.4 Step 3: License agreement

To pass the pre-installation check:

1. Verify that all items in the pre-installation checklist are marked Yes.

   If any of the items in the pre-installation checklist are displayed in red, the Joomla installation will fail. To correct these settings, see Appendix A, "Local and Remote Servers" before continuing with the installation process.

2. Review the recommended settings.

   Some of these settings are recommended but not required. If your actual settings differ from these recommendations, Joomla still operates normally. For administrative and security reasons, however, we highly recommend that you conform your settings to the Joomla list whenever possible.

3. After correcting the required settings, click Check Again.

4. Repeat this process until all items in the pre-installation checklist are marked Yes, as shown in **Figure 1.3**.

5. Click Next.

To accept the license agreement:

1. Read through the license agreement (**Figure 1.4**).

2. If you agree with the terms, click Next to continue.

   If you do not agree with the GPL/GNU licensing agreement, the installation will not continue.

To configure your web site's database:

1. From the Database Type menu, choose mysql.

   The settings on this page create your web site's database and enable Joomla to communicate with the database.

2. In the Host Name field, type *localhost.*
3. In the Username field, type your MySQL database user name.
4. In the Password field, type your MySQL database password.
5. In the Database Name field, type a name for your database.

   You don't have to be creative; shorter is better. Use a piece of your domain name; for example, if my domain name is www.mywebsite.com, I would create the database name mywebsitedb (**Figure 1.5**).

6. Do not alter the advanced settings. These settings are used when you have an existing database that needs to be either replaced or deleted before continuing.
7. Click Next to continue.

✔ Tip

- A database prefix is used when you want to run more than one web site from a single Joomla installation, or in some cases it can be required by your hosting provider. Never use *bak* as a database prefix. This prefix is already used by Joomla to create backups of your database tables.

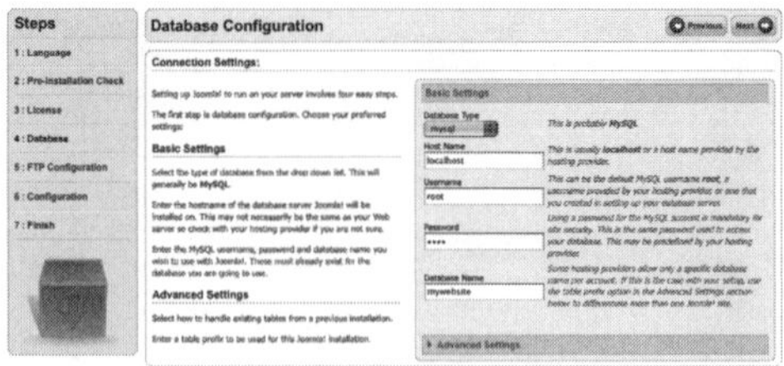

Figure 1.5 Step 4: Database configuration

Database User Names and Passwords

The MySQL server installs with a user name of root, and a password of root. For security reasons, developers change the default user name and password. For more information on how to change the user name and password, see Appendix A, "Local and Remote Servers."

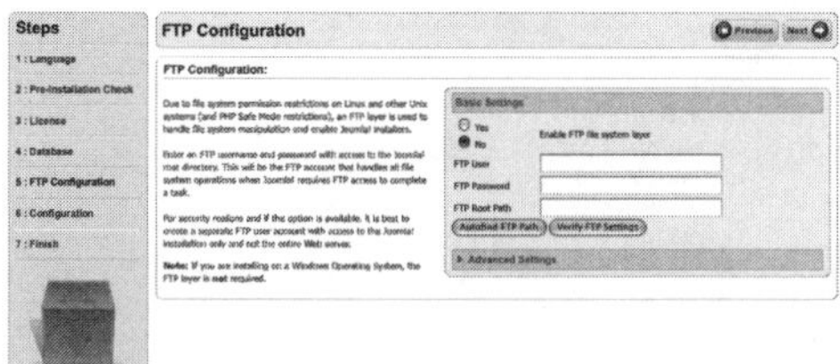

Figure 1.6 Step 5: FTP configuration

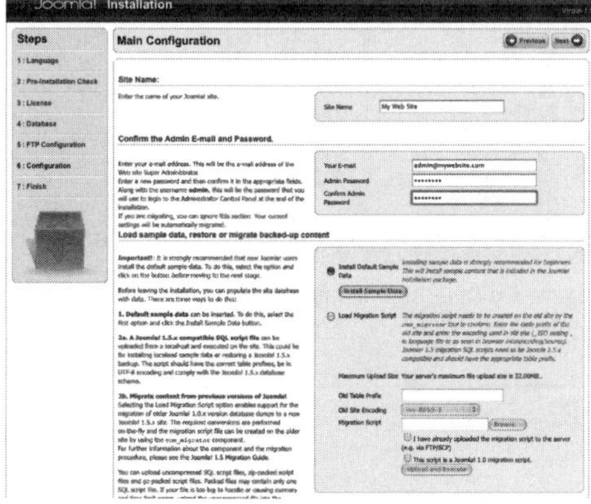

Figure 1.7 Step 6: Main configuration

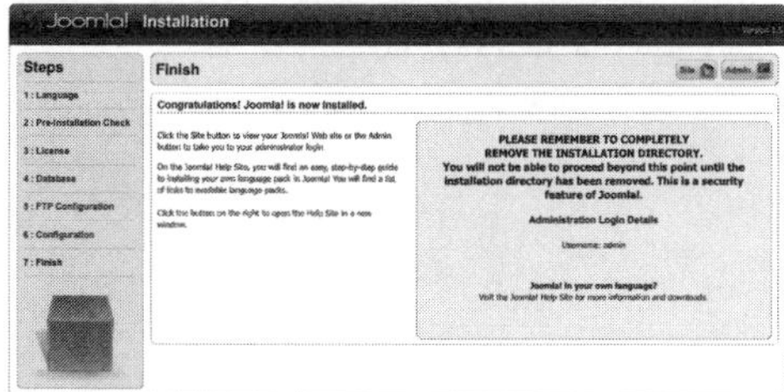

Figure 1.8 Installation complete

To configure FTP settings:

1. Click No to disable the FTP system layer (**Figure 1.6**).

   Due to issues with file permissions on Linux and Unix servers, an FTP layer was introduced in Joomla 1.5.x.

   Specific FTP settings are too varied to cover here. Check with your hosting provider for FTP information specific to your account.

   For now leave these fields blank. This information can be modified later from the administrative control panel.

2. Click Next to continue.

To configure the main settings:

1. In the Site Name field, type the name of your web site (**Figure 1.7**).

2. In the Your E-mail field, type an e-mail address for the super administrator of your web site.

3. In the Admin Password field, type a password.

4. The remaining information is for installing sample data, migrating a prior version, or importing an existing database. We are creating a new site so leave the defaults.

5. Click Next to continue. A box will open warning there is no sample data being installed. Click OK.

   Joomla is now installed, and your database tables have been created. However, you have one more thing to do. For security reasons you *must* delete the *install.php* file and the *installation* folder (**Figure 1.8**).

continues on next page

6. Go back to your root folder and delete the install.php file, as well as the folder named *installation* (**Figure 1.9**).

✔ Tip

- Be sure you write down your password! You will need it to log into the administrative back end of Joomla. The default super administrator is assigned the user name admin. You are able to change this later if needed, but not until after your initial login.

To view your new web site:

1. Open a web browser.
2. Type `http://localhost/mywebsite` and press Enter (**Figure 1.10**).

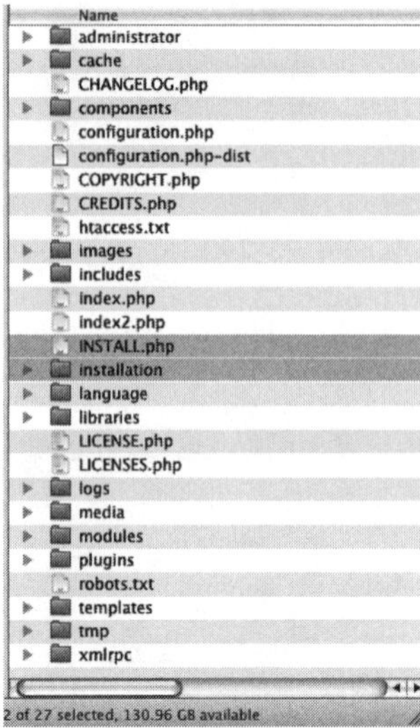

Figure 1.9 Deleting the install files

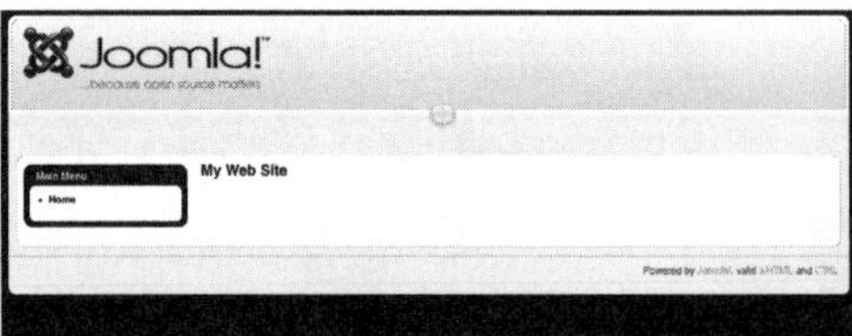

Figure 1.10 Your new web site

2

GETTING STARTED

The benefit of a web content management system, such as Joomla, is that all the code is handled for you as you enter content, build modules, enable components, and add navigation. Anyone familiar with computers, the web, and software applications can create a complete, interactive web site that displays in any standards-compliant browser without knowing a single line of code.

You create and manage your web site through what is called the administrative *back end*. Only super administrators, administrators, and managers can access the back end of the web site. All other users access the web site from the *front end* and can only add, edit, or delete content when you provide permission (see Chapter 8, "Engaging Your Users").

This chapter will familiarize you with the administrative back end navigation and where each feature is located. There are many ways to navigate through Joomla, however, and as you become more familiar with the program, you will develop your own way of moving around.

Starting Joomla

To access the back end of Joomla, you need to log in as one of the administrator types. An initial super administrator account was created during the installation process.

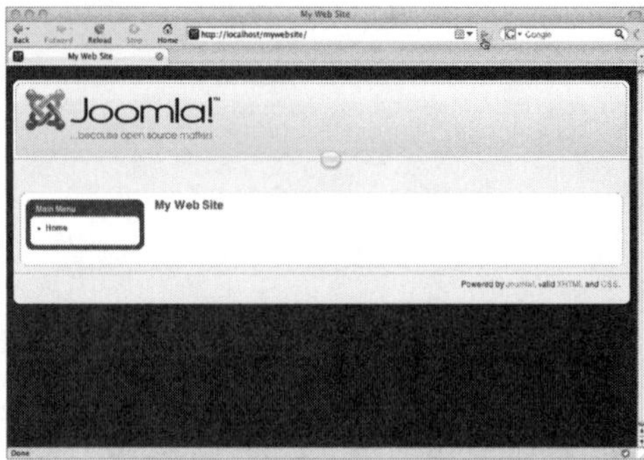

Figure 2.1 The home page

Figure 2.2 The administrative login form

To log in to the back end:

1. Open a web browser.
2. Type `localhost/mywebsite`, and then press Enter.

   The front end of your web site opens to the home page (**Figure 2.1**).

   Right now, there is no visible way to log in to the front or back end of the web site. Even without a login form or link created yet, however, you can still access the administrative login page.

   For creating front and back end login forms, see Chapter 6, "Extending Your Site."
3. In the browser address field, type `localhost/mywebsite/administrator`, and then press Enter.

   The super administrator login page opens (**Figure 2.2**).
4. In the Username field, type `admin`.
5. In the Password field, type the administrative password you created during the installation process.
6. Click Login. You must have a local server running before you can open Joomla.

Administrative User Types

- **Super administrators:** Have access to the entire site, back and front ends, and can perform any function.
- **Administrators:** Have access to the front and back end but cannot install extensions or modify super administrator accounts.
- **Managers:** Have access to the front and back end but are limited to media, content, components, and the main menu.

Using the Control Panel Page

When you first log in as an administrator, the Control Panel page opens (**Figure 2.3**). Joomla looks like any standard web page and consists of menus, toolbars, and icons. The icons are shortcuts to the most common tasks performed when creating content for your site. To learn what each icon does, consult the menu description of the same name.

To access the Control Panel page at any time:

- Choose Site > Control Panel.

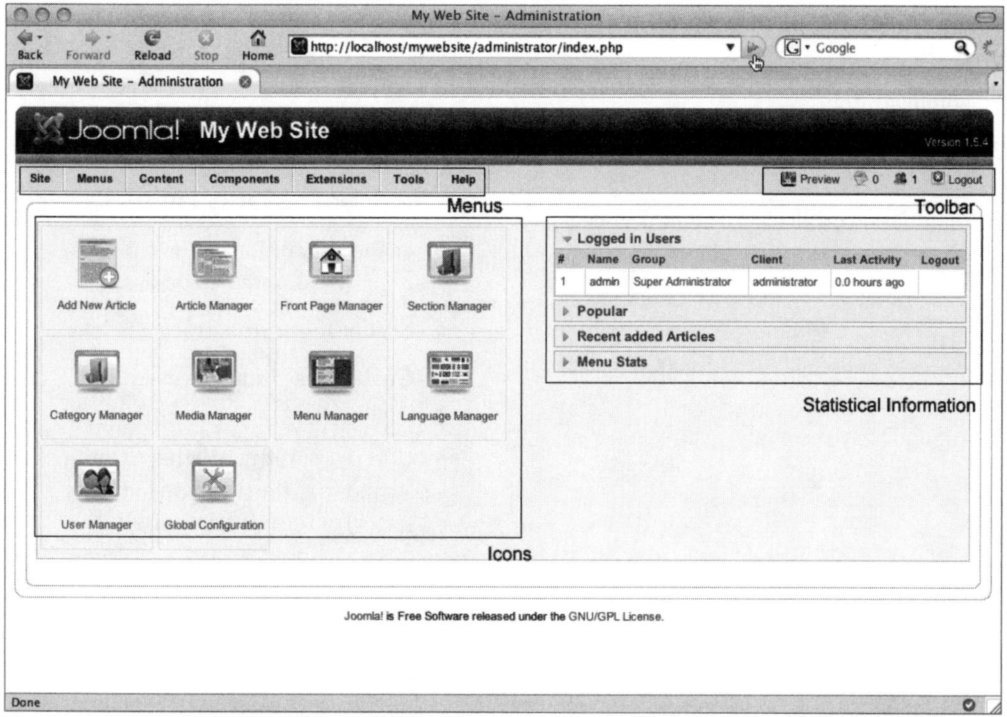

Figure 2.3 The Control Panel page

Viewing Site Information

On the right side of the Control Panel page is a list of statistical information related to your web site, such as who is currently logged in, the most popular articles on the site, the most recently added articles, and the number of items contained in your menus (**Figure 2.4**).

These statistics come in very handy while managing your site. Understanding how your site is being used helps you to create a better experience for your users.

For example, if you see a user that has not logged in for a few months, you can delete that user; you can send an inquiry e-mail; or you can watch for possible spammers.

Keeping track of popular and recently added articles helps manage when an article should be archived, or possibly put on the front page, and so on.

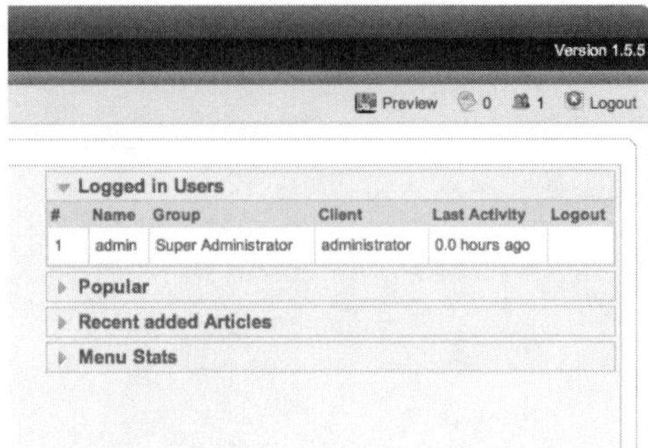

Figure 2.4 Web site statistics

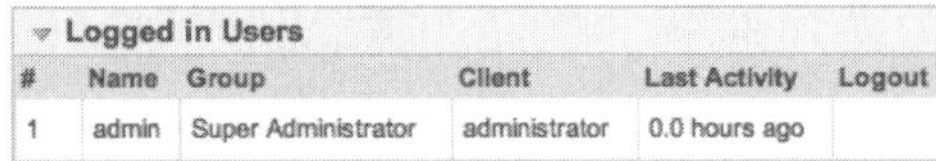

Logged in Users

#	Name	Group	Client	Last Activity	Logout
1	admin	Super Administrator	administrator	0.0 hours ago	

Figure 2.5 Logged in Users panel

To view user status information:

1. Log in to the back end as a super administrator.
2. Click the arrow next to "Logged in Users" (**Figure 2.5**).
   Information on all logged in users appears.

User Status Fields

- **#:** The item ID for this user. This is used by the system database.
- **Name:** The username used to login.
- **Group:** The group this user belongs to.
- **Client:** Identifies whether the user logged in to the back end (administrator) or the front end (site).
- **Last Activity:** The last time this user was logged in.
- **Logout:** A checkmark in this field shows the user is currently logged out of the site.

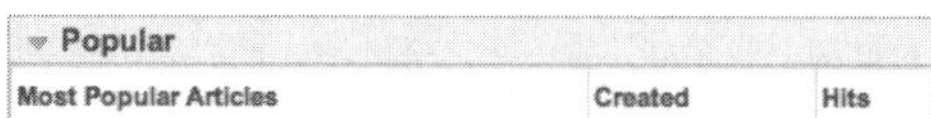

Figure 2.6 Most popular articles panel

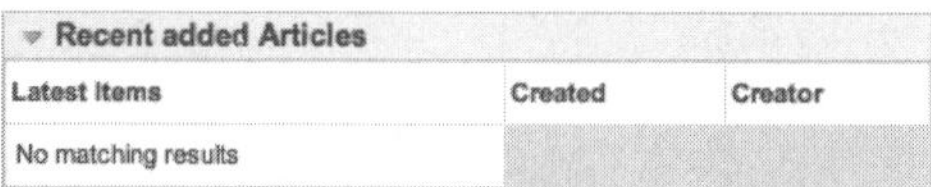

Figure 2.7 Recently added articles

Figure 2.8 Menu statistics

Popular Articles Fields

- **Most Popular Articles:** Lists the title of the most popular articles on the site. These are the articles that are getting the most views from users.
- **Created:** This is the date the article was created.
- **Hits:** The total number of hits this article has received.

Recent Added Article Fields

- **Latest Items:** The titles of the last number of articles added to the site.
- **Created:** The date the article was created.
- **Creator:** The user name of the person who created the article.

To view the most popular articles:

1. Log in to the back end as a super administrator.
2. Click the arrow next to Popular (**Figure 2.6**).

To view the most recently added articles:

1. Log in to the back end as a super administrator.
2. Click the arrow next to Recent Added Articles (**Figure 2.7**).

To view all current menus:

1. Log in to the back end as a super administrator.
2. Click the arrow next to Menu Stats.

   The list displays all the menus on your site and the number of menu items contained in each menu (**Figure 2.8**).

Using the Toolbar

The toolbar contains three links: Preview, Mail, and Logout. In addition, an icon shows the number of users logged in (**Figure 2.9**).

The Users Logged In icon tells you the total number of registered users currently logged in to your site. You can then use the "Logged in Users" panel to find out more information about these users. (For creating and managing user accounts see Chapter 3, "Adding Your Content.")

Figure 2.9 The control panel toolbar

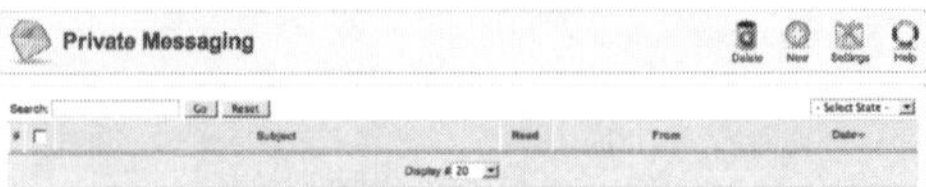

Figure 2.10 The super administrator Private Messaging Mail Manager

To preview the front end:

1. Log in to the back end as a super administrator.
2. Click the Preview icon.

   The Preview icon enables you to preview the front end of your web site from anywhere within the back end as you are making changes to the site.

To view super administrator system mail:

1. Log in to the back end as a super administrator.
2. Click the Mail icon.

   The Private Messaging page displays the number of messages you have in your inbox (**Figure 2.10**). For using the administrative mail feature, see Chapter 7, "Modifying Global Settings."

To log out of the back end:

- Click the Logout icon.

  This logs you out of the administrative back end and displays the front end.

Using the Site Menu

The Site menu contains options for managing and configuring sitewide settings. This menu contains links to the main Control Panel page, User Manager, Media Manager, and Global Configuration page (**Figure 2.11**).

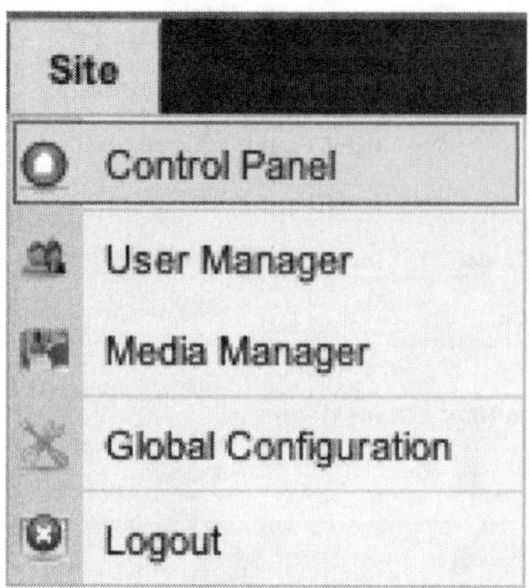

Figure 2.11 The Site menu

To open the Control Panel page:

- Choose Site > Control Panel.

To view the User Manager:

1. Log in to the back end as a super administrator.
2. Choose Site > User Manager.

   The User Manager lists *all* registered users on your web site (**Figure 2.12**).

   If the sample data was not installed, the web site currently has one user, the super administrator.

continues on next page

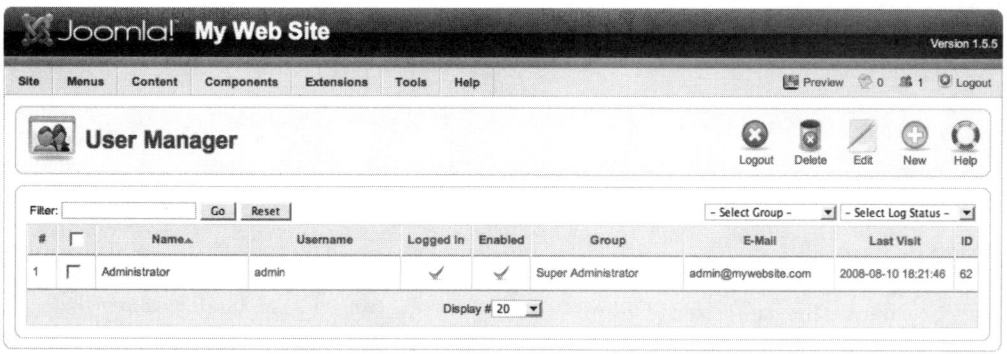

Figure 2.12 The User Manager

3. Click Administrator.

   This opens the User details screen (**Figure 2.13**).

4. In the User Details area, enter your name in the Name field.

   If you want to be known as Administrator when adding articles or sending e-mails, you can leave this as is.

   Leave all other fields at the default settings for now. For creating and managing user details, see Chapter 3, "Adding Your Content."

5. Click Save.

   Your full name is now displayed as a user that is part of the super administrator group (**Figure 2.14**).

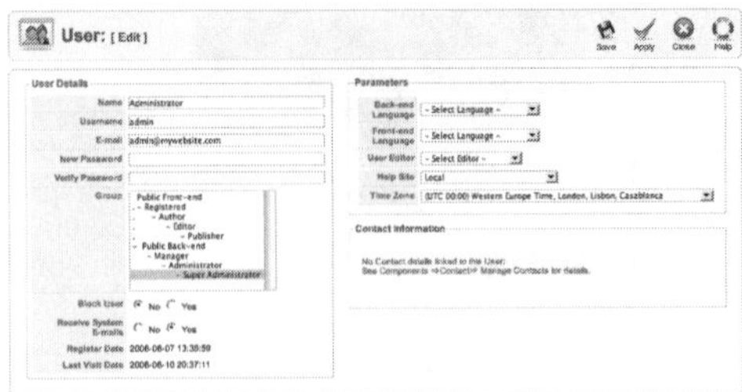

Figure 2.13 The User details page

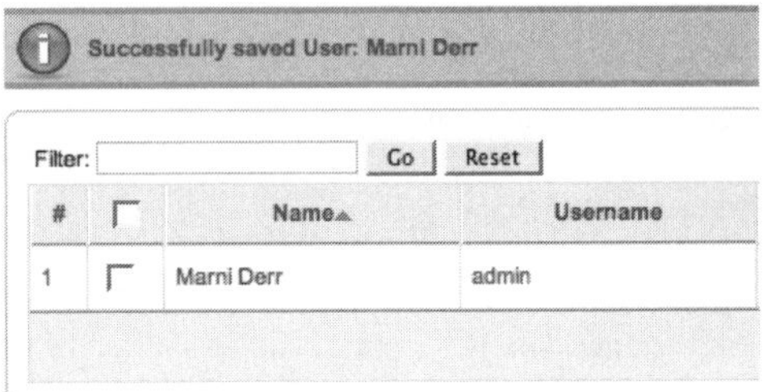

Figure 2.14 Administrator name change

User Manager Fields

- **Name:** The full name of the user. Clicking the name opens that user's details for editing.
- **Username:** The name used to log in.
- **Logged In:** A checkmark in this field means the user is currently logged in to the site.
- **Enabled:** A checkmark in this field means the user account is active.
- **Group:** Displays the group this user belongs to.
- **E-Mail:** Displays the user's email address. Clicking the address opens your email program to send this user a message.
- **Last Visit:** The date and time this user last logged in to the web site.
- **ID:** The database ID number for this user.

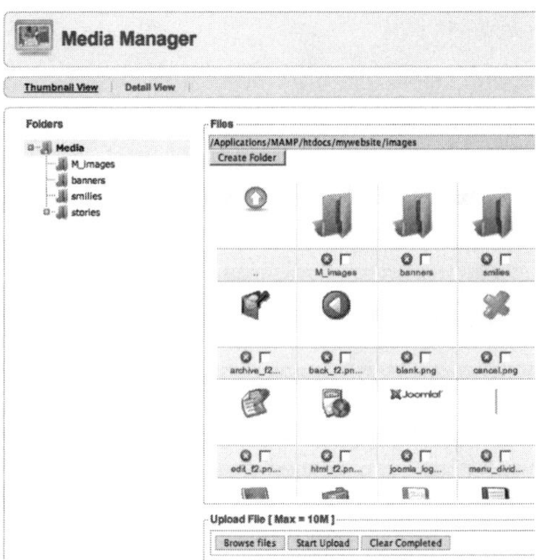

Figure 2.15 The Media Manager

To view the Media Manager:

1. Log in to the back end as a super administrator.
2. Choose Site > Media Manager.

   The Media Manager is a complete directory of all the media files stored on your site. You will see all the images currently used by the Joomla front and back ends (**Figure 2.15**).

   From here you can upload new media files, delete media files, and create media file directories (see Chapter 3, "Adding Your Content").
3. Click the Detail View link.

   This view displays the image name, file dimensions, and file size.

To view the Global Configuration pages:

1. Log in to the back end as a super administrator.
2. Choose Site > Global Configuration (**Figure 2.16**).

   There are three types of global configuration pages: Site, System, and Server.
3. Click the Site link.

   Site settings are *about* your site. Taking the site online or offline, entering metadata information used by search engines, and the system-wide search engine optimization (SEO) settings are all set under Site global configuration. (see Chapter 7, "Modifying Global Settings").

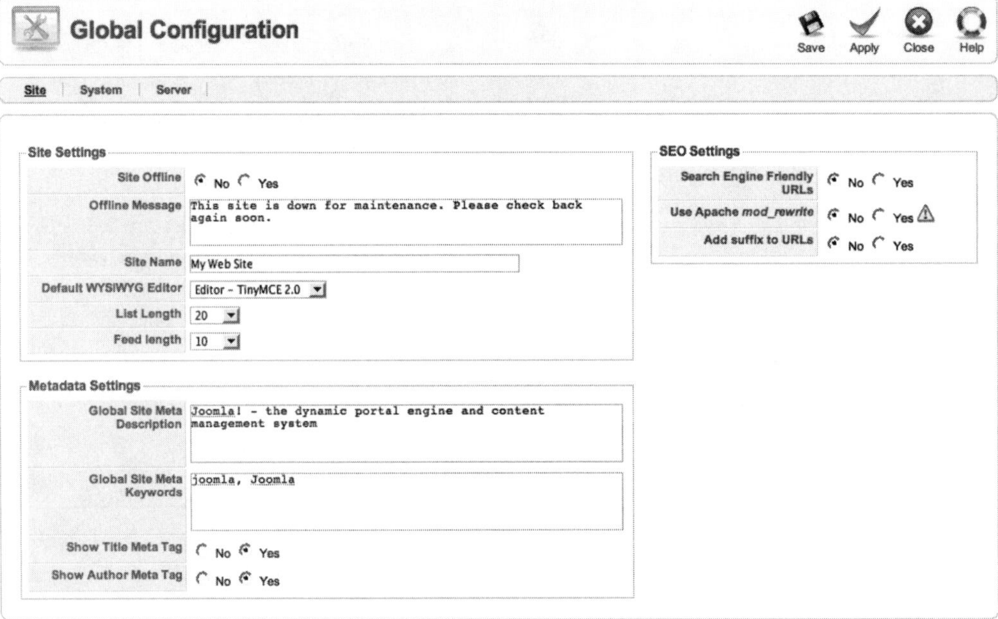

Figure 2.16 The Global Configuration pages

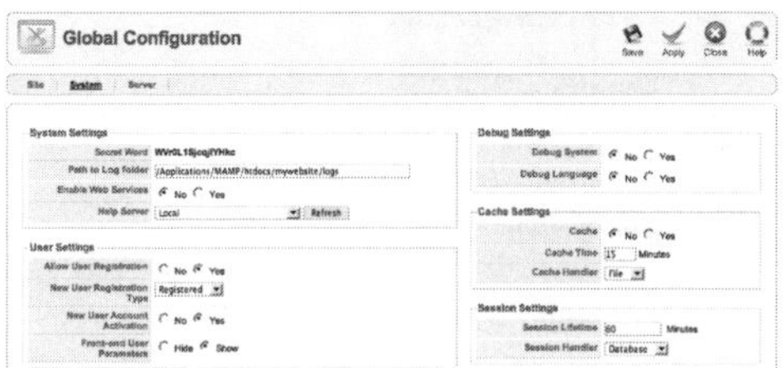

Figure 2.17 The System Global Configuration page

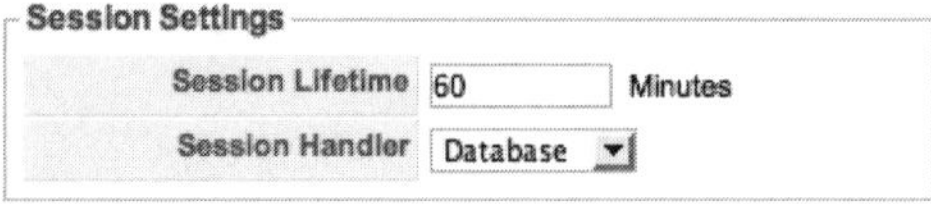

Figure 2.18 The Session Lifetime field

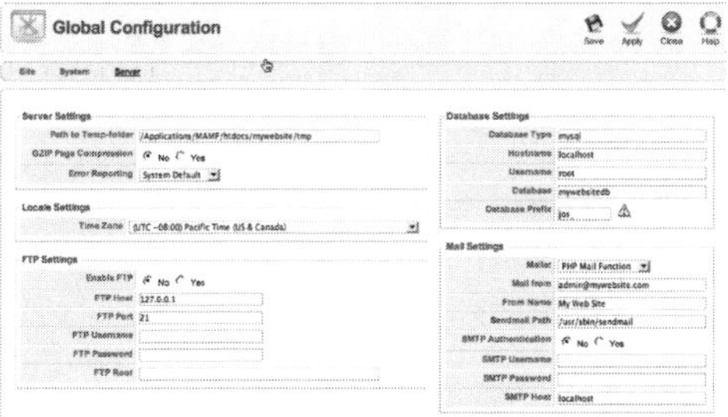

Figure 2.19 The Server Global Configuration page

Figure 2.20 Setting the web server time

4. Click the System link.

   System settings are global controls for your site, enabling user registration, media controls, debugging, web server cache settings, and sessions settings (**Figure 2.17**).

5. In the Session Settings area, enter `60` in the Session Lifetime field.

   This is the maximum amount of time a user remains logged in to the web site with no activity (**Figure 2.18**).

6. Click Apply.

7. Click the Server link.

   These are the settings that allow Joomla to communicate with your web server (**Figure 2.19**). You should recognize these settings from the installation. Generally these settings are not modified unless you are uploading your site to a remote server, or your FTP or mail settings have changed (see Chapter 7, "Modifying Global Settings").

8. In the Locale Settings area, select your time zone (**Figure 2.20**).

   This sets the base time for your web site. For example, you need to bring the site down for maintenance and state the site would be live again by 4:00 pm. This is the base for your *server* time.

9. Click Save.

To log out of the back end:

- Choose Site > Logout to log out of the back end of the web site and return to the front end home page.

Using the Menus Menu

The Menus menu contains the Menu Manager, Menu Trash, and all the menu modules you create for your web site (**Figure 2.21**). This menu changes and grows as you add new menu types. For example, most web sites have a main menu, a user menu, a footer menu, and some specialized menus.

Figure 2.21 The Menus menu

One of the more difficult concepts about a web content management system is that the menus control everything that appears on the pages of your web site. Menus link to sections, components, modules, and content. Without a menu link, content cannot be called from the database to display on a page.

To view the Menu Manager:

1. Log in to the back end as a super administrator.
2. Choose Menus > Menu Manager.

   If the Joomla installation was installed without sample data, the menu and the Menu Manager will have only one menu module already created, the Main Menu (**Figure 2.22**).

   From the Menu Manager you can copy, delete, edit, or add new menu modules (see Chapter 4, "Making Your Site Dynamic with Menus").

   The Main Menu is generally the top level of navigation, although you can give menus any name you like. As you add menus, they will appear in this list.

Figure 2.22 The Menu Manager

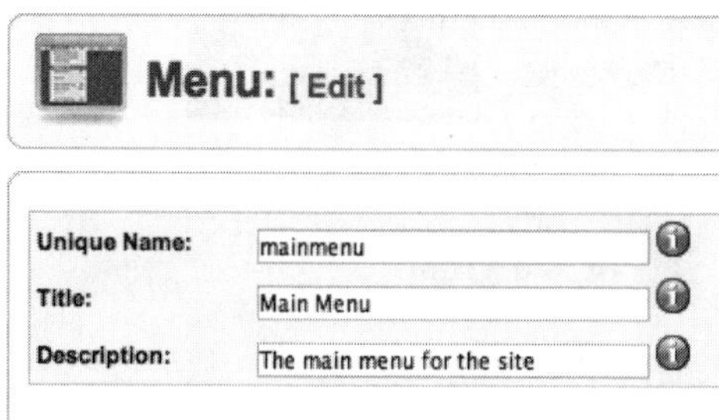

Figure 2.23 The menu details screen

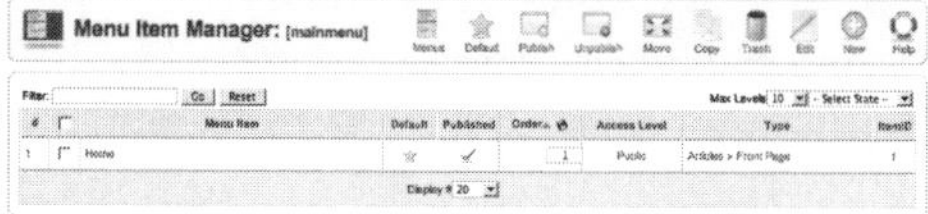

Figure 2.24 The Main Menu Item Manager

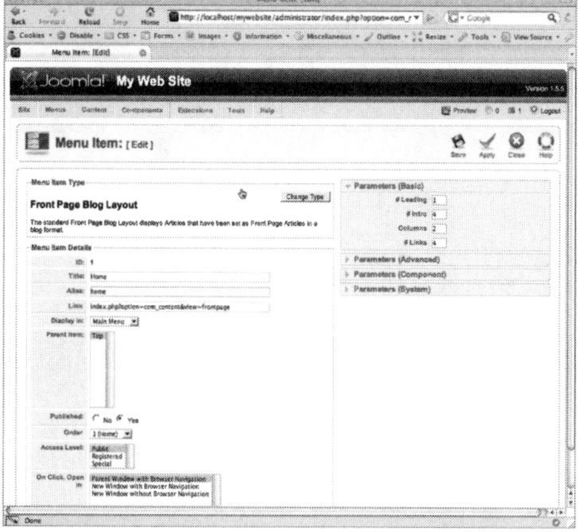

Figure 2.25 The Menu Item details edit page

3. Click the Main Menu link.

   This is where the name, title, and description are set for the main menu (**Figure 2.23**).

4. Click Cancel to go back to the Menu Manager.

To view menu item details:

1. Log in to the back end as a super administrator.

2. Choose Menus > Main Menu.

   This opens the Menu Item Manager for the main menu (**Figure 2.24**). As additional menus are added, selecting the menu link will open the Item Manager for that specific menu (see Chapter 4, "Making Your Site Dynamic with Menus").

3. Click the Home link from the Menu Item Manager (**Figure 2.25**).

Menu Manager Fields

- **Title:** The title of the menu module. Clicking the title will take you to the menu details.
- **Type:** The menu type needed by Joomla to identify this menu.
- **Menu Item(s):** Clicking this icon will take you to the Menu Item Manager.
- **#Published:** The number of published menu items in this menu.
- **#Unpublished:** The number of unpublished items in this menu.
- **#Trash:** The number of menu items in the menu trash.
- **#Modules:** The number of modules associated with this menu.
- **ID:** The database ID number for this menu.

Using the Content Menu

The Content menu provides access to the managers that organize the content on your web site (**Figure 2.26**).

Because Chapter 3, "Adding Your Content" covers sections, categories, and articles in detail, this section just lists the highlights.

The Content menu choices are:

- **Article Manager:** The Article Manager lets you manage all the *articles*, or content, on your site. From the Article Manager you can archive, publish, move, edit, delete, change parameters, assign articles to sections and categories, or add new pieces of content (**Figure 2.27**).
- **Article Trash:** The Article Trash behaves just like a computer trash or recycle bin. If you delete an article but decide later you really wanted to keep that content after all, you can go to the Article Trash Manager and restore it. If you delete an article from the Trash Manager, however, just like emptying your trash, it will be completely deleted from your database.

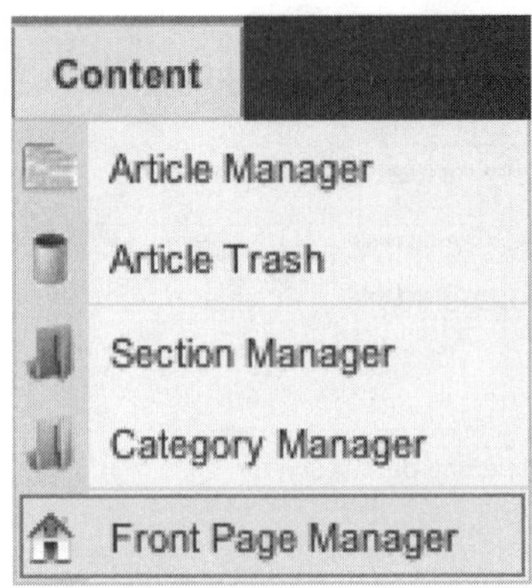

Figure 2.26 The Content menu

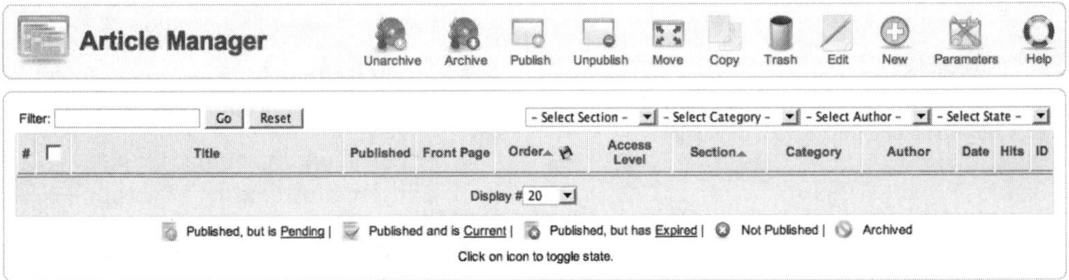

Figure 2.27 The Article Manager

- **Section Manager:** The Section Manager lists all the sections created for your site. You can add, publish, copy, edit, or delete sections (**Figure 2.28**).
- **Category Manager:** The Category Manager lists all the categories created for your sections. You can publish, move, copy, delete, edit, and add new categories (**Figure 2.29**).
- **Front Page Manager:** The Front Page Manager lists all the content assigned to display on the *home* page of your web site. The Front Page is actually a *section* of your web site (**Figure 2.30**).

✔ Tip

- In previous versions of Joomla, articles were referred to as *content items.*

Figure 2.28 The Section Manager

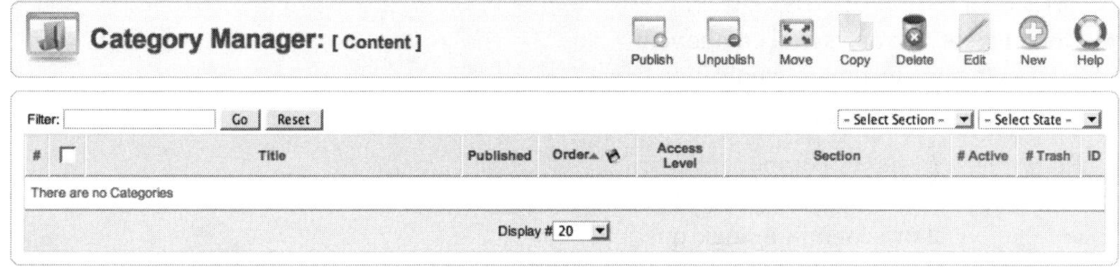

Figure 2.29 The Category Manager

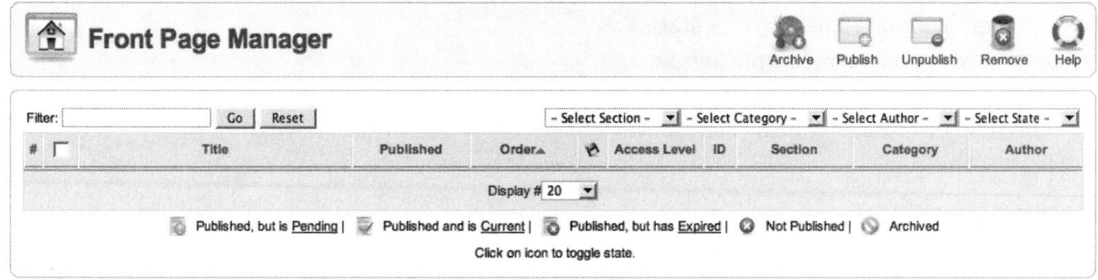

Figure 2.30 The Front Page Manager

Using the Components Menu

The Components menu lists all the components installed on the site. You can think of components as mini applications running inside your web site. For example, a forum or a product catalog could be a component. There are many third-party component extensions available for Joomla.

Because Chapter 5, "Working with Modules," covers components in detail, this section just lists the highlights (**Figure 2.31**).

Figure 2.31
The Components menu

The Components menu choices are:

- **Banner:** The banner component can be used for advertising banners, or as you will see later in the book, you can modify banners to fit many different needs.
- **Contacts:** The contact component manages all contacts for your web site. Users are not automatically added to the contact component.
- **News Feeds:** The news feed component is for managing incoming syndication or RSS feeds to your web site.
- **Polls:** Polls is a survey component that users see and vote on. The Joomla poll component allows for only a single question with up to 12 options as an answer.
- **Search:** This search component is not to be confused with a web site search box. The search component provides statistics for your web site. Here Joomla logs what users are searching for on your site, the search terms used, and how often they are searching.
- **Web Links:** Create and manage a web link or resource page containing useful links to other web sites.

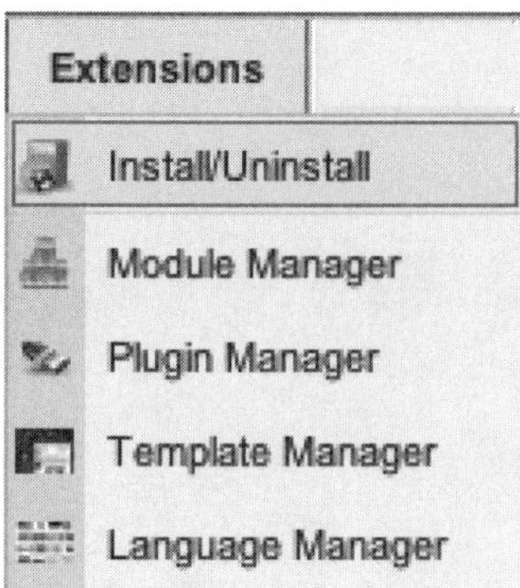

Figure 2.32 The Extensions menu

Using the Extensions Menu

The Extensions menu is used to install, uninstall, and manage third-party components, modules, plugins, templates, and language packages (**Figure 2.32**).

To install/uninstall an extension:

1. Log in to the back end of the site as a super administrator.

   Only super administrators can install or uninstall extensions.

2. Choose Extensions > Install/Uninstall.

   All extensions can now be installed or uninstalled from this page (**Figure 2.33**). In prior versions of Joomla extensions, components, modules, plugins, and templates were installed from separate pages (see Chapter 6, "Extending Your Site").

continues on next page

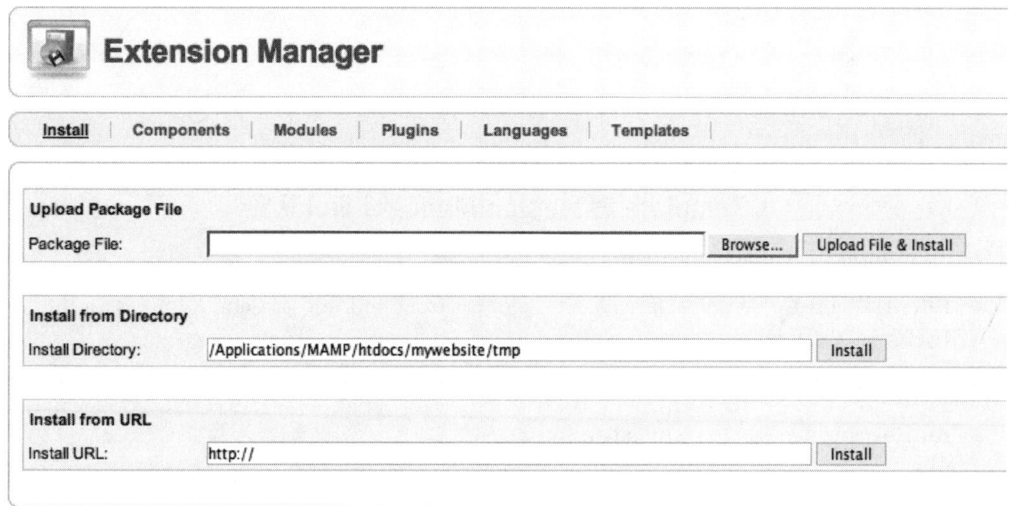

Figure 2.33 The Install Extension Manager

3. Click the Templates link.

   There are currently four templates that come preinstalled with Joomla: Beez, JA_ Purity, rhuk_milkyway, and Khepri. The templates, or any extension, that is grayed out cannot be uninstalled (**Figure 2.34**).

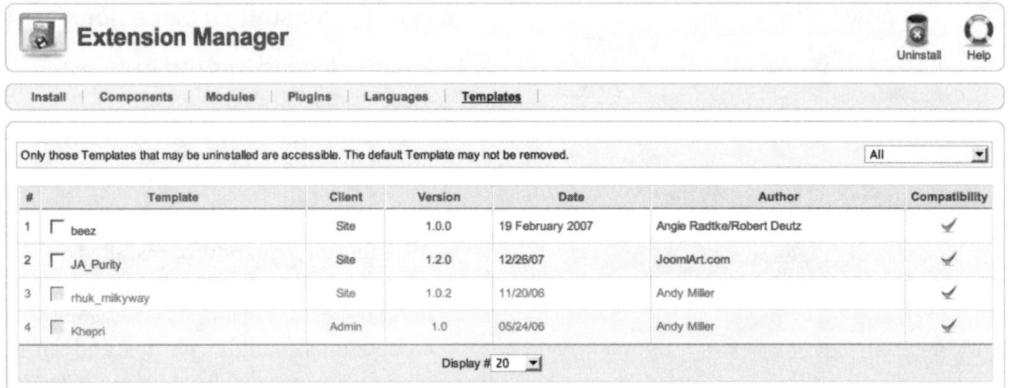

Figure 2.34 The Template Extension Manager

Template Extension Manager Fields

- **Template:** The name of the template.
- **Client:** Where the template is used. Site is for the front end web site, and Admin is for the back end interface.
- **Date:** The date the template was created by the template creator.
- **Author:** The name of the template creator.
- **Compatibility:** A green checkmark in this field means this template is fully compatible with this version of Joomla.

To open the Module Manager:

1. Log in to the back end as a super administrator.
2. Choose Extensions > Module Manager.

   The Module Manager lists all modules installed or created on your site. Here you can add, enable or disable, copy, configure, or delete modules (**Figure 2.35**).
3. Click the Administrator link.

   The back end administrative interface is also a web site that has its own components, modules, and templates. Unless you are an advanced user, you won't ever modify the back end interface.

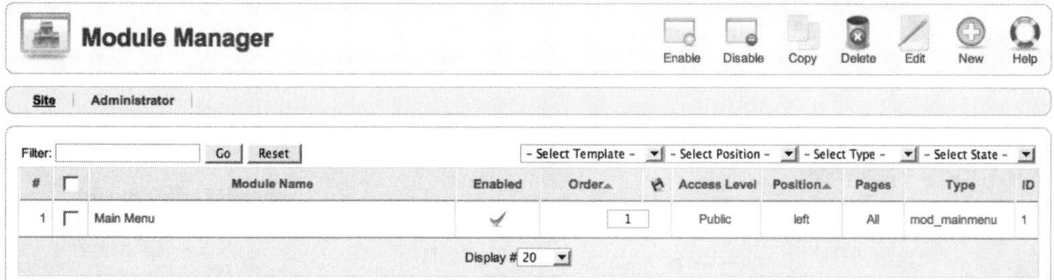

Figure 2.35 The Module Manager

Module Manager Fields

- **Module Name:** The name of the module. Clicking the module name opens the module details for editing.
- **Enabled:** A green checkmark means this module is enabled on the web site. A red circle with an X means the module is not currently enabled on the site.
- **Order:** This is the order in which the module will display on the site in a given position, that is, top, left, right, and so on.
- **Access Level:** The access level required by the user to see this module.
- **Position:** The position assigned to this module. (Plugins do not have positions.)
- **Pages:** Lists which pages of the site this module displays on.
- **Type:** Used by Joomla to identify what type of module this is.
- **ID:** The database ID number for this module.

To open the Plugin Manager:

1. Log in to the back end as a super administrator.
2. Choose Extensions > Plugin Manager.

   Modules and components can function independently. Plugins are extensions for modules and components (**Figure 2.36**).

   Currently only 20 items display on a single page (**Figure 2.37**). All managers can have the number of items to display changed.
3. In the Display # drop-down menu, choose 50.

   All of the plugins are displayed on a single page, and the navigation goes away.

   The preinstalled Joomla plugins are explained in Appendix B, "Resources."

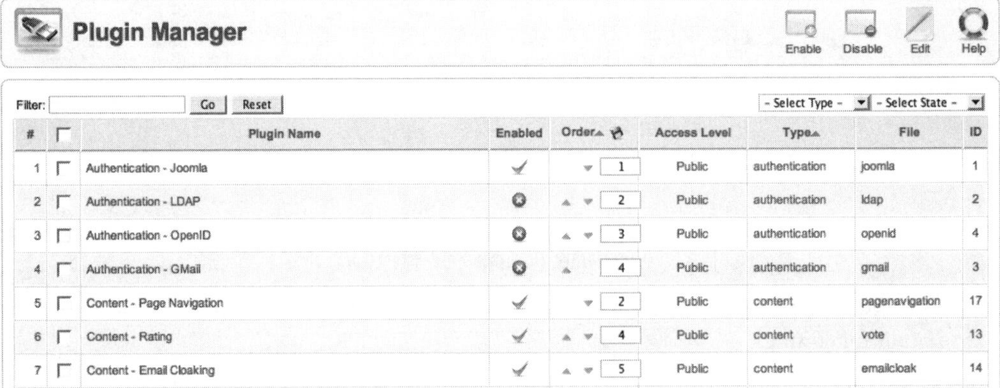

Figure 2.36 The Plugin Manager

Figure 2.37 The Display # drop-down menu

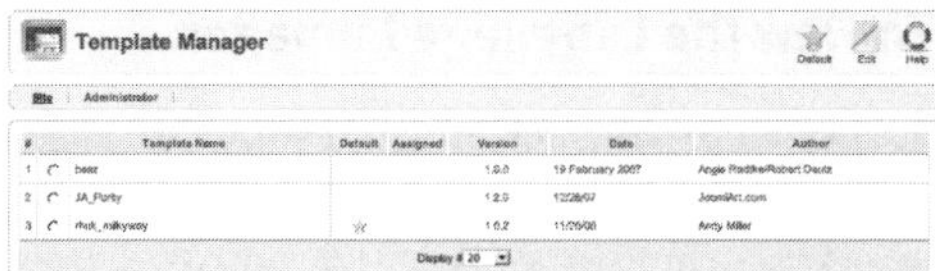

Figure 2.38 The Template Manager

Joomla Templates

The Joomla template system is one of the best Joomla features for a designer. Unlike most content management systems, Joomla does not integrate templates into the framework itself but keeps the presentation (the template) completely separate and self-contained in its own file structure. What this means is any standard HTML/CSS design can be easily implemented or converted to be used with Joomla. (See Chapter 9, "Creating Joomla Templates" for more details.)

For even more flexibility, Joomla allows multiple templates and multiples styles within the same template, then with a few clicks you can assign a specific design to any page of your web site. You can use any of the default templates in Joomla's library, download templates, or create your own.

To change the default template:

1. Log in to the back end as a super administrator.
2. Choose Extensions > Template Manager (**Figure 2.38**).

   The Template Manager opens, displaying the default templates. Notice you are currently in the Site Template Manager. These are the templates that are used for the public front end of the web site. The Administrator Template Manager is the template for the administrative back end and contains only one template. Do not modify, add, or alter this in any way.
3. Click the radio button next to the second template, JA_Purity.
4. Click the Default icon.

   The star in the Default column moves opposite JA_Purity to signify this is the new default template for the entire web site.

continues on next page

5. Click Preview to see that the new template has been applied.

   Preview is a great way to see how the changes you just made in the administrative back end impact your web site (**Figure 2.39**).

✔ Tip

- You can find many free and commercial templates available for Joomla web sites online; just search on the phrase *Joomla Templates.* Be sure the templates are Joomla 1.5; prior versions will not work.

To view the Language Manager:

1. Log in to the back end as a super administrator.
2. Choose Extensions > Language Manager.

   The Language Manager lists all the language packages installed on the web site (**Figure 2.40**).

Figure 2.39 The new default template applied to the home page

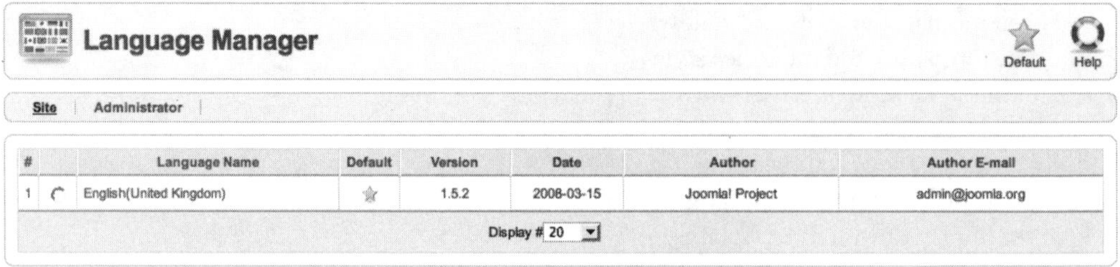

Figure 2.40 The Language Manager

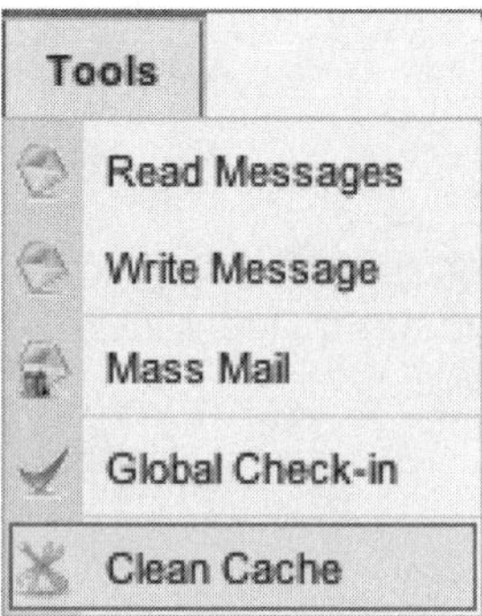

Figure 2.41 The Tools menu

Using the Tools Menu

The Tools menu provides access to global web site functions (**Figure 2.41**). These will be covered in more detail later in the book (see Chapter 7, "Modifying Global Settings").

The Tools menu choices are:

- **Read Messages:** Accesses the super administrator's private messaging system. Read Messages lists all messages sent to you from other administrators.
- **Write Messages:** Sends private messages to other administrators.
- **Mass Mail:** Creates mass e-mail messages that will go out to user groups you specify.
- **Global Check-in:** Tells Joomla to check in any content currently checked out for editing or locked items.
- **Clean Cache:** Deletes all cached files from your web server.

Using the Help Menu

The Help menu links to the help system and provides a summary of your web server's system information (**Figure 2.42**).

The Help menu choices are:

- **Joomla Help:** Opens the help documentation for Joomla from the web.
- **System Info:** Displays the system information for your web server (**Figure 2.43**). This information will be different on different server configurations. If you have problems with your Joomla installation and the server, check here to verify your web server settings are configured correctly.

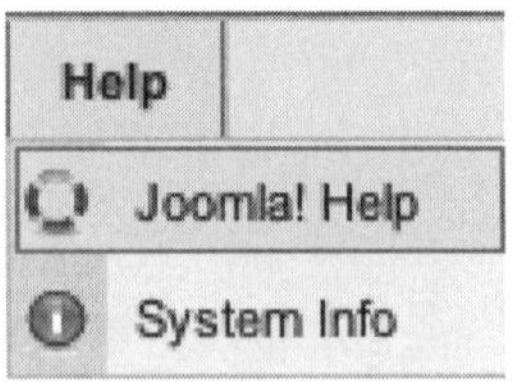

Figure 2.42 The Help menu

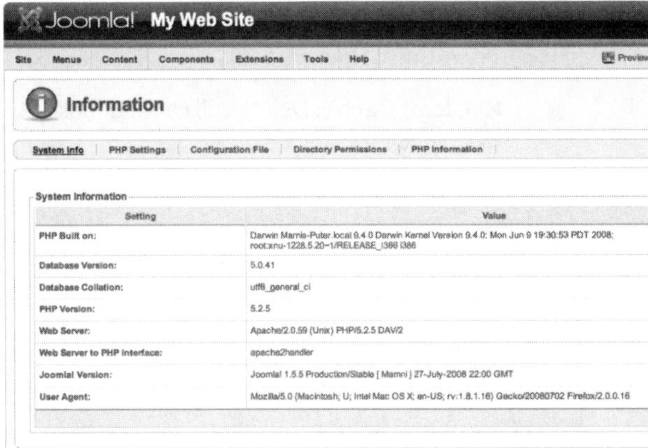

Figure 2.43
The System Info pages

System Information

- **System Info:** Displays a brief outline of some high-level PHP and database information.
- **PHP Settings:** Displays the PHP configuration settings for the web server.
- **Configuration File:** Displays the configuration.php file information.
- **Directory Permissions:** Displays each directory in Joomla and whether that directory is writable (you can make changes) or unwriteable (you cannot make changes).
- **PHP Information:** Displays the version and configuration of your web server's PHP installation.

3 Adding Your Content

Before content management systems, and the popularity of Web 2.0, web sites were commonly a series of static pages. To create a dynamic site required developers with coding and database skills and a team to update and maintain them. Now, with content management systems, sites are dynamic and accessible to everyone. Static pages meant content generally lived on a single page, with a single link to that page. To have flexible content meant maintaining that content in multiple places. With a content management system, content is created as individual pieces contained in a database and can appear on a single page or multiple pages with a simple click of a button.

Joomla is so flexible that you can start adding content, menus, or extensions before ever designing or organizing your site. Resist the temptation, however, because the best practice is to have a plan in place before you start. Without a plan, or at least a basic concept of how the site is organized, you can spend hours modifying work already done.

Joomla organizes content by sections, categories, and articles. *Sections* are the top level, *categories* are the second level, and *articles* are where most of your actual content lives.

This chapter covers how to organize and add content to your web site, as well as how to create sections, categories, and articles.

Designing a Web Site

Before diving in and creating a web site, you should have a plan, whether it's an outline, a rough hand sketch, or something more elaborate centered around a graphical design. If you start with a clear idea of what your site should look like, what your site will be about, and the most efficient way your users will get around, you can set up a web site in a few hours without having to write a single line of code. In addition, taking the time to plan ahead can save hours of rework and reorganization later.

We designed this book around a typical family blog site. **Figure 3.1** illustrates the site design we brainstormed before we began.

Once you have a site design, think about how it translates into levels of organization for a Joomla site. For example, events is a section. The events section, in turn, will contain categories of birthdays, anniversaries, vacations, and reunions (**Figure 3.2**). In each of these categories, you will add articles.

✔ Tip

- One term that can be a little tricky for first-time Joomla users is an article. The term *article* is Joomla's term for content. Any content you add to your site will be added through the Article Manager. When you see the word *article,* think web site content.

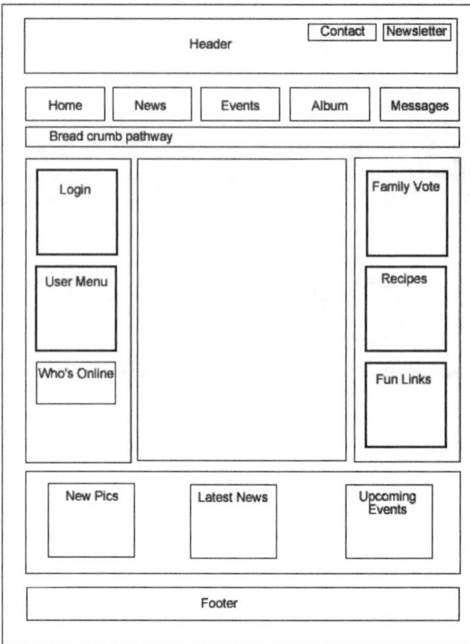

Figure 3.1 A wireframe of a web site

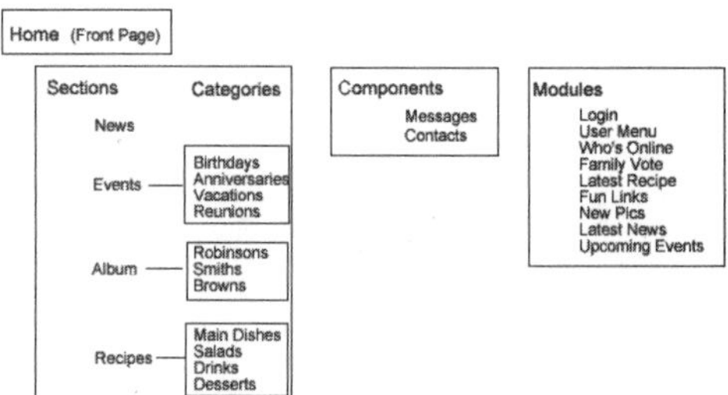

Figure 3.2 A site map in outline form

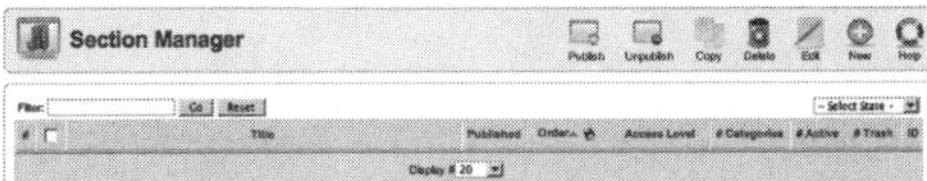

Figure 3.3 The Section Manager

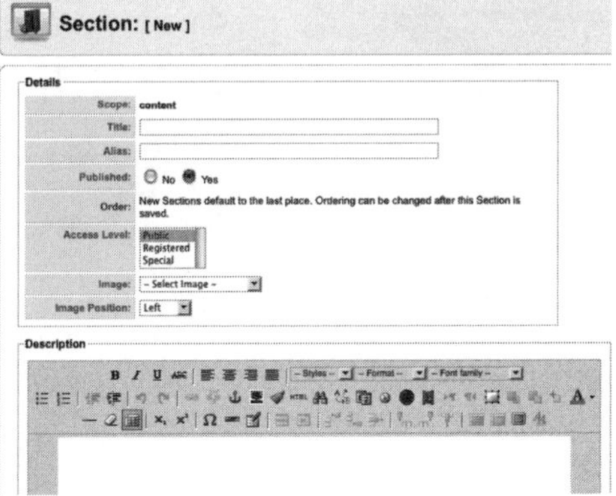

Figure 3.4 The New Section screen

Creating and Managing Sections

Web sites can have one section or multiple sections, depending on what best suits your site's purpose and function. For example, personal blog sites generally have a single section that contains many links to photos, older entries, and so on. A real estate site, by comparison, might have multiple sections that organize the content into the specific areas clients would look for, such as buyers or sellers, residential properties, commercial properties, or buildable land, and so on.

To create and manage the sections you need for your web site, you must be logged into the back end as a super administrator.

To create a section:

1. Choose Content > Section Manager.

   The Section Manager opens (**Figure 3.3**).

2. On the toolbar, click New.

   This opens the New Section Editor with a Details and Description area (**Figure 3.4**).

3. Under Details, in the Title field, type `News`.

4. Leave the Alias field blank.

   The information in the Alias field is used in the URL when the option for Search Engine Friendly URLs is set to Yes in the Global Configuration settings (see Chapter 7, "Modifying Global Settings"). Joomla automatically fills in the Alias field when you save your settings. If you want some-thing other than the default, you can enter it in all lowercase with no blank spaces. You can use hyphens between the words.

continues on next page

5. In the Published field, click Yes (**Figure 3.5**).

   Choosing Yes for Published, for any piece of content, means this item is visible on the web site.

6. In the Order field, leave the default 1(News).

   This field controls the order in which items display on the site. The Order option is visible only when you create your first section. Subsequent sections are added to the bottom of the order by default. After you save a section, you can change the ordering.

7. In the Access Level field, select Public.

8. From the Image drop-down menu, choose articles.jpg.

   The image you specify here will display below the section title if you set the Description Image parameter to Show in the Menu Manager (see Chapter 4 "Making Your Site Dynamic with Menus"). You can also use this field to place an image at the top of your section, instead of a title.

   The image must be in the database or you will not be able to select it here. The Media Manager is covered later in this chapter.

9. In the Image Position field, leave the position set to Left.

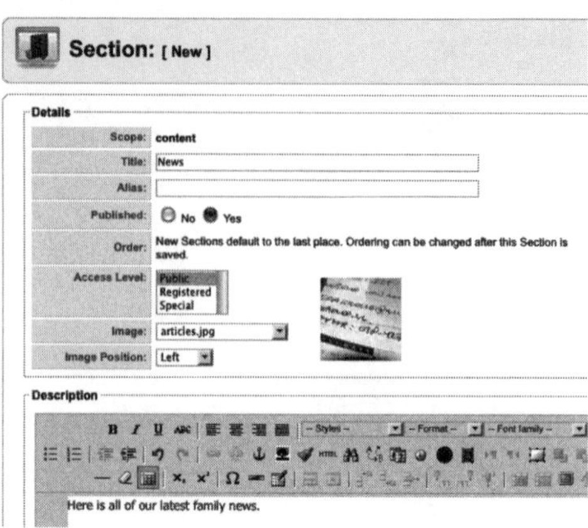

Figure 3.5 The completed New Section screen

Access Levels

- **Public:** This section is visible to any user.
- **Registered:** This section is visible only to people who are registered users.
- **Special:** This section is visible to users with an access level of author or above.

Figure 3.6 The Apply button on the toolbar

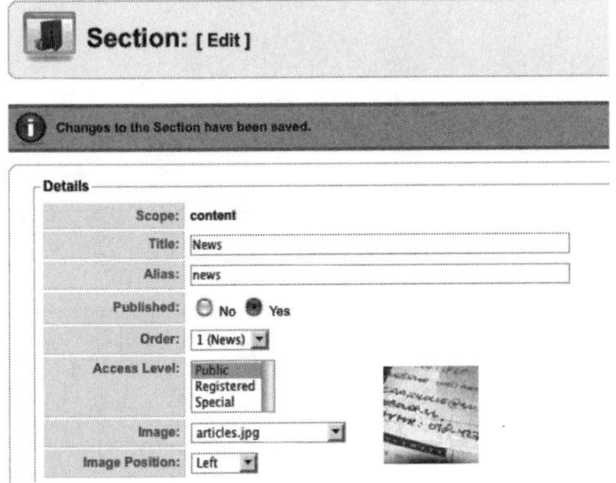

Figure 3.7 The Section Editor after the clicking the Apply button

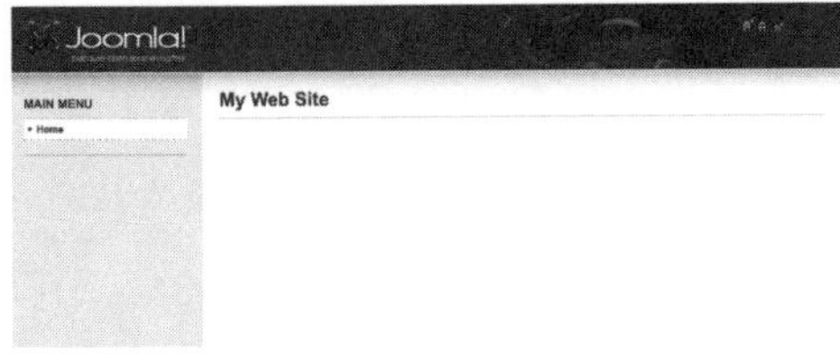

Figure 3.8 A preview of your web site

10. In the Description field, type `Here is all of our latest family news.`

    If you have the Description parameter set to Show in your Menu Manager, the description you type here displays right below the section title.

11. Click Apply (**Figure 3.6**).

    Apply saves your changes immediately but does not take you out of the page you are working on (**Figure 3.7**).

12. Click Preview.

    Note that your section does not yet display on the site. Nothing is visible on the site unless it is linked through a menu. You will learn about menus in the next chapter (**Figure 3.8**).

13. Repeat steps 2 through 11 to add three more sections titled `Events`, `Our Albums`, and `Recipes`. Leave all fields at the defaults.

To use the Section Manager:

1. Choose Content > Section Manager.

   You now have five sections created for your web site (**Figure 3.9**). The fifth section is the Front Page, which is discussed later.

2. Click any section title.

   That section opens for editing.

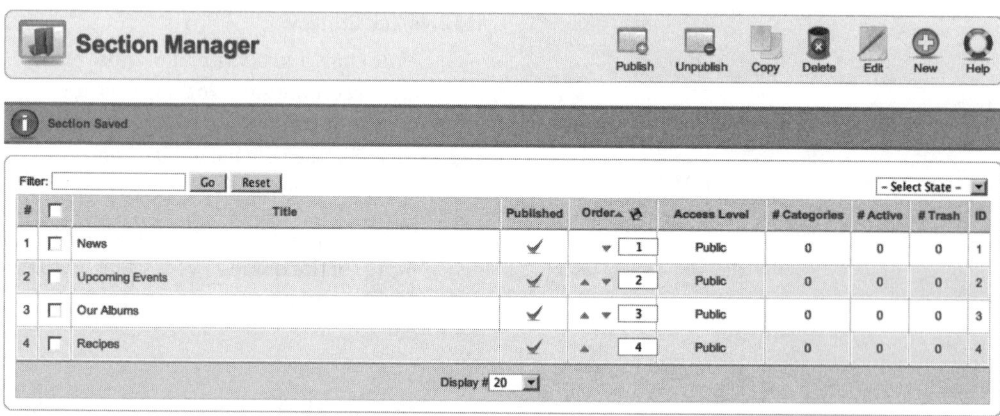

Figure 3.9 The Section Manager displaying the new sections

Section Manager Field Titles

- **Title:** The title given to the section.
- **Published:** A green checkmark means the section is published and visible on the site. A red circled X means the section is not visible on the site.
- **Order:** The display order of the section.
- **Access Level:** The current required access level for this section.
- **#Categories:** The number of categories assigned to this section.
- **#Active:** The number of active articles for this section.
- **#Trash:** The number of categories and articles assigned to this section that are in the trash.
- **ID:** The database ID number for this section.
- **Display #:** The number of items to display on this section's page. If more than this number of items are assigned to this section, the Previous and Next navigation buttons display.

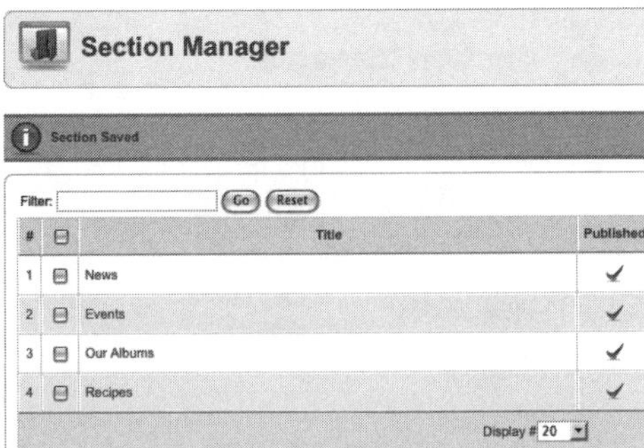

Figure 3.10 Making the News section unpublished

Figure 3.11 Publish and Unpublish Icons

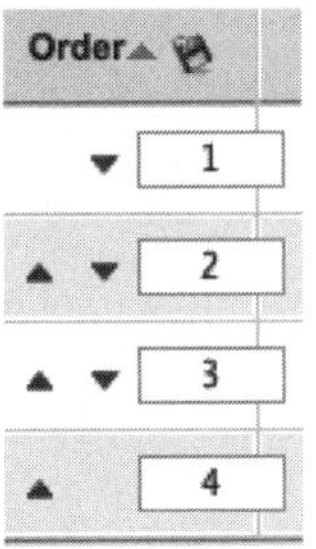

Figure 3.12 The Order column

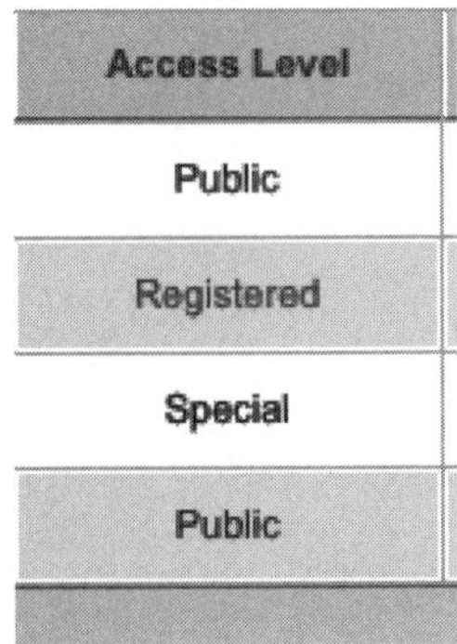

Figure 3.13 The Access Level field

To modify section settings:

1. Choose Content > Section Manager.

   You can easily change the order of sections, publish or unpublish a section, and change the section access level from the Section Manager.

2. To change the published status of the News section, click the checkmark in the Published column. The status toggles to unpublished. Click it again and it toggles back to published (**Figure 3.10**).

   You can also select the checkbox next to the section title and then click the Publish or Unpublish icon on the Section Manager toolbar (**Figure 3.11**).

3. To change the order of the sections, click the up or down arrow buttons to the left of the order number. This moves the section up or down in the list and changes the order in which it appears on the site page.

   You can also change the order by typing the order number next to each section, and then clicking the save icon at the top of the column (**Figure 3.12**).

4. To change the access level for a specific section, click the current Access Level link —that is, Public, Registered, or Special— in that section's row. For example, if you click Public once, in the News section row, the access level changes to Registered. Click again and it changes to Special. Click a final time and it returns to Public (**Figure 3.13**).

To edit a section:

1. Choose Content > Section Manager.
2. Click the section title News (**Figure 3.14**).
3. Change the Image drop-down list to Select Image.
4. Click Save.

   You just removed the image you chose for the News section title.

To copy a section:

1. Choose Content > Section Manager.
2. Click the box to the left of the News section, and then click the Copy button.

   The Section Copy Editor opens (**Figure 3.15**).

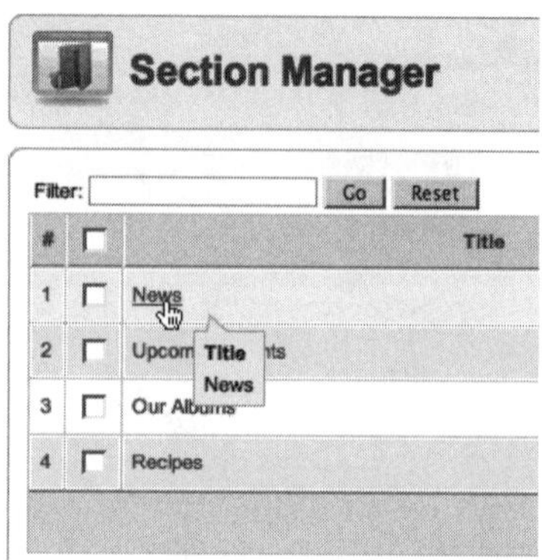

Figure 3.14 Selecting the section title name

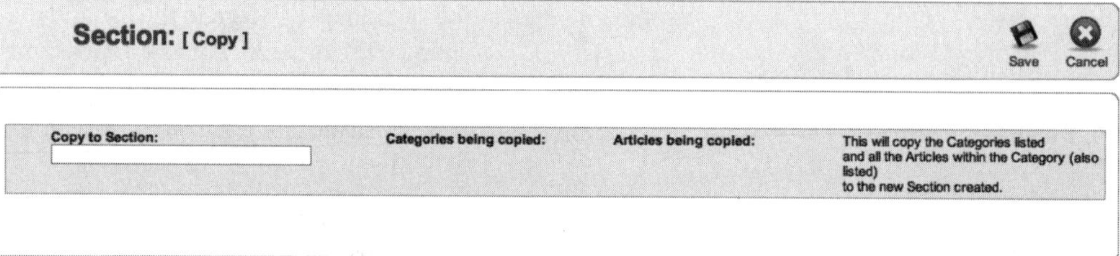

Figure 3.15 The Section Copy dialog box

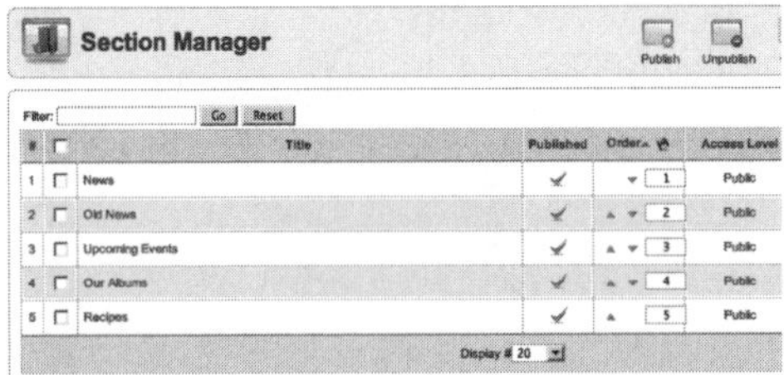

Figure 3.16 The new section added using the Copy function

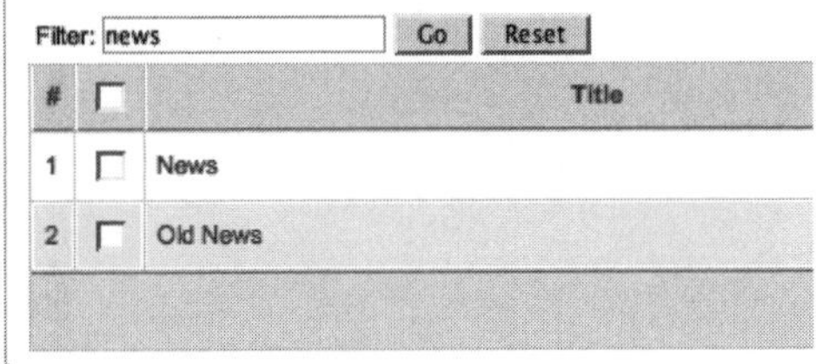

Figure 3.17 Sections listed by filtering for the word News

Figure 3.18 Selecting section filtering by State

3. In the "Copy to Section" field, type `Old News` as the new section name.

   If this section contained categories and articles, they would be listed as available to copy over with the new section.

4. Click Save.

   Notice that the new section keeps the Published and Access Level settings of the original section that was copied. The new section also has an order of 2 and was placed right after the section that you copied it from (**Figure 3.16**).

To filter sections:

1. Choose Content > Section.

2. In the Filter field, type `News`, and then click Go.

   The only sections you see are the ones with the word *News* in their titles (**Figure 3.17**).

3. Click the Reset button to see all of the sections again.

4. At the top right of the Section Manager, choose Unpublished from the Select State list (**Figure 3.18**).

   Notice that no sections are listed, because they are all published.

5. Select Published in the Select State list so that all of your sections display again.

To delete a section:

1. Choose Content > Section Manager.
2. Select the checkbox to the left of the Old News section.
3. On the toolbar, click the Delete icon.

   The section is now gone (**Figure 3.19**). Notice that the order is now off. You may want to reorder these sections so they are 1 through 4.

✔ Tip

- You can't delete a section if it has categories or articles assigned to it. You must first delete or move the articles, then categories, then the section can be deleted.

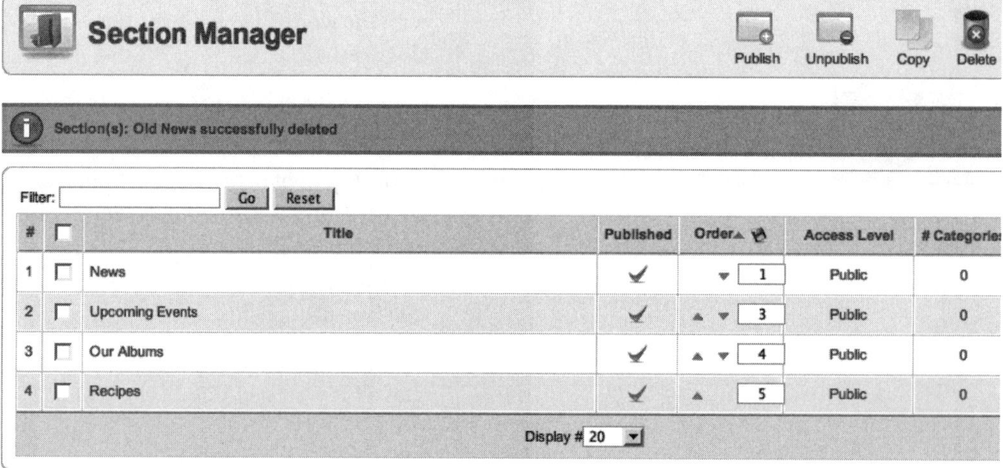

Figure 3.19 Deleting a section

Linking Sections to the Main Menu

Before you can see any of the sections you create, you must link them to a menu. Menus control everything that displays on your web site. No matter how many sections you add, nothing will appear until it is linked to a menu. In this example, you will link your sections to the menu items on the main menu. Joomla adds the main menu to your web site automatically; you don't have to do anything special. The main menu already contains your Home page section (Front Page).

Chapter 4, "Making Your Site Dynamic with Menus," discusses menus in detail. For now, this example illustrates the basics of adding the sections you just created to your main menu so you can begin to see how a web site is built.

To add a section to a menu:

1. Choose Menus > Main Menu.

   As you can see, the Home page is the first menu item by default. You cannot delete the Home menu item because it already contains the section Front Page (**Figure 3.20**).

continues on next page

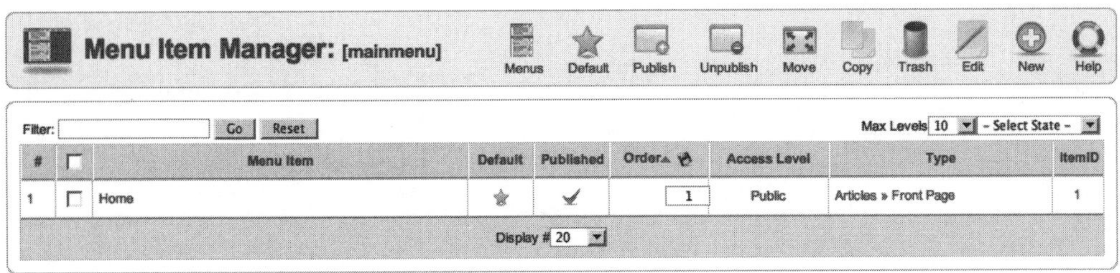

Figure 3.20 The Menu Item Manager

2. On the toolbar, click the New icon.

   The Menu Item page appears (**Figure 3.21**).

   The selections you make in this screen control how your page is going to look. You will learn much more about the selections on this page in Chapter 4, "Making Your Site Dynamic with Menus."

3. Click the Articles link to display a list of selections (**Figure 3.22**).

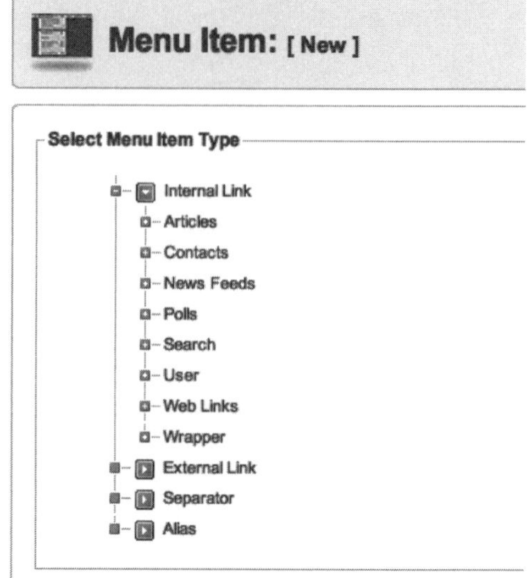

Figure 3.21 The Menu Item types

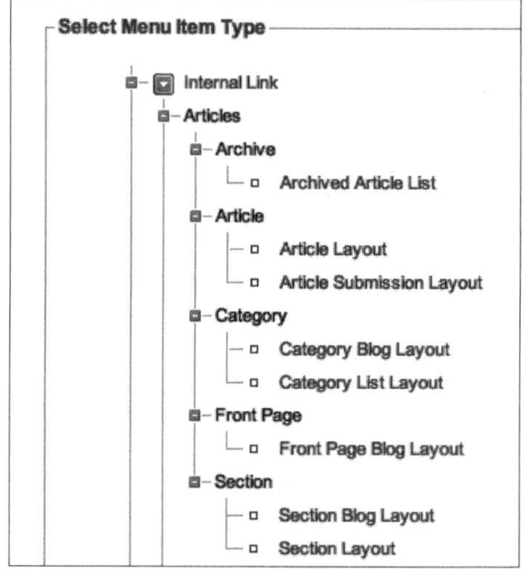

Figure 3.22 Selecting a Menu Item type

4. Click Section Blog Layout.

   The Menu Item page appears. This page is where you enter the details about your menu item. This screen is also covered in Chapter 4, so for now you will just make a few selections (**Figure 3.23**).

5. In the Title field, type `News`.

   The Title field is the name of the menu item that appears on your web site.

6. Choose News from the Section drop-down menu (**Figure 3.24**).

   This makes the News section one of your menu items. Any content you link to the News section will appear when you click the News link in your main menu.

continues on next page

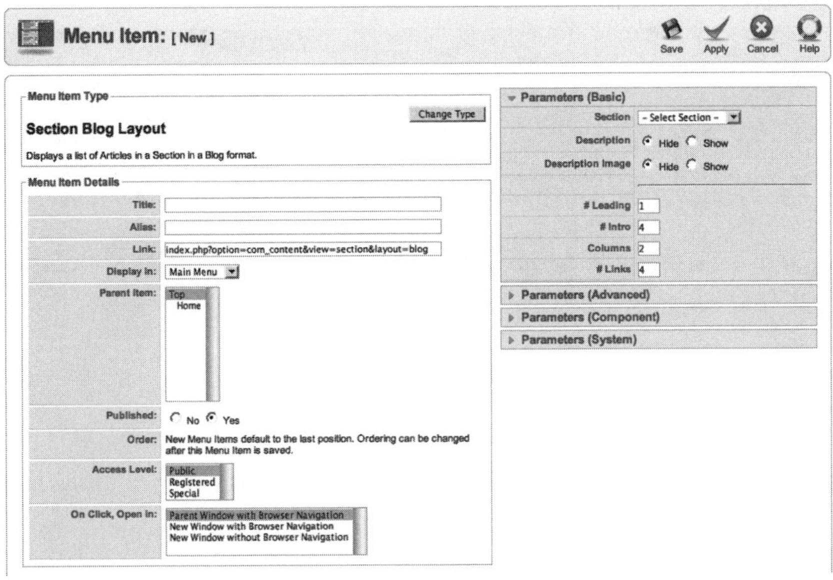

Figure 3.23 The New Menu Item Editor

Figure 3.24 Selecting the section for the menu item

7. Click Apply.

   Apply saves your changes without exiting the screen.

8. Click Preview.

   News is now the second menu item below Home. You have now added a section and an active menu link to that section on your site (**Figure 3.25**).

9. Repeat steps 1 through 8 to add menu items for each section: Events, Our Albums, and Recipes (**Figure 3.26**).

10. Click Preview.

    The main menu now looks like **Figure 3.27**.

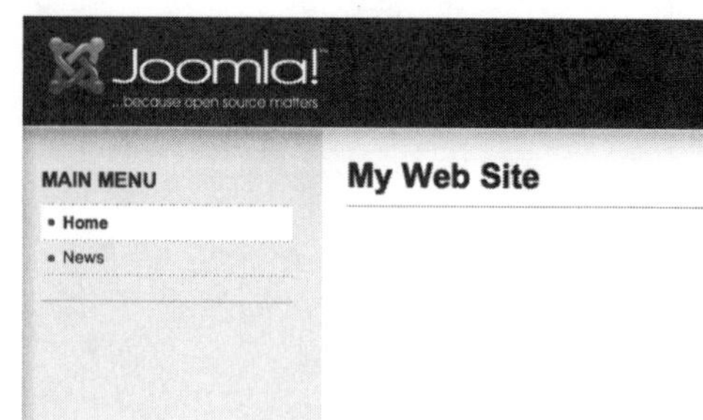

Figure 3.25 News added to the main menu on the web site

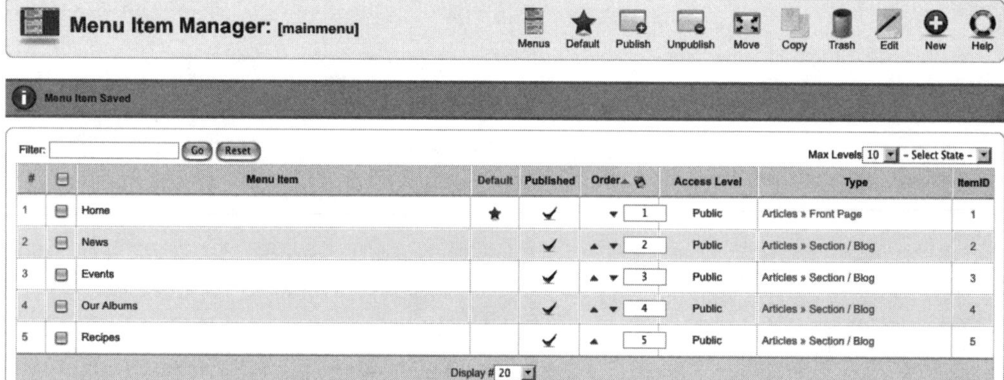

Figure 3.26 The Menu Item Manager with all the new sections added

Figure 3.27 The main menu on the Home page

Creating and Managing Categories

Categories help to further organize the information contained in your sections. A category can be assigned to a single section only, but it can have many articles assigned to it. It is the middle level of the organization. You create, edit, and manage categories through the Category Manager.

To create a category:

1. Choose Content > Category Manager.

   The Category Manager opens (**Figure 3.28**).

continues on next page

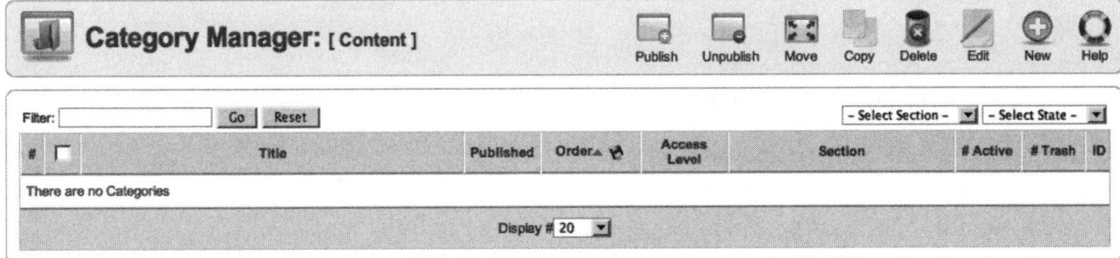

Figure 3.28 The Category Manager

Category Manager Fields

- **Title:** The title given to this category.
- **Published:** A green checkmark shows this category is published to the site. A red circled X means this category is unpublished.
- **Order:** The order in which the category will appear on the site.
- **Access Level:** The current required access level for this section.
- **Section:** The section this category is assigned to.
- **#Active:** The number of active articles assigned to this category.
- **#Trash:** The number of articles assigned to this category that are in the trash.
- **ID:** The database ID number for this category.

2. Click the New icon.

   This opens the Category Editor (**Figure 3.29**).

3. In the Title field, type `Birthdays`.

   You can show or hide the title when you select the article parameters. You'll learn more about this when you create articles.

4. Leave the Alias field blank.

   The same rules apply in categories as in sections. Joomla will create the default alias, or you can type your own. Be sure to use all lowercase with no spaces.

5. In the Published field, click Yes.

6. In the Section field, select Events.

7. In the Access Level field, select Public.

8. Leave the Image and Image Position fields at their defaults.

   You will be working with images in Chapter 5, "Working with Modules."

9. In the Description field, type `Here are all of our birthdays! Please add yours to the list if it is not already here`.

   The Category Editor now looks like **Figure 3.30**.

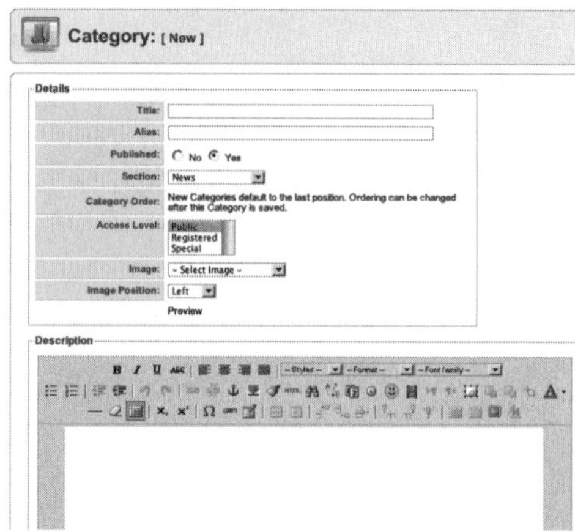

Figure 3.29 The Category Editor

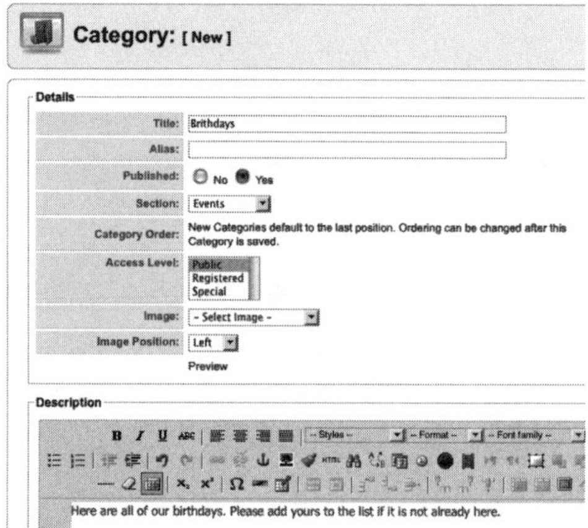

Figure 3.30 The updated Category Editor

10. Click Save.

11. Repeat steps 2 through 10 to add categories for:
    - ▲ Reunions, Graduations, and Anniversaries in the Events section.
    - ▲ Main Dishes, Desserts, Salads, and Drinks in the Recipes section (**Figure 3.31**).
    - ▲ Family Happenings, Vacations, and Trips to the News Section.

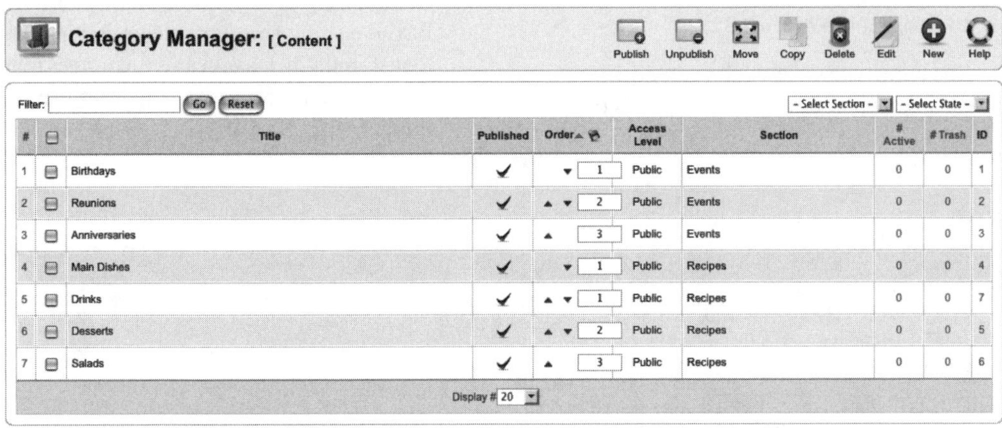

#		Title	Published	Order	Access Level	Section	# Active	# Trash	ID
1		Birthdays	✓	1	Public	Events	0	0	1
2		Reunions	✓	2	Public	Events	0	0	2
3		Anniversaries	✓	3	Public	Events	0	0	3
4		Main Dishes	✓	1	Public	Recipes	0	0	4
5		Drinks	✓	1	Public	Recipes	0	0	7
6		Desserts	✓	2	Public	Recipes	0	0	5
7		Salads	✓	3	Public	Recipes	0	0	6

Figure 3.31 All the new categories created

To modify category settings:

1. Choose Content > Category Manager.

   You can quickly change the order of the categories, their published status, and the category access level from the first screen of the Category Manager.

2. To change the published status, click the Published column next to the Birthdays category.

   The status toggles to not published. Click it again to toggle the status back to published (**Figure 3.32**).

3. To change the order of the categories, click the up or down arrow buttons to the left of the order number. This moves the category up or down in the list and changes the order in which it appears on the site page.

   You can also change the order by typing the order number next to each category, and then clicking the save icon at the top of the column (**Figure 3.33**).

4. To change the access level for a specific category, click the current Access Level link—that is, Public, Registered, or Special — in that category's row. For example, if you click Public once in the Birthdays row, the access level changes to Registered. Click again and it changes to Special. Click a final time and it returns to Public (**Figure 3.34**).

#		Title	Published
1		Birthdays	

Figure 3.32 Changing the published state of a category

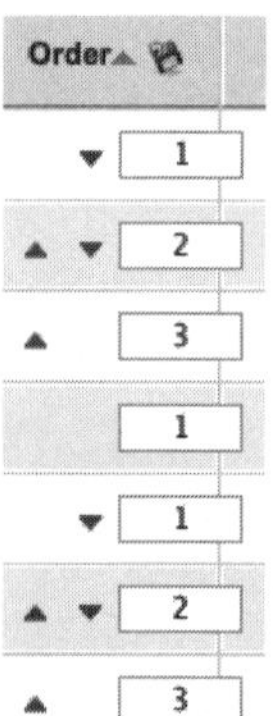

Figure 3.33 Changing the order of the categories

#		Title	Published	Order	Access Level
1		Birthdays	✓	1	Registered

Figure 3.34 Changing the access level of a category

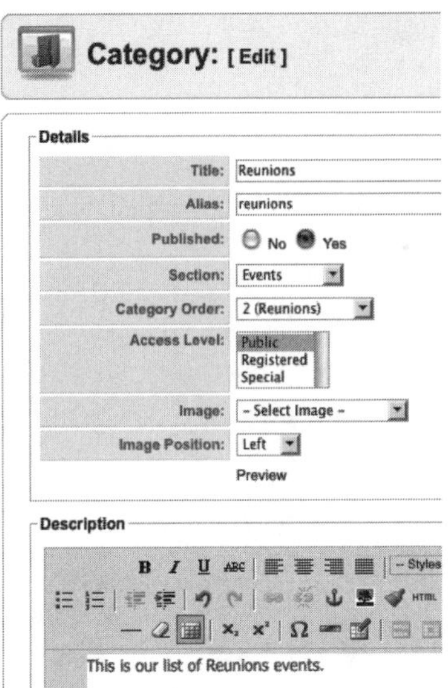

Figure 3.35 Editing a category

To edit a category:

1. Choose Content > Category Manager.
2. Click the Reunions category.

   The Category Editor appears, allowing you to edit the category details.
3. In the Description field, type `This is our list of Reunion events.`
4. Click Save (**Figure 3.35**).

   Your changes are saved.

To copy a category:

1. Choose Content > Category Manager.
2. Click the box to the left of the Birthdays category, and then click the Copy icon.

   The copy Category Editor opens. Here you select the section to copy the category to and any articles assigned to this category (**Figure 3.36**).
3. Select Our Album from the "Copy to Section" list.
4. Click Save.

   There is now a copy of the Birthday categories in the Our Album section.

continues on next page

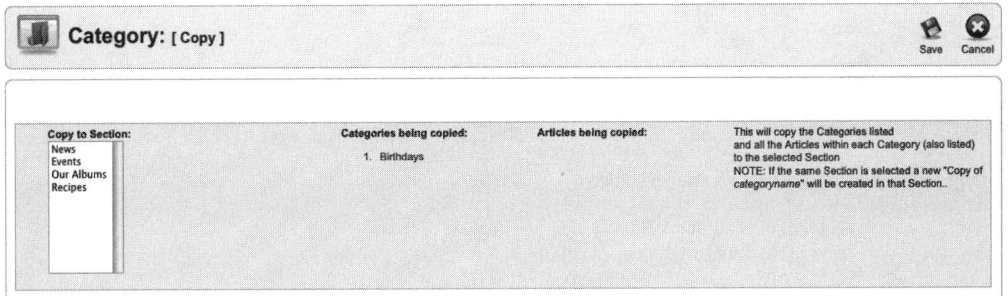

Figure 3.36 The Category Copy dialog box

5. Click the “Copy of Birthdays” link.

   The Category Editor opens (**Figure 3.37**).

6. Change the title to `Birthday Pictures`.
7. Delete the Description text.
8. Click Save.

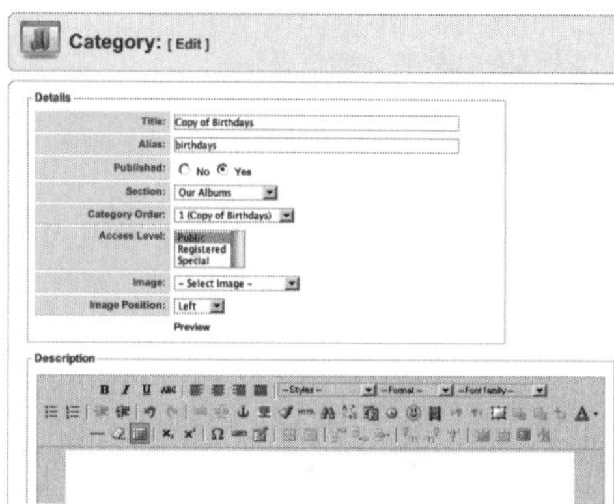

Figure 3.37 Editing the category title

To filter categories:

1. Choose Content > Category Manager.
2. In the Filter field, type `Birthdays`, and then click Go.

   The only category you see is Birthdays. You will not see Birthday Pictures because the word *Birthday* lacks an *s*, and the filter search must match at least one word exactly to display (**Figure 3.38**).

3. Click the Reset button to see all of the categories again.
4. At the top right of the Category Manager, choose News from the Select Section list.

   Because the News section contains no categories, the list is empty (**Figure 3.39**).

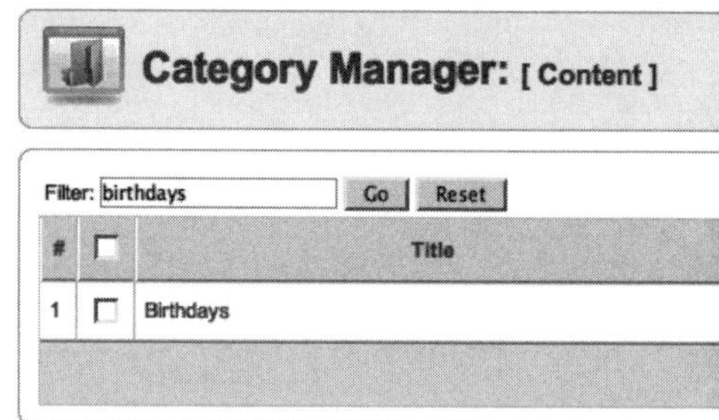

Figure 3.38 Category content filtered by keyword

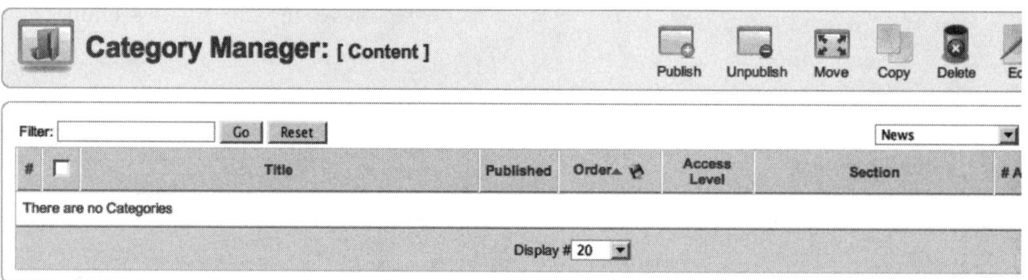

Figure 3.39 The empty Category Manager screen

5. Click the Reset button to see all of the categories again.
6. Choose Unpublished from the Select State list.

   Notice that all the sections are gone because they are all published.
7. Click Reset to display all the categories for the site again.

To delete a category:

1. Choose Content > Category Manager.
2. Click the box to the left of the Birthday Pictures category.
3. Click the Delete icon (**Figure 3.40**).

✔ Tip

- You cannot delete a category if there is an article assigned to it.

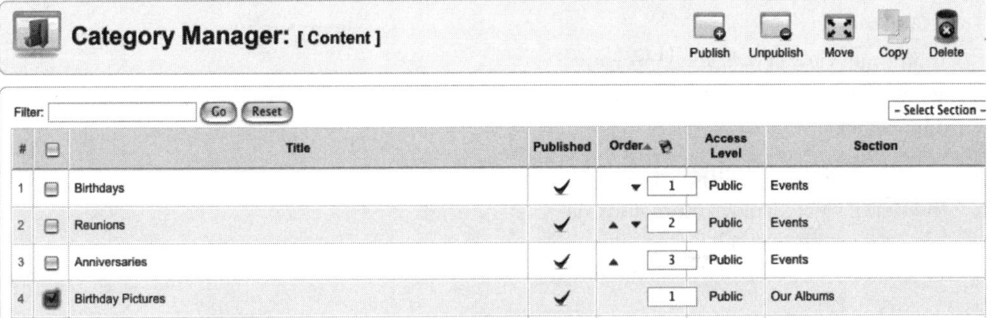

Figure 3.40 Deleting a category from the Category Manager screen

Using the Media Manager

With the Media Manager you can organize and store all the media files for your web site: images, movies, and sound files. Before you can use any type of media on your site or in articles, you must upload it to the Media Manager. It's a good idea to give some thought to how you want to organize your media before starting to upload your files. You may not want to load all of your media into one folder, for example, because individual items may be hard to find later when you have a large number of files. Instead, you should create folders that identify the media. For example, family_pictures, recipe_pictures, events, and so on.

Figure 3.41 Thumbnail view

Figure 3.42 Detail view

To open the Media Manager:

1. Choose Site > Media Manager.

   The Media Manager opens.

2. Click the Thumbnail View link. This is the default view.

   Thumbnail view shows you a preview image of graphic files and directories (**Figure 3.41**).

3. Click the Detail View link.

   The Detail view displays more information on each file: a small image, filename, dimensions, and size of the media file (**Figure 3.42**).

   At the bottom of the Media Manager page, the maximum size for media uploads on your site is displayed. The default is 10 MB. You can change the maximum media upload size in the global configuration pages (see Chapter 7, "Modifying Global Settings").

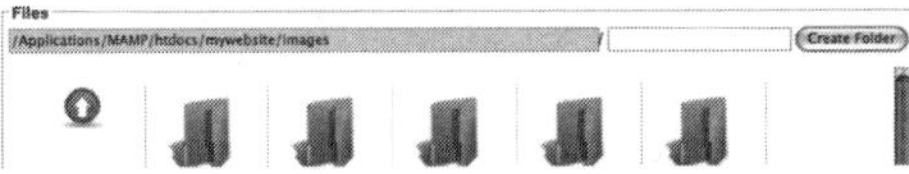

Figure 3.43 Create Folder field

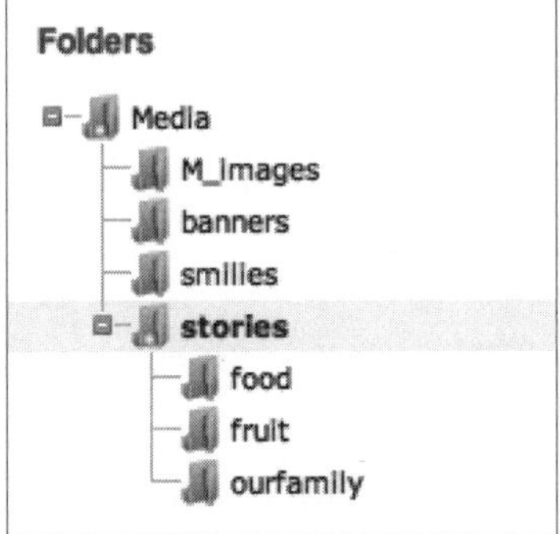

Figure 3.44 New folder

Figure 3.45 Browse files button

To create a new media directory (folder):

1. Choose Site > Media Manager.
2. Select the stories folder to open this directory.

   All images you want available to your articles through the Article Editor must be contained in the stories folder.
3. In the Create Folder field, type `ourfamily` (**Figure 3.43**).
4. Click the Create Folder button.

   A new folder called ourfamily is created to store the family pictures used on your web site (**Figure 3.44**).

   The folder is currently empty, but you can add some photos if you'd like.

To upload files to your site:

1. Choose Site > Media Manager.
2. Click the ourfamily folder.

   You are now in the ourfamily folder, which is currently empty.
3. Click the "Browse files" button at the bottom of the page (**Figure 3.45**).

   This will open an Explorer (Windows) or Finder (Mac) window. If you downloaded the sample files from the companion web site, the examples use the images provided there. If you have not downloaded the files, you can pick any small picture and continue.

continues on next page

4. Browse to the ourfamily folder on your computer.
5. Open the folder, select all the images, and then click Select.

   As long as you do not exceed the maximum total file size, you can upload multiple images at one time.
6. Click the Start Upload button (**Figure 3.46**).

   The images are now stored in the ourfamily folder and are available for use on your web site (**Figure 3.47**).

Figure 3.46 Upload Media files

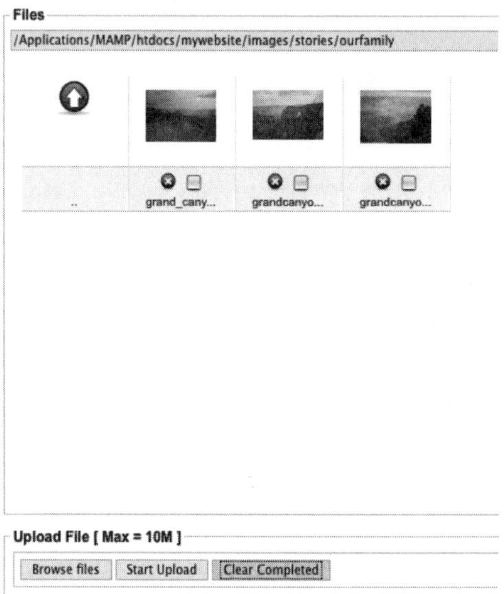

Figure 3.47 Uploading media files

✔ Tip

- Clicking any graphic gives you a preview of how that graphic will appear on your site.

To delete media files:

1. Choose Site > Media Manager.
2. Select the folder that contains the media file, in this case, the ourfamily folder.
3. Click the checkbox below the media file, and then click Delete (**Figure 3.48**).

Figure 3.48 Media files deletion

Article Manager Fields

- **Title:** The title of the article.
- **Published:** Shows whether this article is published or not.
- **Front Page:** Shows whether this article is displayed on the Home page of the site.
- **Order:** Lists the order in which this article will appear on the site.
- **Access Level:** Displays what access level users need to view this article.
- **Section:** Displays the section this article is assigned to.
- **Category:** Displays which category this article is assigned to.
- **Author:** Displays the name of the author of this article.
- **Date:** Displays the date this article was created.
- **Hits:** Displays the number of times this article has been viewed. This is tracked by the number of menu clicks received to view the article.
- **ID:** The database ID number for this article.

Writing Articles

Using the Article Manager you can add content to your site. Articles can be assigned to a category or a section, or they can be uncategorized. If you have a small site, you can leave articles uncategorized, but it is best practice to anticipate growth and organize them accordingly now, rather than later.

The Article Manager enables you to set global article parameters and specific parameters for individual articles. Usually, you will leave most of the settings at the default of Use Global settings, but you have a lot of versatility to change settings.

To view the Article Manager:

- Choose Content > Article Manager.

  The Article Manager opens. Here you manage all the written content on your web site (**Figure 3.49**).

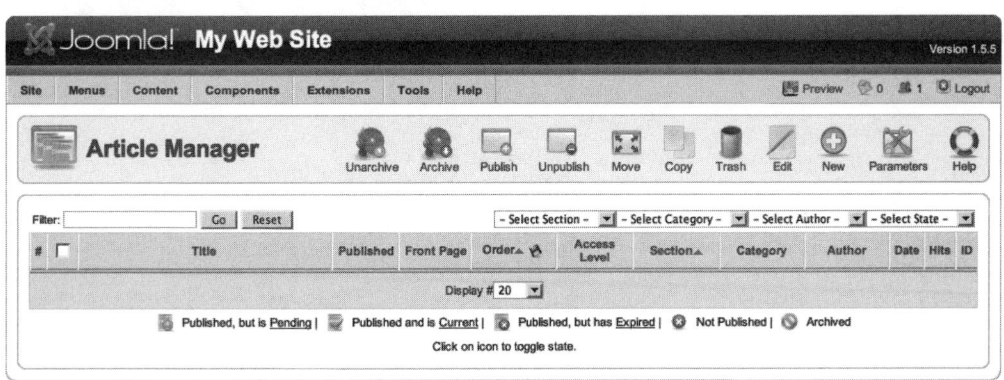

Figure 3.49 The Article Manager

To set global article parameters:

1. Choose Content > Article Manager.
2. Click the Parameters icon.

   The Articles Global Configuration screen opens. This screen sets the default parameters for all of the articles on your site. As you'll see later, you can change specific parameters for different articles. Setting global parameters means you have to set most parameters only once, and then only modify specific items that relate directly to the individual articles on the Article Editor page. Article parameters set in the Article Editor will override the global article parameters (**Figure 3.50**).
3. Change any parameters desired, and then click Save.

Figure 3.50 The global parameters

Article Global Configuration Parameters

- **Show Unauthorized Links:** Selecting Yes displays all article links independent of user access level.
- **Show Article Title:** Shows or hides the article title.
- **Title Linkable:** Makes the title link to the article.
- **Show Intro Text:** Shows or hides a few lines of introductory text for the articles.
- **Section Name:** Shows or hides the section name that the article is assigned to.
- **Section Title Linkable:** Makes the section title a link that takes the user to the section the article is assigned to.
- **Category Title:** Shows or hides the category title that the article is assigned to.
- **Category Title Linkable:** Makes the category title an active link to the category the article is assigned to.
- **Author Name:** Shows or hides the author's name.
- **Created Date and Time:** Shows or hides the date and time the article was created.
- **Modified Date and Time:** Shows or hides the date and time the article was modified.
- **Show Navigation:** Displays navigation between articles.
- **Read More Link:** Shows or hides the Read More link.
- **Article Rating/Voting:** Shows or hides a hit rating for the article.
- **Icons:** Shows or hides the PDF, print, and e-mail icons. Selecting these icons makes a PDF, print, or e-mail of the article for the user.
- **PDF Icon:** Shows or hides the PDF icon next to the article.
- **Print Icon:** Shows or hides the Print icon next to the article.
- **E-mail Icon:** Shows or hides the E-mail icon next to the article.
- **Hits:** Shows or hides the number of hits for each article.
- **For each feed item show:** Displays either the Intro Text or the Full Text of the article.
- **Filtering options:** Allows you to filter content that you receive from content authors.
- **Filter groups:** Selects the group that you want.
- **Filter type:** Specifies the filter type. Blacklist allows all tags except those in the blacklist field. Whitelist allows only the tags in the Filter tags and Filter attributes fields. No HTML removes all HTML tags from the article.
- **Filter tags:** List all tags that you want to allow when selecting one of the filtering options.
- **Filter attributes:** List all additional attributes separating each one with a space or comma.

To create an article:

1. Choose Content > Article Manager.
2. On the toolbar, click the New icon.

   The Article Editor opens (**Figure 3.51**).
3. In the Title field, type `Gordon's Chocolate Smootie`.

   You can show or hide the title in the article parameters.
4. Leave the Alias field blank.
5. In the Section drop-down menu, choose Recipes.

   Assigning an article to a section tells Joomla which page to display this article on. If this article is left uncategorized, it will not show up anywhere until added to either a section, a category, or both. Uncategorized items can only appear on the Front Page.
6. Next to Published, select Yes.

   If you select No, the article stays in your database but doesn't appear anywhere on your web site. If you want to publish it later, you can always go back and change the Published status to Yes.
7. Next to Front Page, select No.

   This article won't appear on the Home page of your web site.
8. From the Category list, choose Drinks.
9. In the Text field, type:

   ```
   Gordon's Chocolate Smoothie
   1 Cup chocolate soy milk
   1 small banana
   1 cup strawberries
   1 Tbsp protein powder
   1 Tbsp Ground Flax Seed
   Blend until smooth
   ```

   This recipe is for illustration purposes only (**Figure 3.52**).

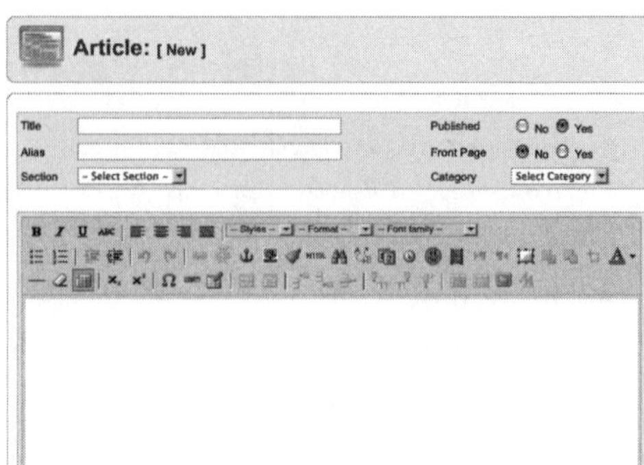

Figure 3.51 The Article Editor

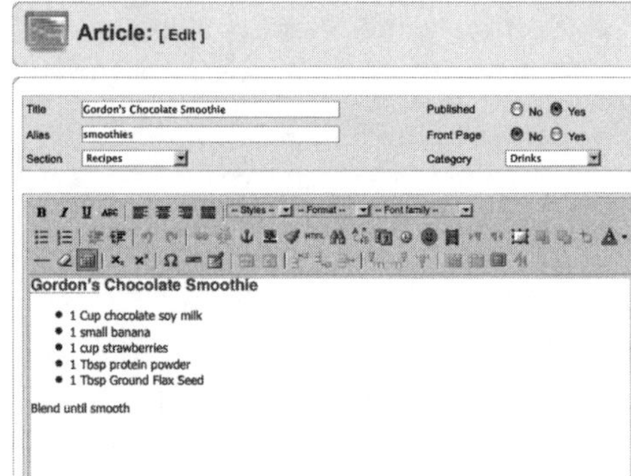

Figure 3.52 An example article

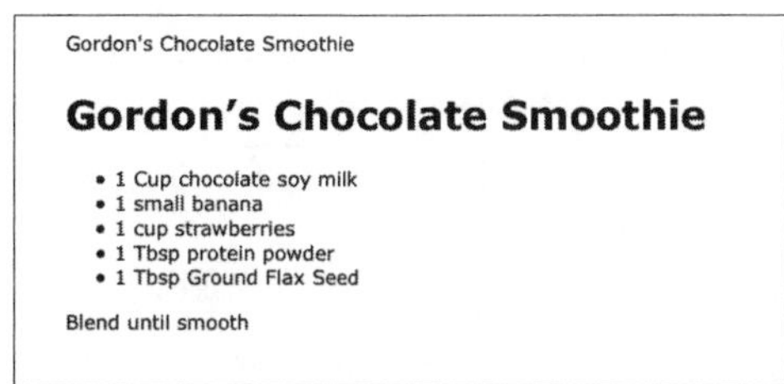
Gordon's Chocolate Smoothie

Gordon's Chocolate Smoothie

- 1 Cup chocolate soy milk
- 1 small banana
- 1 cup strawberries
- 1 Tbsp protein powder
- 1 Tbsp Ground Flax Seed

Blend until smooth

Figure 3.53 Preview of your article

Figure 3.54 Preview of your web site

10. Click Apply.
11. On the Article Editor toolbar, click the Preview icon.

    If you click the Preview icon next to the Save button, you preview the article. The upper Preview link previews the entire web site.

    A small box appears, displaying what your article will look like on your site (**Figure 3.53**).
12. Close the article preview, and then select the site Preview link.
13. Click the Recipes menu link.

    You can now see how the recipe will display on the web site. Users can see who created the article and when it was created, and they can choose to save the article as a PDF, print the article, or e-mail the article (**Figure 3.54**).

To set individual article parameters:

1. Choose Content > Article Manager.
2. Click the title of the article to open in the Article Editor.

continues on next page

3. Click the arrow next to Parameters (Article) to expand the article parameters list (**Figure 3.55**).

   You set an article's individual parameters from the Article Editor. Any parameters that you change in this screen are changed only for the specific article. If you want to change global parameters, go to the article's Global Configuration Parameters page.

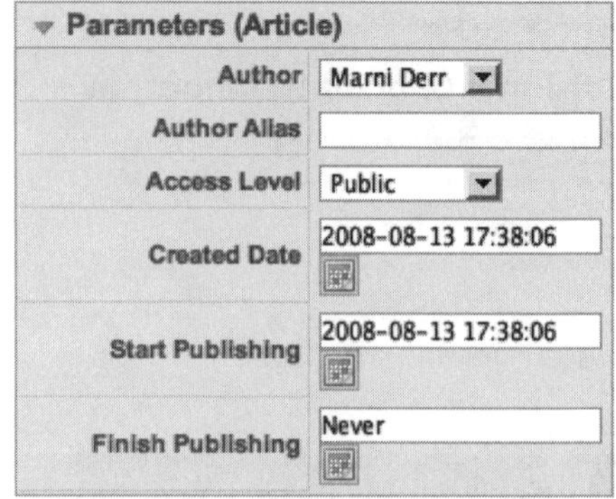

Figure 3.55 Article parameters

Article Parameters

- **Author:** Assigns an author to the article.
- **Author Alias:** Enables you to display a different name for the article's author.
- **Access Level:** Defines the access level a user needs to read this article.
- **Created Date:** Enables you manually to set the date an article was created. You can use this if you are planning to publish an article in the future.
- **Start Publishing:** Enables you to set a date and time when you want to start publishing the article.
- **Finish Publishing:** Enables you to set the date and time when you want to stop the article from displaying on the site. If you do not select a date in this field, the article stays on the site until you remove it.

You can use the Start and Finish Publishing dates for articles that you want to publish periodically. For example, if you have a back-to-school article, you can start publishing it in August and end publishing in September. Each year, you can change the year and republish the article.

Figure 3.56 Advanced article parameters

4. Click the arrow next to Parameters (Advanced) (**Figure 3.56**).

   These parameter definitions are the same as the global article configuration parameters, with the exceptions listed in the sidebar.

5. Click the arrow next to Metadata Information.

   Metadata information is used by search engines to identify an article and its relevance to a user keyword search (**Figure 3.57**).

Metadata Information
Description
Keywords
Robots
Author

Figure 3.57 Article metadata information

Advanced Article Parameters

- **Content Language:** Selects the article language.
- **Key Reference:** Sets a text key that can be used to reference this article.
- **Alternative Read:** Specify alternative text that you want to display next to the Read More text. The default text that shows up is the article title.

Article Metadata Info

- **Description:** Enter the meta description for the article.
- **Keywords:** Enter the meta keywords for the article.
- **Robots:** Enter keywords available to search engine robots.
- **Author:** Enter the author name for the meta information.

To format article content:

1. Choose Content > Article Manager.
2. Click the Smoothies article title.

   This opens the Article Editor.

   By default, the Article Editor uses the Tiny MCE 2.0 editor for entering content. It works similarly to most other word processing programs. You can customize the look of your content with bold, italics, underline, centering text, and much more. If you are an HTML coder, you can also click the HTML button and type HTML directly into the editor (**Figure 3.58**).
3. Highlight *Gordon's Chocolate Smoothie*, and choose Heading 1 from the Format list.

   The title is now styled as a Heading 1. These styles are controlled by the current template's CSS.
4. Highlight the ingredients and click the Bullets button.

   Now all of your ingredients are formatted as bullets (**Figure 3.59**).
5. Click Save.
6. Click Preview.

   Notice that your article is now styled on the site (**Figure 3.60**).

✔ Tips

- To edit the HTML code directly in the Article Editor, click the HTML icon.
- If you want to use a different editor than the default to format your article, you can specify the editor in the Global Configuration settings. See Chapter 7 "Modifying Global Settings" for more information about this editor.

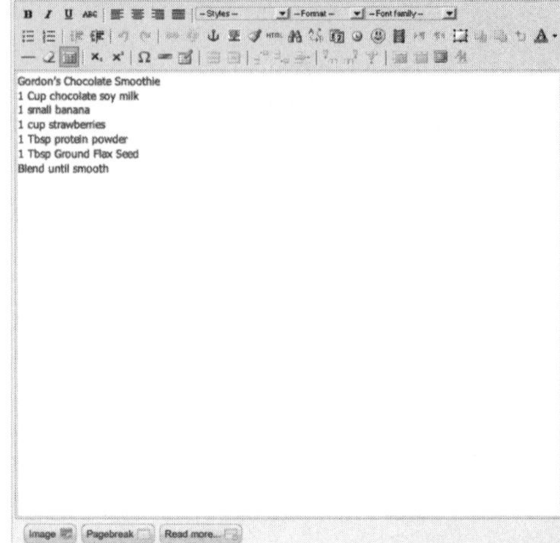

Figure 3.58 Editing content in the Article Editor

Figure 3.59 Formatting article text

Figure 3.60 Preview a formatted article

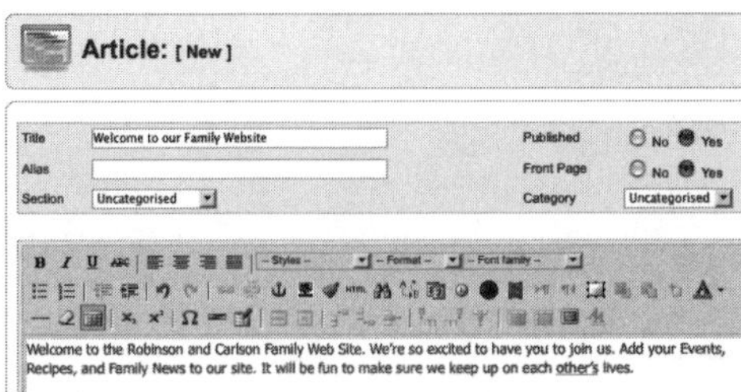

Figure 3.61 Adding a front page article

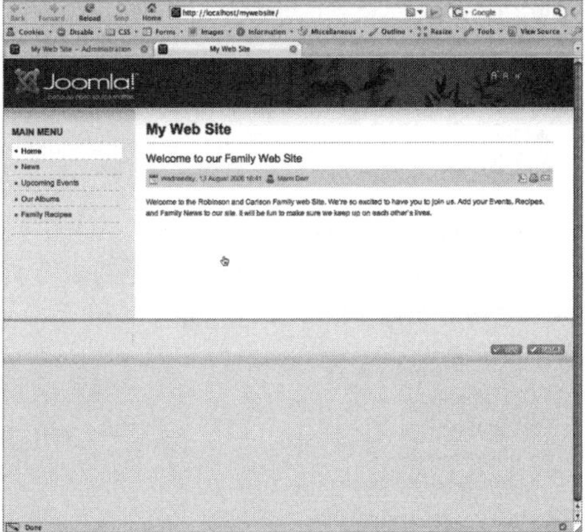

Figure 3.62 Preview of the front page

To add an article to the front page:

1. Choose Content > Article Manager.
2. Click New to create a new article.
3. In the Title field, type `Welcome to our Family Web Site`.
4. In the Section drop-down menu, choose Uncategorized.

   Notice that the Category field automatically changes to Uncategorized. You can't select a category if you choose Uncategorized in the Section menu.
5. Click the Yes radio button next to Front Page.

   Your article will now appear on the Home page of your web site.
6. In the text field, type

   `Welcome to the Robinson and Carlson Family Web Site. We're so excited to have you to join us. Add your Events, Recipes, and Family News to our site. It will be fun to make sure we keep up on each other's lives.` (**Figure 3.61**)
7. Click Save.
8. Click Preview (**Figure 3.62**).

To add an image to an article:

1. Choose Content > Article Manager.
2. Click the Gordon's Chocolate Smoothie article.

   This opens the Gordon's Chocolate Smoothie article in the Article Editor.
3. At the bottom of the Article Editor, click the Image button.

   You may have to scroll down to see this button. This opens a smaller version of the Media Manager (**Figure 3.63**).
4. Select the ourfamily folder.

   You set this folder up earlier.
5. Select an image, and then click the Insert button.
6. Click Save.
7. Click Preview (**Figure 3.64**).

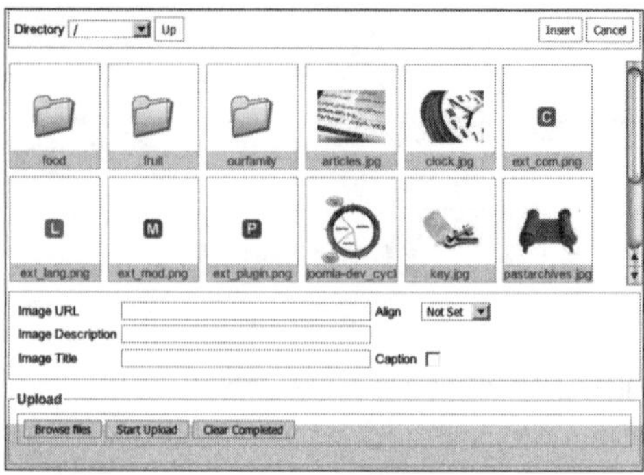

Figure 3.63 A smaller version of the Media Manager

Figure 3.64 Preview of article with image

✔ Tip

- You can use the Article Image Manager in the same way you use the Media Manager, with the exception that you cannot create new file directories.

Article Image Fields

- **Directory:** This is the images/stories directory in your Joomla Media Manager directory. Select the directory where your image is located.
- **Insert:** After selecting an image, click Insert to insert this image into the article.
- **Cancel:** Exits the article Image Manager.
- **Image URL:** After you select an image, the directory path is filled in this field.
- **Image Description:** A brief description for this image, used as a caption if the Caption checkbox is selected.
- **Image Title:** The title entered in this field will show when the user hovers over the image with the mouse.
- **Align:** Aligns the image left or right of the article.
- **Caption:** Select if you want the image title to display below the image.
- **Browse files:** Select browse to upload an image to this directory.
- **Start Upload:** Click to upload the image to the database.
- **Clear Completed:** Removes the completed message displayed after uploading an image.

To add a Read More link:

1. Choose Content > Article Manager.
2. In the Article Manager, click the "Welcome to Our Web Site" article.

   The Article Editor screen appears so you can edit the article parameters.
3. Add the following information to the text underneath the image:

   `The Robinsons live on the West Coast and enjoy surfing and beach activity. They love to go back to Minnesota to visit the Carlsons.`

   `The Carlsons live in Minnesota and spend a lot of time on lakes. They also enjoy the winter sports. Lots of cross country skiing and snowmen are built during the winter months.`
4. Click Apply, and then click Preview to see the article on the front page (**Figure 3.65**).
5. Go back to the Article Editor.
6. Place your cursor in front of the paragraph that starts with *The Carlsons live* (**Figure 3.66**), and then click the Read More button.

   Joomla inserts a Read More link on the page at the cursor's location. A red line appears, marking the link's location (**Figure 3.67**).
7. Click Save, and then click Preview.

   You now see the entire article. By adding a Read More link you can hide the last sentence with a Read More button. Users must click the button to access the rest of the article (**Figure 3.68**).

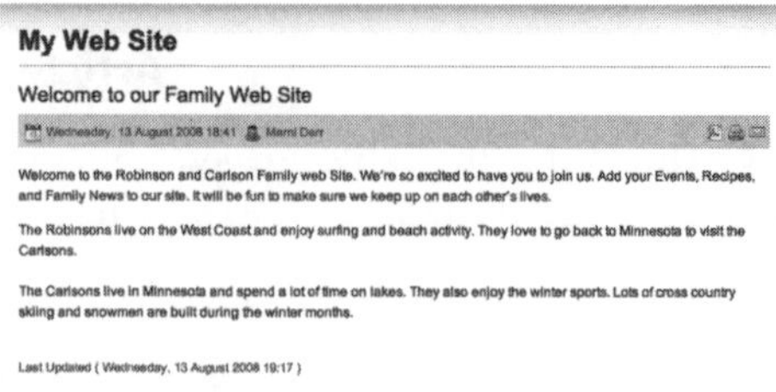

Figure 3.65 Preview of long article

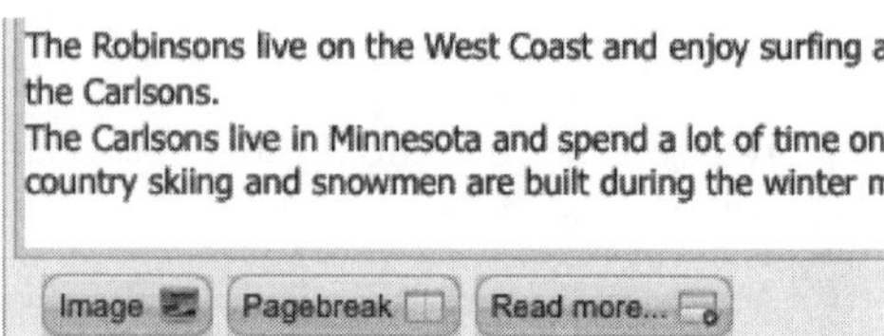

Figure 3.66 Read More link

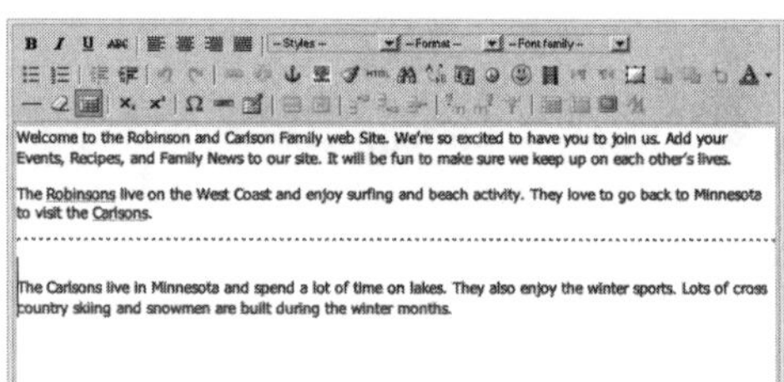

Figure 3.67 The entire article

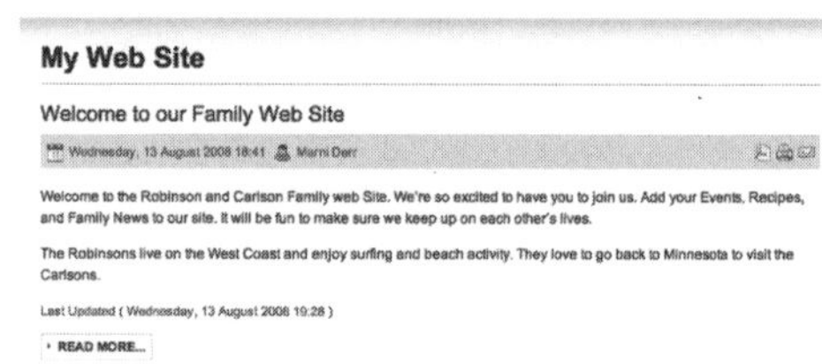

Figure 3.68 Preview the article with a read more link

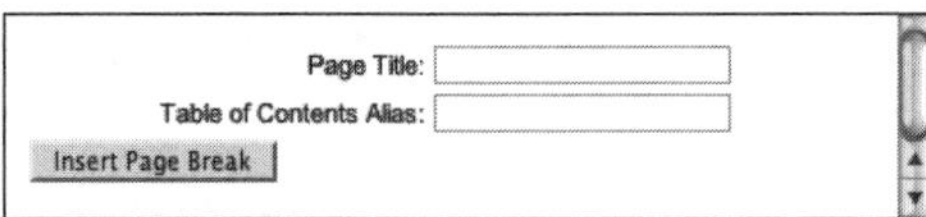

Figure 3.69 Insert Page Break box

Figure 3.70 Completed Insert Break box

Figure 3.71 Preview the Article Index link

To create an article index with page break:

1. Choose Content > Article Manager.
2. In the Article Manager, click the "Welcome to Our Web Site" article.

   The Article Editor opens.
3. Place your cursor in front of the paragraph that starts with *The Robinsons live*, and then click the Page Break button.

   The Insert Page Break box opens (**Figure 3.69**).
4. In the Page Title field, type `About the Robinsons`.
5. In the Table of Contents Alias field, type `The Robinsons`.
6. Click the Insert Page Break button.
7. Place your cursor in front of the paragraph that starts with *The Carlsons live*, and then click the Insert Page Break button.
8. In the Page Title field, type `Carlsons`.
9. In the Table of Contents Alias field, type `About the Carlsons` (**Figure 3.70**).
10. Click the Insert Page Break button.
11. Click Save, and then click Preview.

    This creates an Article Index and adds page navigation to the bottom of the article (**Figure 3.71**).
12. Click The Robinsons link.

    Only the paragraph about the Robinsons appears.
13. Click through the different links to see how the table of contents works.

To filter articles:

1. Choose Content > Article Manager.
2. Select a filter option (**Figure 3.72**).

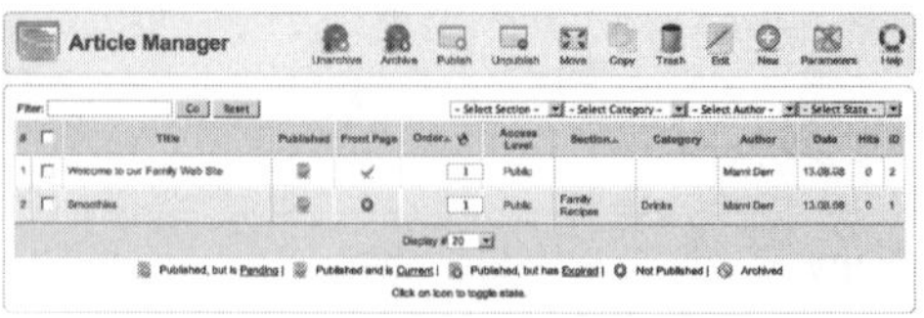

Figure 3.72 Article filter options

To copy an article:

1. Choose Content > Article Manager.
2. Click the checkbox next to the Smoothies article title, and then click the Copy icon.

   This opens the Copy Articles selections.
3. Choose Recipes / Desserts from the Copy to Section/Category list (**Figure 3.73**).
4. Click Save.

Figure 3.73 Copy Articles screen

To move an article

1. Choose Content > Article Manager.
2. Click the checkbox next to the Smoothies article in the Recipes/Desserts section/ category.
3. Click the Move icon.
4. Select Recipes / Main Dishes from the Move to Section/Category list (**Figure 3.74**).
5. Click Save.

Figure 3.74 Move Articles screen

Article Filter Options

- **Filter:** Enter a sort word or title and click Go. This displays only the articles with that word.
- **Select Section:** Lists only articles assigned to the section you specify.
- **Select Category:** Lists only articles assigned to the category you specify.
- **Select Author:** Lists only articles written by the author you specify.
- **Select State:** Lists only articles with a status of Published, Unpublished, or Archived, depending on your selection.

Figure 3.75 The Trash Icon

To move an article into the Trash Manager:

1. Click the checkbox next to the Smoothies article in the Recipes/Main Dishes section/category.
2. Click the Trash icon (**Figure 3.75**).

   You have now removed the article from the Article Manager, but it won't be completely removed from your system until you delete it from the Trash Manger.

To delete an article from your site:

1. Choose Content > Article Trash.

   After you have moved the article into the Trash Manager, you must delete it from the Trash Manager to completely remove the content from your site (**Figure 3.76**).

2. Click the checkbox next to the Smoothies article.

3. Click the Delete icon.

   The Permanently Delete Items screen appears (**Figure 3.77**).

4. Click the Delete button to permanently delete the listed articles from your site's database.

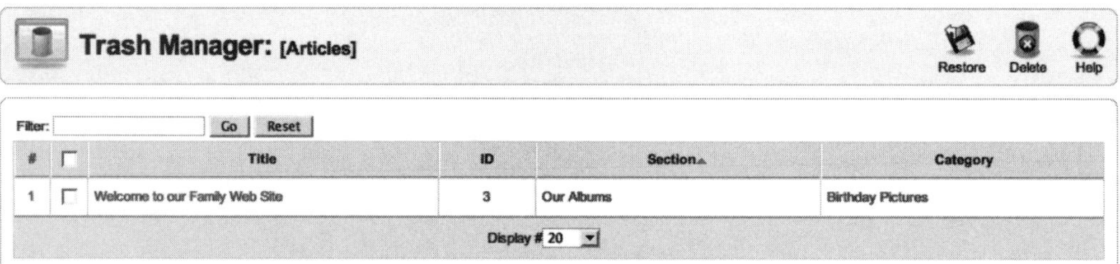

Figure 3.76 Trash Manager

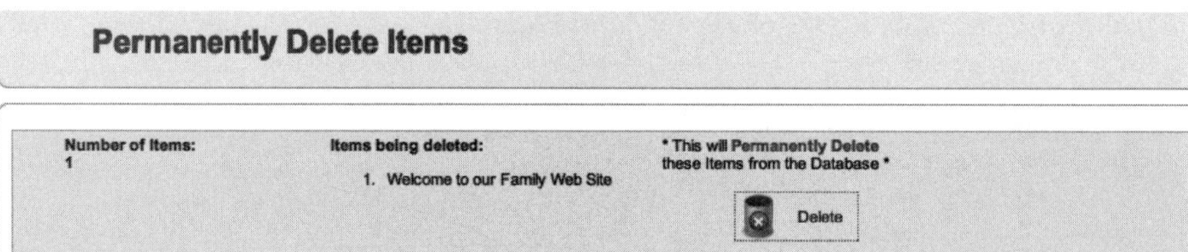

Figure 3.77 Permanently Delete Items screen

To restore an article from the article trash:

1. Choose Content > Article Trash.
2. Click the checkbox next to the article you want to restore.
3. Click the Restore icon.

   If you have not deleted an article from the Trash Manager, you can still restore it to your site. After you restore an article from the Trash Manager, it is placed in its original section and category but is in an unpublished state. You will need to publish it if you want it to show on your site (**Figure 3.78**).
4. Click the Restore icon.

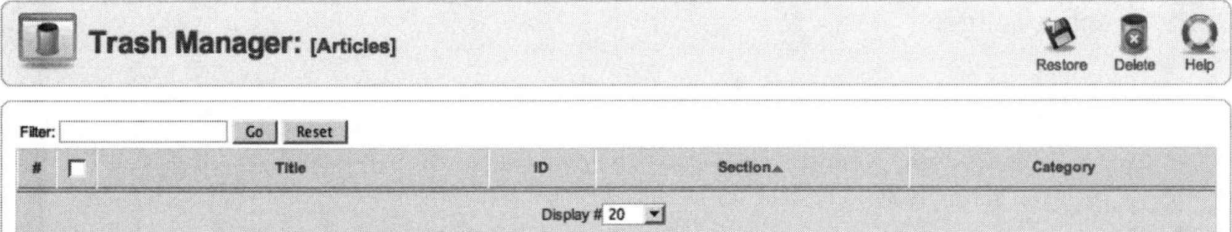

Figure 3.78 Trash Manager after restore

To archive/unarchive an article:

1. Choose Content > Article Manager.
2. Click the checkbox next to the article you want to archive or unarchive.
3. Click the Archive icon to archive an article.

   This moves the articles out of the front end article list, but you can still access them on the site. You can add a link so users can access these older articles (**Figure 3.79**).
4. Click the Unarchive icon to unarchive the article.

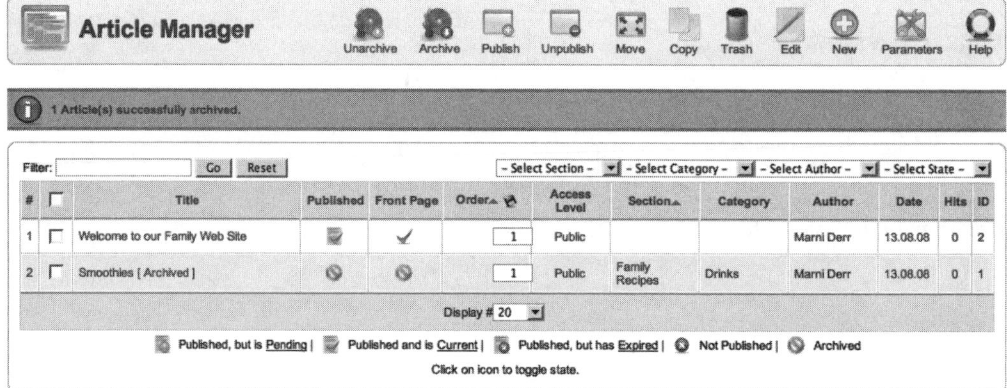

Figure 3.79 Archiving in the Article Manager

Assigning Items to the Front Page

Use the Front Page Manager to manage your Home page content. The front page is actually a section and can contain components, modules, content, and menus like any other section. You can quickly change the published status, order, or access level of the article from the first screen of the Front Page Manager (**Figure 3.80**).

To assign content to the Home page:

1. Choose Content > Article Manager.
2. Click the Front Page column until you see the checkmark.

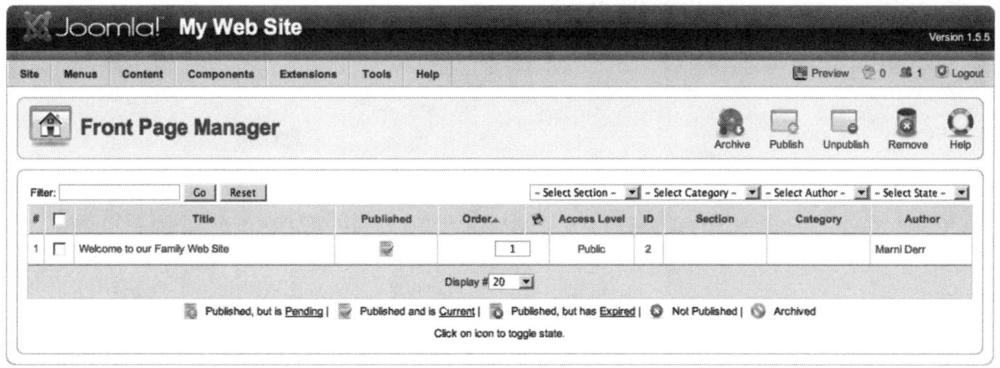

Figure 3.80 The Front Page Manager

To modify Front Page settings:

1. Choose Content > Front Page Manager.
2. To change the published status of an item, click the checkmark in the Published column. The status toggles to unpublished. Click it again and it toggles back to published.
3. To change the access level for a specific item, click the current Access Level link (Public, Registered, or Special) in that section's row. For example, if you click Public once, in the item's row, the access level changes to Registered. Click again and it changes to Special. Click a final time and it returns to Public.
4. To change the access level, click the access level next to the article that you want to change, and the level toggles among the three access levels.

Front Page

The front page is generally thought of as containing "static" content. Although technically nothing is static when using a CMS. The items assigned to the front page are generally things you want a user to see immediately and consistently on your site, like the front cover of a book. The Front Page is the Home Page, and needs to give the user the what, where, and why for the site.

Additional Content

There is additional article content on the companion web site, www.writingyourdreams.com, to make it easy for you to add some sample data. Adding these articles will enhance the look of the web site and help you when you are going through the rest of the book.

Making Your Site Dynamic with Menus

Menus are the most important part of setting up a Joomla web site, because you use menus to display content. Menus not only control navigation but literally *define* how the content is laid out and presented to the user. Nothing appears on the web site without being linked to a menu item. Because your visitors access and view all information through the menu clicks, it's vitally important to get them right. The menu modules control the placement (position) of the menu items on the site, and the menu items control the presentation and layout of the content being displayed.

The good news is, you can easily edit and change menus—like anything else created in Joomla—as you create the site. To add a menu, you must do three things:

1. Create a menu module.
2. Configure and enable the menu module in the Module Manager.
3. Add menu items to the menu module.

Creating Menus

It's important to understand how menus and modules are related. All menus are modules that contain menu items (links). After you create a menu, you must configure and enable the menu in the Module Manager. Often, when creating and modifying menus, you will find yourself going back and forth between the Menu Item Manager and the Module Manager. You will learn more about other types of modules in Chapter 5, "Working with Modules."

To create a menu module:

1. Choose Menus > Menu Manager.
   The Menu Manager opens (**Figure 4.1**).

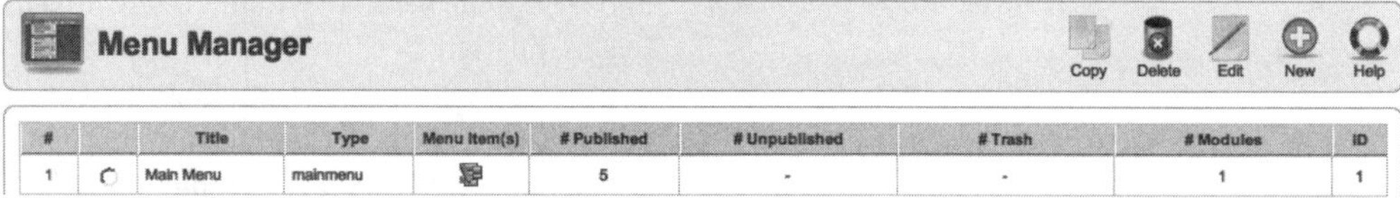

Figure 4.1 The Menu Manager

Menu Manager Fields

- **Title:** The menu title that displays above the menu when Show Title is set to Show.
- **Type:** The unique identifier Joomla uses to identify this menu module.
- **Menu Items icon:** Opens the Menu Item Manager for this menu module.
- **# Published:** Displays the number of published menu items in this menu.
- **# Unpublished:** Displays the number of unpublished menu items in this menu.
- **# Trash:** Displays the number of menu items in the trash for this menu. Deleted menu items are held in the trash until permanently deleted. If you delete a menu module, however, it is deleted immediately.
- **# Modules:** Displays how many other modules are contained in this menu module. Menu modules can contain other modules.
- **ID:** Displays the database ID number for this menu module.

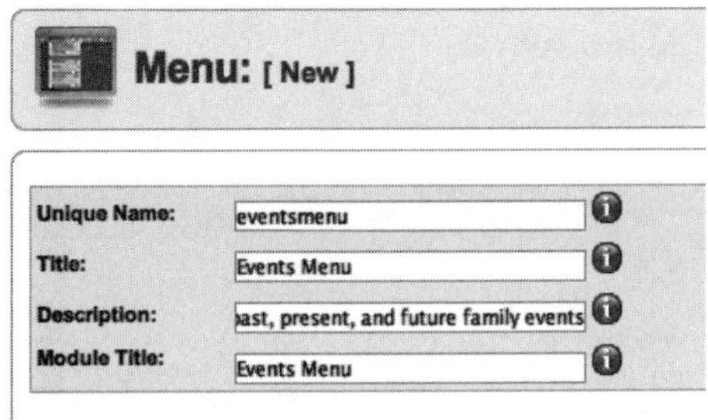

Figure 4.2 The Create New Menu Module page

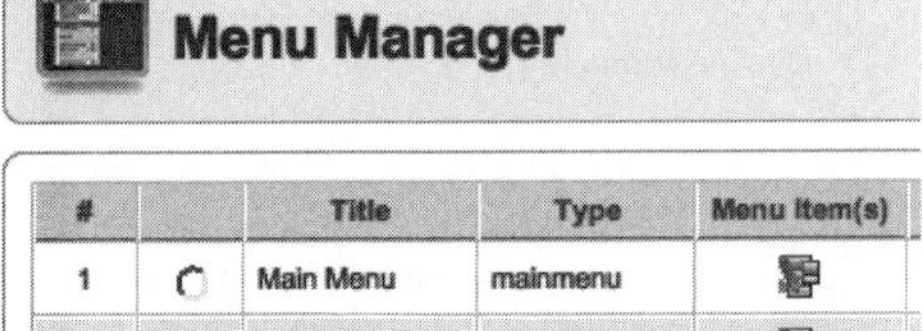

Figure 4.3 The new menus listed in the Menu Manager

2. On the toolbar, click New.

   The New Menu page appears; this is where you create the new menu module.

3. In the Unique Name field, type `eventsmenu`.

   Joomla uses this name to identify the menu, so it must be unique. Use only alphanumeric characters without spaces. You can put underscores between words instead of spaces.

4. In the Title field, type `Events Menu`.

   This is the title of the menu that displays on your web site. You can choose to hide or show the title of the menu through the Module Manager.

5. In the description field, type:

   `A place for past, present,`
   `and future family events.`

6. In the Module Title field, type `Events Menu`.

   This is the name of the menu module, and it will be added to the Module Manager. If you leave this field blank, the menu will not be accessible (**Figure 4.2**).

7. Click Save.

8. Repeating steps 1 through 7, create two more menus—one titled `Albums Menu` and one titled `Recipes Menu`.

   The menus have been added and are now listed in the Menu Manager, but until they are enabled they will not show up on the site (**Figure 4.3**).

✔ Tip

- For small or simple sites, the main menu may be all you need. For large or more complex sites, duplicating the main menu with individual menu modules may be necessary to speed up the loading of your site. The choice comes down to personal preference and the site's design.

To enable a menu module:

1. Choose Extensions > Module Manager.

   The Module Manager page opens (**Figure 4.4**). The newly created menu modules are all listed, but they aren't enabled yet. (For a refresher on Module Manager fields, see Chapter 2, "Getting Started.")

2. In the Enabled column, click the red circled X for each menu module.

   The Menu Modules are now enabled, as indicated by the green checkmarks in the Enabled column (**Figure 4.5**).

3. Click the Preview link.

   The menus are all listed on the front page (**Figure 4.6**). The menus may not be in the order you want them to appear, but you can change that by using *positions*.

✔ Tip

- Positions are used to place modules anywhere around the main body of the page. All modules can be assigned to specific positions defined by the template. Currently all menu modules are in the Left position. You can have multiple modules assigned to positions and control the order in which they appear using the Module Manager.

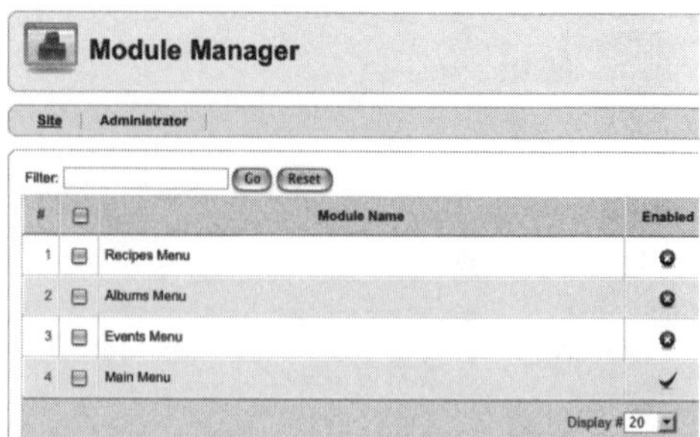

Figure 4.4 The Module Manager with the menus disabled

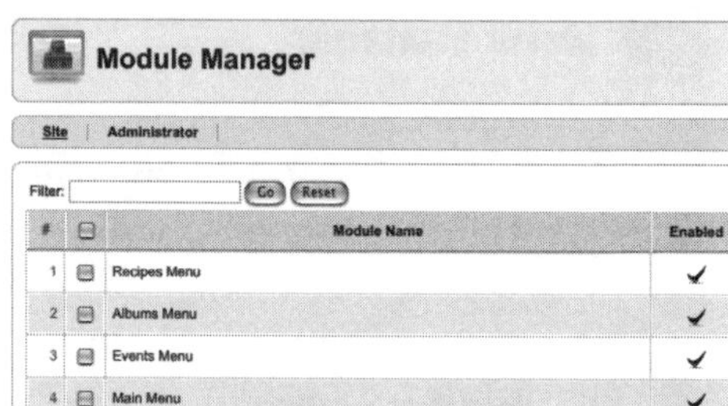

Figure 4.5 The Module Manager with the menus enabled

Figure 4.6 The site with the new menus

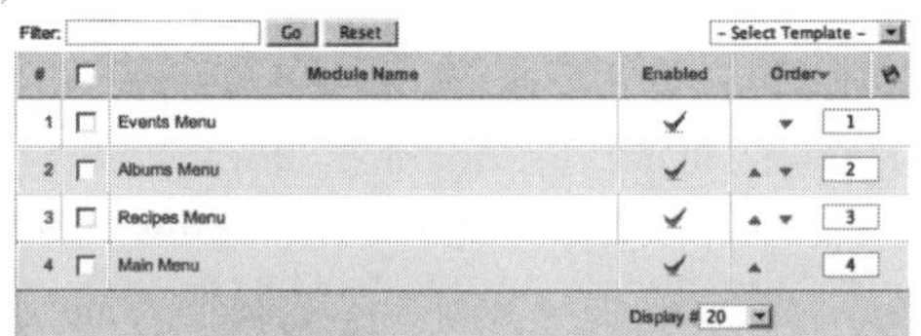

Figure 4.7 The Module Manager showing the creation order of the menus

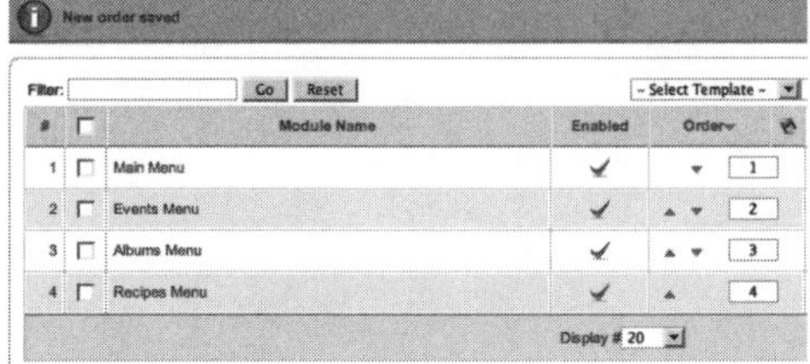

Figure 4.8 The Module Manager showing the menu ordering changed

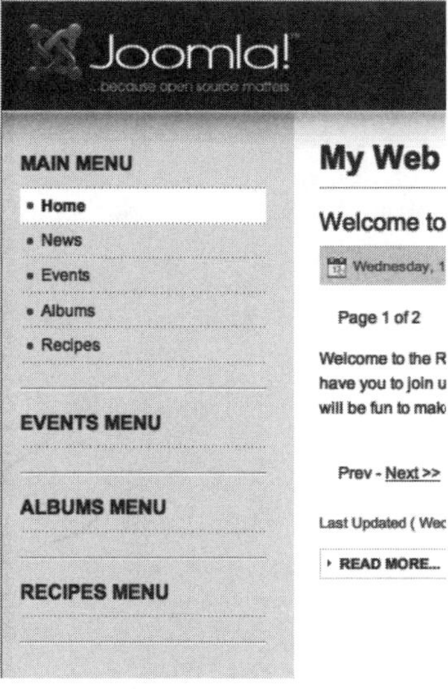

Figure 4.9 The front page with the menus displayed in order

To change the display order of menu modules:

1. Choose Extensions > Module Manager.

   The Module Manager opens. Because the main menu is the main navigation for the site, you want this menu to display first. The menus are currently in the order they were created (**Figure 4.7**).

2. For the Main Menu, type 1 in the Order column.

3. For the Events menu, type 2 in the Order column.

4. For the Albums menu, type 3 in the Order column.

5. For the Recipes menu, type 4 in the Order column.

6. Click the Save icon next to the Order column header.

   You can also change the order by using the arrows next to the order number. This can be a more efficient way to reorder your modules when you have many modules and those modules are all in different positions. For now the four menus are in the correct order (**Figure 4.8**).

7. Click Preview.

   The new menu ordering is reflected on the front page (**Figure 4.9**).

To change a menu position:

1. Choose Extensions > Module Manager.

   The Module Manager opens with a list of all modules created or installed on your site.

   The current design trend is to place the main navigation of a web site horizontally across the top, so you are going to change the position of this menu to place it across the top of the web site.

2. Click the Main Menu link to open the Module Editor (**Figure 4.10**).

   You will use the Module Editor to configure all settings for the menu module. Each of the module settings will be covered throughout this chapter; for now you simply need to change the position of the main menu.

3. In the Details area, choose hornav from the Position drop-down menu (**Figure 4.11**).

   The position and the menu's style are defined by the template.

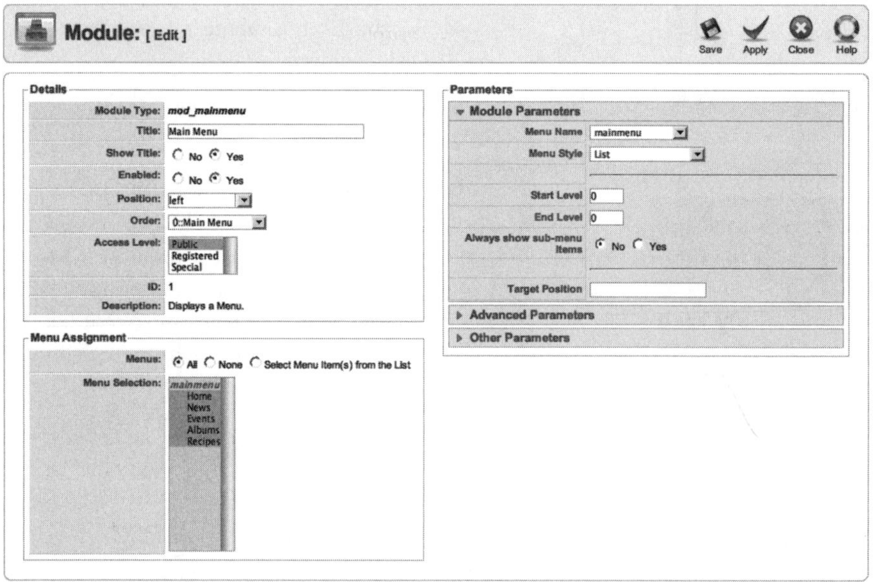

Figure 4.10 The Module Editor

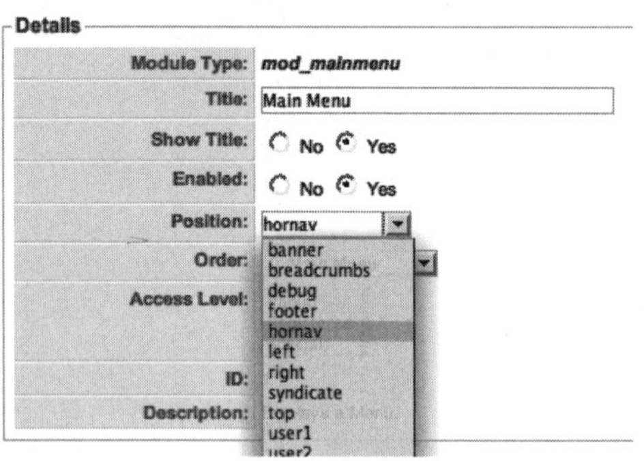

Figure 4.11 Choosing hornav for the Main Menu position

CREATING MENUS

Figure 4.12 The front page displays the Main Menu in the horizontal position defined in your template

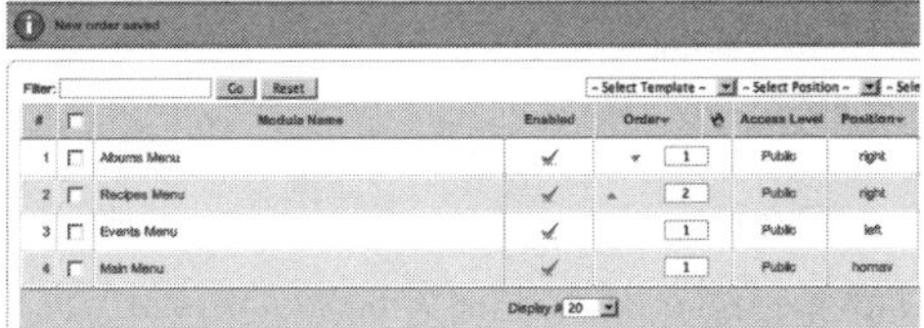

Figure 4.13 The new menu position ordering

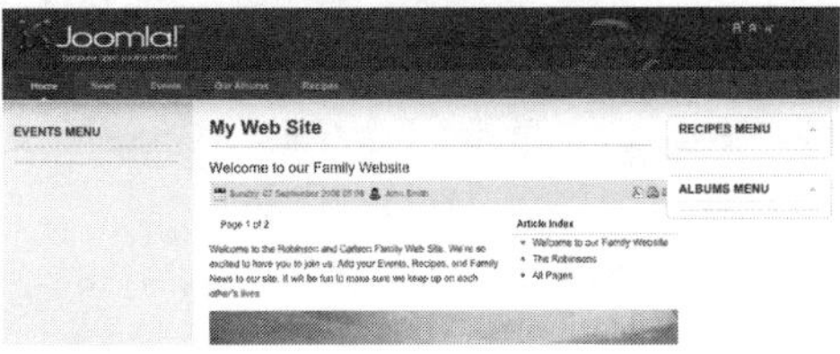

Figure 4.14 The new menus positioned on the front page

4. Click Save, and then click Preview.

   You have just moved the main menu to the horizontal position styled by the template (**Figure 4.12**).

5. Change the Albums and Recipes menus to the Right position.

   The menu ordering changes as you group menus into different positions. Notice each menu is assigned an order according to the position (**Figure 4.13**).

6. Click Preview to see your changes (**Figure 4.14**).

   To learn how to use the positions for your template, as well as how to create your own positions, see Chapter 9, "Creating Joomla Templates."

✔ Tip

- Templates define the positions for the web site. If you want to see where all the positions are located, from the front page of your web site type `www.mywebsite.com?tp=1` (**Figure 4.15**). The positions are all labeled on your web page.

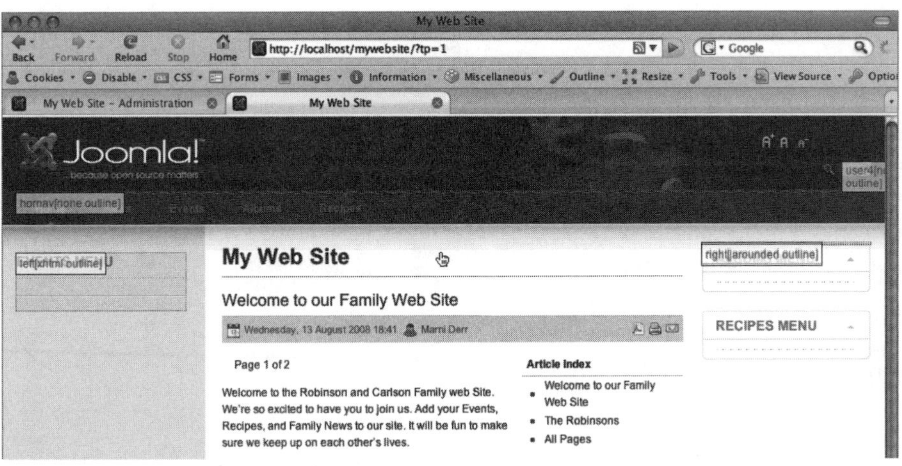

Figure 4.15 Using the `?tp=1` command to display the positions of your template

To edit menu module details:

1. Choose Extensions > Module Manager.

   The Module Manager opens with a list of all modules created or installed on your site.

2. Click the Main Menu link to open the Module Editor.

   The Module Editor is where you configure the module details, menu assignments, and parameters. The module details control the display functions (**Figure 4.16**).

3. Click the No radio button for Enabled.

   The menu is no longer enabled, so it won't show on the web site.

4. Click Apply, and then click Preview (**Figure 4.17**).

   Notice that the menu no longer displays on the web site.

5. Now re-enable the menu by clicking the Yes radio button for Enabled.

6. Click Save, and then click Preview (**Figure 4.18**).

To use menu assignment:

1. Choose Extensions > Module Manager.

   The Module Manager opens with a list of all modules created or installed on your site.

2. Click the Events Menu link to open the Module Editor.

   The default is to assign menu modules to all menu items. Menu assignment tells Joomla when this menu module is to display on the page (**Figure 4.19**).

3. In the Menu Assignment area, click the "Select Menu Item(s) from the List" radio button.

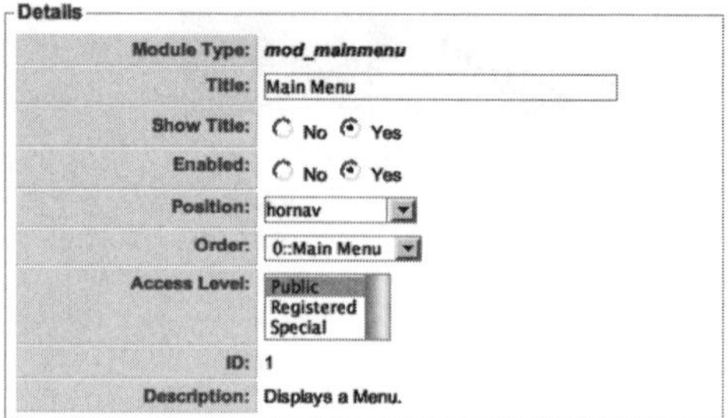

Figure 4.16 The menu module details

Figure 4.17 A preview of the web site without a main menu

Figure 4.18 A preview of the web site with a main menu enabled

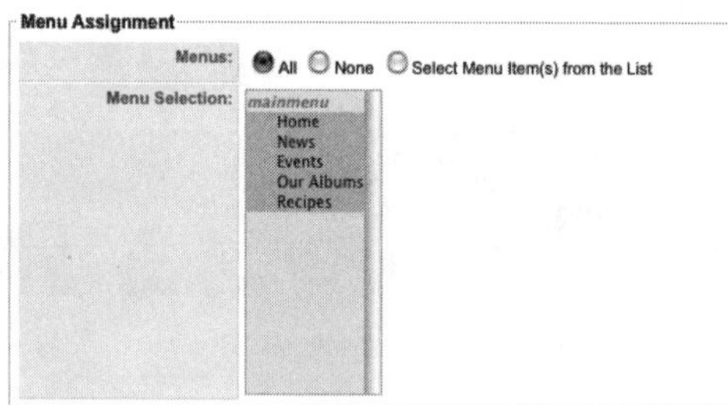

Figure 4.19 The menu assignment selections

Creating Menus

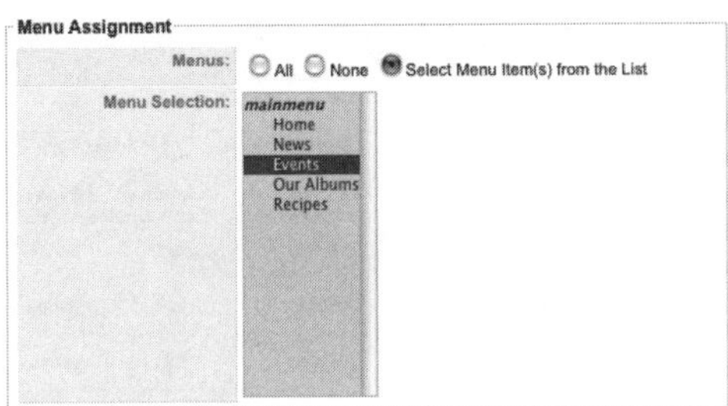

Figure 4.20 Assigning the Events menu module to the main menu Events link

4. From the Menu Selections, choose Events.

   Assigning the Events menu module to the Events menu item tells Joomla to display this module only when the user clicks the Events link in the Main Menu (**Figure 4.20**).

5. Click Save.

6. Repeat steps 2 through 5 to assign the Albums menu module to the Home and Our Albums menu items.

continues on next page

Module Editor Details

- **Module Type:** Identifies the kind of module.
- **Title:** The title of the module.
- **Show Title:** Shows or hides the module title. Selecting Yes shows the Title at the top of the module; selecting No hides the title.
- **Enabled:** Enables the module to be used on the web site.
- **Position:** Places the module in the position selected and uses the CSS styling from the template.
- **Order:** Sets the order of this module and how it is displayed on the site.
- **Access Level:** Defines who can see the module on the site according to their access level.
- **ID:** The database ID number for this module.
- **Description:** A brief description of the module.

Menu Assignment

- **All:** Displays the menu on all pages.
- **None:** Does not display the menu on any page. None is generally used to hide a menu. You can use hidden menus to display content on a specific page, yet not display a menu with links you may not want available to the user.
- **Select:** Allows you to select specifically the pages you want this menu displayed on.

7. Repeat steps 2 through 5 to assign the Recipes menu module to the Home and Recipes menu.

   As shown in steps 6 and 7, you can assign menu modules to multiple menu items. Command-click (Mac) or Control-click (Windows) to select multiple menu items.

   The module assignment for each menu module is listed in the Pages column. All indicates the menu module is assigned to all menu items, and Varies indicates that it is assigned to some menu items (**Figure 4.21**).

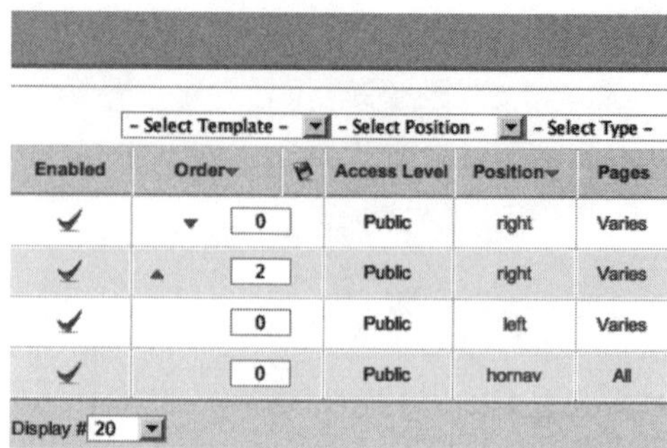

Figure 4.21 Pages column showing which pages the menu module is assigned to

8. Click Preview.

   Click each of the links in the main menu to see the results. When you click Events, the Events Menu appears. When you click Albums, the Our Albums menu appears (**Figure 4.22**).

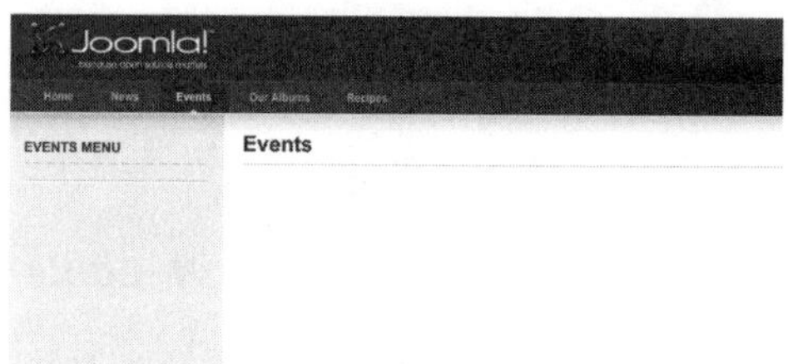

Figure 4.22 A preview of the Events menu on the Events section page

✔ Tip

- In summary, the menu module is a container for the menu items. This allows the module and the items to be styled individually by the template, and it lets you place the menus in positions on the page and assign what pages the menus will or will not appear on.

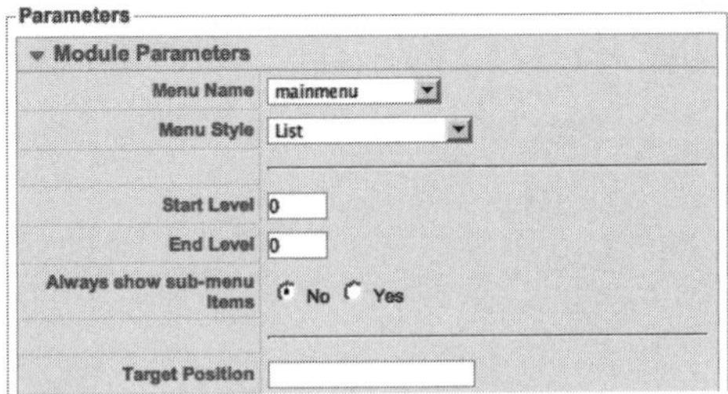

Figure 4.23 Menu module basic parameters

Menu Module Parameters

Menu module parameters control how a menu module appears on your site and works with your template. From the parameter settings, you control the menu style and name, whether the menu has submenus, and so on. This section covers an overview of the Menu Module parameter settings.

To access the menu module parameters:

1. Choose Extensions > Module Manager.

   The Module Manager opens with a list of all modules created or installed on your site.

2. Click the Main Menu link to open the Module Editor.

3. Click the arrow next to Module Parameters to expand the Module Parameters panel.

   The Module Parameters panel is where you can change your parameter settings. You won't be changing any of these settings right now (**Figure 4.23**).

continues on next page

Menu Module Parameters (Basic):

- **Menu Name:** This is the current menu name for this menu module.
- **Menu Style:** The List menu selection is the default. The other menu styles are for supporting legacy Joomla 1.0.x templates and should not be used for Joomla 1.5.x native templates.
- **Start Level/End Level:** This allows you to break up a long or multilevel menu into separate modules. Zero is the top level.
- **Always show sub-menu Items:** Clicking Yes means submenu items are displayed whether or not the parent (top level) of the menu is active. Clicking No means the user must click the parent item to display the submenu.
- **Target Position:** Specifies the locations of drop-down and pop-up menus. Set in pixels.

4. Click the arrow next to Advanced Parameters to expand the Advanced Parameters panel.

   These parameters are used for XHTML and CSS coding purposes and will be covered in Chapter 9, "Creating Joomla Templates" (**Figure 4.24**).

5. Click the arrow next to Other Parameters.

   The Other Parameter settings are for menus that contain submenus (**Figure 4.25**).

   These parameters are discussed later in the chapter as you create more menu modules.

6. Click Close to exit the screen.

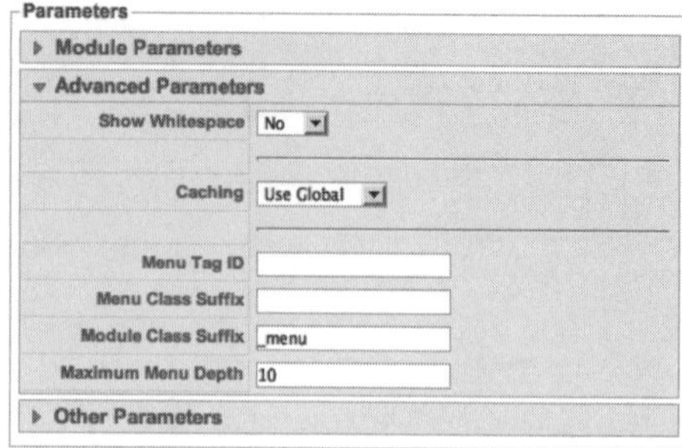

Figure 4.24 Menu module Advanced parameters

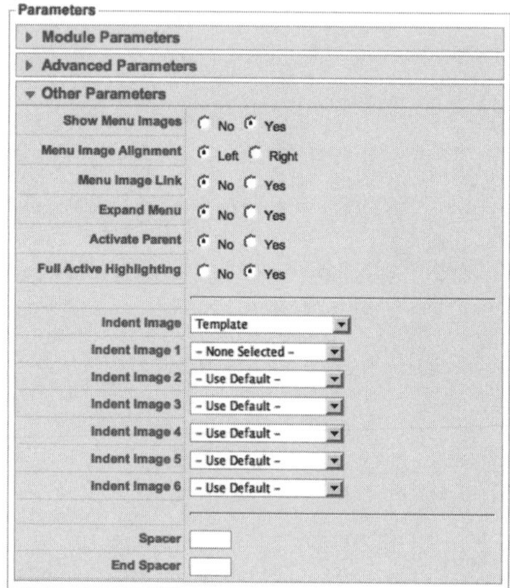

Figure 4.25 Menu module Other parameters

Menu Module Parameters (Advanced)

- **Show Whitespace:** This is used for viewing the actual XHTML source code generated by the menu, and it does not affect the way the menu displays on the page.
- **Caching:** Use Global uses the global configuration cache setting for this menu. No Caching does not cache the menu module.
- **Menu Tag ID:** For coding purposes, you can assign an optional `id` attribute for the HTML `<ul>` tag.
- **Menu Class Suffix:** The CSS class applied to each menu item.
- **Module Class Suffix:** The CSS class to be applied to the menu module.
- **Maximum Menu Depth:** The maximum number of submenu levels this menu is allowed.

Adding Menu Items

All menu items are added to, or contained in, modules. Although menu items are essentially links telling Joomla what to present on the page, like any standard link used in web sites, they literally define how that content is to be presented. What this means is menu items are more than just links contained in a module—you need to have a clear idea of how you want the content presented when creating a menu link. So if menu modules control the placement (position) and look of the menu container on the site, and the menu items control the presentation and layout of the content being called, how do you know what layout to use? This section covers each of the layouts provided by Joomla. As with any other function, menu items contain details and parameters that help modify presentation.

To access the Menu Item Manager:

- Choose Menus > Recipes Menu to open the Menu Item Manager (**Figure 4.26**).

  Each menu module contains its own Menu Item Manager. From here you create all the menu items that will be contained in this menu module (**Figure 4.27**).

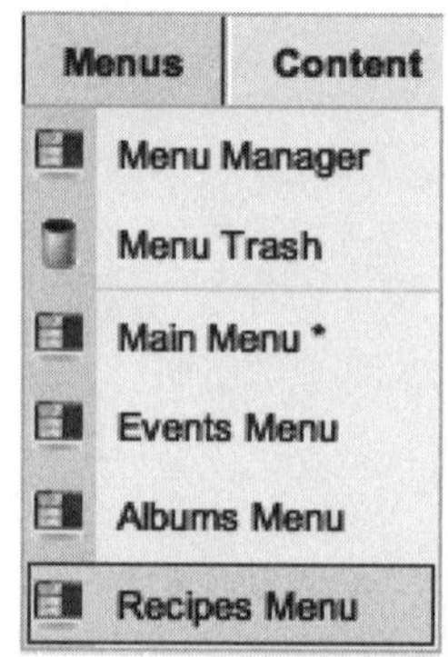

Figure 4.26 Selecting the Recipes menu

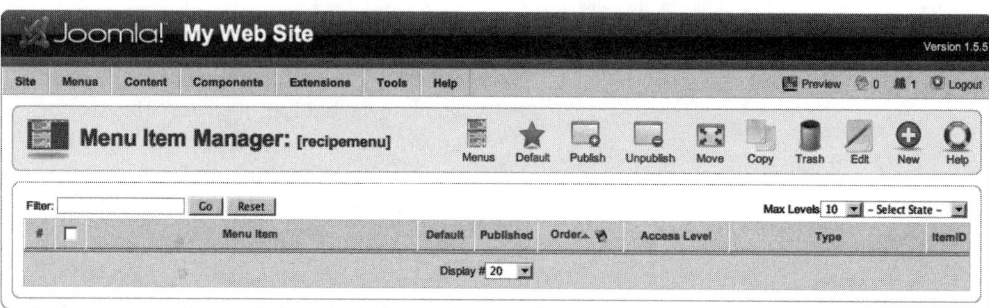

Figure 4.27 The Menu Item Manager

Menu Item Manager Fields

- **Menu Item:** This displays the name of the menu item. When clicked, it opens the Menu Item Editor for this menu item.
- **Default:** A star in this row sets the default menu item (focus) for this menu module.
- **Published:** Displays whether this menu item is published or unpublished.
- **Order:** Shows the current order of the menu items contained in this menu.
- **Access Level:** Displays the access level required to see this menu item.
- **Type:** Displays the menu item type for this menu item.
- **ItemID:** Displays the database ID for this menu item.

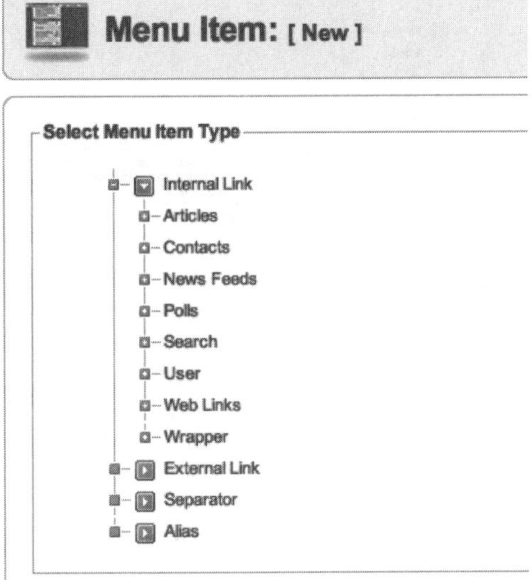

Figure 4.28 Selecting a menu item type

Selecting Menu Item Types

Menu item types are organized into four groups. Each group contains layouts for each menu item type you are using. If you install third-party components and modules, new layout types will be added to the Menu Item Type list (**Figure 4.28**).

- **Internal Links:** Used to display the content on your site.
- **External Links:** Used to link to sites outside your web site.
- **Separators:** Used to place separator items, such as graphics or lines, between your menus.
- **Alias:** Alias links are used to link back to existing menu items.

  Each menu item type has various layouts. In this section we cover the most common types of layouts used, the details and parameters you can set with each layout, and examples of what the layouts will look like on the site. However, it is impossible to cover every variation. As you work with menu item types and their parameters, you will become familiar enough to develop and customize the look you are going for.

To create an archived article list layout:

1. Choose Menu > Recipes Menu.
2. Click the New icon to open the New Menu Item selection page.

   Hovering over a menu item type displays a pop-up describing the layout (**Figure 4.29**).
3. Choose Internal Link > Articles > Archive > Archived Article List.

   The Menu Item Editor opens, where you configure all the settings for this layout type. At the top of the page is the name of the layout type selected for this menu item. You can change the layout type at any time by coming back to the Menu Item page (**Figure 4.30**).

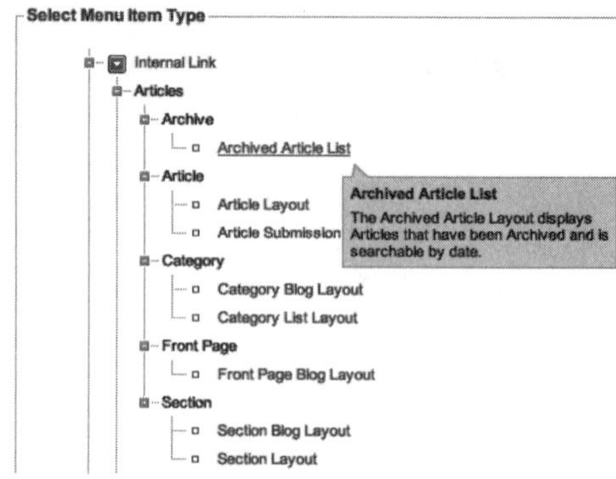

Figure 4.29 A pop-up description of the layout

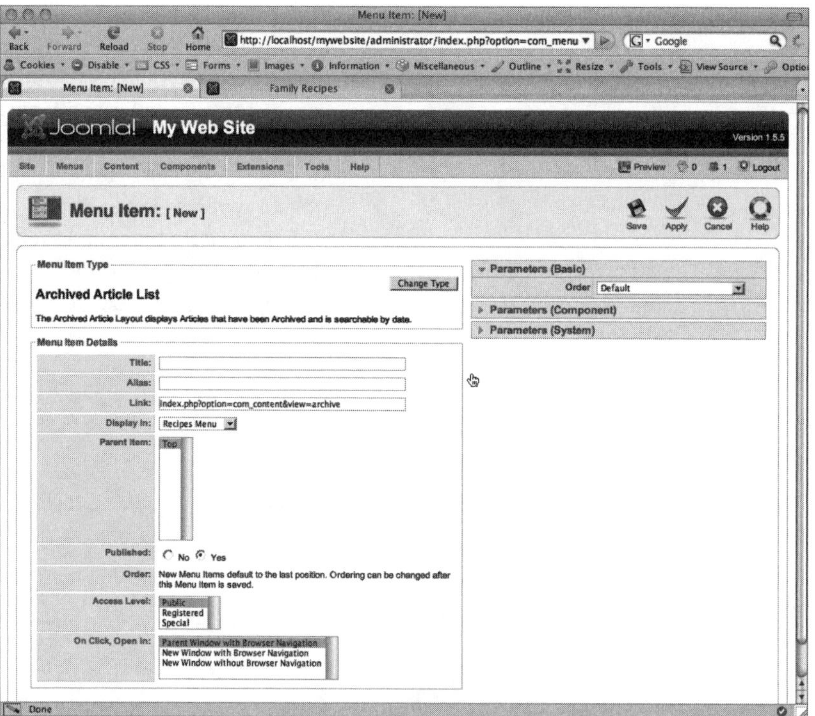

Figure 4.30 The Menu Item Editor for the Archived Article List

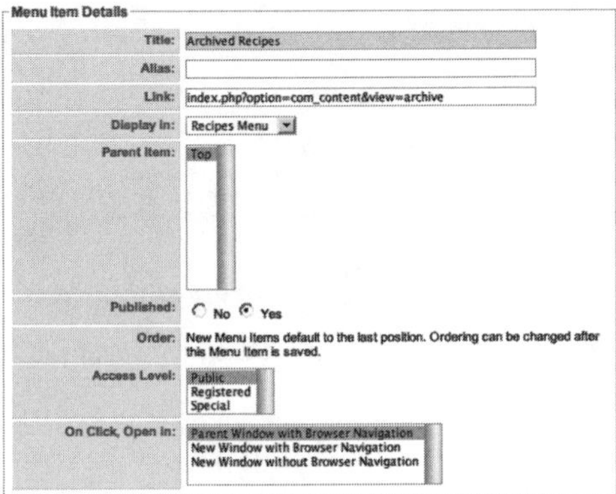

Figure 4.31 The menu item details settings

4. In the Menu Item Details area, in the Title field, type `Archived Recipes`.

   The title is the name of the link as it will appear in the Recipes Menu module.

5. Leave the Alias field blank.

   The Link field displays the actual *parameterized* URL used by the system to call this page. You cannot modify this field; Joomla fills it in automatically. See Chapter 7, "Modifying Global Settings" for more information about search engine–friendly URLs.

6. Choose Recipes Menu from the Display In drop-down menu.

   Your choice determines in which menu module this link appears.

7. In the Parent Item list, leave Top highlighted, because this is a top-level parent menu item.

8. Click the Yes radio button for Published.

   If you don't publish your menu item, it won't appear in your menu. Select No if you plan to publish the menu item later or for hidden menu items.

9. In the Access Level list, choose Public.

10. In the "On Click, Open In" list, choose Parent Window with Browser Navigation.

    This selection opens your menu item in the current window without opening a new browser window (**Figure 4.31**).

11. Click Apply.

To set article archived list parameters:

1. Choose Menu > Recipes Menu.
2. Click Archived Recipes.
3. Under Parameters (Basic), choose "Most recent first" from the Order drop-down menu (**Figure 4.32**).

   Archived article lists have only one basic parameter: the order in which you want the list sorted. Most order settings are self-explanatory with the following exceptions:

- **Order:** Sorts the articles by the order they appear in the Article Manager. Use this when you want to choose the order for your articles.
- **Default:** Sorts by most recent archived article first.

4. Click the arrow next to Parameters (Component) to expand the list.

   Component parameters set to Use Global use the article's Global Configuration parameters (**Figure 4.33**). Changing the parameters here will override the article's parameters for this menu item only. These parameters were covered in detail in Chapter 3, "Adding Your Content."
5. Click the arrow next to Parameters (System).
6. In the Page Title field, type `Our Older Recipes.`

   This places a page title above the article list.

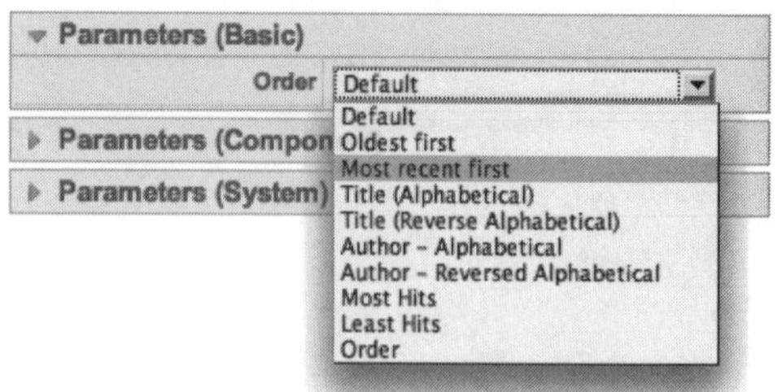

Figure 4.32 Article archived list basic parameters

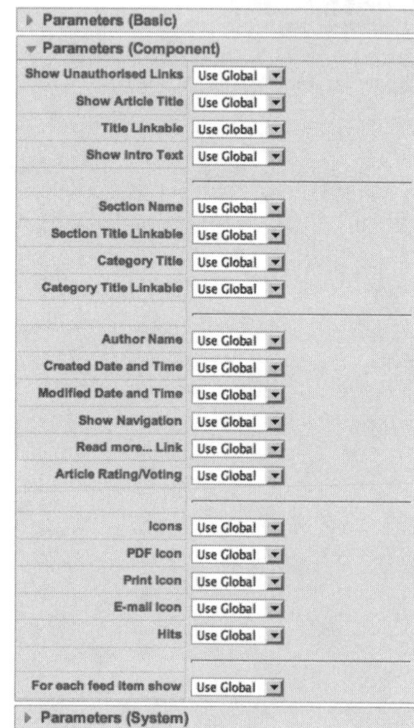

Figure 4.33 Article archived list component parameters

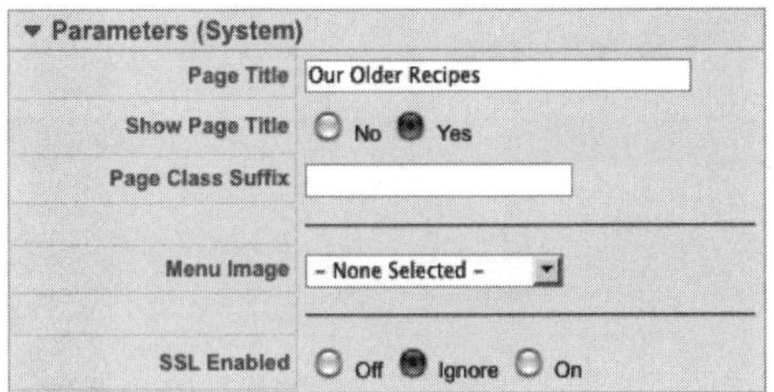

Figure 4.34 Article archived list system parameters

Figure 4.35 The Archived Recipes menu item added to the Recipes menu module

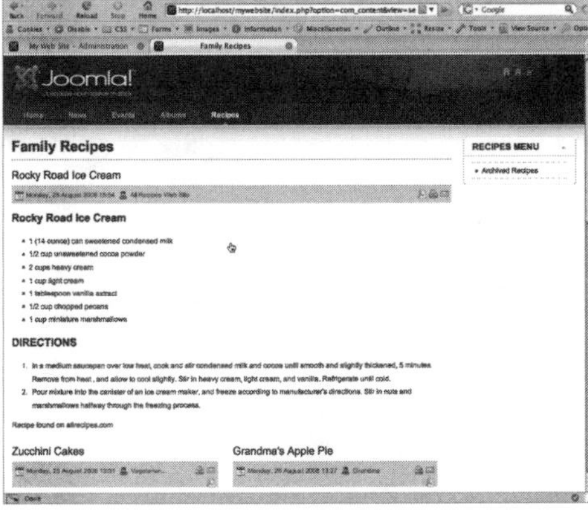

Figure 4.36 The web site Recipe section

7. Click the Yes radio button for Show Page Title (**Figure 4.34**).

   Leave all other system parameters at their defaults:

   ▲ **Page Class Suffix:** Assigns a CSS class from your template.

   ▲ **Menu Image:** Places an image next to this menu item link.

   ▲ **SSL Enabled:** Is used by Joomla to allow SSL connections.

8. Click Save, and then click Preview.

   The first menu item is now in the Recipes Menu module. If you cannot see the link, click the arrow next to Recipes Menu to expand the list (**Figure 4.35**).

   This creates a menu item (link) so the user can access any archived recipes, but it also will control how the archived recipes are laid out.

9. Choose Recipes from the main menu.

   The Recipes section opens, displaying all of the current recipes, with a Recipes menu on the right to help users navigate through all the recipes contained on the site (**Figure 4.36**).

continues on next page

10. In the administrative back end, choose Content > Article Manager.
11. Select the checkbox for three recipes and click the Archive button.

    The three articles you chose are now grayed out and archived (**Figure 4.37**). If you do not create a menu item for archived items, your users have no way of accessing or viewing content that has been archived on the site.
12. Return to the Recipe page of the web site, click Refresh, and then choose the Archived Recipes menu item.

    A list off the archived recipes is displayed, along with a filter to search through the archives (**Figure 4.38**). The archived articles list layout defined how this content will be presented to the user.

Figure 4.37 Archiving recipes

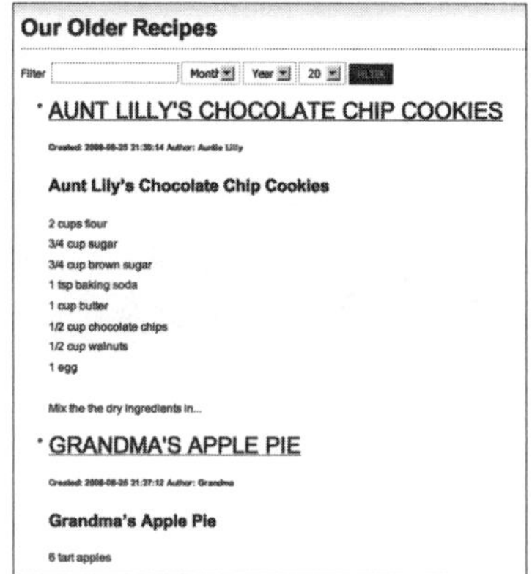

Figure 4.38 The archived list layout

To create an article layout menu item:

1. Choose Menus > Recipes Menu.
2. On the Menu Item Manager toolbar, click the New icon.
3. Choose Internal Link > Articles > Article Layout.

   The Menu Item Editor opens (**Figure 4.39**).

   Unlike all the other layouts, the article layout type displays only a single article.
4. In the Title field, type `Today's Recipe`.

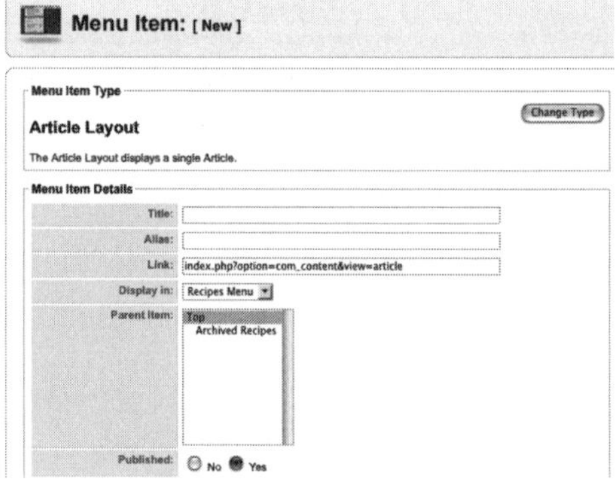

Figure 4.39 The article layout

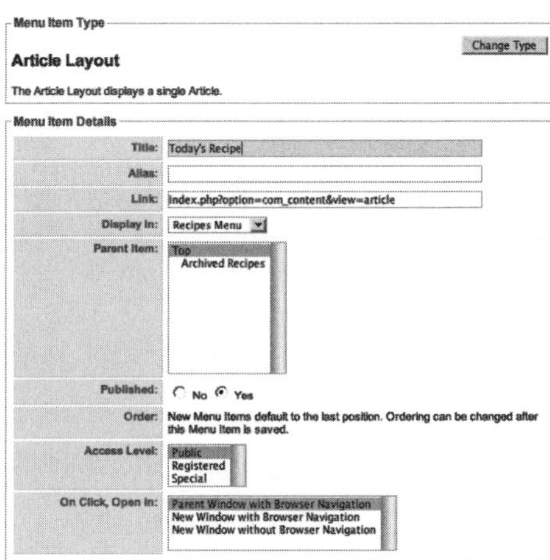

Figure 4.40 Creating an article layout

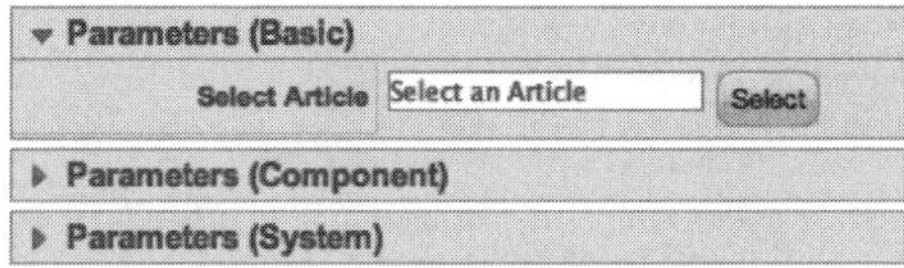

Figure 4.41 Selecting an article

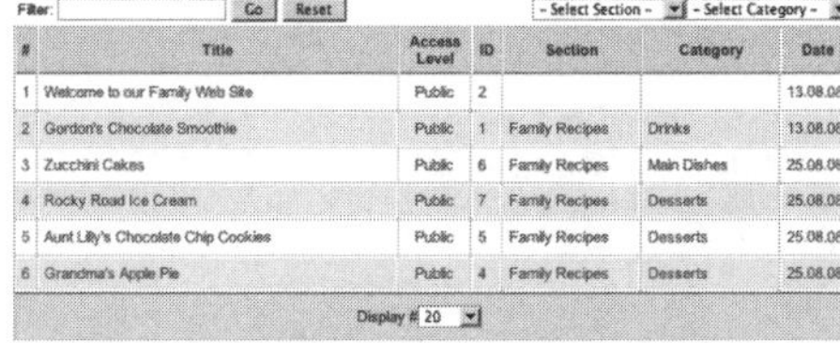

#	Title	Access Level	ID	Section	Category	Date
1	Welcome to our Family Web Site	Public	2			13.08.08
2	Gordon's Chocolate Smoothie	Public	1	Family Recipes	Drinks	13.08.08
3	Zucchini Cakes	Public	6	Family Recipes	Main Dishes	25.08.08
4	Rocky Road Ice Cream	Public	7	Family Recipes	Desserts	25.08.08
5	Aunt Lilly's Chocolate Chip Cookies	Public	5	Family Recipes	Desserts	25.08.08
6	Grandma's Apple Pie	Public	4	Family Recipes	Desserts	25.08.08

Figure 4.42 A list of created articles

Figure 4.43 A single article using article layout

5. Leave all other fields in the Menu Item Details at their defaults (**Figure 4.40**).

6. Under Parameters (Basic), click the Select button (**Figure 4.41**).

   A small window appears, displaying all articles created (**Figure 4.42**).

7. Click the Zucchini Cakes title.

   Do not change the Component Parameters unless you want to override the Global Configuration parameters set for this article. System Parameters allow you to add a title to the page, define a custom CSS class, and enable SSL connections.

8. Click Save, and then click Preview.

   Another menu item, Today's Recipe, is added to the Recipes menu.

9. Click Today's Recipe to see an example of an article layout (**Figure 4.43**).

To create a category blog layout menu item:

1. Choose Menus > Recipes Menu.
2. On the Menu Item Manager toolbar, click the New icon.
3. Choose Internal Link > Articles > Category > Category Blog Layout (**Figure 4.44**).
4. In the Menu Item Details area, type `Desserts` in the Title field.
5. Leave all other fields in the Menu Item Details at their defaults (**Figure 4.45**).
6. Continue setting category blog parameters.

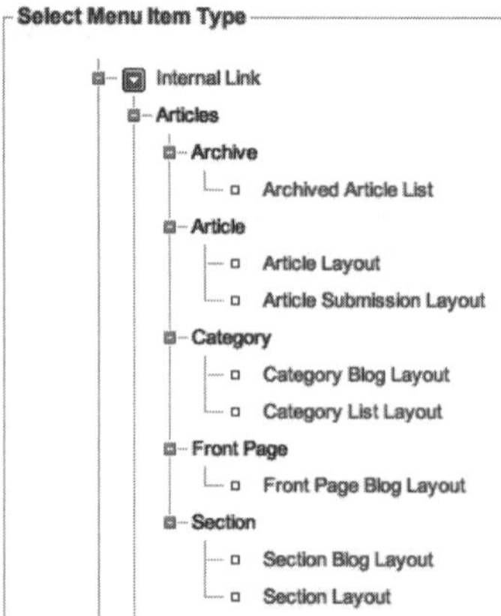

Figure 4.44 The blog layouts

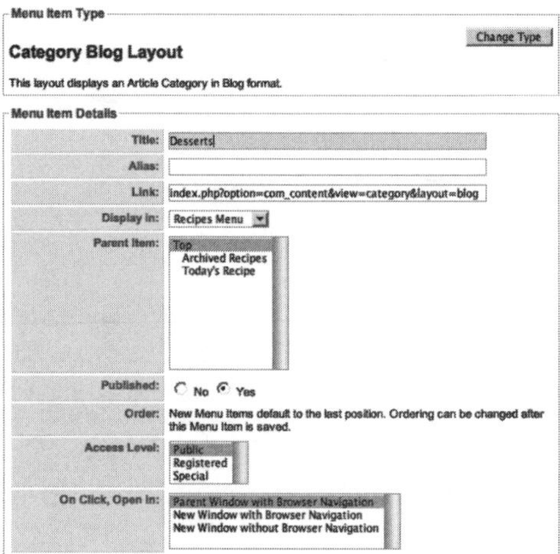

Figure 4.45 Category blog layout details

Blog Layout Types

The Category, Front Page, and Section blog layouts are all very similar. All the blog layouts contain a leading area, intro area, and an area for links within the main body of the page.

- **Category Blog Layout:** This layout displays all articles assigned to the category selected in the menu item parameters.
- **Front Page Blog Layout:** This layout displays all articles assigned to the front page.
- **Section Blog Layout:** This layout displays all articles assigned to the section selected in the menu item parameters.

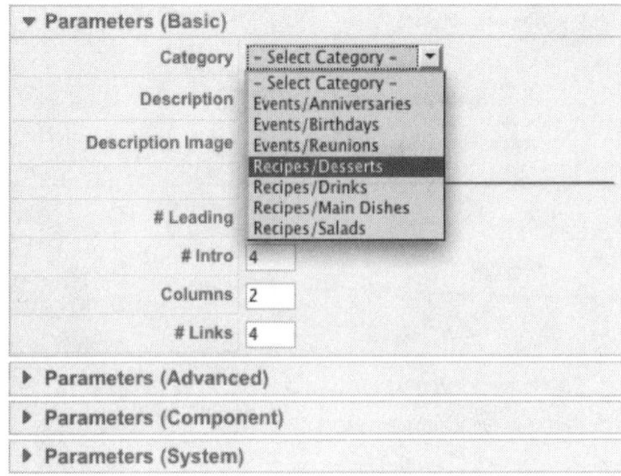

Figure 4.46 Selecting the section and category

To set category blog parameters:

1. Choose Menus > Recipes Menu.
2. Click the Desserts menu item.
3. Click the arrow next to Parameters (Basic).
4. Choose Recipes/Desserts from the Category drop-down menu (**Figure 4.46**).

   This tells Joomla the section and the category to pull the articles from.
5. Click the Hide radio button for Description.

   Selecting Show displays the section and category descriptions set in the category and section managers. Selecting Hide does not display the descriptions.
6. Leave Description Image set to Hide.

   If an image was created for the section and category descriptions, you could set this to Show to display the images.

continues on next page

Basic Parameters

- **# Leading:** Determines how many leading articles display at the top of the main body on the page. A setting of 0 displays a leading article the full width across the page.
- **# Intro:** Determines the number of articles to display after the leading article.
- **Columns:** Determines how many columns of articles display. This is only for the main body of the page. For example, a setting of 2 means two articles at a time will display side by side after the intro article.
- **# Links:** Determines the number of links to display at the bottom of the main page. This is useful when there are too many articles to display on a single page, and it provides access to the rest of the articles in this section and category.

7. Leave the rest of the parameters at their defaults (**Figure 4.47**).

   You can alter these numbers to see the affect on the layout.

8. Click Save, and then click Preview.

9. In the Recipes Menu, click the Desserts link.

   You use the parameters to alter the layout and override any article global parameters set, such as hiding the date and author info, and so on (**Figure 4.48**).

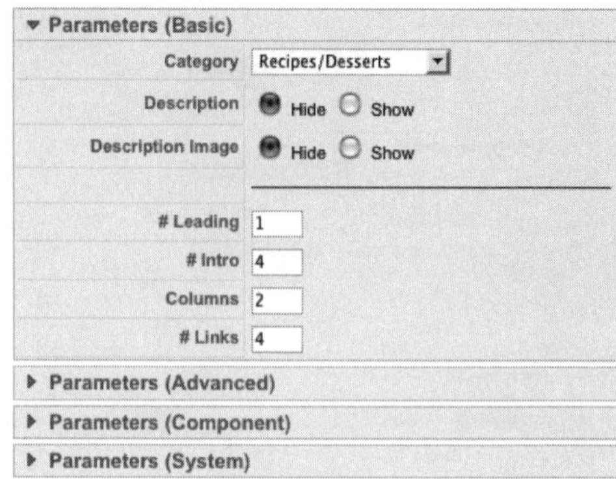

Figure 4.47 Category blog layout parameters

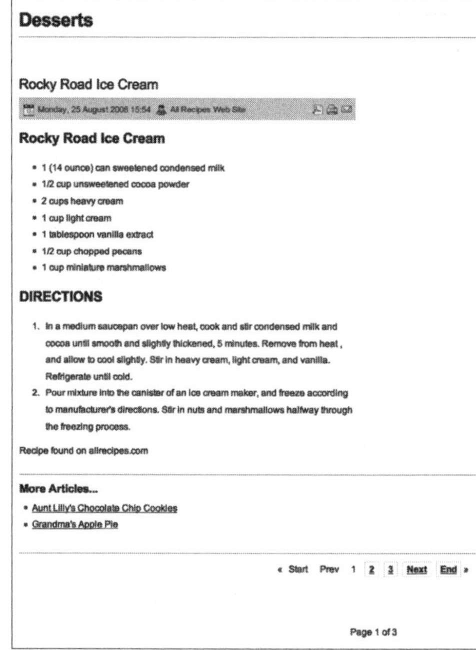

Figure 4.48 A category blog layout on the site

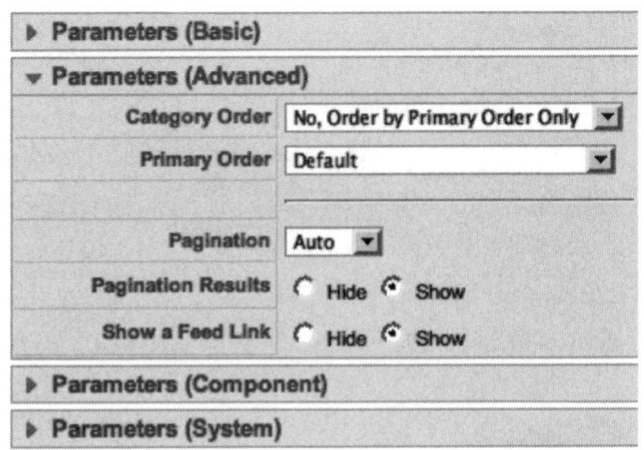

Figure 4.49 Category blog layout advanced parameters

Figure 4.50 The Change Type button

To set category blog advanced parameters:

1. Choose Menus > Recipes Menu.
2. In the Menu Item Manager, click Desserts.
   The Menu Item Editor opens for Desserts.
3. Click the arrow next to Parameters (Advanced) (**Figure 4.49**).
4. Change advanced parameters as desired, and then click Save.

To create a category list layout menu item:

1. Choose Menus > Recipes Menu.
2. In the Menu Item Manager, click Desserts.
   The Menu Item Editor opens. To see the difference between layout types, you are going to change the Dessert item's blog layout to a category list layout.
3. In the Menu Item Type area, click the Change Type button (**Figure 4.50**).
   The Change Menu Item page opens.

continues on next page

Category Blog Advanced Parameters

- **Category Order:** Choosing Primary Order sorts the articles using the setting in the Primary Order field. Order sorts the articles by the order specified in the Category Manager; Title sorts alphabetically by title.
- **Primary Order:** Choose Default to sort the most recent articles first. The other settings are self-explanatory.
- **Pagination:** Auto and Show place next and previous links at the bottom of the page if needed. Hide does not place any navigation at the bottom of the page.
- **Pagination Results:** Places numbers on the bottom of the page to tell the user how many more pages of articles they can navigate through.
- **Show a Feed Link:** Hides or shows a feed link. For example, you could receive an RSS feed from allrecipes.com to see new recipes.

  Component and System parameters are the same as covered earlier. Play around with different parameter settings and view the web site to see how your changes affect the layout.

4. Choose Internal Link > Articles > Category > Category List Layout (**Figure 4.51**).

   The Category List Layout option shows all the articles belonging to a single category in one list.

5. Click the arrow next to Parameters (Basic) (**Figure 4.52**).

6. Choose Recipes/Desserts from the Category drop-down menu.

7. Leave the Advanced, Component, and System parameters at their defaults (or adjust them to your preference). They are the same as for each of the other menu item types.

8. Click Save, and then click Preview.

9. In the Recipes Menu, click Desserts.

   The list of all articles appears in the Desserts category (**Figure 4.53**).

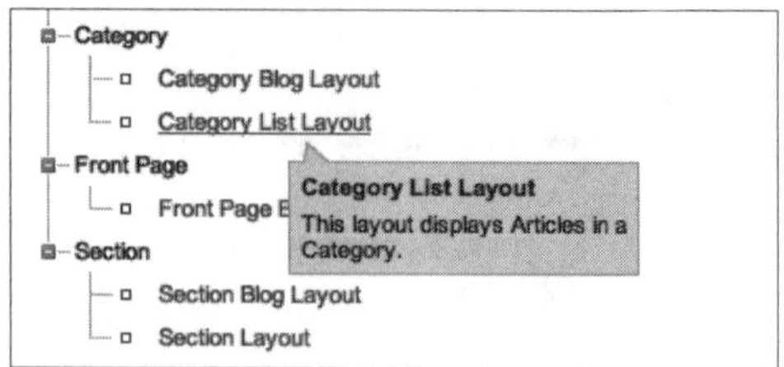

Figure 4.51 Selecting the category list layout

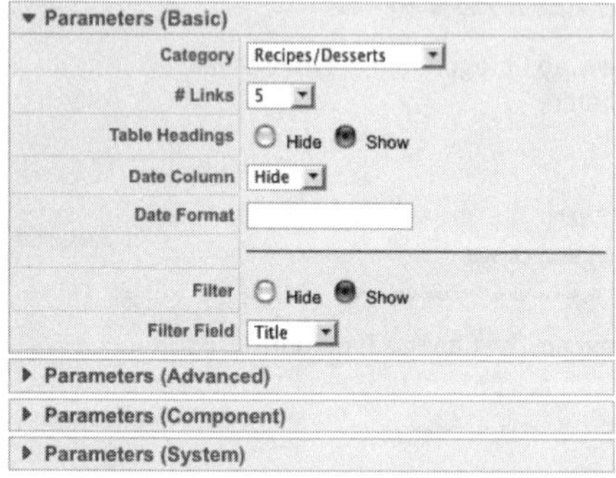

Figure 4.52 Category list basic parameters

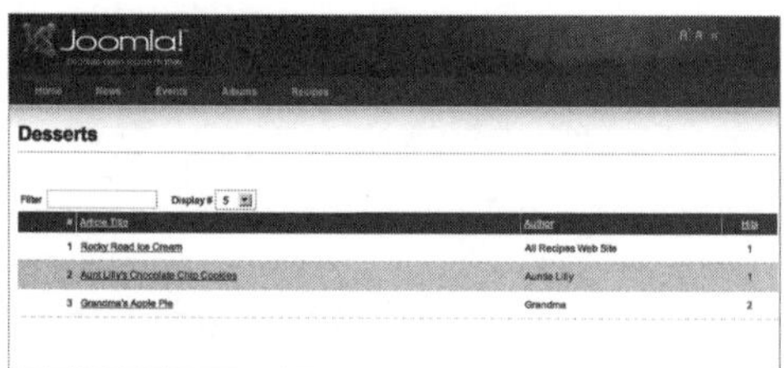

Figure 4.53 The Desserts menu item in category list layout

Category List Layout Basic Parameters

- **# Links:** This sets the number of articles to display as links.
- **Table Headings:** Hides or shows the column headings for the articles in this category.
- **Date Column:** Hides or shows the date column.
- **Date Format:** If left blank, the date will use the default date format for your web site.
- **Filter:** Hides or shows the filter options for the articles. Showing a filter field lets the user sort and find specific articles faster.
- **Filter Field:** Selects the field used as the sort option.

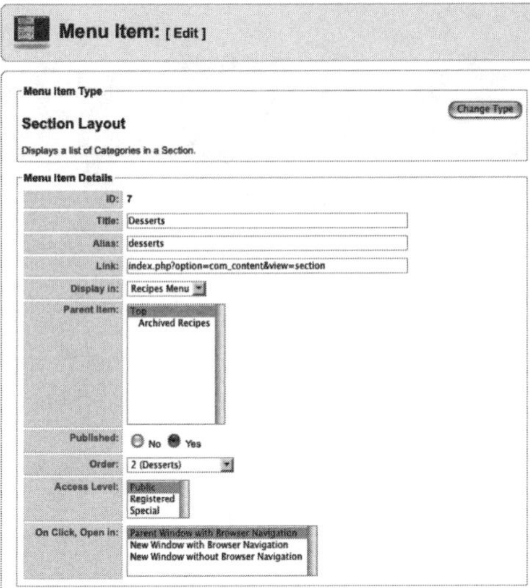

Figure 4.54 The section layout settings

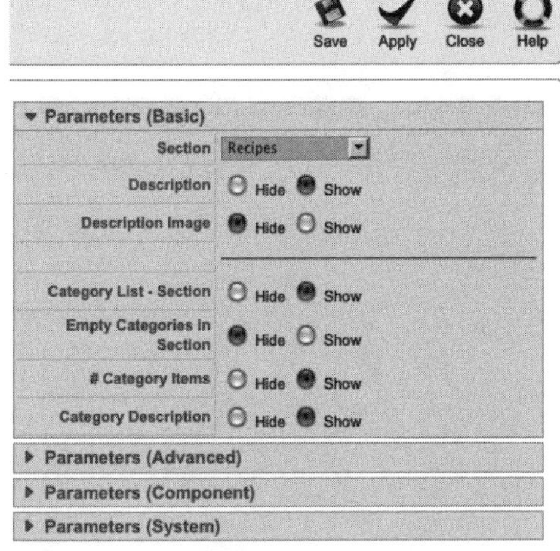

Figure 4.55 The Section layout basic parameters

To create a section layout menu item:

1. Choose Menus > Recipes Menu.
2. Click the Desserts menu item.

   The Menu Item Editor opens so you can change the layout type to a section layout.
3. In the Menu Item Type area, click the Change Type button.
4. Choose Internal Links > Articles > Section > Section Layout.

   A section layout show all the articles, arranged by categories, in a single section. The category titles are links, and they display the number of articles each category contains (**Figure 4.54**).
5. Under Parameters (Basic), choose Recipes from the Section drop-down menu (**Figure 4.55**).
6. Click Save, and then click Preview.

continues on next page

7. Click the Desserts link from the Recipes Menu.

   The section title, Family Recipes, is at the top of the page, along with the section description, and the categories for this section are all listed as links. Next to the category links are the number of articles contained in each category (**Figure 4.56**).

8. On the Desserts page, click the Desserts link.

   A category list layout is displayed automatically, allowing the user to search the available recipes (**Figure 4.57**).

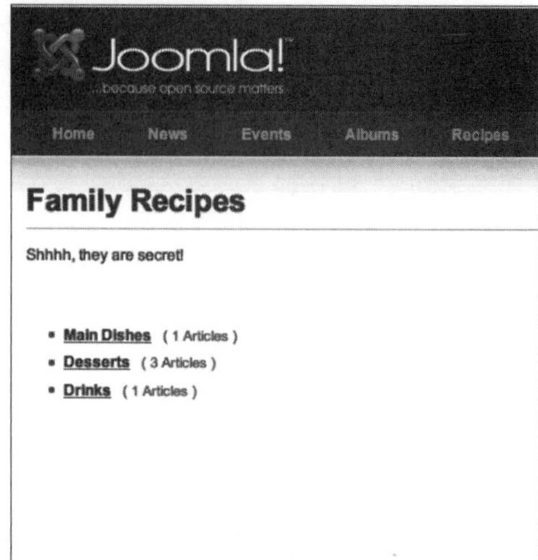

Figure 4.56 The section layout viewed on the site

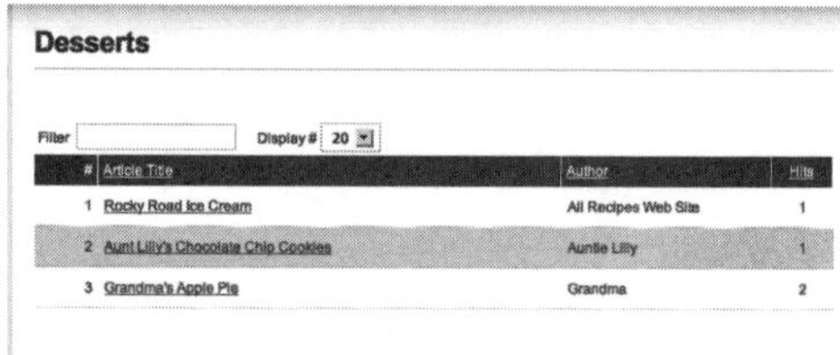

Figure 4.57 Selecting a category link

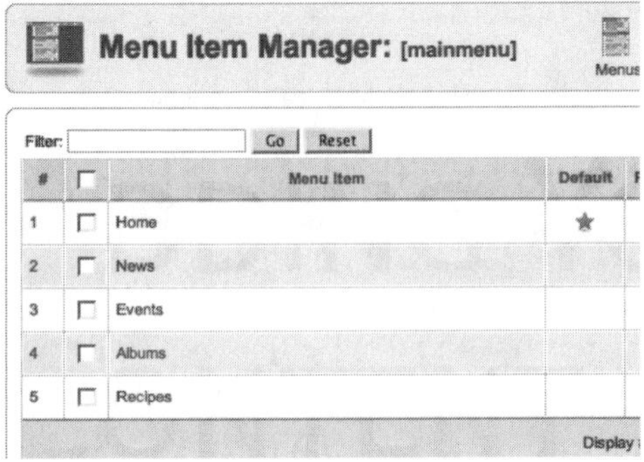

Figure 4.58 The Home menu item as the current default

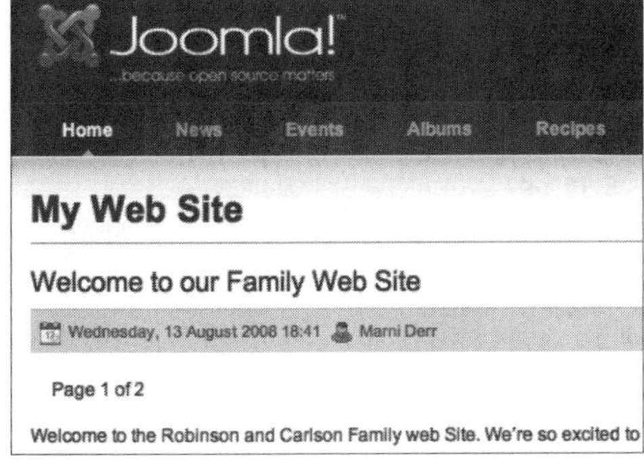

Figure 4.59 The Home menu item as active

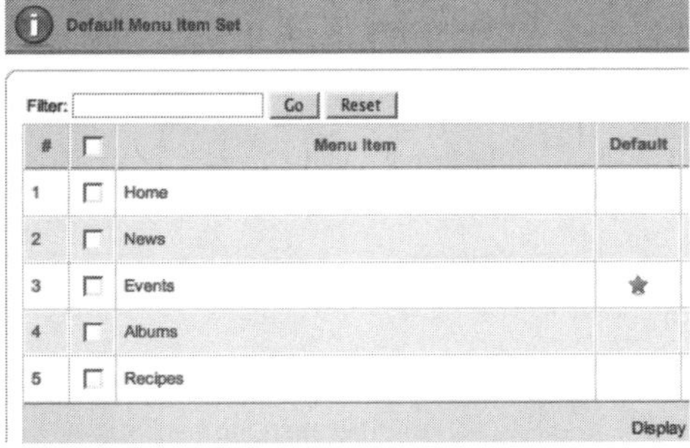

Figure 4.60 The Events menu changed to default

Modifying Menu Items

As you have learned, it is easy to change menu items without re-creating them from scratch. In addition to changing the menu item type, you can move, copy, delete, publish, and unpublish items. You can also change the default menu item.

To change the default menu item:

1. Choose Menus > Main Menu.

   The Menu Item Manager page appears, listing all of the menu items for the Main menu (**Figure 4.58**).

   The Home menu item is currently the default for the main menu. This means the Home menu item has what web developers term as *focus*. A user goes to the web site, and the Home menu item is active. In this template, the Home link is highlighted with a small triangle (**Figure 4.59**).

2. In the Menu Item Manager, click the box to the left of the Events menu item.

3. Click the Default icon.

   The Default icon moves to the Events menu item, making Events the new default (**Figure 4.60**).

4. Click Preview.

   Notice that the Events menu item is now the default menu item, and the Events section is the first page that displays.

5. Change the default menu item back to the Home menu item.

To copy a menu item:

1. Choose Menus > Recipes Menu.

   The Menu Item Manager for the Recipes menu opens so you can choose a menu item to copy (**Figure 4.61**).

2. Click the box to the left of the Desserts menu item, and then click the Copy icon.

   The Copy Menu Item(s) page opens, listing all the menus available on the site (**Figure 4.62**).

3. In the Copy to Menu list, select recipemenu.

4. Click the Copy icon.

   A duplicate of Desserts is now in the Menu Item Manager. The new menu item keeps all the same settings as the original. This comes in handy when you want another menu item with the same settings; simply make a copy, change the name, and the item is ready. Copying is useful when you need to provide access to a menu item from multiple menu modules.

5. Click the Desserts menu item you copied.

   The Menu Item Editor opens.

6. Change the Title to `Main Dishes`, and then delete the text in the Alias field.

7. Change the menu item type to Category Blog Layout.

8. From the Category drop-down menu, choose Recipes/Main Dishes.

9. Click Save, and then click Preview (**Figure 4.63**).

10. Click the Main Dishes menu item to see the new menu item.

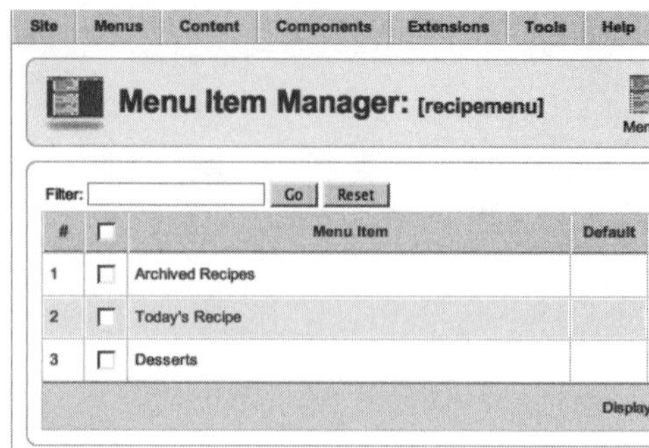

Figure 4.61 The Menu Item Manager for the Recipes menu

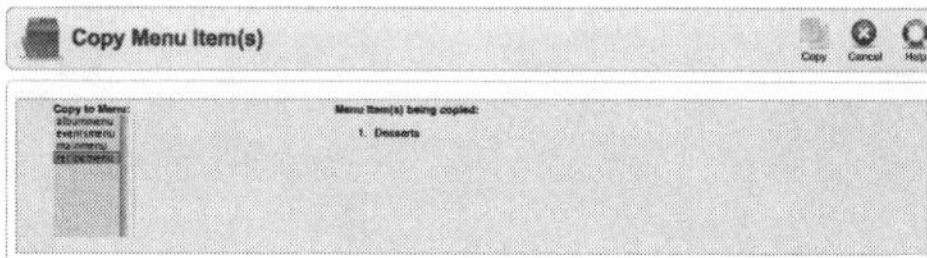

Figure 4.62 Copy Menu Item(s) page

Figure 4.63 The copied menu item after editing

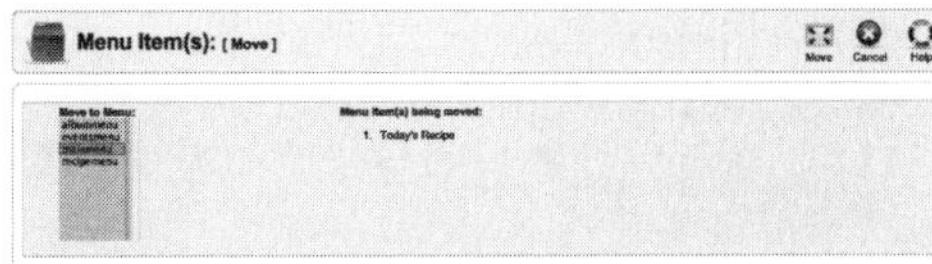

Figure 4.64 The Menu Item(s) Move page

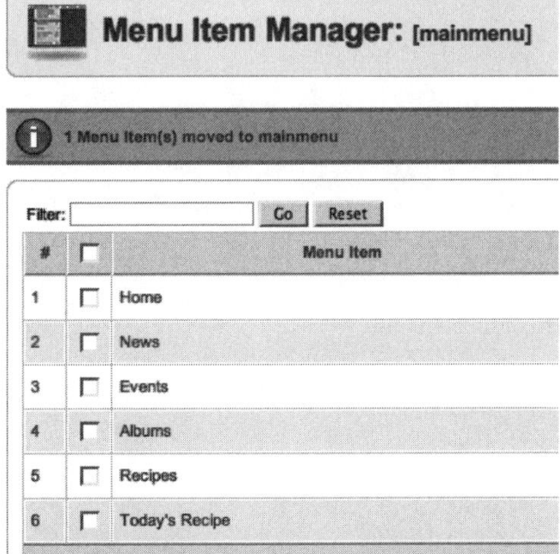

Figure 4.65 Today's Recipe moved to the Main Menu

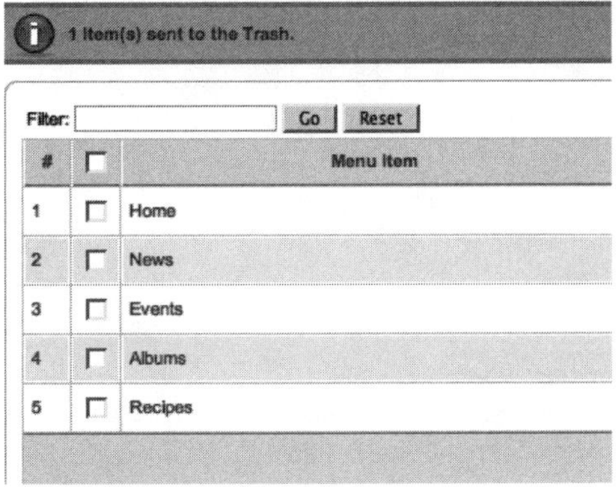

Figure 4.66 Menu item sent to the trash

To move a menu item:

1. Choose Menus > Recipes Menu.
2. Click the box to the left of the Today's Recipe menu item, and then click the Move icon.

   The Menu Item(s) Move page opens (**Figure 4.64**).
3. In the Move to Menu list, select mainmenu.
4. Click the Move icon.

   The Today's Recipe menu item is moved to the Main Menu, and the Menu Item Manager for the Main Menu opens (**Figure 4.65**).

To delete or restore a menu item from the Trash Manager:

1. Choose Menus > Main Menu.
2. Click the box to the left of Today's Recipe.
3. Click the Trash icon to move the menu item to the trash.

   Moving a menu item to the trash does not completely delete it from the system. To delete it permanently, you must delete it from the Menu Trash (**Figure 4.66**).

continues on next page

4. Choose Menus > Menu Trash.

   The Trash Manager opens with a list of all menu items that have been sent to the trash but not yet deleted from the database. From here you can select to restore an item or delete an item (**Figure 4.67**).

5. Click the checkbox next to Today's Recipe.

6. Click Delete.

   Clicking Delete removes the menu item permanently from your system, but first you will be asked if you are sure you want to permanently delete this item (**Figure 4.68**).

7. Click Cancel.

   For this example, you don't want to delete Today's Recipe. Instead, you are going to restore the item in the next step.

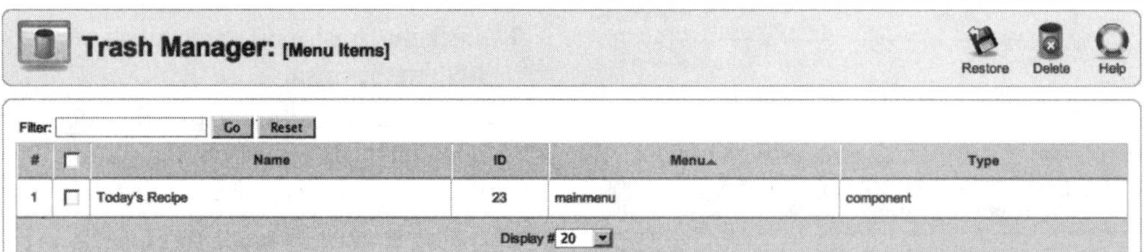

Figure 4.67 The Trash Manager

Figure 4.68 The Permanently Delete Items page

8. Click the checkbox next to Today's Recipe, and then click Restore.

   The Restore Items page opens asking if you want to restore the item (**Figure 4.69**).

9. Click Restore, and when the system asks you yet again if you're sure, click OK.

10. Go back to the Main Menu to see that the Today's Recipe item has been restored.

    When restored from the Trash Manager, an item defaults to unpublished with an item order of 999999. You need to publish the item before it appears on the site, and you also need to adjust its order.

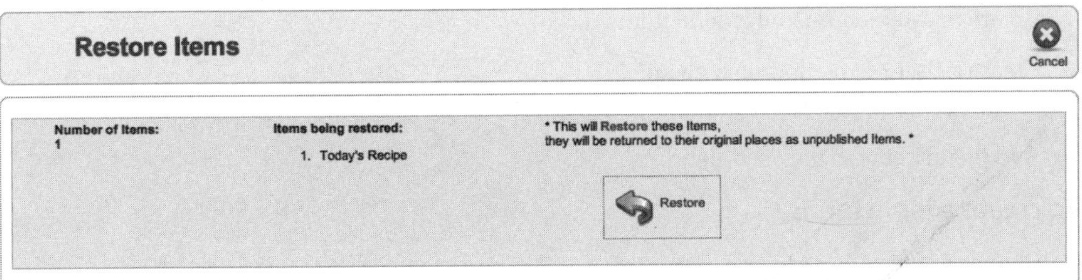

Figure 4.69 The Restore Items page

Creating Registered User Menus

When a menu module is set to Registered, the menu and all menu items are viewable only by registered users after they log into the site. By creating a user menu, you can have menu items to add or edit content, modify user profiles, and so on, that are available only to this user.

Before users can log in, however, the site needs a front end login form. In this section, you will:

- Create a Login Form module for registered users.
- Create registered user-only menu items.
- Create a User Menu module with an access level of Registered.
- Add menu items to the user menu.

To create a login form:

1. Choose Extensions > Module Manager.

   The Module Manager opens, displaying all the current modules created and installed on the site (**Figure 4.70**).

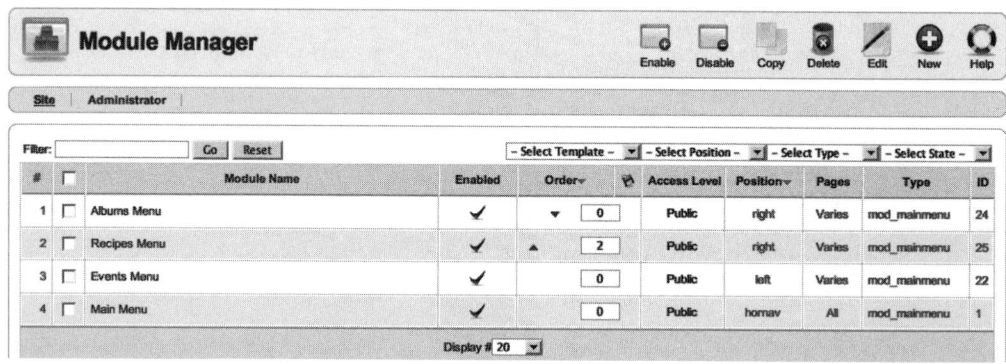

Figure 4.70 The Module Manager

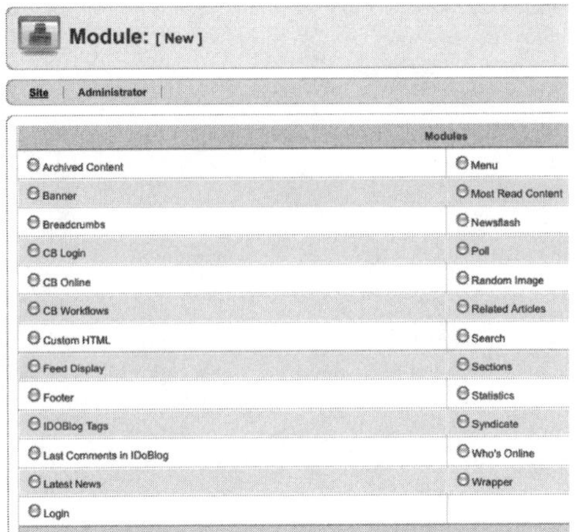

Figure 4.71 The module types you can create

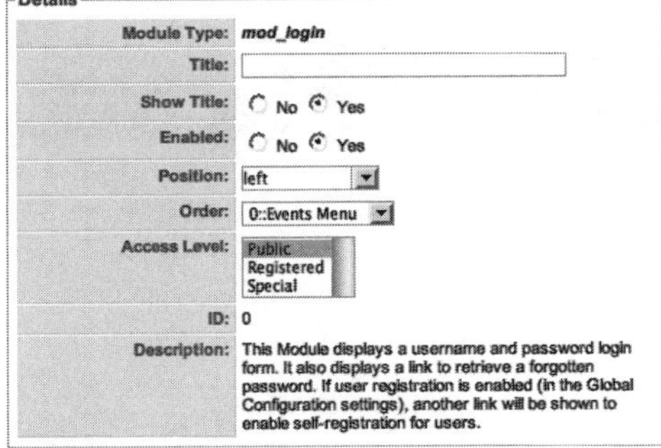

Figure 4.72 Login module details

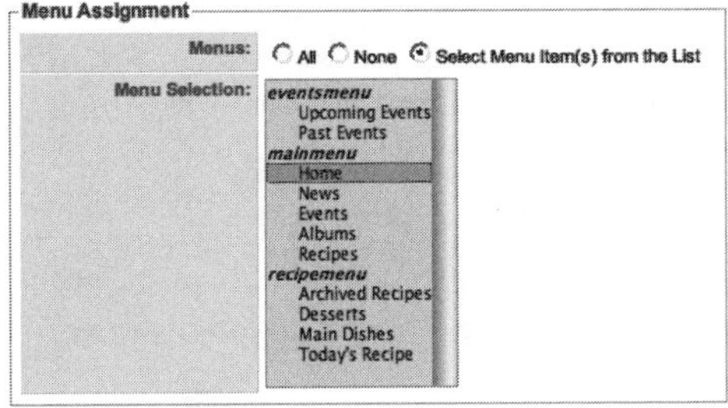

Figure 4.73 Selecting a menu assignment

2. Click New.

   The New Module page opens. This page displays all the module types you can create for your site (**Figure 4.71**). You can also install third-party extensions, some which may expand this list by adding additional module types. See Chapter 6, "Extending Your Site."

3. Click the Login radio button, and then click Next.

   The Login module creates a login form so that a user can log in to the front end of the web site.

   The Module Edit page opens with the details, menu assignment, and parameters specific to the Login module.

4. In the Details area, type `Login Form` in the Title field.

5. Make sure the Position is set to Left, and leave all other fields at their defaults for now (**Figure 4.72**).

6. In the Menu Assignment area, select the "Select Menu Item(s) from the List" radio button for Menus.

   You want this module to appear only on the home page, so you are going to choose the Home menu item from the list.

7. Select the Home menu (**Figure 4.73**).

continues on next page

8. Set any login form parameters (**Figure 4.74**).
9. Click Save, and then click Preview.

   A login form is created and appears on the home page for users to log in (**Figure 4.75**).

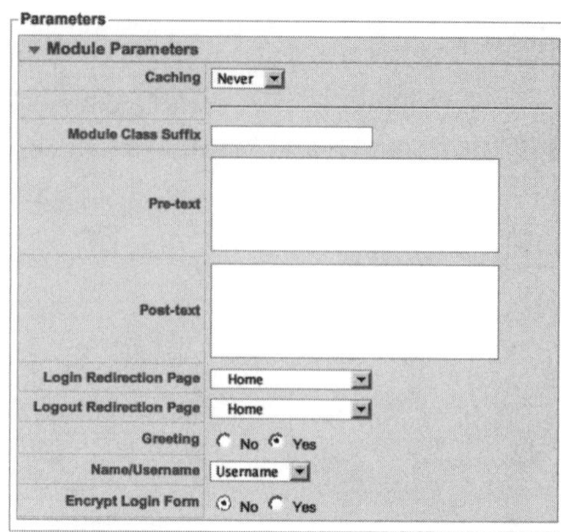

Figure 4.74 Login form module parameters

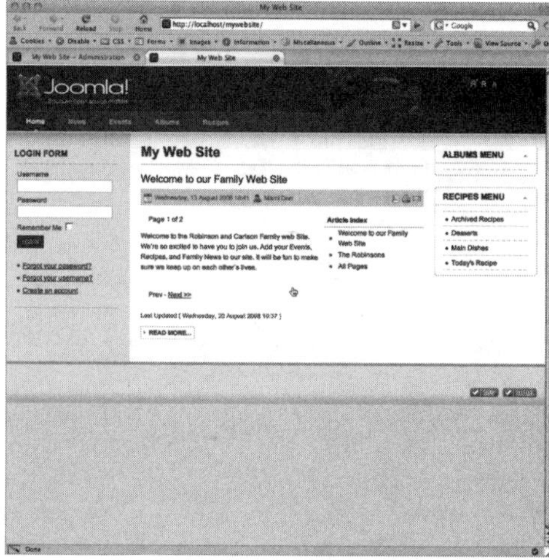

Figure 4.75 The login form on the home page

Login Form Parameters

- **Caching:** Sets whether or not to cache this module. A login form cannot be cached.
- **Module Class Suffix:** This is the CSS class to apply from the template.
- **Pre-text:** Text typed into this field displays above the login form.
- **Post-text:** Text typed into this field displays below the login form.
- **Login Redirection Page:** When a user logs in, this is the first page that displays.
- **Logout Redirection Page:** When a user logs out, this page displays.
- **Greeting:** Selecting Yes displays the simple greeting text. Selecting No will not display greeting text.
- **Name/Username:** Once logged in, the form displays the name or the username as selected here.
- **Encrypt Login Form:** This uses the SSL encryption method. If your site does not have https capability, leave No selected.

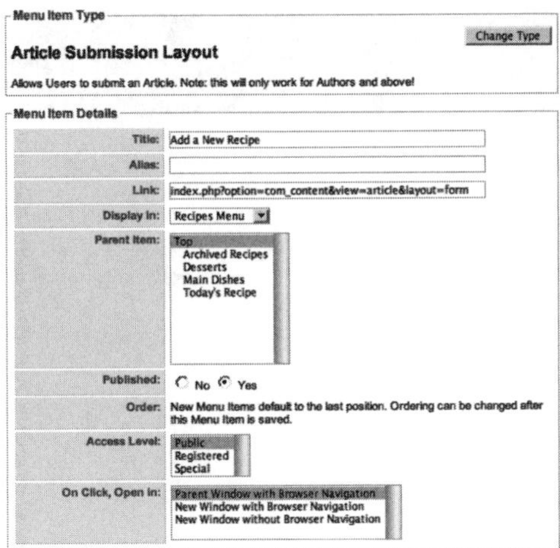

Figure 4.76 Article submission layout menu item details

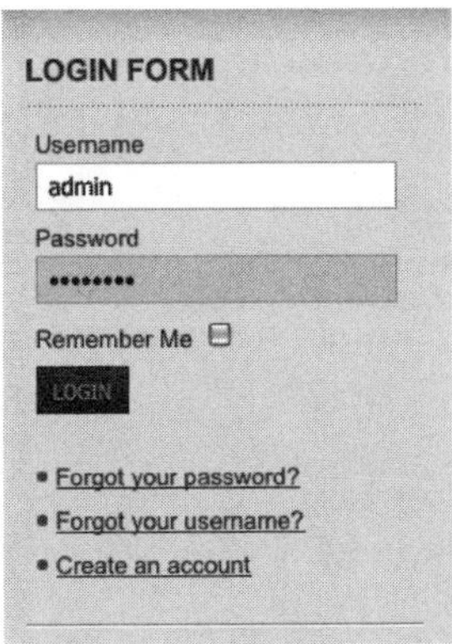

Figure 4.77 The login form on the web site

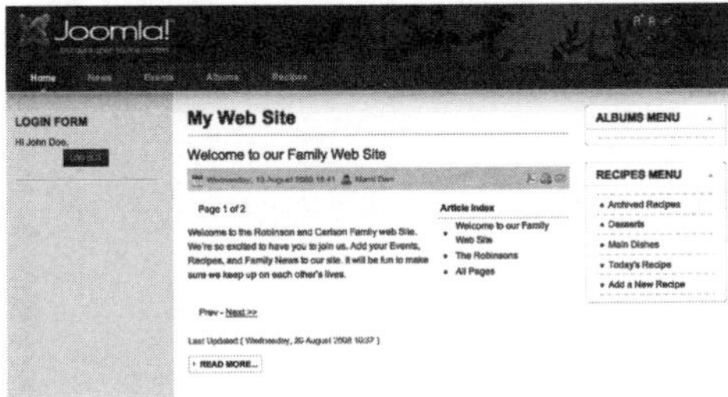

Figure 4.78 The login form after a user has logged in

To create an article submission menu item:

1. Choose Menus > Recipes Menu.
2. On the Menu Item Manager toolbar, click the New icon.
3. Choose Internal Link > Articles > Article > Article Submission Layout.

   Creating an Article Submission menu item creates a submission form page for users with Author, Publisher, or Editor access level to submit articles.
4. In the Title field, type `Add a New Recipe`.
5. Leave all other fields in the Menu Item Details area at their defaults (**Figure 4.76**).

   There are no basic or advanced parameters for an article submission form. The component and system parameters are the same as other layouts.
6. Click Save, and then click Preview.
7. In the Login form, type `admin` as the user, and then type your administrative password (**Figure 4.77**).
8. Click the Login button.

   The user is logged in, and the greeting appears where the login form was (**Figure 4.78**).

continues on next page

9. From the Recipes menu, click the "Add a New Recipe" link.

   You are now logged in and can create a recipe (submit an article).

   An example of the article submission menu item layout is shown in **Figure 4.79**.

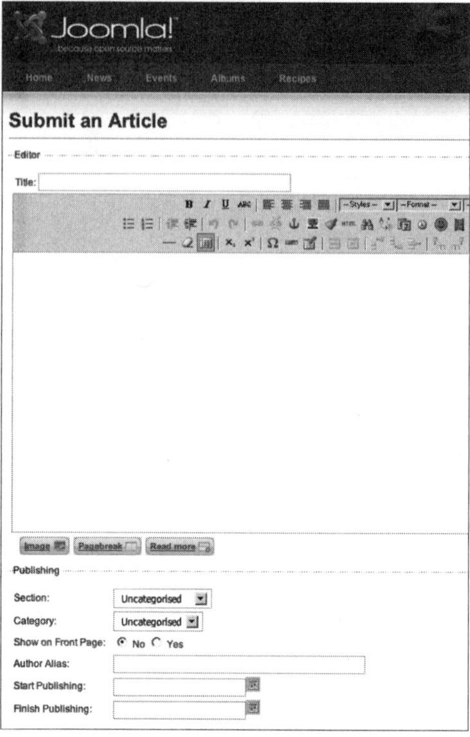

Figure 4.79 The submission form web page

To create a user menu module:

1. Choose Menus > Menu Manager.
2. From the Menu Item Manager, click New.
3. Set the Menu New page fields as shown in **Figure 4.80**:
   - Unique Name: `usermenu`
   - Title: `User Menu`
   - Description: `This is a user details menu.`
   - Module Title: `User Menu`
4. Click Save.
5. Choose Extensions > Module Manager to open the Module Manager.
6. Click the User Menu.

   The User Menu Editor opens.
7. In the Details area, click the Yes radio button for Enabled (**Figure 4.81**).
8. Click Save.

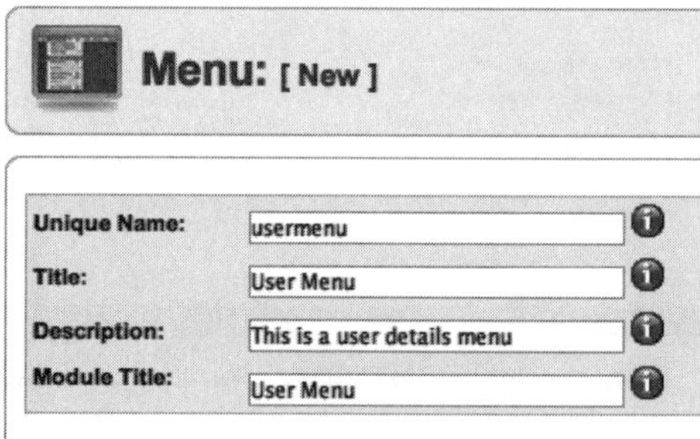

Figure 4.80 Create a new user menu

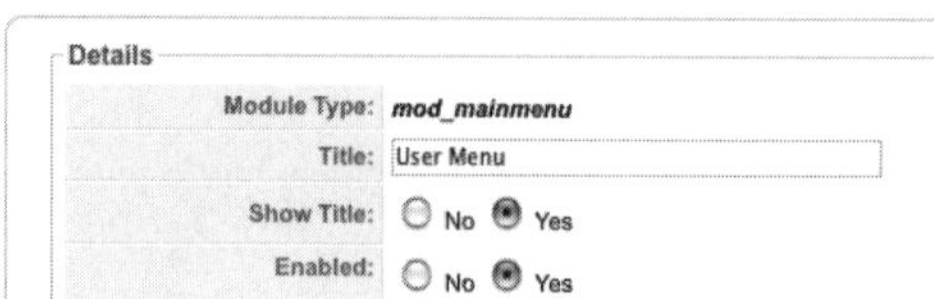

Figure 4.81 Enabling the User Menu

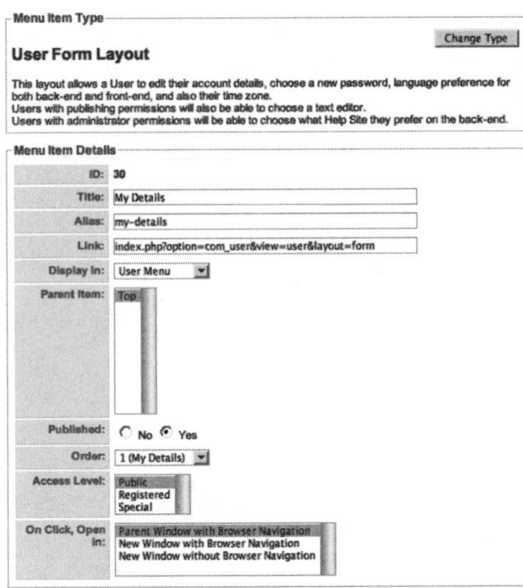

Figure 4.82 User form layout details

Figure 4.83 The user menu

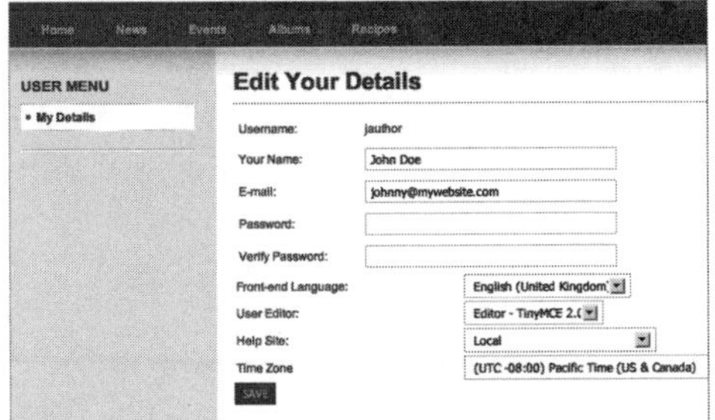

Figure 4.84 The Edit Your Details page

To create an author details menu item:

1. Choose Menus > User Menu.
2. From the Menu Item Manager, click New.

   In this procedure, you will add a way for the front end authors to edit their account details, such as password, language, name, and so on.
3. Choose Article > User > User Form Layout.

   The User Form Layout page enables users to edit their account information (**Figure 4.82**).
4. In the Title field, type `My Details`.

   This title is the menu link. Leave the Alias field blank. This is filled in automatically by Joomla.
5. Choose User Menu from the "Display in" drop-down menu.
6. In the Access Level list, select Registered.
7. Click Save, and then click Preview.

   The User Menu appears, displaying a link to the user details. You need to be logged in to see this menu (**Figure 4.83**).
8. Click the My Details link.

   The Edit Your Details page opens, where you can modify your user settings (**Figure 4.84**).

To create a web link submission menu item:

1. Choose Menus > User Menu.
2. From the Menu Item Manager, click New.
3. Choose Web Links > Web Link > Web Link Submission Layout.

   The Web Link Submission Layout page creates a form through which users can submit web links to the front end of the web site (**Figure 4.85**).
4. In the Title field, type `My Interesting Links`.
5. In the Access Level list, select Registered.
6. Click Save, and then click Preview.

   Your web link submission menu link is now the second item on this menu. Clicking the link opens the Submit A Web Link form (**Figure 4.86**).

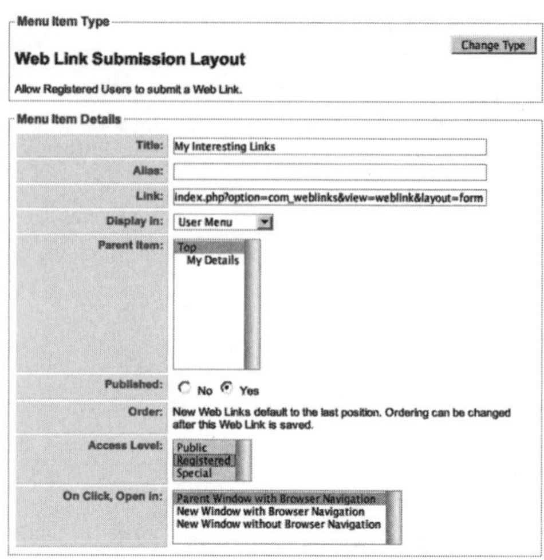

Figure 4.85 Web Link Submission Layout page

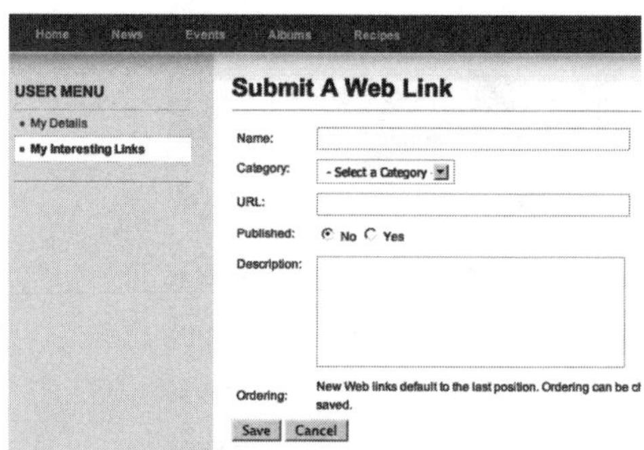

Figure 4.86 Web submission form

Creating Submenus

Creating a second-level menu, a *submenu*, is as easy as creating all the other menus. The difference is that a submenu is contained in the same menu module as its parent menu.

You make submenus by simply creating new menu items and assigning them to be children of a parent menu item or by copying entire menu items into another menu item.

To create a drop-down submenu:

1. Choose Menus > Recipes Menu.
2. Select all the menu items in the Menu Item Manager for recipemenu.
3. Click Copy.
4. In the Copy to Menu list, select mainmenu.

   This copies all the menu items into the mainmenu, preserving all the item layout types (**Figure 4.87**).
5. Click Copy.

   The menu items all are copied over to the Main menu, and the Main Menu Item Manager opens.
6. Click the Today's Recipe link.

continues on next page

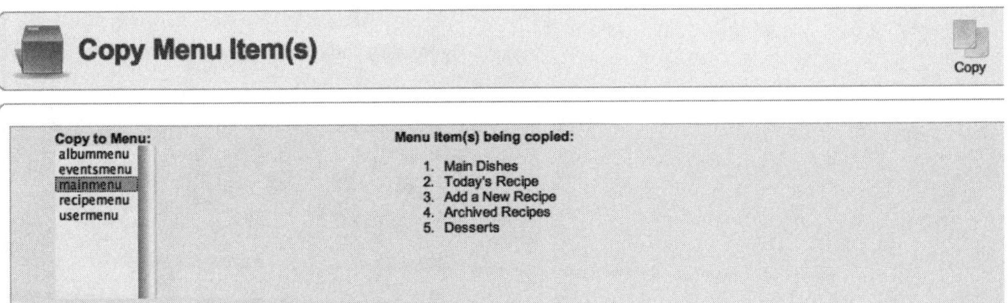

Figure 4.87 The Copy Menu Items page

7. In the Menu Item Details area, select Recipes from the Parent Item list, and leave all other items at their defaults.

   By selecting Parent, you are telling Joomla that all the menu items need to be submenus of the Recipes menu item (**Figure 4.88**).

8. Click Save.

   Today's Recipe now displays under its parent menu item of Recipes (**Figure 4.89**).

9. Copy the menu items Main Dishes and Desserts by repeating steps steps 6 through 8, so the remaining copied menus items are submenus under Recipes.

10. Click Preview.

    When you hover over Recipes in the Main menu, the submenu appears (**Figure 4.90**).

✔ Tip

- If you cannot see the submenus under Recipes, open the Recipes Menu module under Extension > Module Manager. Under the Module Parameters, ensure the setting Always show sub-menu items is set to Yes.

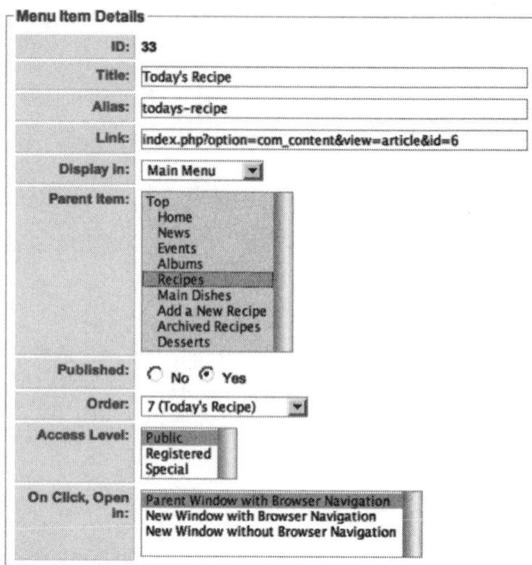

Figure 4.88 Changing the parent item

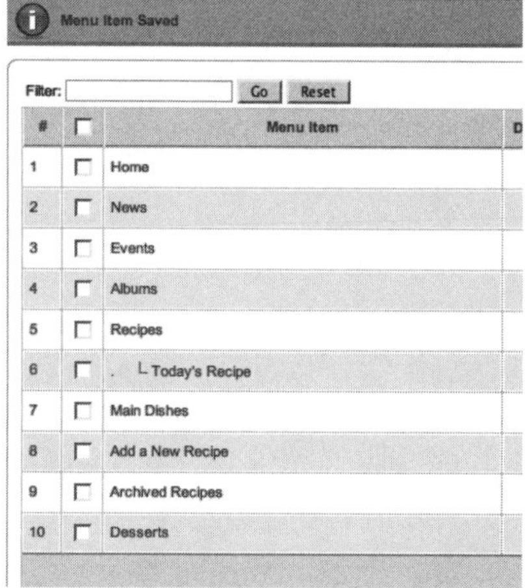

Figure 4.89 Today's Recipe as a submenu

Figure 4.90 Hovering over the Recipes menu

5 Working with Modules

As you've seen throughout this book, using a content management system can greatly benefit you. By storing all your content in a database, Joomla enables you to make your site dynamic and interactive, and it allows you to update it constantly. People are drawn back to dynamic web sites—whether they want to read the latest news or they want to post something of their own. By adding modules to your site, you can enable the kind of interactive features that draw readers in.

You have already worked with modules in Chapter 4, "Making Your Site Dynamic with Menus." This chapter expands your knowledge of module types and walks you through creating and configuring basic modules, assigning modules to positions, and displaying the modules on a site.

So what exactly is a module? Generally, modules control what displays on a site, and they provide the means for a user to interact with the site. For example, a menu module contains the links necessary to display content, and it provides navigation. A Latest News, Archived Content, or Most Read module also displays links to display specific content. Components also contain content, but without a module, that content will not display. Chapter 6, "Extending Your Site," takes a closer look at this theory and details how modules, components, and plugins interact together.

Creating Modules

Modules add interactive elements to your site. Some work independently, such as a news flash or search bar, and some work in combination with components or other elements on your site.

Modules can contain links, content, or images, as well as perform interactive functions. Although content (articles) and components display in the main body of the page, modules do not. Modules usually appear *around* the main body of the page. For example, the Login module is usually in the right or left column. The footer is on the bottom of the page; banners are usually at the top or bottom, but they are not in the main body.

To create and manage modules, you use the Module Manager. Although it contains links for creating two main categories of modules—Site and Administrator—you will be working with Site modules only. Site modules, such as Breadcrumbs, Menus, Most Read Content, and so on, appear on your web site's front end, whereas Administrator modules are used for back end functions. Do not change the Administrator modules, because you might inadvertently make the back end inaccessible.

Menu modules are covered in Chapter 4, "Making Your Site Dynamic with Menus." Advanced modules and component combinations are covered in Chapter 6, "Extending Your Site."

Creating an Archived Content Module

An Archived Content module displays a list of links to archived articles. The links are in the form of calendar months. Each month will link to a display of article titles for that month.

To create an Archived Content module:

1. Choose Extensions > Module Manager.

   The Module Manager opens. Here you enable, disable, copy, delete, edit, or create all modules.

2. On the toolbar, click New.

   The Module page opens. This is a list of all the module types currently available. If you add third-party extension that contains modules, they also appear in this list (**Figure 5.1**).

continues on next page

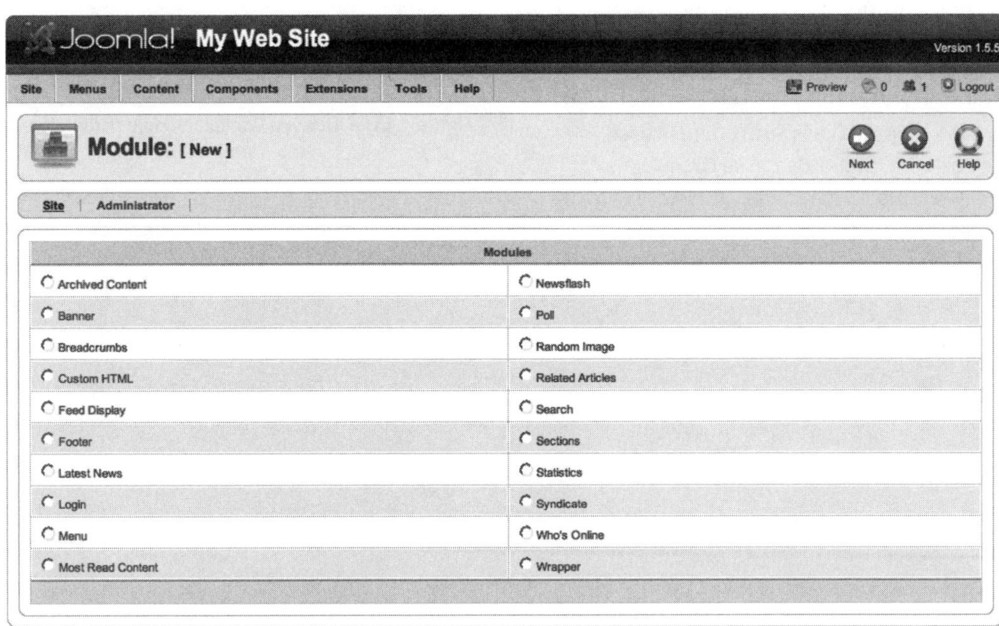

Figure 5.1 The list of modules you can create

3. Click the Archived Content radio button, and then click Next.

   The Module Editor opens.

4. In the Title field, type `Old News`.

   Each type of module can have its own set of parameters; however, Details and Menu Assignment parameters are common across most modules.

5. Leave all other Details settings at their defaults.

6. In the Menu Assignment area, click the "Select Menu Item(s) from the List" radio button for Menus.

7. In the Menu Selection list, under mainmenu, choose Home.

   This sets the Archive Content module to display on any page you choose. In this step, you restrict the module to display only on the Home page (**Figure 5.2**).

8. Under Module Parameters, in the Count field, leave the default of 10 (**Figure 5.3**).

   This tells the module how many archived articles to display.

9. Leave the Module Class Suffix field blank.

   The Module Class Suffix field is used to assign a CSS class (see Chapter 9, "Creating Joomla Templates" for more information).

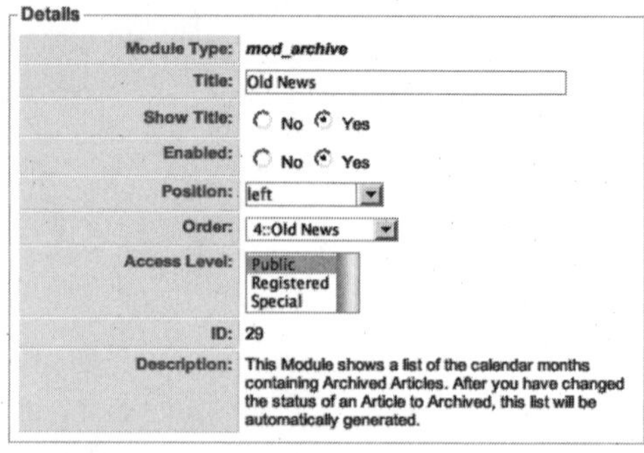

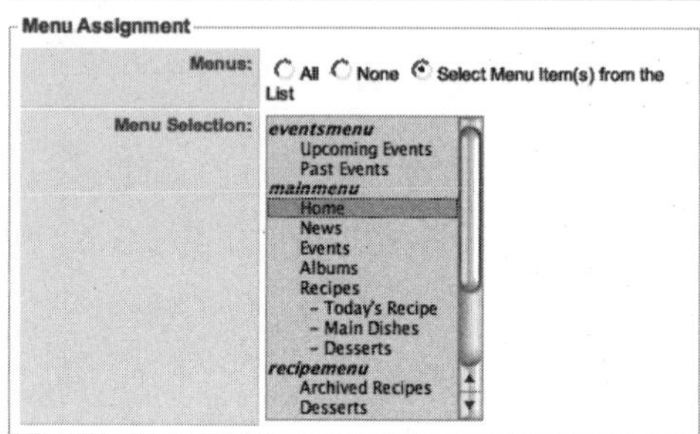

Figure 5.2 The New Module Editor

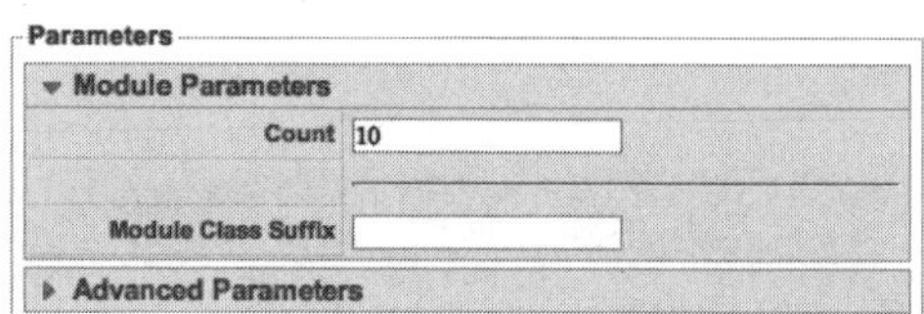

Figure 5.3 The Archived Content module parameters

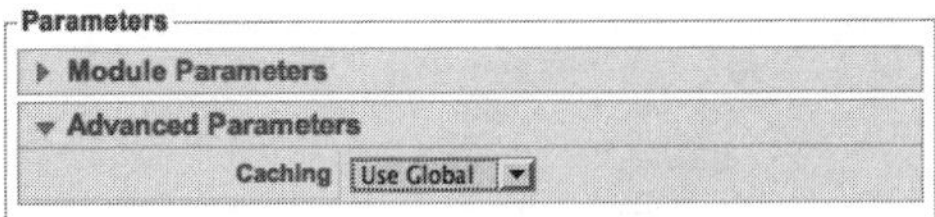

Figure 5.4 The Archived Content module advanced parameters

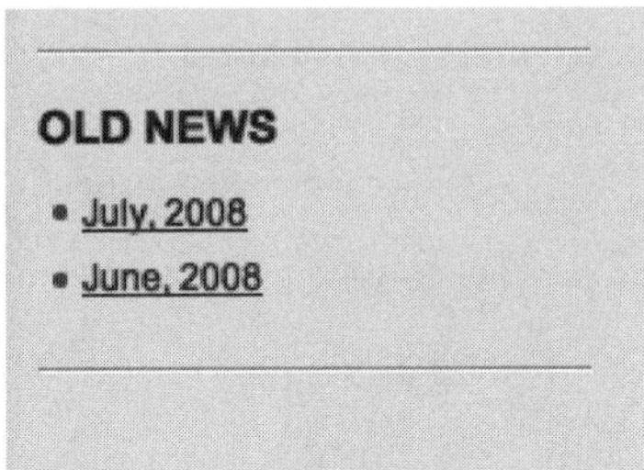

Figure 5.5 The Archived Content module as it appears on the site

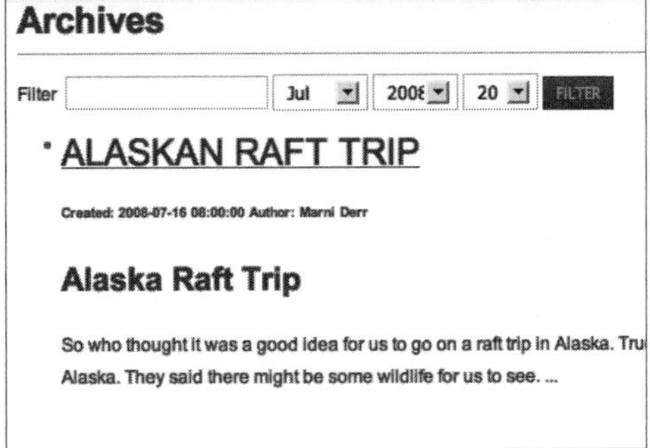

Figure 5.6 Selecting a link from the Archived Content module

10. Click the arrow next to Advanced Parameters. Leave Caching set to the default Use Global (**Figure 5.4**).

The Archived Content module has only one advanced parameter, which specifies whether or not to cache the module using the global cache settings. Caching makes the module load faster so the browser doesn't have to refresh all of the information.

11. Click Save, and click then Preview.

The Old News module displays on the Home page of the web site (**Figure 5.5**). Users now can access all archived articles through this module. The links are generated automatically by Joomla by month/year.

Once a month link is clicked, all archived articles for that month are displayed. You can use the filter to search archived articles (**Figure 5.6**).

✔ Tip

- An archived article left uncategorized will not display through the Archived Content module.

Creating a Breadcrumb Module

Breadcrumbs are often referred to by two different names: *breadcrumbs* and *pathways*. When creating CSS styles, Joomla uses the class .pathway. Breadcrumbs keep a linear trail of links from the Home page to where the user currently is on the site. This makes returning to various places in the site easy for a user to navigate. Breadcrumbs are generally positioned above the main body of content on the site.

To create a Breadcrumbs module:

1. Choose Extensions > Module Manager to open the Module Manager.
2. On the toolbar, click New to open the New Module page.
3. Click the Breadcrumbs radio button, and then click Next.

   The Edit Module page opens to set the details and parameters for the Breadcrumb module.
4. In the Title field, type `Breadcrumbs`.
5. Choose breadcrumbs from the Position drop-down menu.

   Most Joomla templates have a position and styling for breadcrumbs/pathways. Position controls where the module displays on the page. The placement of the positions are controlled by the template.
6. Leave the rest of the Details and Menu Assignment parameters at their defaults.

   Breadcrumbs are generally set to display on all pages of a web site, making it easier for users to navigate from anywhere (**Figure 5.7**).

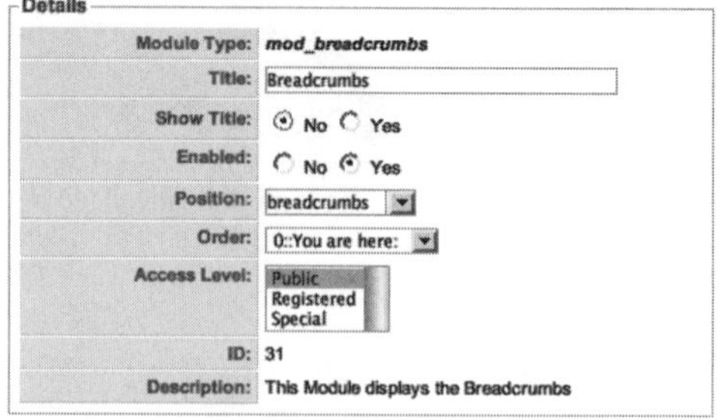

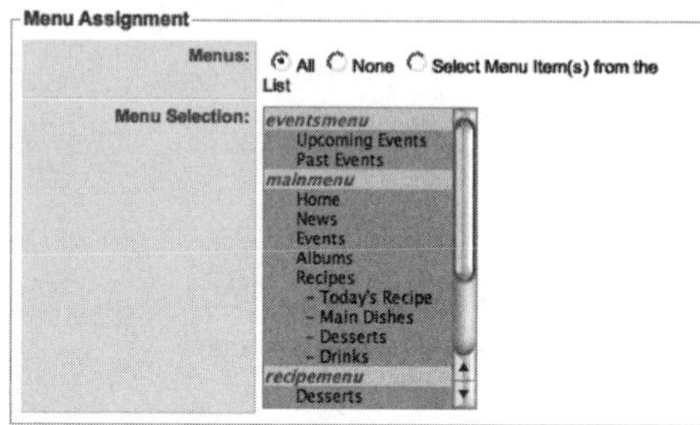

Figure 5.7 The Breadcrumb module details

Showing Template Positions

You can show template positions by typing `?tp=1` at the end of your URL. For example, type `mysebsite.com?tp=1` to display the template-defined positions.

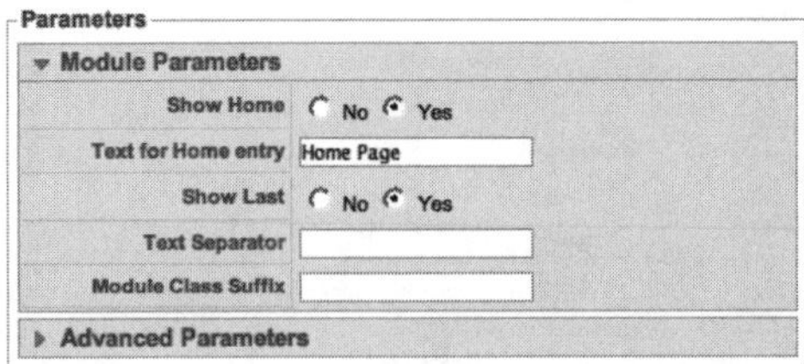

Figure 5.8 Setting the text for the Home page link

Figure 5.9 The Breadcrumb module as it appears on the site

7. Under Module Parameters, leave Show Home set to Yes.

   Selecting Yes places the Home page link at the beginning of the breadcrumb navigation links.

8. Click the Yes radio button for Show Last.

   This displays the last link as the user's current location on the site.

9. In the "Text for Home entry" field, type `Home Page`.

   The text in this field displays as the Home page link (**Figure 5.8**).

10. Leave the Text Separator field blank.

    Leaving this field blank places a ">" in between each link.

11. Click Save, and then click Preview.

    Click through the menus to see the breadcrumbs trail (**Figure 5.9**).

Creating Custom HTML Modules

Custom HTML modules can be used to display text, images, or a piece of content you want to display outside the main body of the page. Joomla comes with 20 different module types to choose from. Installing extensions adds even more modules to this list. A custom HTML module gives you the freedom to create your own modules.

To create a Custom HTML module:

1. Choose Extensions > Module Manager to open the Module Manager.
2. On the toolbar, click New to open the New Module page.
3. Click the Custom HTML radio button, and then click Next.

   A Custom HTML module has the same Details and Menu Assignment fields as all other modules (**Figure 5.10**).

   The custom HTML module has a single parameter, Module Class Suffix, that lets you use a custom CSS class suffix to customize the look of this module (**Figure 5.11**).

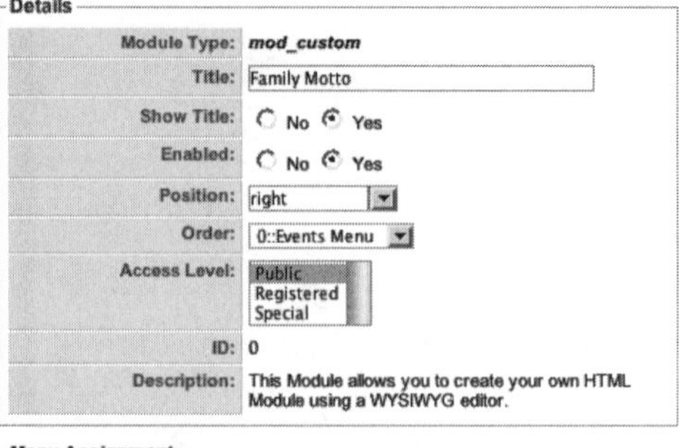

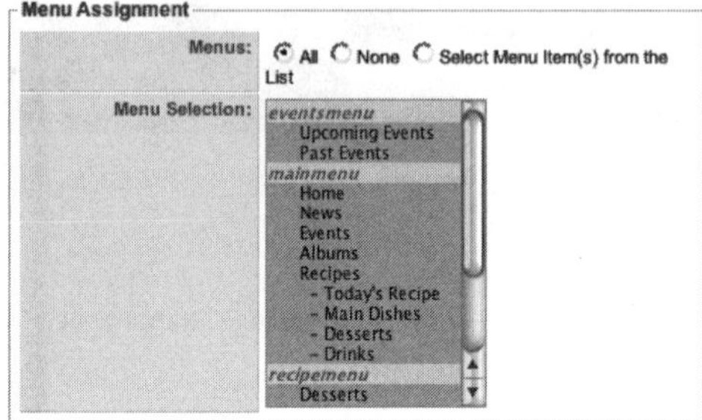

Figure 5.10 The Custom HTML module details

Figure 5.11 The Custom HTML module parameters

The Custom HMTL module gives you the freedom to create any type of module you want using a WYSIWYG editor. The TinyMCE editor does have restrictions on the type of HTML you can use. If you prefer, you can choose No Editor in the global configuration pages, or install another editor extension allowing more HTML flexibility (**Figure 5.12**).

4. In the Title field, type `Family Motto`.
5. Choose right from the Position drop-down menu.
6. In the Custom Output field, type `Our Family is ready for fun.`

continues on next page

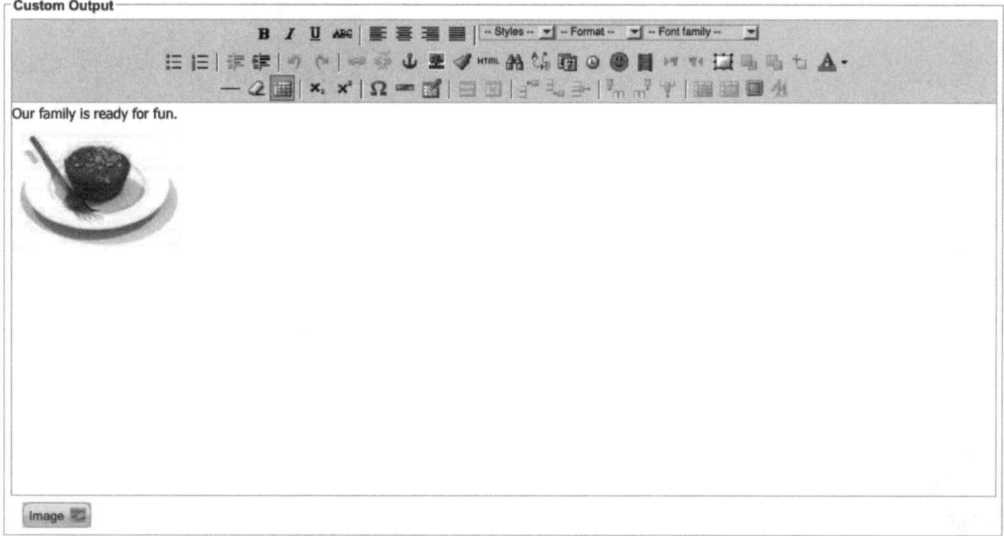

Figure 5.12 The Custom module WYSIWYG editor

7. Click the Image button.

   A small version of the Media Manager opens so you can insert an image into the module.

8. Choose an image, and then click the Insert button.

   You can insert text, an image, or both. You can position the image before or after the text (**Figure 5.13**).

9. Click Save, and then click Preview.

   The site now has a small Family Motto module displayed on the front page (**Figure 5.14**).

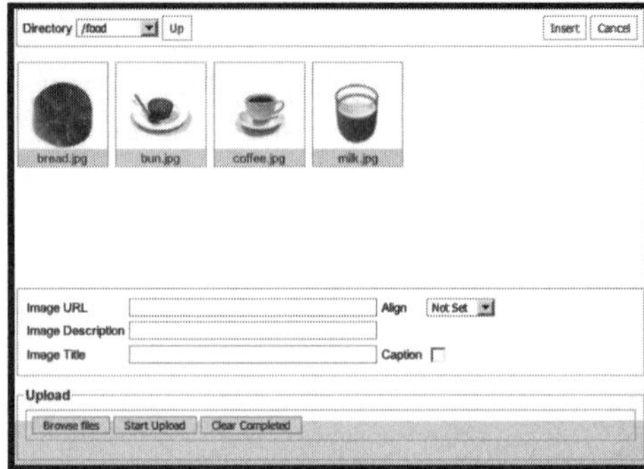

Figure 5.13 Adding an image to the Custom module

Figure 5.14 The Family Motto module

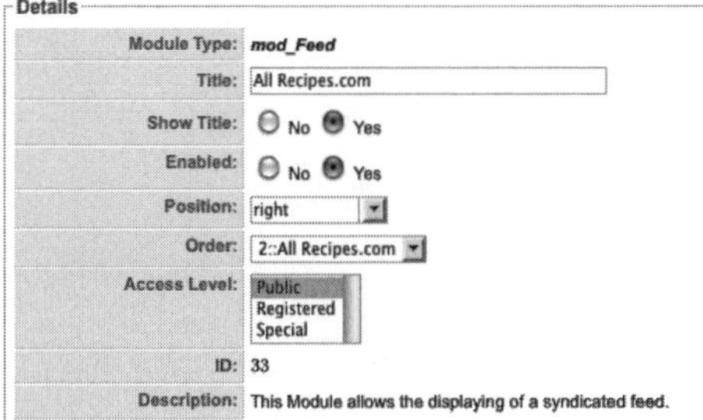

Figure 5.15 The Feed Display details

Creating a Feed Display Module

The Feed Display module creates a single RSS feed from another web site into your web site. Feeds are referred to as RSS feeds, news feeds, and syndication by the web community. However, although all feeds provide the same function, there are two separate modules in Joomla (Feed Display and Syndicate) and one component (News Feed), so it can be confusing.

- **Feed Display:** A Feed Display module creates a single feed from another web site to your web site.
- **Syndicate:** A Syndicate module creates an RSS feed link for a specific page of the web site, allowing users to create a news feed for the current page. This feed allows users to watch items on this page in their own news aggregator.
- **News Feed component:** This is a component that creates a news feed page (see Chapter 6, "Extending Your Site" for more information).

To create a Feed Display module:

1. Choose Extensions > Module Manager.
2. On the toolbar, click New to open the New Module page.
3. Click the Feed Display radio button, and then click Next.
4. In the Title field, type `All Recipes.com`.
5. Choose right from the Position drop-down menu.

   This feed will display below the Recipe menu on the Recipes pages (**Figure 5.15**).

continues on next page

6. In the Menu Assignment area, click the "Select Menu Item(s) from the List" radio button for Menus.

7. Under Menu Assignment, choose Recipes > Today's Recipe, Main Dishes, Desserts, and Drinks (**Figure 5.16**).

8. Under Module Parameters, type the following in the Feed URL field: `http://rss.allrecipes.com/daily.aspx?hubID=84`.

   This is one of the feed display URLs provided by allrecipes.com. Most web sites that syndicate have a page that will give you a list of their RSS feed URLs and any XML you need to easily display their information. Feed Title, Description, and Image are fed from the original site.

9. In the Items field, type 3.

   This is the number of feed article titles to display in the Feed Display module.

10. Click the Yes radio button for Item Description to place a brief description under the Feed Article link.

11. In the Items field, enter the number of words you want to display from the description (**Figure 5.17**).

12. Click Save, and then click Preview.

13. Click Recipes from the Main menu.

    RSS feeds are live; if you are working on a local server and not connected to the Internet, you may see an error. If you don't see the module right away, wait a few seconds for it to appear. You now have a live feed from another web site (**Figure 5.18**).

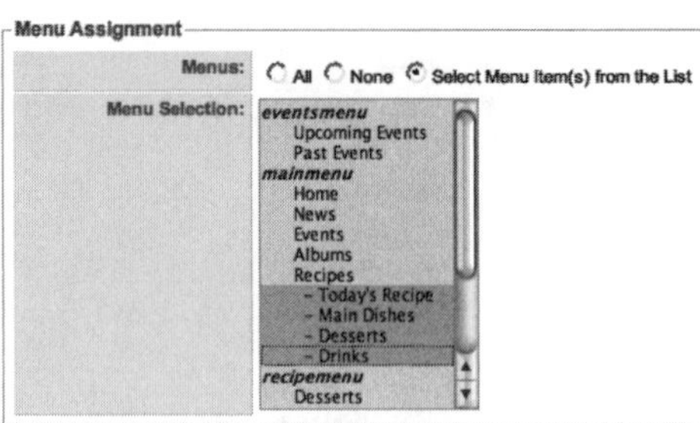

Figure 5.16 The Feed Display menu assignment

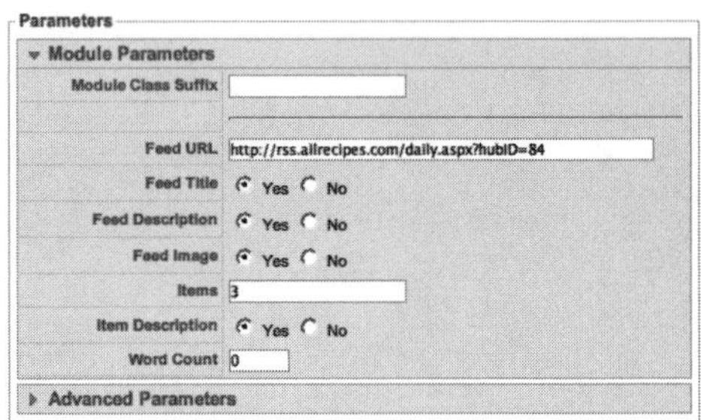

Figure 5.17 The Feed Display parameters

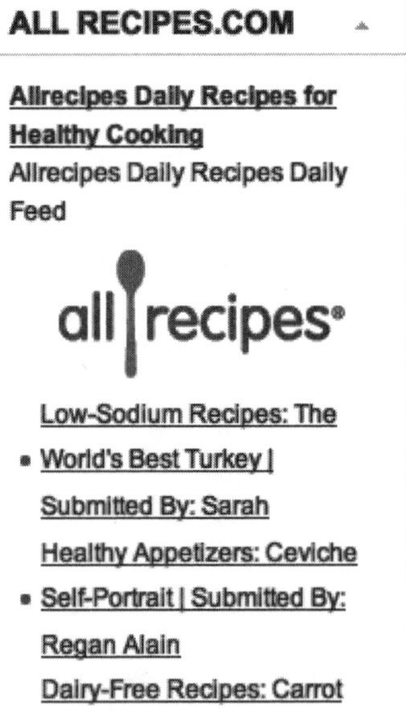

Figure 5.18 The RSS feed from allrecipes.com pulled into your site

CREATING A FEED DISPLAY MODULE

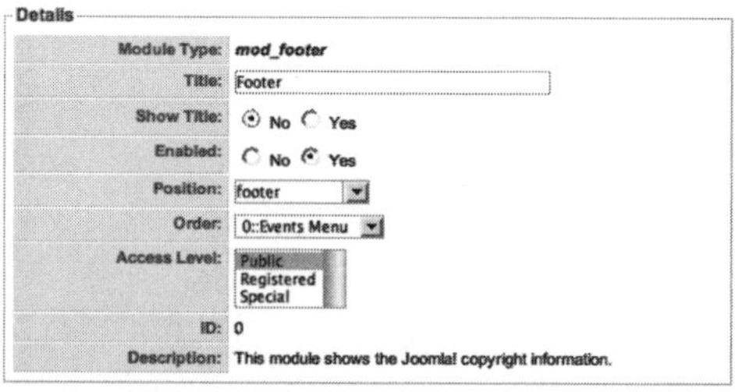

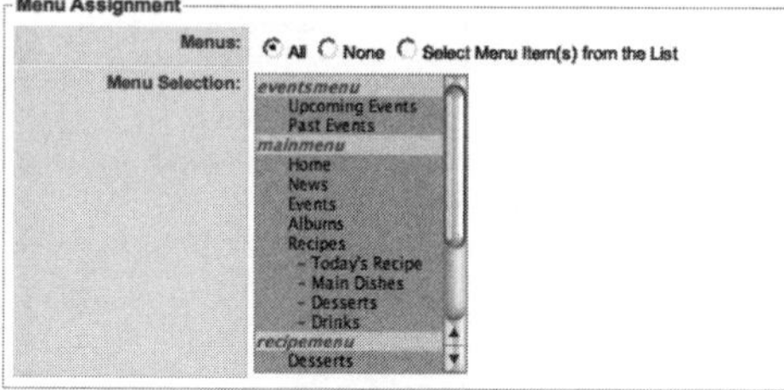

Figure 5.19 The Footer module details

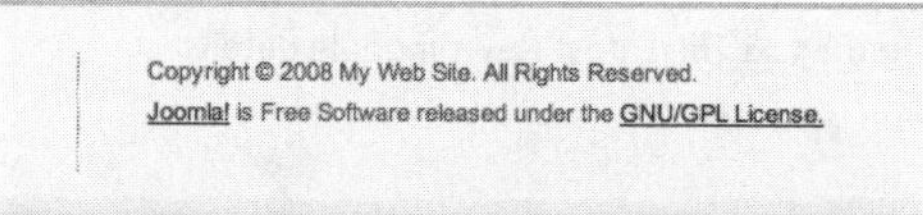

Figure 5.20 The Footer module added to the site

Creating a Footer Module

The Footer module contains copyright and Joomla information from a .php include file in the Joomla application. This will pull your site name from the global configuration site name field and display a Joomla link and Joomla GPL statement. To modify this information, you must make changes in the include file. If you want to create your own footer information with menu links, create a Footer *Menu* module, not the Footer module found in the Module Manager.

To create a Footer module:

1. Choose Extensions > Module Manager to open the Module Manager.
2. On the toolbar, click New to open the New Module page.
3. Click the Footer radio button, and then click Next.
4. In the Title field, type `Footer`.
5. Click the No radio button for Show Title.
6. Choose footer from the Position drop-down menu.

   Leave all other settings at their defaults, including the All selection from the Menu Assignment details. This ensures the footer is displayed on all pages of the site (**Figure 5.19**).
7. Click Save, and then click Preview.

   The footer appears at the bottom of the web site (**Figure 5.20**).

✔ Tip

- The Footer module is not the same as a Footer menu. Most web sites contain a footer area for such links as privacy notices, webmaster information, and legal notices. To create a Footer menu with menu item links, create a Footer Menu module through the Menu Manager.

Creating a Latest News Module

The Latest News module is used to display links to the most recently added articles created on the site. This is similar to the behavior of the Archived Content module, except with Latest News you can be very specific in filtering which articles to display in the list. You use this module to target specific sections and/or categories of content.

To create a Latest News module:

1. Choose Extensions > Module Manager to open the Module Manager.
2. On the toolbar, click New to open the New Module page.
3. Click the Latest News radio button, and then click Next.
4. In the Title field, type `Latest News`.
5. Choose user2 from the Position drop-down menu.

   This places the Latest News module in the user2 position defined by the template. Joomla template designers generally use common position names: right, left, user1 through user9, and so on. As you will see in Chapter 9, "Creating Joomla Templates," you can create positions with unique or more descriptive names and then place them anywhere on the web page.
6. In the Menu Assignment area, click the "Select Menu Item(s) from the List" radio button for Menus.
7. In the Menu Selection list, choose all the menu items under mainmenu only (**Figure 5.21**).

   Leave the default parameters for now (**Figure 5.22**). We will create another Latest News module and restrict it to a specific section and category.

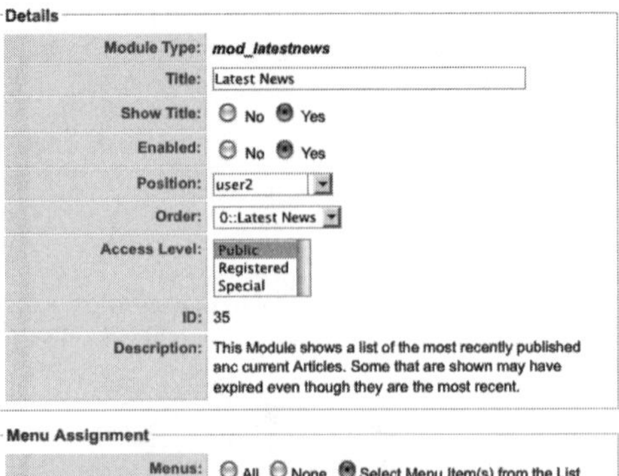

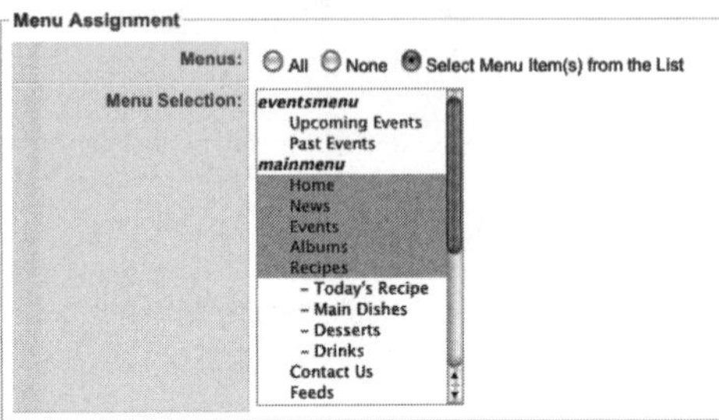

Figure 5.21 The Latest News module details

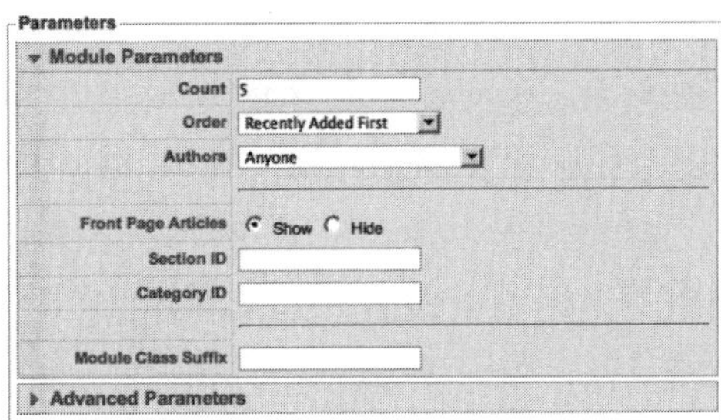

Figure 5.22 The Latest News module parameters

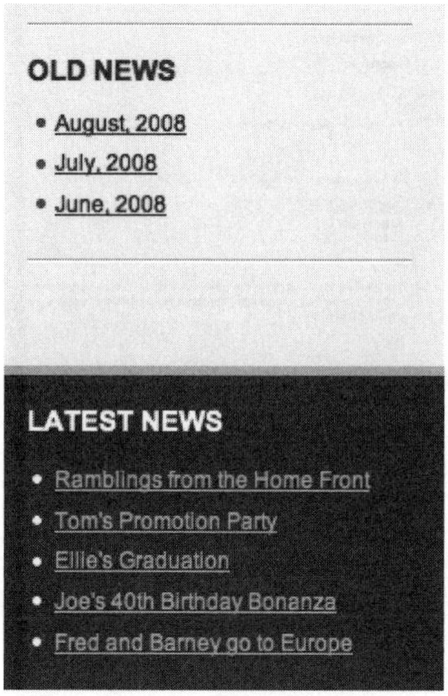

Figure 5.23 The Latest News module on the web site

8. Click Save, and then click Preview.

   The module is now in the user2 position defined by the template, and it lists five of the most recently added articles (**Figure 5.23**).

To create an Upcoming Events module using Latest News:

1. Choose Extensions > Module Manager to open the Module Manager.
2. On the toolbar, click New to open the New Module page.
3. Click the Latest News radio button, and then click Next.

   You're using the Latest News module, but you are going to customize it so it displays upcoming events only.
4. In the Title field, type `Upcoming Events`.

continues on next page

Latest News Parameters

- **Count:** Specifies the number of article links to display in the list.
- **Order:** Sets the order in which the latest news article links appear in the module.
- **Authors:** Specifies whether you want all articles for all authors to appear, only articles by the currently logged-in user or all articles except the currently logged-in user. You could use this field if you are the administrator, for example, and you don't want your articles to appear in the latest news links.
- **Front Page Articles:** Includes or excludes articles assigned to the front page from the latest news links.
- **Section ID:** Uses the unique database ID number for a specific section and displays only article links contained in that specific section.
- **Category ID:** Use the unique database ID number for a specific category and displays only article links contained in that category.
- **Module Class Suffix:** Uses a CSS class from the template to customize the look of this module.

5. Choose user1 from the Position drop-down menu.
6. In the Menu Assignment area, click the "Select Menu Item(s) from the List" radio button for Menus.
7. In the Menu Selection list, choose Upcoming Events under eventsmenu and choose Home, New, and Events under mainmenu (**Figure 5.24**).

   For the Upcoming Events module, you want only upcoming events to display. Selecting just the section ID for upcoming events ensures no other article links appear in this module.
8. Click Save.
9. Choose Content > Section Manager.

   The Section Manager opens.

   Look in the ID column for the Upcoming Events row: The ID number in **Figure 5.25** is 2. Your site may vary, as ID numbers are assigned by the database in the order they are created. When defining or assigning only a specific section, category, article, and so on, you need to use the ID number to tell Joomla what content is being called from the database.

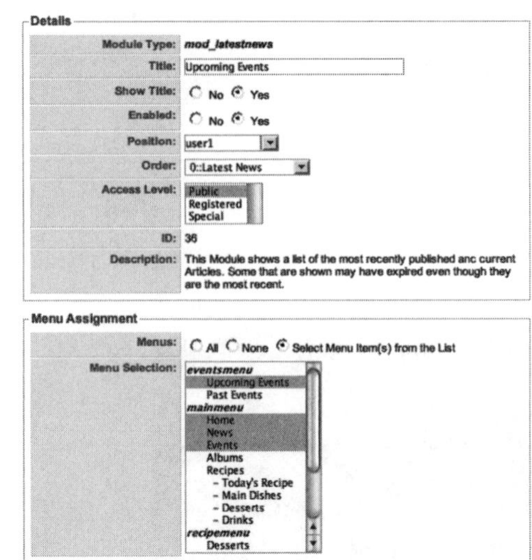

Figure 5.24 The Upcoming Events details

#		Title	Published	Order	Access Level	# Categories	# Active	# Trash	ID
1		News	✓	1	Public	3	7	0	1
2		Upcoming Events	✓	3	Public	4	0	0	2

Figure 5.25 Locating the Section ID number

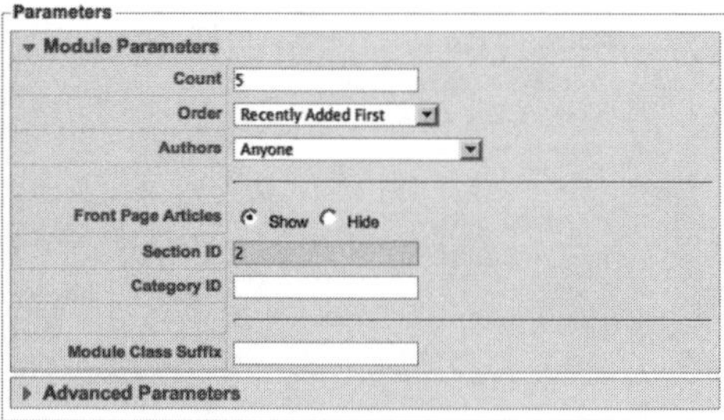

Figure 5.26 Setting the section ID

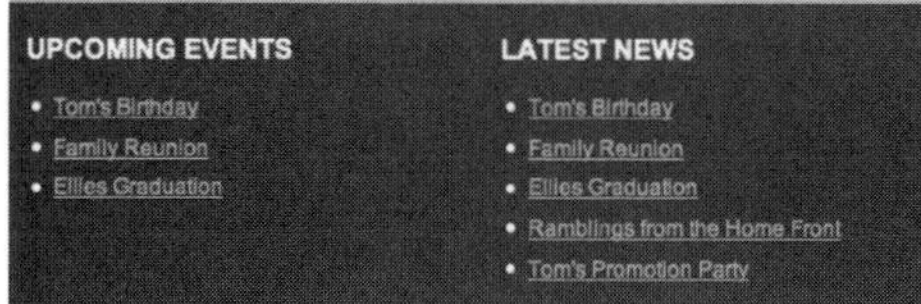

Figure 5.27 The Upcoming Events module displayed on the web site

10. Close the Section Manager.

11. Choose Extensions > Module Manager.

12. Click the Upcoming Events module link (the module you just created).

    The Upcoming Events module Editor page opens.

13. Under Module Parameters, in the Section ID field, type the section ID number you looked up in step 9.

    This field tells Joomla to display only articles from the events section. If you wanted more than one section to show here, you could enter multiple section IDs separated by commas (**Figure 5.26**).

14. Leave the Category ID field blank to show events from all categories.

    If you want only selected categories to show, you could enter their category IDs separated by commas.

15. Click Save, and then click Preview.

    You can use modules to create any type of information you want displayed. The module name *Latest News* does not mean it has to display the latest news only. It can be used to display any recently added content for any section, multiple sections, or categories. This example shows how flexible Joomla can be when it comes to displaying information on your site (**Figure 5.27**).

Creating a Most Read Content Module

The Most Read Content module displays a list of articles that have been read more than any other content on the site. You can narrow this list by selecting articles in only a specific section or a specific category.

To add a Most Read Content module:

1. Choose Extensions > Module Manager to open the Module Manager.
2. On the toolbar, click New to open the New Module page.
3. Click the Most Read Content radio button, and then click Next.
4. In the Title field, type `Favorite Recipes`.
5. Choose left from the Position drop-down menu.
6. In the Menu Assignment area, click the "Select Menu Item(s) from the List" radio button for Menus.
7. In the Menu Selection list, choose Recipes, and all its submenu items under the mainmenu (**Figure 5.28**).
8. Under Module Parameters, in the Section ID field, type `4`.

   This number is the section ID number for the Recipes section (**Figure 5.29**). You can find this ID in the Section Manager.
9. Click Save, and then click Preview.
10. Click Recipes from the Main menu.

    Now when users look at the recipes section, they can see the top five recipes listed in the favorite recipes module. Currently the site contains only four recipes, however, as more are added, only five would show at a time (**Figure 5.30**).

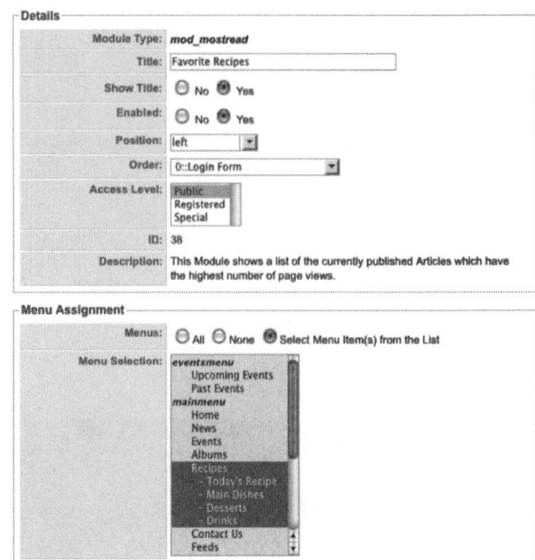

Figure 5.28 The Most Read Content details and menu assignment

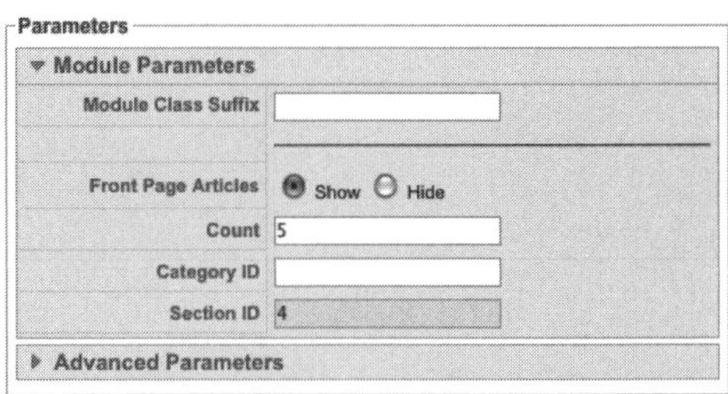

Figure 5.29 The Most Read Content parameters

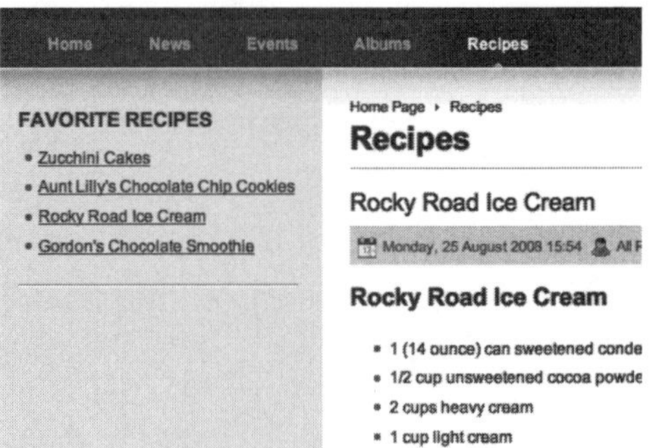

Figure 5.30 The Top Five Recipes module

Creating a Newsflash Module

A Newsflash module displays random information, such as a single article, or multiple articles from a single category. Each time the page is refreshed, a different article appears in the module.

To create a Newsflash module:

1. Choose Extensions > Module Manager to open the Module Manager.
2. On the toolbar, click New to open the New Module page.

continues on next page

Newsflash Parameters

- **Category:** Displays only items from the section/category selected in this field.
- **Layout:** Determines the layout of the articles. "Randomly choose one at a time" displays a single random article from the category selected. "Horizontal or Vertical" displays the number of articles defined in the # of Articles field, as a horizontal or vertical list, respectively.
- **Show Images:** Determines whether images display in the article. Choose Yes to show images in the article; choose No to leave them out.
- **Title Linkable:** Choose Yes to make the article title linkable, choose No to make the article title not a link, or choose Use Global to use the article global setting.
- **Show last separator:** Choose Yes to include an article separator after the last article. Choose No for no separator after the last article.
- **Read more... Link:** Displays a Read More link in the Newsflash module to let the user know there is more content for this article.
- **Article Title:** Determines whether the article title displays. Choose Yes to display the article title; choose No to not display the article title.
- **# of Articles:** Sets the number of articles to display if you choose "Horizontal or Vertical" in the Layout drop-down menu.
- **Module Class Suffix:** Uses a CSS class from the template to customize the look of this module.

3. Click the Newsflash radio button, and then click Next.
4. In the Title field, type `News Flash`.
5. Choose left from the Position drop-down menu.
6. Leave the Menus radio button set to All (**Figure 5.31**).
7. Under Module Parameters, choose News/Family Happenings from the Category drop-down menu.

   News flash items can come from a single category only.
8. Choose "Randomly choose one at a time" from the Layout drop-down menu (**Figure 5.32**).
9. Click Save, and then click Preview.

   Click through the news flash articles by clicking on the titles (**Figure 5.33**).

✔ Tip

- For long articles, if you do not have a Read More link, the news flash will span the entire length of the article. It is best practice for news flashes to either be short descriptive content or longer content with a Read More link leading to the full article.

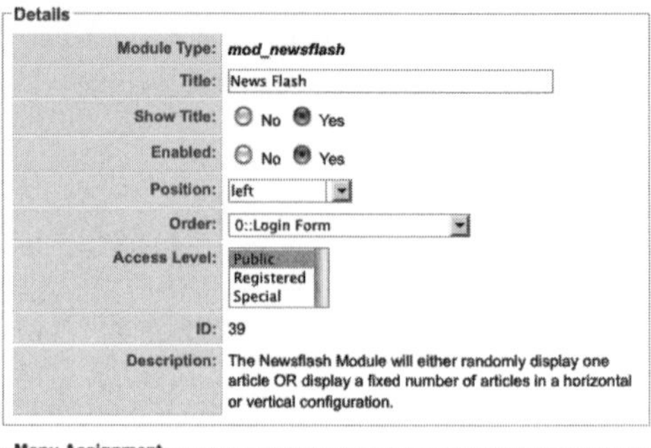

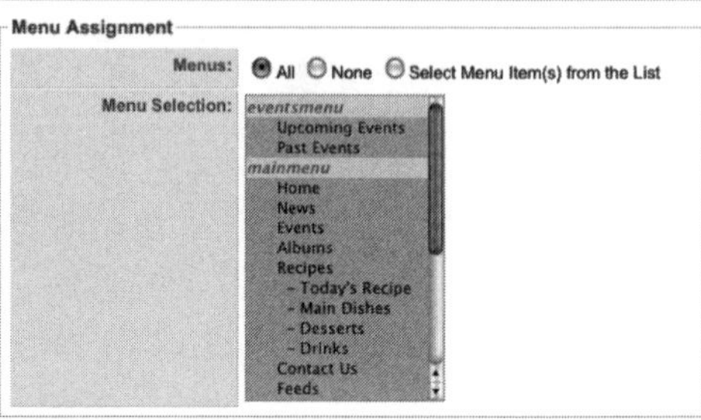

Figure 5.31 The Newsflash module details

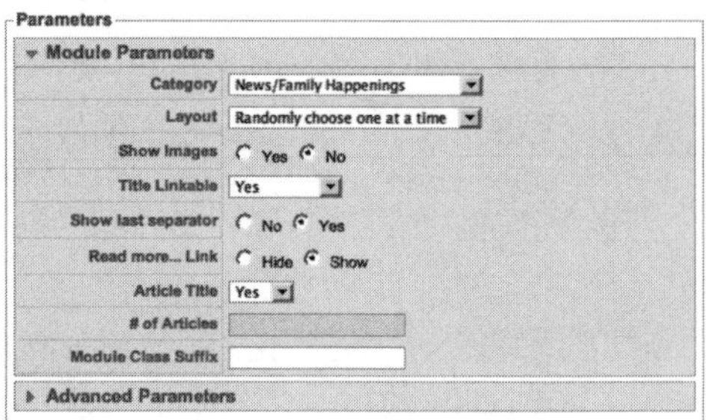

Figure 5.32 The Newsflash parameters

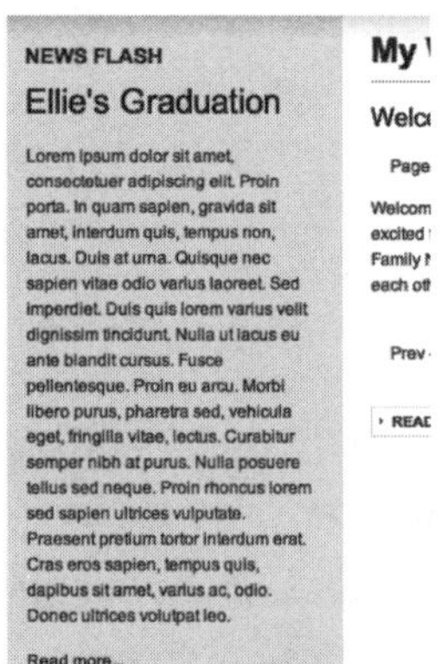

Figure 5.33 The news flash displayed on the site

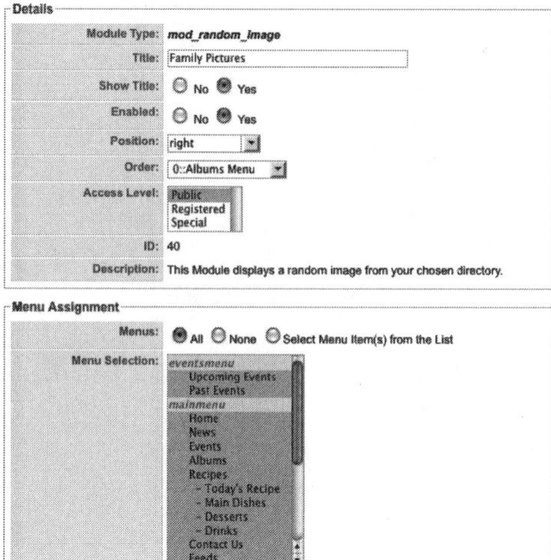

Figure 5.34 The Random Image module details

Creating a Random Image Module

The Random Image module displays random images stored in the Media Manager. You will be able to choose the image type, image folder to use, and the size of the images displayed in the module.

To create a Random Image module:

1. Choose Extensions > Module Manager to open the Module Manager.
2. On the toolbar, click New to open the New Module page.
3. Click the Random Image radio button, and then click Next.
4. In the Title field, type `Family Pictures`.
5. Choose right from the Position drop-down menu (**Figure 5.34**).
6. In the Image Type field, type `jpg`.

   This is the file type of the image. You can use only jpg, png, or gif for this module.
7. In the Image Folder field, type `images/stories/ourfamily`.

   This is the media directory path to where the images are stored. Images are stored in the images/stories directory. Directories (file folders) containing uploaded images will be in the stories directory.

continues on next page

8. Set the Width and Height amounts to `200`.

   These fields set the maximum width and height of the image. Regardless of the size of the original image, the random image module will reduce the graphic to this size in pixels. It is best practice however to have the image the same size as it will appear on the web site (**Figure 5.35**).

9. Leave the Module Class Suffix field blank.

   The CSS class is used by the template to customize the style of the module.

10. Click Save, and then click Preview.

   A small module displaying random images is now on the site, much like a Newsflash module displaying random articles (**Figure 5.36**).

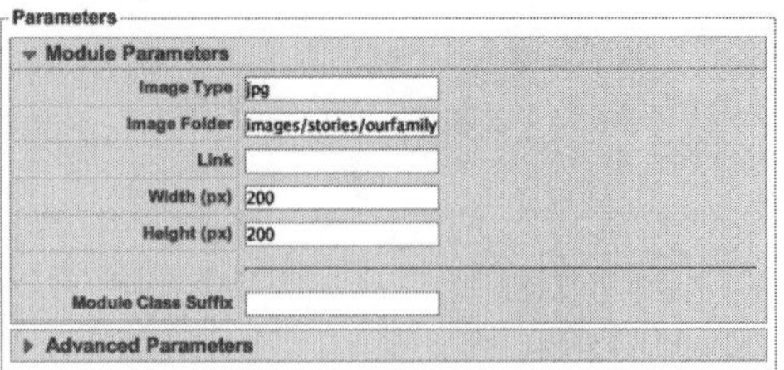

Figure 5.35 The Random Image parameters

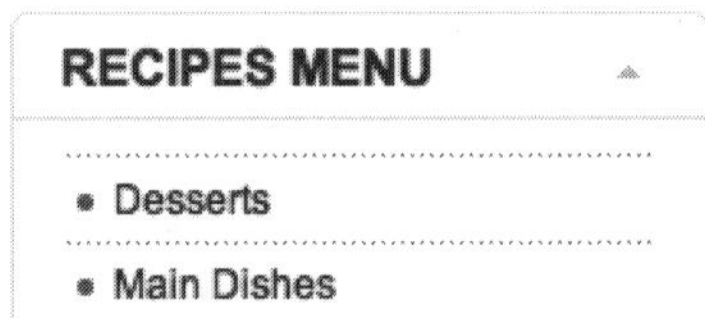

Figure 5.36 The Random Image displayed on the site

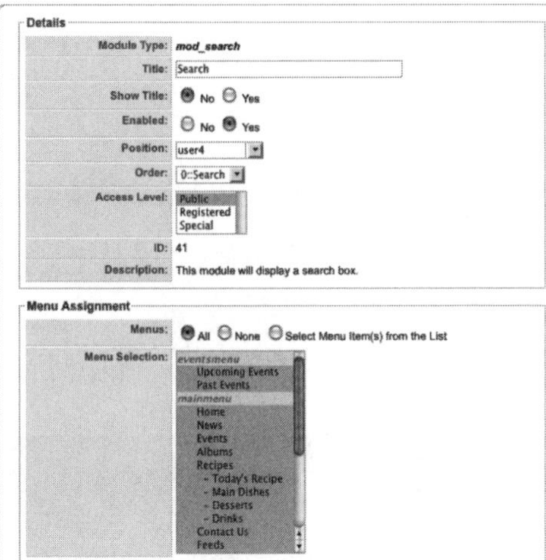

Figure 5.37 The Search module details

Creating a Search Module

The Search module is basically a search box that you can place anywhere on your site. The search box styling is controlled by the CSS in your template; you assign the position in the Search module details. Most designers will place a position in templates for the search box above or in the main body of a web page. A user can use the search box to search for any content on your site.

To create a Search module:

1. Choose Extensions > Module Manager to open the Module Manager.
2. On the toolbar, click New to open the New Module page.
3. Click the Search radio button, and then click Next.
4. In the Title field, type `Search`.
5. Choose user4 from the Position drop-down menu.
6. Under Menu Assignment, choose All.

   Because a search box searches everything on your site, it is best to make a search box available on all pages (**Figure 5.37**).
7. Under Parameters, in the Box Width field, type `30`.

   This field determines the number of characters allowed in the search box.
8. In the Text field, type `Enter Search`.

   This text displays in the search box.

continues on next page

9. Click the Yes radio button for "Search button."

   If you choose Yes, a search button is displayed for the user to click. If you choose No, the user has to start the search by pressing the Enter key.

10. Choose Right from the Button Position drop-down menu.

    Button Position determines where the search button will be in relation to the search box.

11. For "Search button as image," leave No selected.

    If you have a specific search button, you can click the Yes radio button. If you want an image in this field, it must be named *searchButton.gif*, and it must be located the *images/M_images* folder.

12. In the Button Text field, type Go.

    This text displays on the search button (**Figure 5.38**).

13. Click Save, and then click Preview.

    A search box appears placed on the web site, allowing users to search the entire site for desired items (**Figure 5.39**).

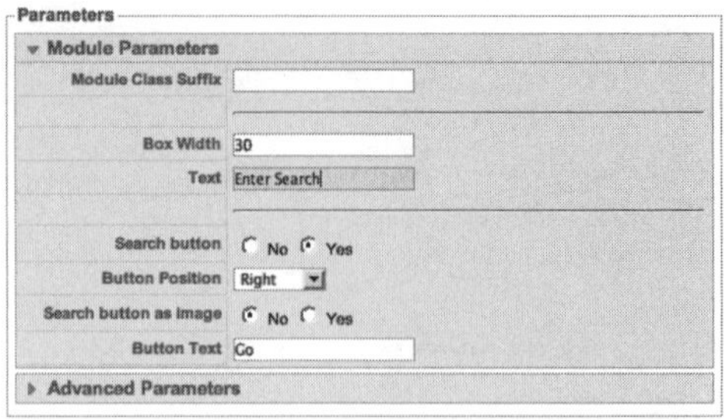

Figure 5.38 The Search module parameters

Figure 5.39 The search box displayed on the site

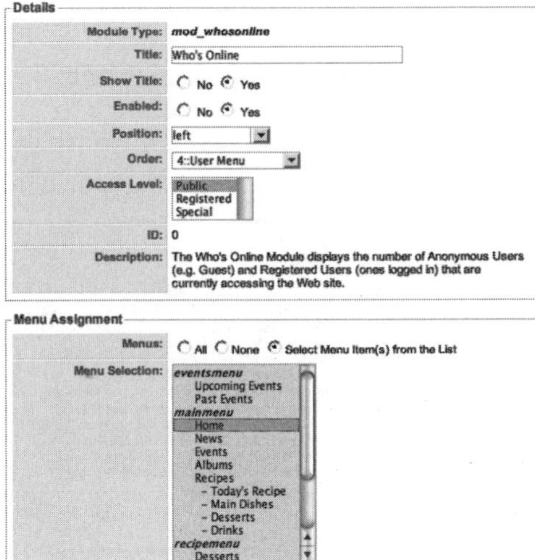

Figure 5.40 The Who's Online module details

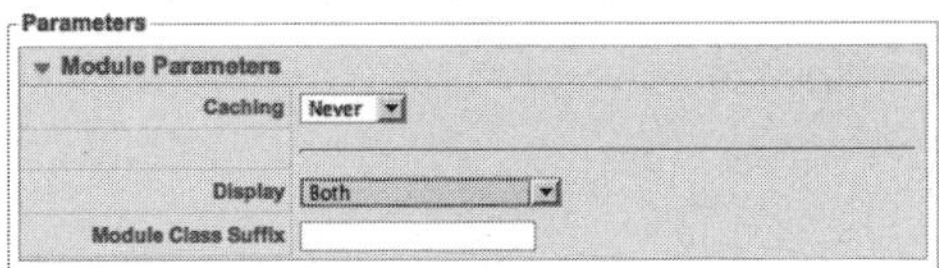

Figure 5.41 The Who's Online parameters

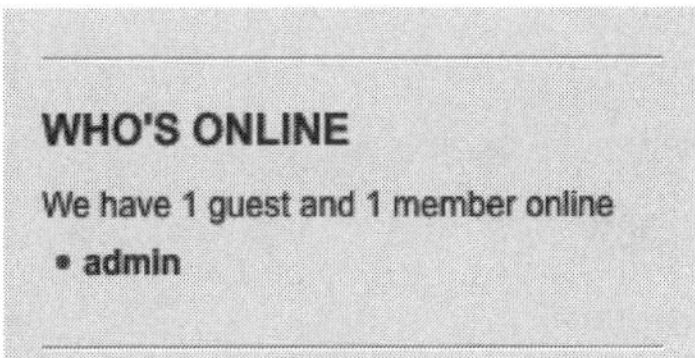

Figure 5.42 The Who's Online module displayed on the site

Creating a Who's Online Module

The Who's Online module displays a module that lets users see who is currently viewing the web site or is logged in. A list of logged-in user names will display in the Who's Online module. Users not logged in will display as guests.

To create a Who's Online module:

1. Choose Extensions > Module Manager to open the Module Manager.
2. On the toolbar, click New to open the New Module page.
3. Click the Who's Online radio button, and then click Next.
4. In the Title field, type `Who's Online`.
5. Choose left from the Position drop-down menu.
6. Choose "4::User Menu" from the Order drop-down menu.

   This places the Who's Online module beneath the user menu.
7. In the Menu Assignment area, click the "Select Menu Item(s) from the List" radio button for Menus.
8. In the Menu Selection list, choose Home under mainmenu.

   Choosing Home means that this module appears only on the Home page (**Figure 5.40**).
9. Under Module Parameters, choose Both from the Display drop-down menu.

   Choosing Both means that both the number of guests/members and the names of the members appear (**Figure 5.41**).
10. Click Save, and then click Preview (**Figure 5.42**).

Creating a Related Articles Module

The Related Articles module will display a list of articles that are related to the current article displayed on the page. Articles are related by their keywords. If an article has keywords assigned in the metadata information field that match other article keywords, links to the other articles display in the module. The metadata information is entered in the Article Manager for each article.

To create a Related Articles module:

1. Choose Extensions > Module Manager.
2. On the toolbar, click New to open the New Module page.
3. Click the Related Articles radio button, and then click Next.
4. In the Title field, type `Vacations`.
5. Leave all other items under Details and Menu Assignment at the defaults.

   You have created a module that looks at all vacation articles with similar metadata keywords, and it displays links to those articles (**Figure 5.43**).
6. Under Parameters, click the Show radio button for Show Date.

   If you have many articles with matching keywords, you can sort them by date for your users (**Figure 5.44**).
7. Click Save, and then click Preview.
8. Choose Events from the Main menu.
9. Choose Past Events from the Events menu.
10. Click the title *Fred and Barney go to Europe.*

    The Related Articles module displays as soon as you view an article with similar keywords (**Figure 5.45**).

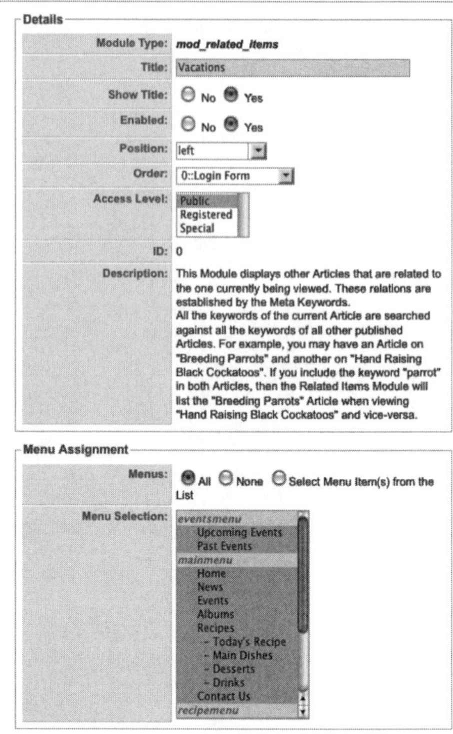

Figure 5.43 The Related Articles module details

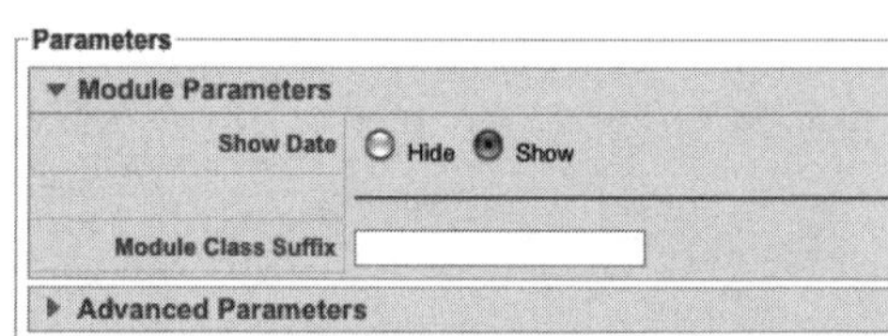

Figure 5.44 The Related Articles module parameters

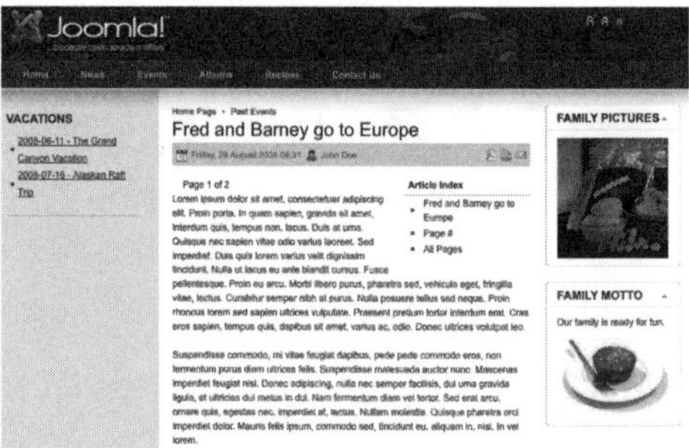

Figure 5.45 The Related Articles module on the site

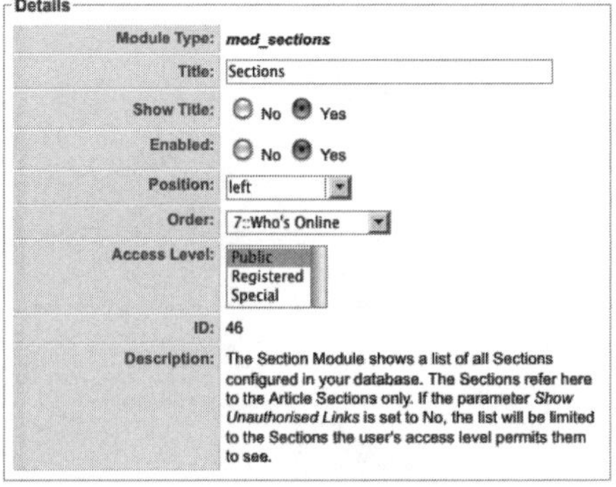

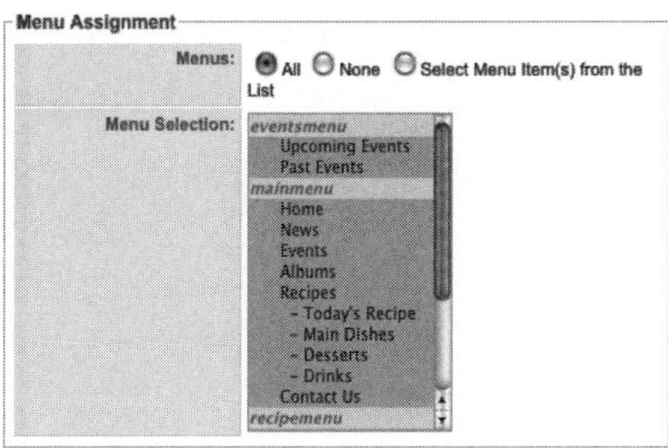

Figure 5.46 The Sections module details

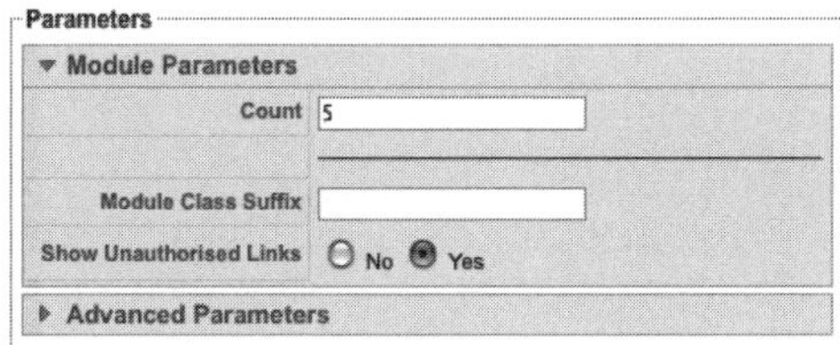

Figure 5.47 The Sections module parameters

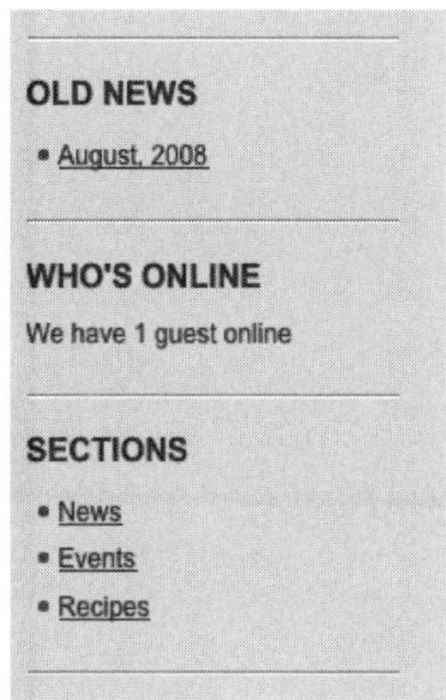

Figure 5.48 The Section module displayed on the site

Creating a Section Module

A Section module creates a list of links to every article section contained on the site. If a section contains no articles, a link to that section does not display.

To create a section module:

1. Choose Extensions > Module Manager.
2. On the toolbar, click New to open the New Module page.
3. Click the Sections radio button, and then click Next.

   The New Module page opens.
4. In the Title Field, type `Sections`.
5. Leave all other details and menu assignments at the defaults (**Figure 5.46**).
6. Under Parameters, in the Count field, type 5.
7. Click the Yes radio button for Show Unauthorized Links.

   This shows all the sections, regardless of a user's access level. When set to No, only those sections a user has access to will show (**Figure 5.47**).
8. Click Save, and then click Preview.

   A list of sections displays. Only those sections that have articles display. Notice Albums is not a link in the Sections module; this is because we have not created an article assigned to the Albums section (**Figure 5.48**).

Creating a Syndicate Module

Syndication is another name for live RSS feeds. What sets syndication apart from the news feeds earlier in the chapter is the Syndicate module sends feeds from your site to the user. When a user subscribes using the Syndicate module they can use a news aggregator or the bookmarks in their browser to see when new information is posted to the site.

The Syndicate module sends information based on the page the user subscribes to. For example, if a user is viewing the Recipes page and clicks the Subscribe link, the user has subscribed to the Recipe's page. Only when new recipes are added will the user see new information.

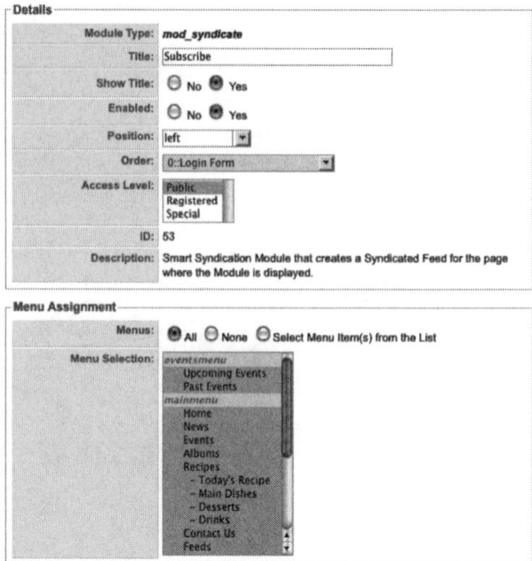

Figure 5.49 The Syndicate module details

To create a Syndicate module:

1. Choose Extensions > Module Manager.
2. On the toolbar, click New to open the New Module page.
3. Click the Syndicate radio button, and then click Next.

   The New Module page opens.
4. In the Title Field, type `Subscribe`.
5. Leave all other details and menu assignments at the defaults

   You want users to be able to subscribe to any page on the site, so leave the menu assignment on All (**Figure 5.49**).

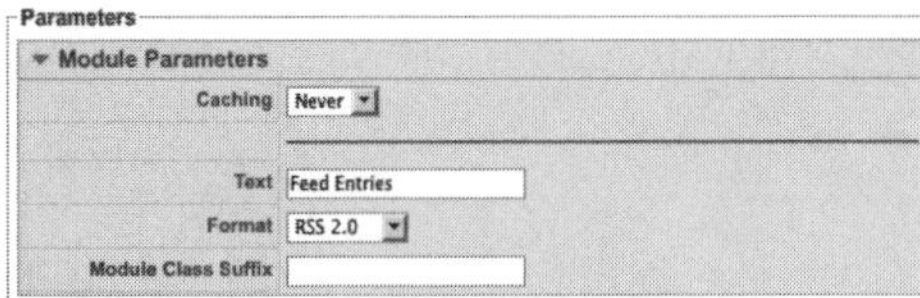

Figure 5.50 The Syndicate module parameters

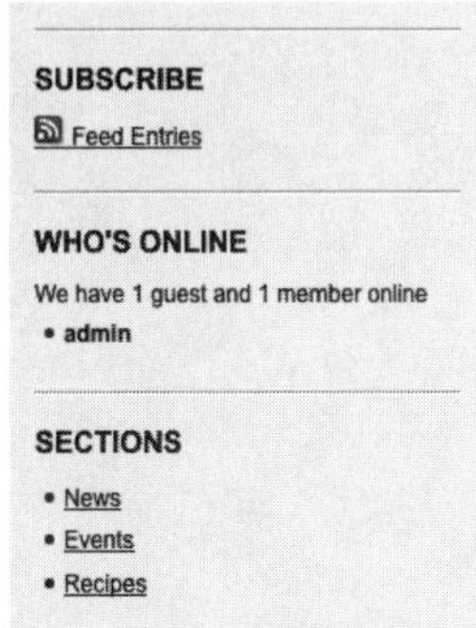

Figure 5.51 The Syndicate module on the web site

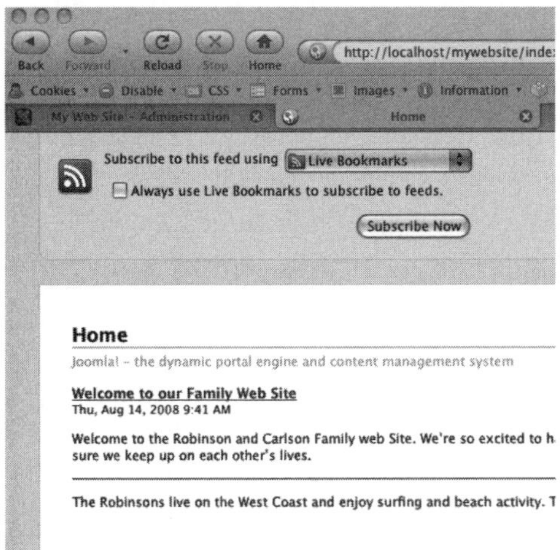

Figure 5.52 The subscription selection page

6. Leave the Module Parameters at the defaults.

   Joomla supports both RSS 2.0 and Atom 1.0 feed types (**Figure 5.50**).

7. Click Save, and then click Preview.

   The site now displays a Subscribe link on every page (**Figure 5.51**).

8. Click Feed Entries from the Home page.

   A new browser window opens, allowing the user to subscribe to entries on the Home page (**Figure 5.52**).

Extending Your Site

In previous chapters you learned how modules provide interactivity and navigation to your site and that articles contain 99% of all content on your site. In this chapter we show you how to extend a site further by using some of Joomla's built-in components as well as installing third-party extensions and plugins.

One of the more difficult concepts is to understand the differences between modules, components, and plugins. Because most components, modules, and plugins work together, it is difficult to draw a definitive line between them.

Components, unlike modules, display only in the main body of the page. A component is an individual feature, function, or page that extends your site's capabilities. For example, in the previous chapter you created a News Feed module. The module displayed a single feed that displayed on the right side of the page. The News Feed *component*, created in this chapter, displays a list of multiple feeds, all categorized, and then displayed in the main body of the page.

✔ Tip

- Some components work independently, and others require modules in order to display on the site—similar to the way articles cannot display without menu items to define the way the article is laid out. Unlike articles, which can be left uncategorized, most components require at least one category before you can use them. These components also need either a module or a menu item in order to display on the site.

Adding Banners

You can use the Banner component to create advertising banners on your web site. Like any feature in Joomla, however, it can be used to serve a host of other purposes, as well. For example, a real estate site could use banners to display its hottest properties. A family site, like the one in this book, could use banners to display pictures from various family members. Banners contain clients, for example an advertising banner would contain the business client's information, and categories that must be set up first before using the Banner component. Banner categories are separate from article categories used on the rest of the site.

No matter how you choose to use the Banner component, you must create its elements in the following order:

- Create banner categories.
- Create banner clients.
- Create the banner component.
- Create a banner module.

To add a banner category:

1. Choose Components > Banner > Categories (**Figure 6.1**).

   The Banner Category Manager opens. You can access any of the Banner Managers using the links at the top: Banners, Clients, or Categories (**Figure 6.2**).

2. On the toolbar, click New.
3. In the Title field, type `Carlsons`.

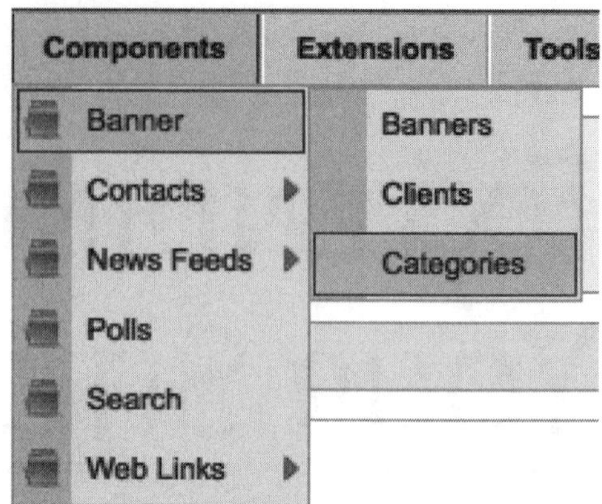

Figure 6.1 The Components > Banner menu

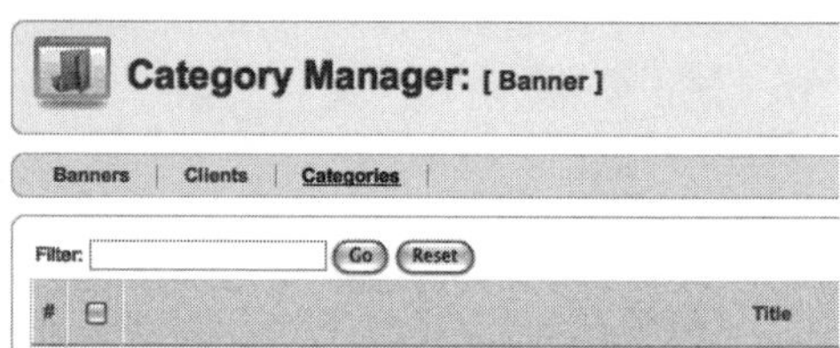

Figure 6.2 The Banner Category Manager

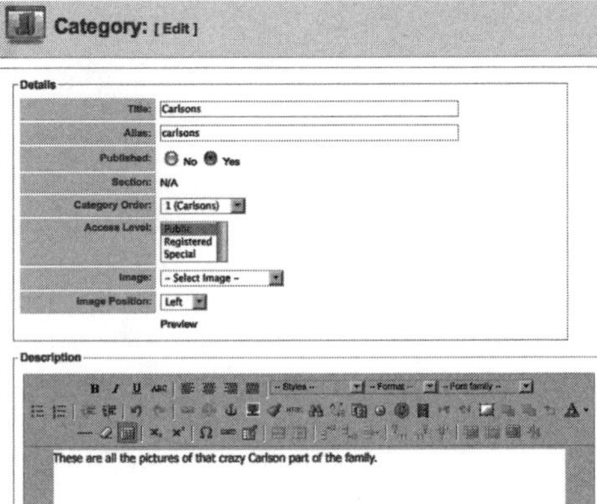

Figure 6.3 The Banner Category edit page

4. Leave the Alias field blank.

   The information in this field is used in the URL when the option for Search Engine–Friendly URLs is set to Yes in the global configuration settings (see Chapter 7, "Modifying Global Settings"). When you click Save, Joomla automatically fills the Alias field. If you want something other than the default, you can enter it in this field, but it must be all lowercase, no blank spaces. You can use hyphens between the words.

5. Click the Yes radio button for Published.

   Leave the rest of the fields at their defaults (**Figure 6.3**).

6. Click Save.

   The next step is to add a banner client.

✔ Tip

- If you want a description to display for a Banner category, you enter it in the Description WYSIWYG editor.

To add a banner client:

1. Choose Components > Banner > Clients.

   The Banner Client Manager opens.

2. On the toolbar, click New.

   Banner clients contain the client information for reference purposes. If you kept advertising banners, you would put all the client's contact information here (**Figure 6.4**).

3. In the Client Name field, type `Carlsons`.

4. In the Contact Name field, type `Rita Carlson`.

5. In the Contact E-mail field, type `ritac@someemail.com`.

6. Click Save.

   You now have clients and categories for your banner and can move on to the final phase of creating a banner.

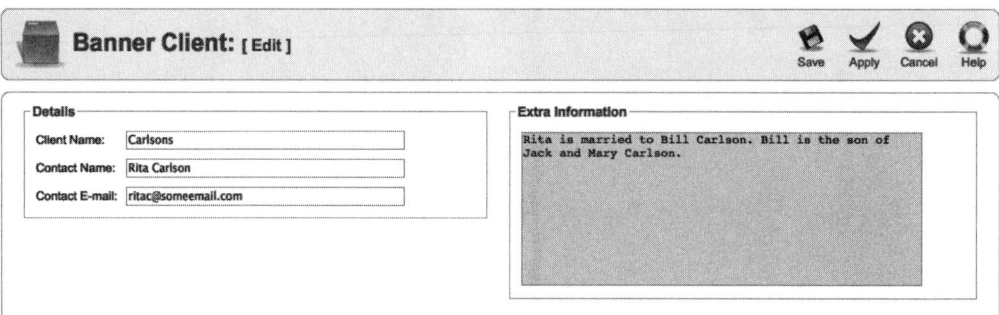

Figure 6.4 The Banner Client edit page

To add a banner:

1. Choose Components > Banner > Banners.
   The Banner Manager opens (**Figure 6.5**).
2. On the toolbar, click New.
   The New Banner edit page opens.
3. In the Name field, type Banner.
4. Leave the Alias field blank.

continues on next page

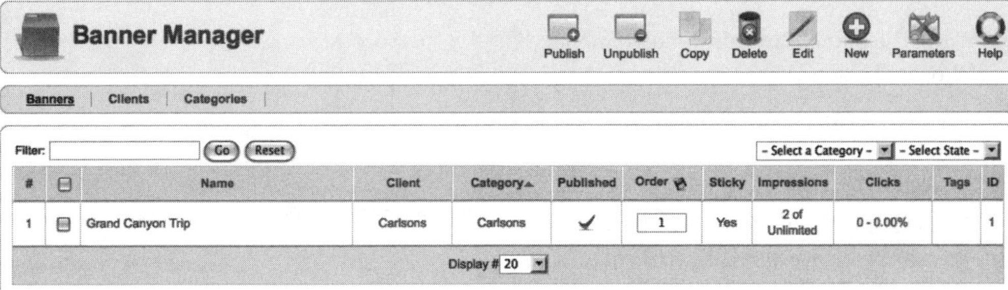

Figure 6.5 The Banner Manager

Banner Manager Fields

- **Name:** The name of the banner.
- **Client:** The name of the client with which this banner is associated.
- **Category:** The category to which this banner is assigned.
- **Published:** A green checkmark in this column means this banner is published.
- **Order:** The order in which the banner will appear, if there is more than one banner.
- **Sticky:** Determines the priority of banners when more than one banner is displayed on the page. Sticky tells the Banner module which priority to assign.
- **Impressions:** Tracks the number of times a banner has displayed on a page.
- **Clicks:** Tracks the number of times a user clicks the banner. The first number tracks how many clicks since the banner was reset to 0, and the second displays a percentage for how many times a user has clicked the banner since it was displayed on the site.
- **Tags:** Displays banners based on keywords in articles.
- **ID:** The database ID number for this banner.

5. Click the Yes radio button for Show Banner.

6. Click the No radio button for Sticky.

   Selecting Yes for Sticky tells the Banner module to give this banner priority if you set multiple banners to show on the same page. A banner set to sticky will be displayed before a banner not sticky. Multiple banners can be set as sticky.

7. In the Order field, type 1.

8. From the Category drop-down menu, choose Carlsons.

9. From the Client Name drop-down menu, choose Carlsons.

10. Choose any image from the drop-down list.

    For now, leave the remaining fields blank. A Banner module needs to be created before the banner can display (**Figure 6.6**).

11. Click Save.

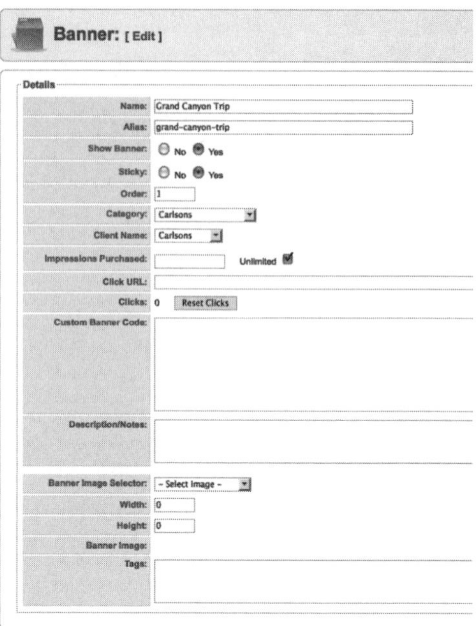

Figure 6.6 The Banner edit details page

To add the Banner module:

1. Choose Extension > Module Manager.

   The Module Manager opens.

2. On the toolbar, click New.

   The New Module screen opens.

3. Click the Banner radio button, and then click Next.

4. In the Title field, type `Banner`.

5. From the Position drop-down menu, choose banner.

6. In the Menu Assignment area, click the All radio button for Menus.

   Just like the Menu module contains the menu items that allow content to display, the Banner module allows your banners to display on the site. (**Figure 6.7**).

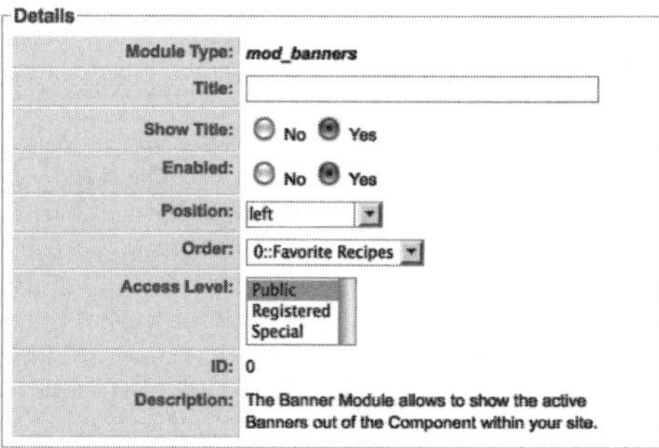

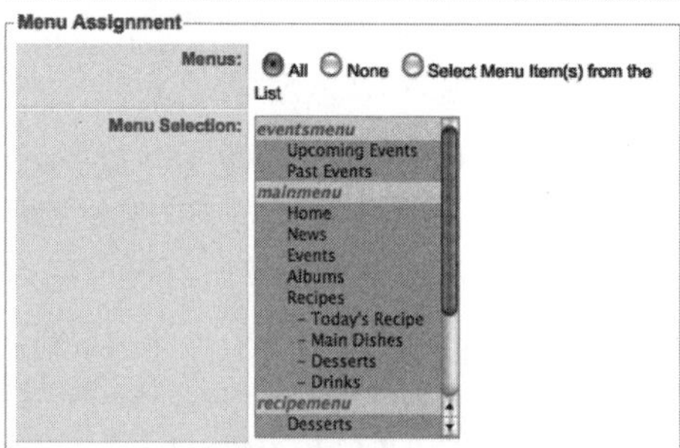

Figure 6.7 The Banner module edit page

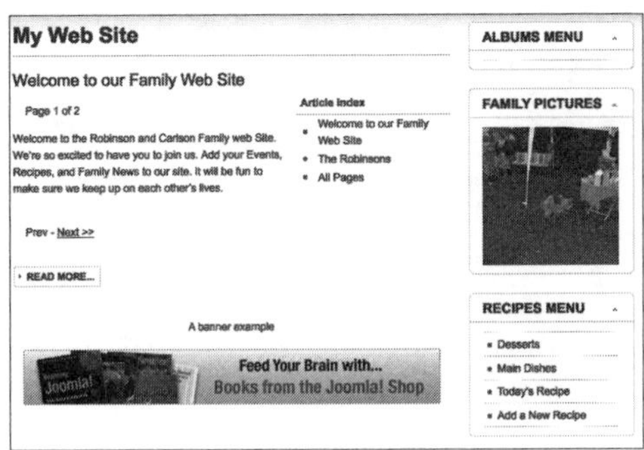

Figure 6.8 The Banner component on the web site home page

7. Click Apply.

8. Click Save, and then click Preview (**Figure 6.8**).

Banner Module Parameters

Figure 6.9 shows the Banner module parameters:

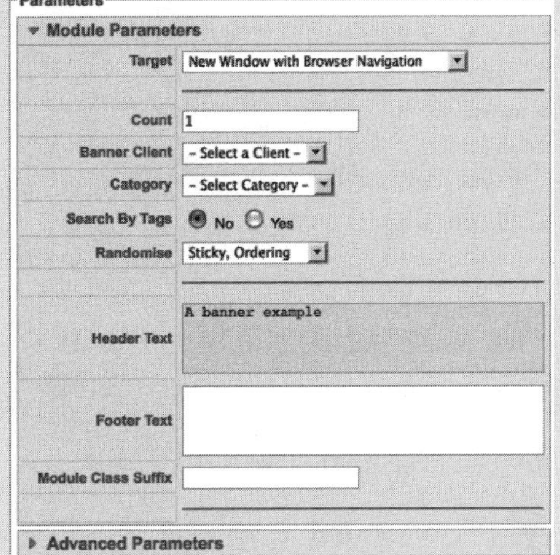

Figure 6.9 The Banner module parameters

- **Target:** Determines whether the banner opens in its own window and features navigation. "Parent Window with Browser Navigation" opens the banner in the current browser page. "New Window with Browser Navigation" opens the banner in a new browser window with forward and back navigation available. "New Window without Browser Navigation" opens the banner in a new browser window without navigation buttons.
- **Count:** The number of banners to display.
- **Banner Client:** Lists all banner clients. Choose the client for the banner.
- **Category:** All banner categories are listed. Choose a category for the banner.
- **Search by Tags:** Tells the Banner module to choose the banners based on keywords used in the articles.
- **Randomize:** Determines the type of banner order. Choose "Sticky, Ordering" to have the banners switch according to the "sticky" ordering created in the banner component. "Sticky, Randomize" displays the banners randomly.
- **Header Text:** Displays the text entered in this field. The text displays above the banner.
- **Footer Text:** Displays the text entered in this field. The text displays below the banner.

Adding Contacts

The Contacts component creates a directory of contacts. This can be used in a variety of ways, but it is generally used to provide users with all the contacts available on your site, or within a company. Using the Contacts component, you can also create a contact form, allowing users to e-mail contacts on the site.

To create a contact directory:

- Create a contact category.
- Create a contact.
- Create a menu item (link).

To add a contact category:

1. Choose Components > Contacts > Categories.

   The New Category screen opens.
2. On the toolbar, click New.
3. In the Title field, type `Administrators`.
4. Leave the Alias field blank.
5. Click the Yes radio button for Published.

   The Description field is used for back end information only and does not display on the contact page (**Figure 6.10**).
6. Click Save.

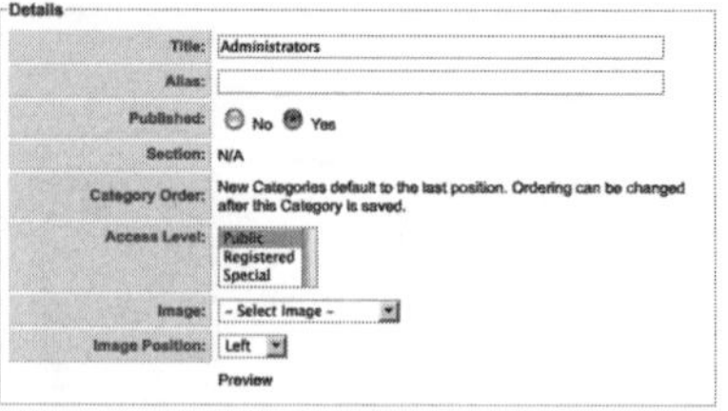

Figure 6.10 The New Category page

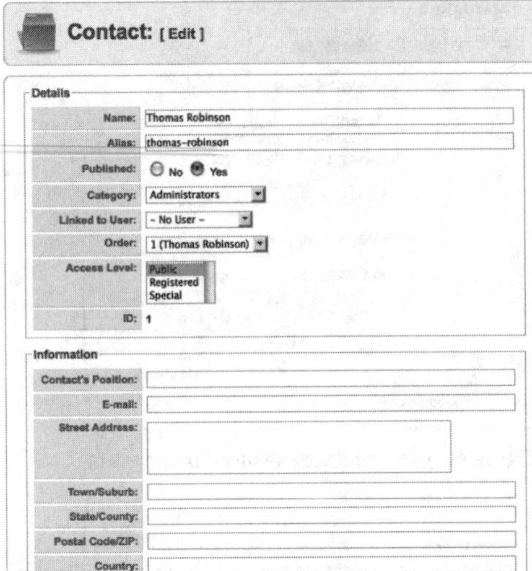

Figure 6.11 The Edit Contact page

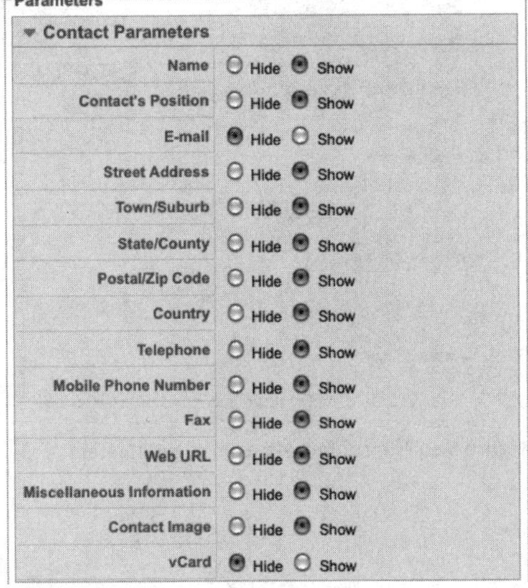

Figure 6.12 The contact basic parameters

To add a contact:

1. Choose Components > Contacts > Contacts.

   The Contact Manager opens.

2. On the toolbar, click New.

   The New Contact page opens.

3. In the Title field, type `Thomas Robinson`.

4. Click the Yes radio button for Published.

   If you select No, this contact will not display on the contacts page.

5. Leave the Alias field blank.

6. From the Category drop-down menu, choose Administrators.

7. Leave Public selected in the Access Level list.

   If you want only registered users to see certain contacts, select Registered.

8. In the "Linked to User" drop-down menu, choose Thomas Robinson.

   This is all the required information for a contact. All other fields and parameters depend on the level of information you need for a contact (**Figure 6.11**).

9. Set the Contact Parameters.

   After entering all the contact information, use the parameters to show or hide any of the contact's information (**Figure 6.12**).

continues on next page

10. Set the Advanced Parameters.

The Advanced Parameters are where you choose the icons that go with each field on the contact page. You can choose an image from the list or use the default images, for example, e-mail icon, phone icon, and so on (**Figure 6.13**).

11. Set the E-mail parameters.

If you want users to be able to contact this person through e-mail, you must click the Show radio button next to E-mail Form. All other fields are optional (**Figure 6.14**).

12. Click Save.

Even though contacts have been added, you will not be able to see contact information or contact forms until you create a menu item link.

✔ Tip

- When creating contacts, you can choose to display only the contact information or choose to have a form added to the end of the contact's information using the Show E-mail Form option.

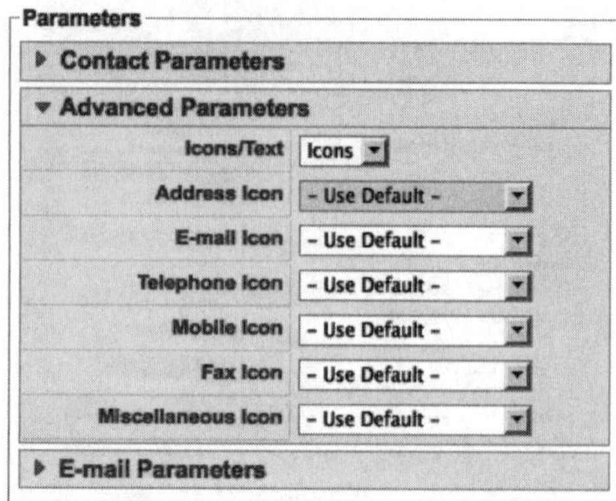

Figure 6.13 The contact advanced parameters

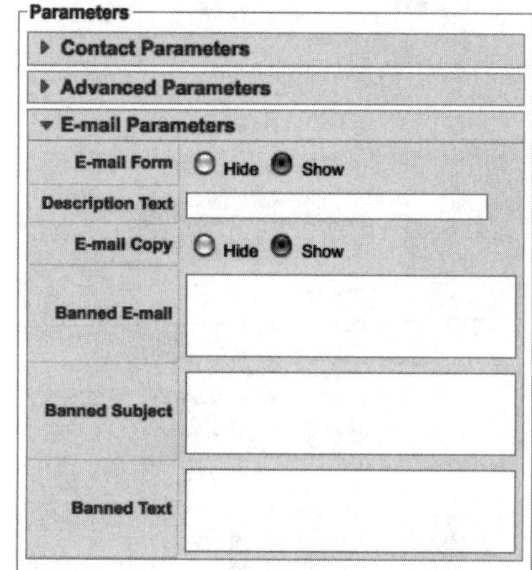

Figure 6.14 The contact e-mail form parameters

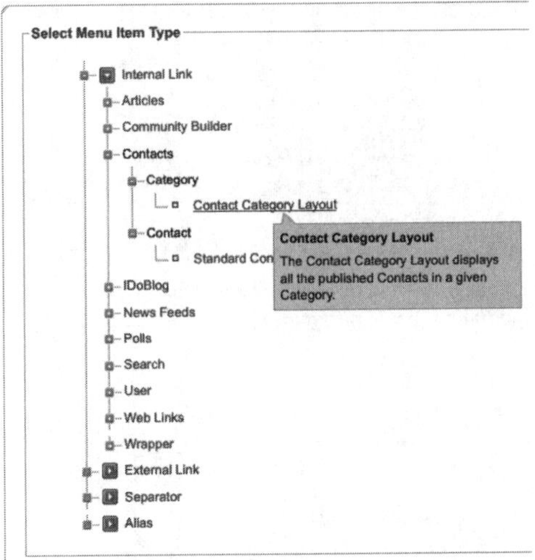

Figure 6.15 The Contact Category Layout menu item

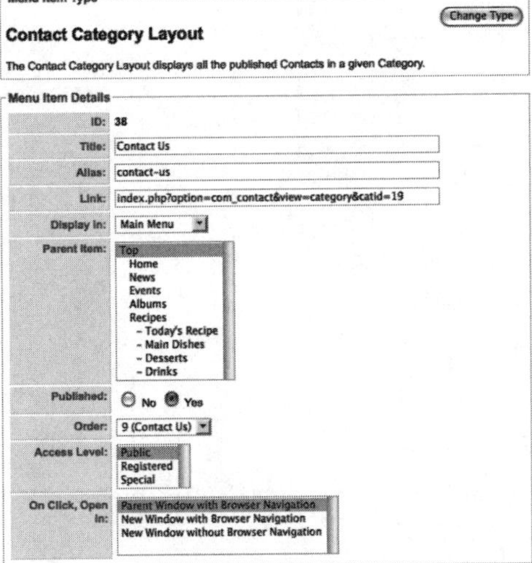

Figure 6.16 The Contact Category Layout menu item page

To add a Contact Us menu item:

1. Choose Menus > Main Menu.
2. On the toolbar, click New.
3. Choose Internal Link > Contacts > Category > Contact Category Layout (**Figure 6.15**).

   The New Menu Item page opens.
4. In the Menu Item Details area, type `Contact Us` in the Title field.

   Leave all other fields at their defaults (**Figure 6.16**).

continues on next page

5. Click the arrow next to Parameters (Basic), and then choose Administrators from the Select Category drop-down menu (**Figure 6.17**).
6. Click the arrow next to Parameters (Component).

   The component parameters will use the default contact parameters set in the Contact Manager, unless you select to override those defaults under Parameters (Component) (**Figure 6.18**).

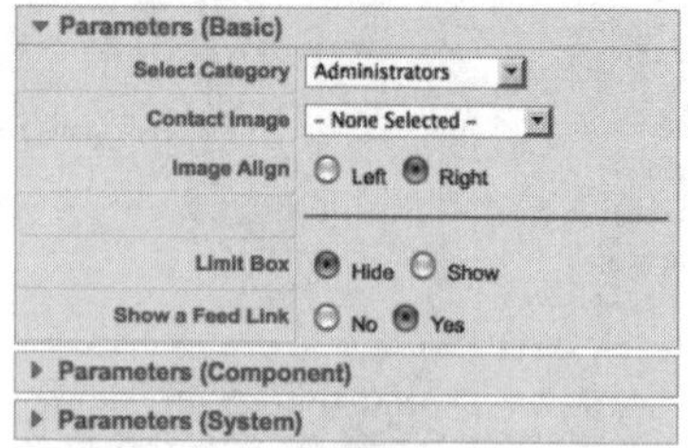

Figure 6.17 The Contact Category Layout menu item basic parameters

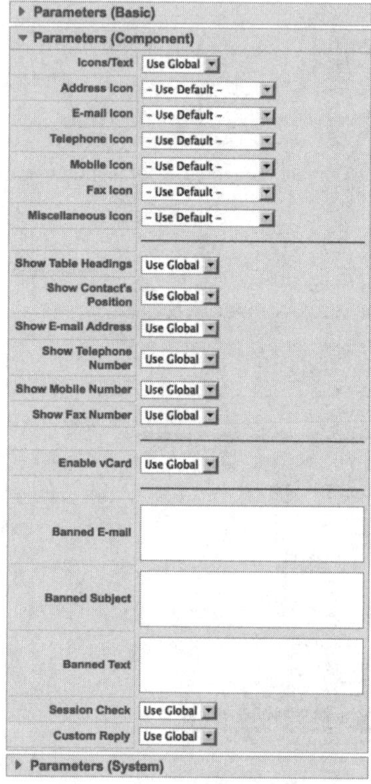

Figure 6.18 The Contact Category Layout menu item component parameters

Contact Category Layout Basic Parameters

- **Select Category:** Choose a category from the list. These categories are created in the Contacts Category manager.
- **Contact Image:** If this contact has a picture or image, you can choose it here. These images must be in the images/stories directory.
- **Image Align:** Align the image to the left or right of the contact's information.
- **Limit Box:** Choose how many contacts to list on a page. You can choose to show or hide the limit box.
- **Show a Feed Link:** Hide or show an RSS feed link.

Figure 6.19 The Contact Category Layout on the web site

Figure 6.20 The Contact Us form

7. Click Save, and then click Preview.
8. Choose Contact Us from the Main menu.

   A contact category layout displays all the contacts for your web site in a list format (**Figure 6.19**).
9. Click the name Thomas Robinson.

   The contact page opens, and a user can now contact Thomas Robinson by e-mail (**Figure 6.20**).

Adding News Feeds

In Chapter 5, "Working with Modules," you created a Feed Display module, which displayed a single feed, fed from the allrecipes.com web site. The News Feed component will display a list of categorized feeds. To use this component you will:

- Create News Feeds categories.
- Create the News Feeds component.
- Create a menu item using the News Feeds layout.

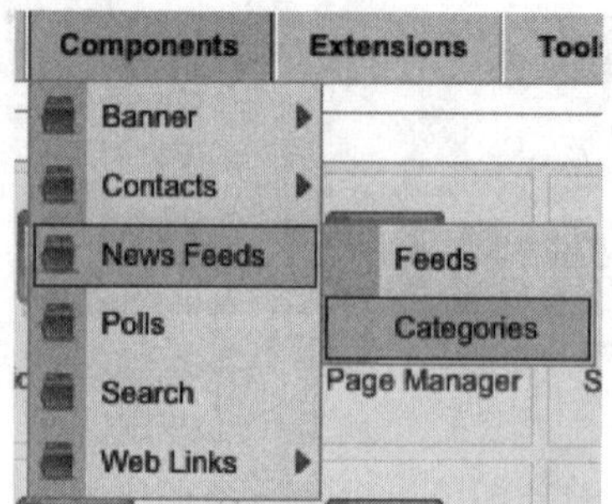

Figure 6.21 The Components > News Feeds menu

To create news feed categories:

1. Choose Components > News Feeds > Categories (**Figure 6.21**).

   The News Feeds Category Manager opens (**Figure 6.22**).

2. Click New.

   The New News Feeds Category Editor opens.

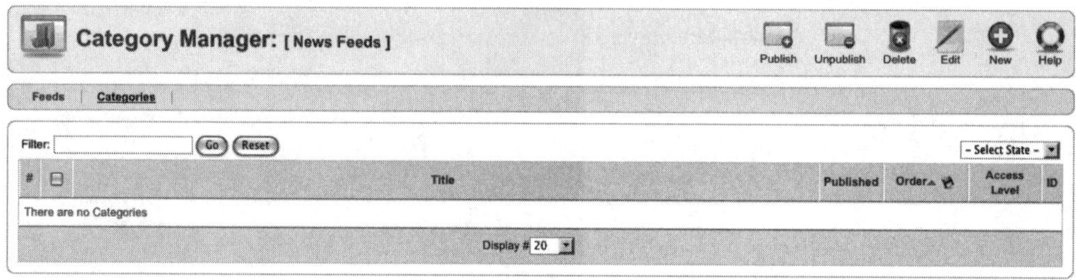

Figure 6.22 The News Feeds Category Manager

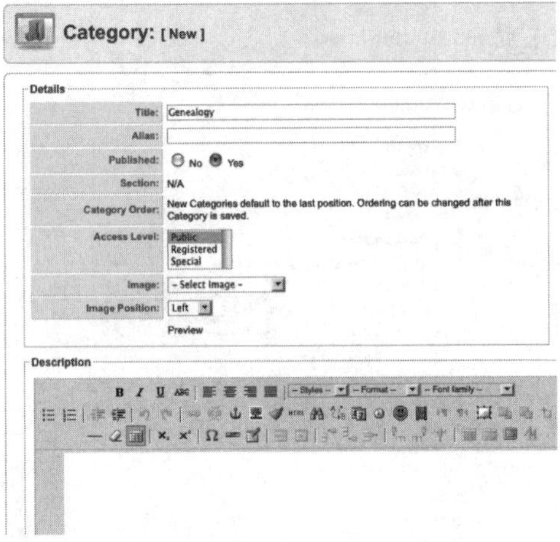

Figure 6.23 The New News Feed Category page

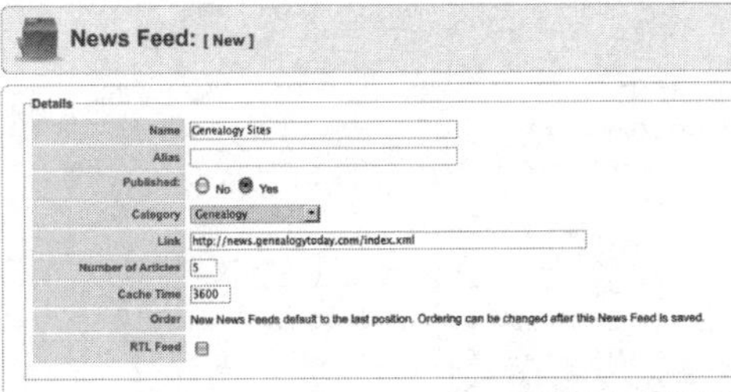

Figure 6.24 The New News Feed page

3. In the Title field, type `Genealogy`.
4. Leave all other fields at their defaults. If you want a description for this feed, enter the text in the Description field (**Figure 6.23**).
5. Click Save.

To create a feed:

1. Choose Components > News Feeds > Feeds.

   The News Feed Manager opens.
2. Click New.

   The New News Feed Editor opens (**Figure 6.24**).
3. In the Name field, type `Genealogy Sites`.
4. From the Category drop-down menu, choose Genealogy.
5. In the Link field, type `http://news.genealogytoday.com/index.xml`

   This adds the news feed link to the site.
6. Click Save.

   You have added a News Feeds component and assigned a feed to a category. Before the page can display on the site, however, it needs a menu item link.

To create a News Feed menu item:

1. Choose Menu > Main Menu.
2. Click New.
3. Choose Internal Link > News Feeds > All Categories > Category List Layout (**Figure 6.25**).
4. In the Title field, type `Feeds`.
5. Leave all other Details at their defaults (**Figure 6.26**).
6. Click Save, and then click Preview.

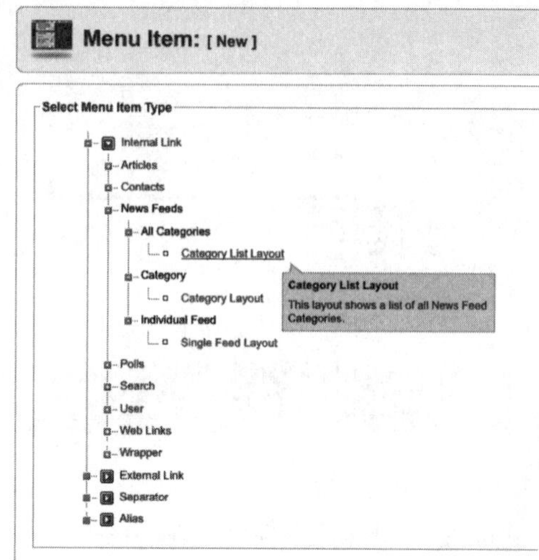

Figure 6.25 The News Feed menu item layout page

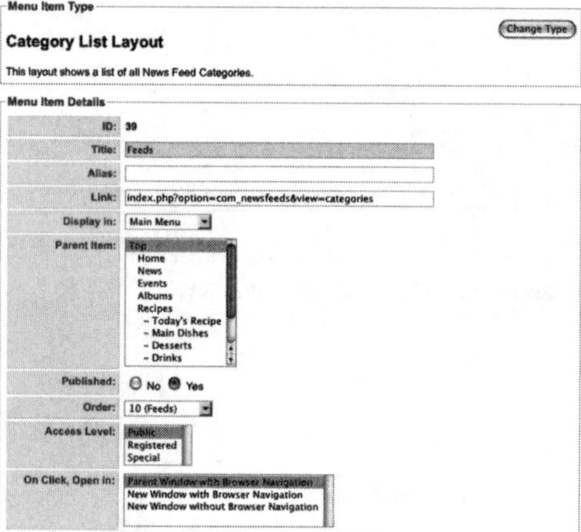

Figure 6.26 The Category List layout menu item edit page

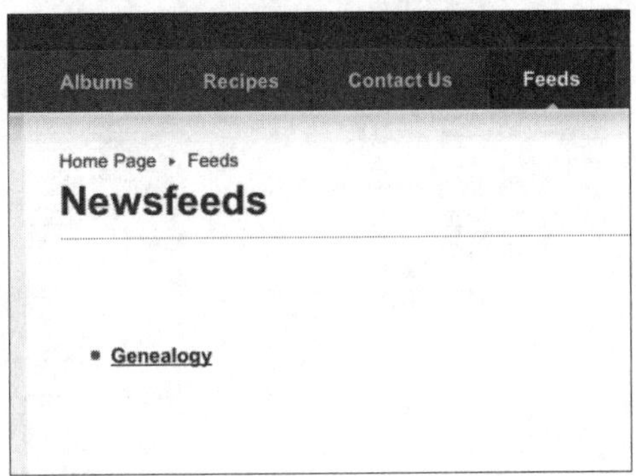

Figure 6.27 The News Feeds component on the web site

Figure 6.28 The Genealogy category link

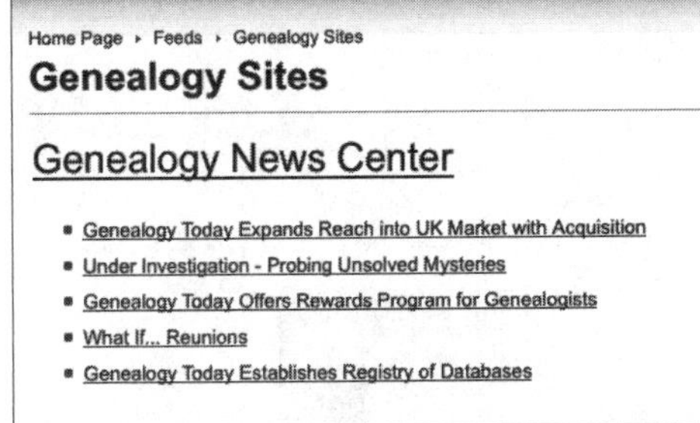

Figure 6.29 The Genealogy News Center feed display

7. Choose News Feeds from the main menu.

   A list of News Feeds categories will display on this page (**Figure 6.27**).

8. Click the Genealogy link.

   Currently there is only one genealogy feed (**Figure 6.28**).

9. Click the Genealogy Sites link.

   The Genealogy News Center feed displays (**Figure 6.29**).

Creating Polls

The Polls component can be used as a rating or voting system for a single item. You can provide up to 12 options and then track the user votes.

To add polls to your site:

- ◆ Create a Poll component.
- ◆ Create a Poll module to display a single poll.
- ◆ Create a menu item link using the Poll layout.

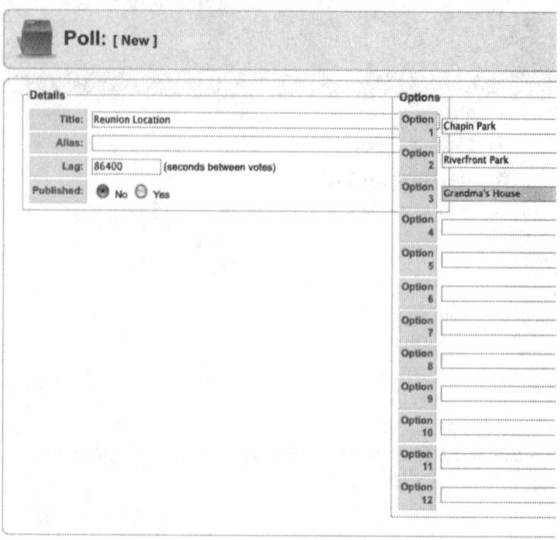

Figure 6.30 The New Poll component page

To create a poll component:

1. Choose Components > Polls.
   The Poll Manager opens.
2. On the toolbar, click New.
3. In the Title field, type `Reunion Location`.
4. Click the Yes radio button for Published.
5. In the Option 1 field, type `Chapin Park`.
6. In the Option 2 field, type `Riverfront Park`.
7. In the Option 3 field, type `Grandma's House` (**Figure 6.30**).
8. Click Save.

To add the Poll module:

1. Choose Extension > Module Manager.
   The Module Manager opens.
2. On the toolbar, click New.
   The New Module screen opens.
3. Click the Poll radio button, then click Next.
4. In the Title field, type `Family Vote`.
5. From the Position drop-down menu, choose right.
6. Leave the Menus radio button at the default All (**Figure 6.31**).

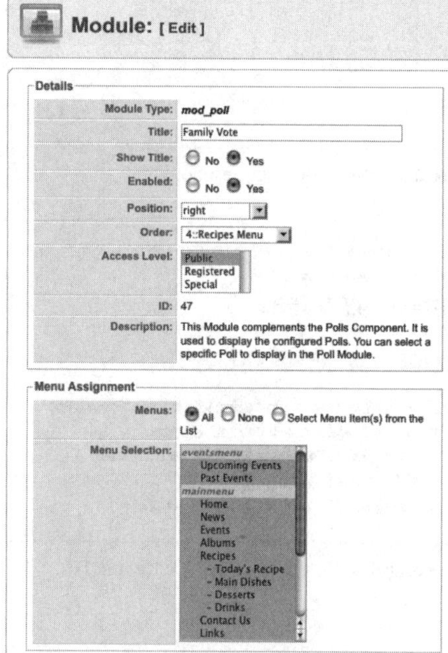

Figure 6.31 The Poll module edit page

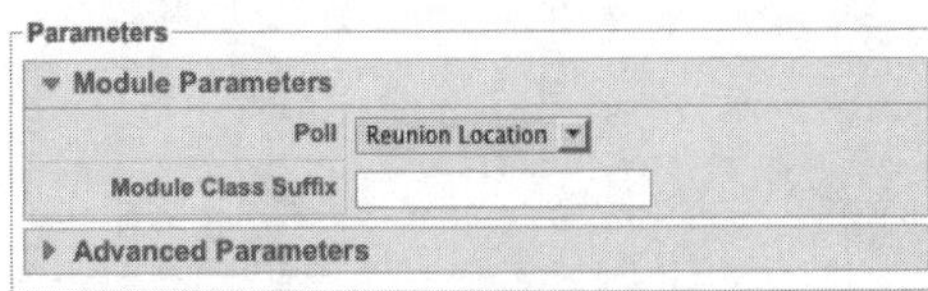

Figure 6.32 The Poll module parameters

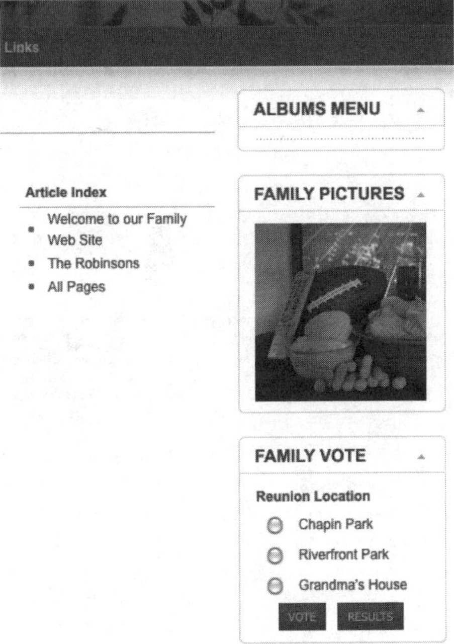

Figure 6.33 The Family Vote Poll module on the web site

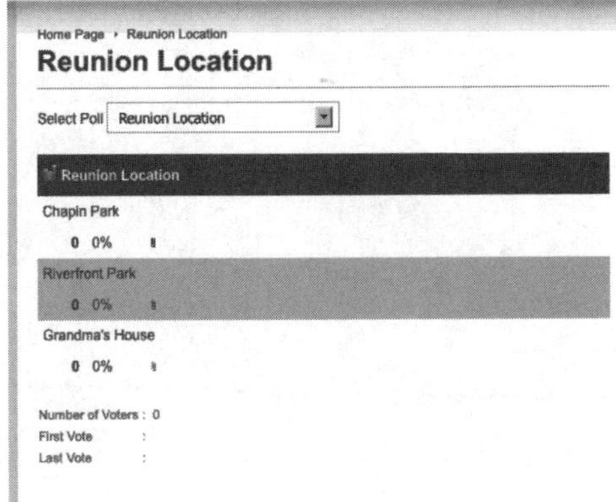

Figure 6.34 The Poll results page

7. Under Module Parameters, choose Reunion Location from the Poll drop-down menu (**Figure 6.32**).

8. Click Save, and then click Preview.

   The Polls module is displayed (**Figure 6.33**).

9. Click the Results button.

   The Polls component displays the results in the main body of the page (**Figure 6.34**). As users vote, the results update. If you had more than one poll, you could select it from the Select Poll list at the top of the page.

Using the Search Component

The Search component allows an administrator to view search statistics for the web site. You must have a Search module enabled on the site in order to collect search information.

1. Choose Components > Search.

   The Search Statistics screen opens (**Figure 6.35**).

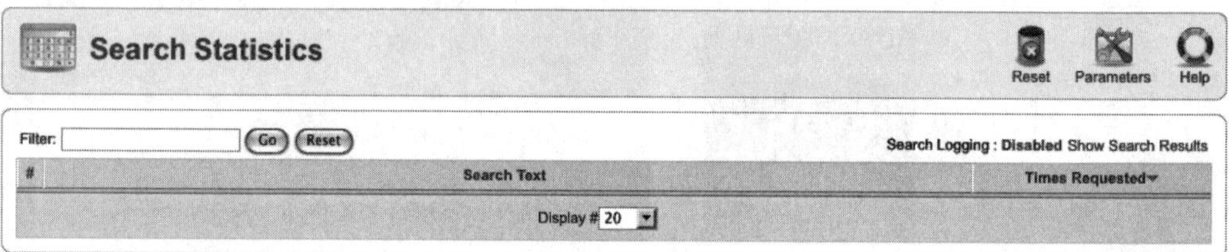

Figure 6.35 The Search Statistics component

2. On the toolbar, click Parameters.
3. Click the Yes radio button for Gather Search Statistics (**Figure 6.36**).
4. Click Save.
5. Click Show Search Results in the Search Statistics Manager (**Figure 6.37**).

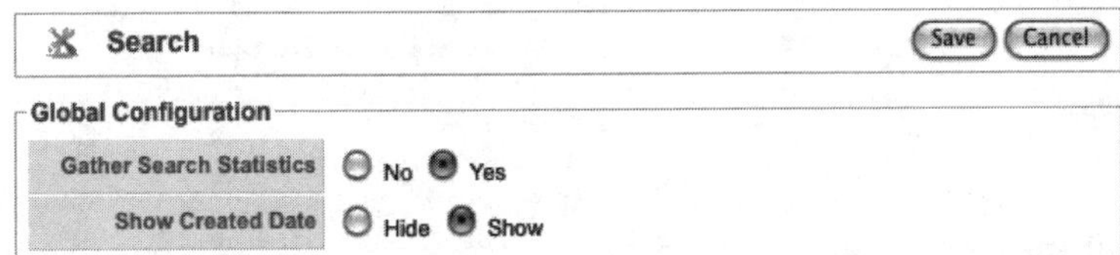

Figure 6.36 The Search Statistics global configuration

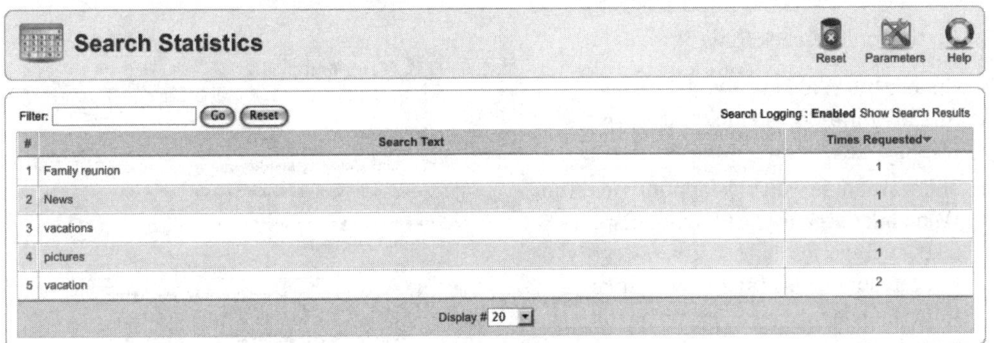

#	Search Text	Times Requested
1	Family reunion	1
2	News	1
3	vacations	1
4	pictures	1
5	vacation	2

Figure 6.37 The Search Statistic results

Adding Web Links

Adding web links to a Joomla site is easy. If you want a web link page that includes categories and the ability for users to add web links, you use the Web Link component. Like other components a Web Link page needs categories and a menu item to display correctly. You can place a link to the web links page in an existing menu module, or you can create a new module. The choice is yours.

In this section you will:

- Add a Web Link menu item to the main menu.
- Create web link categories.
- Create web links.

To add a web link menu item:

1. Choose Menus > Main Menu.
   The Main Menu Items Manager opens.
2. On the toolbar, click New.
3. Choose Internal Link > Web Links > All Categories > Web Link Category List Layout.
   There are three web link layout types. The Web Link Category List Layout displays all the categories in a list. The Category List Layout displays all the web links from a single category. The Web Link Submission Layout enables users to submit web links, similar to the one you created in Chapter 3, "Adding Your Content" (**Figure 6.38**).
4. In the Title field, type `Fun Links`.
   The title is the name of the menu item.
5. Leave all other details and parameters at their defaults (**Figure 6.39**).
6. Click Save.

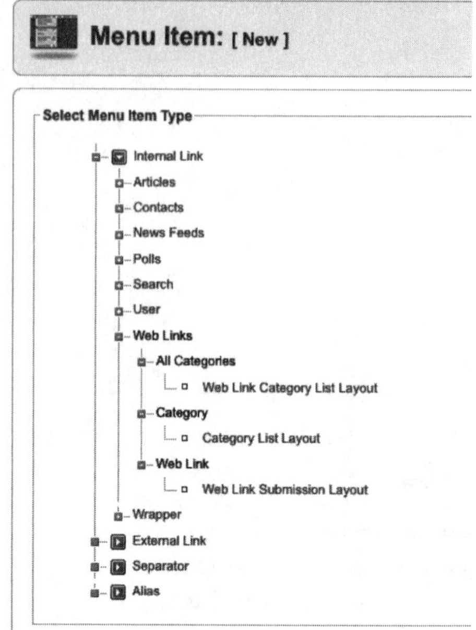

Figure 6.38 The Web Link Category List layout menu item details page

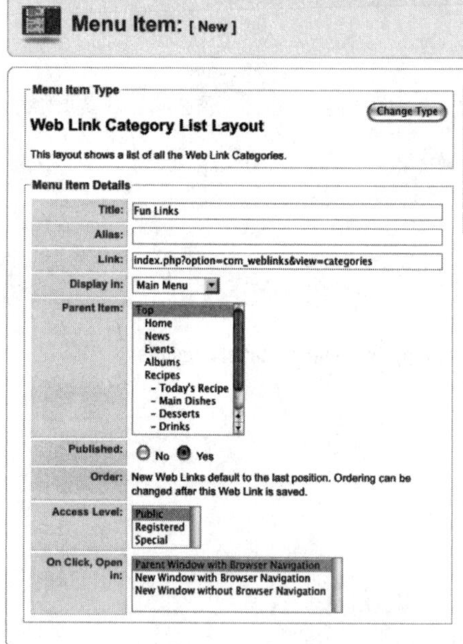

Figure 6.39 The Web Link Category List Layout edit page

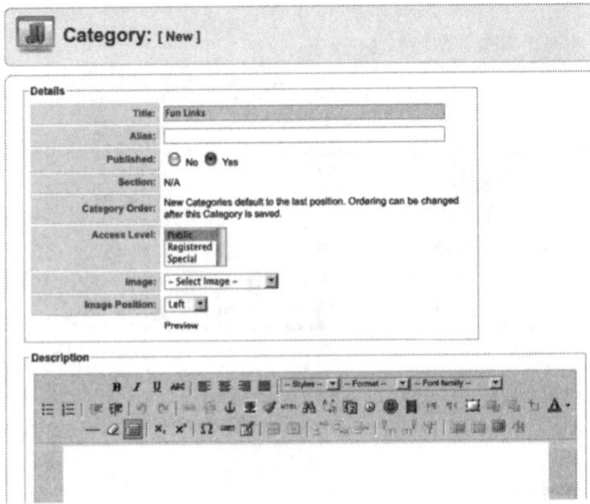

Figure 6.40 The New Category page

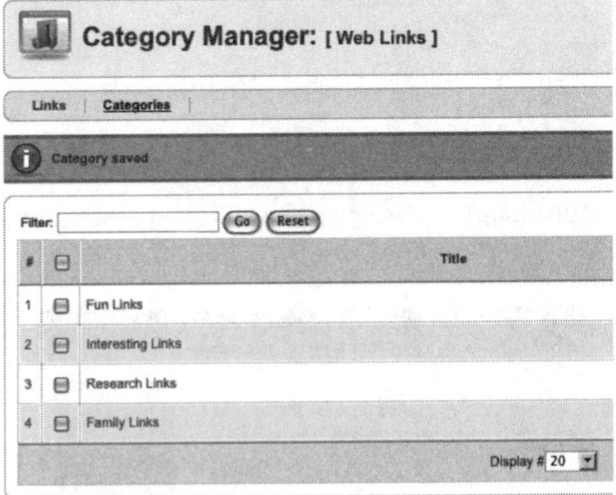

Figure 6.41 The Web Links Category Manager

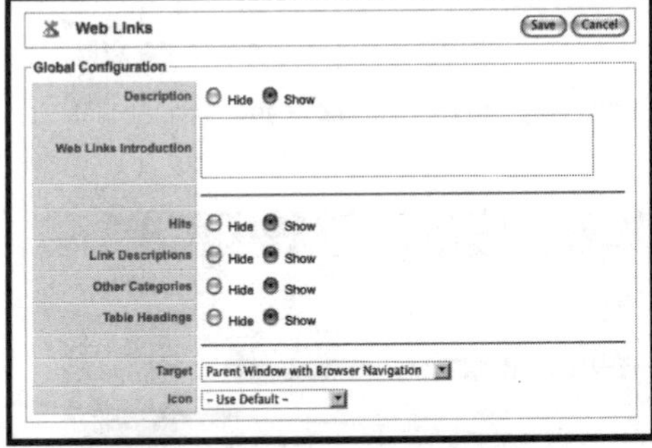

Figure 6.42 The Web Links Global Configuration page

To create web link categories:

1. Choose Components > Web Links > Categories.

   The Category screen opens.

2. On the toolbar, click New.

3. In the Title field, type `Fun Links`.

4. Leave the Alias field blank.

5. Click the Yes radio button for Published.

6. Leave all other details at their defaults (**Figure 6.40**).

7. Click Save.

8. Create a few more categories—Interesting Links, Research Links, and Family Links—by repeating steps 1 through 7 (**Figure 6.41**).

To add web links to the web link page:

1. Choose Components > Web Links > Links.

   The Web Link Manager opens.

2. On the toolbar, click Parameters.

   The Web Links parameters set the global details for the web links component page. You can add a general description and hide or show hits, link descriptions, other categories, and table headings. You can have the page open in a new window or into the main body of the page (**Figure 6.42**).

3. In the Web Links Introduction field, type `These are our links.` To submit a link, you must log into the site and choose My Web Links from the User menu.

4. Click Save.

   You return to the Web Link Manager.

5. On the toolbar, click New.

   The New Web Link screen opens.

continues on next page

6. In the Name field, type `WritersLatte`.
7. Choose Fun Links from the Category drop-down menu.
8. In the URL field, type `http://www.writerslatte.com` (**Figure 6.43**).
9. In the Parameters area, choose Use Global from the Target drop-down menu.
10. In the Description field, type `Fun site for creatives, writers, musicians, poets, and artists` (**Figure 6.44**).
11. Click Save.
12. Using steps 5 through 11 add these two links as well, modifying the Description field as appropriate:
    - ▲ http://www.writingyourdreams.com/
    - ▲ http://www.joomla.org
13. Click Preview.
14. Choose Fun Links from the main menu.

    The Web Link Category List layout displays your global description, and a list of categories to choose from (**Figure 6.45**).
15. Choose Fun Links from the Web Links page.

    The links in the Fun Links category display (**Figure 6.46**).

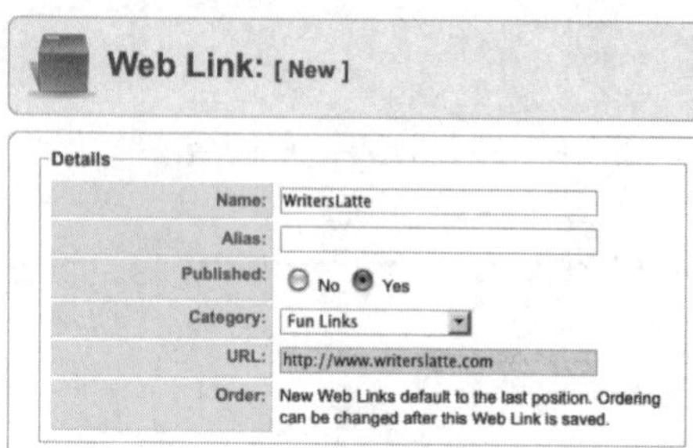

Figure 6.43 The New Web Link page

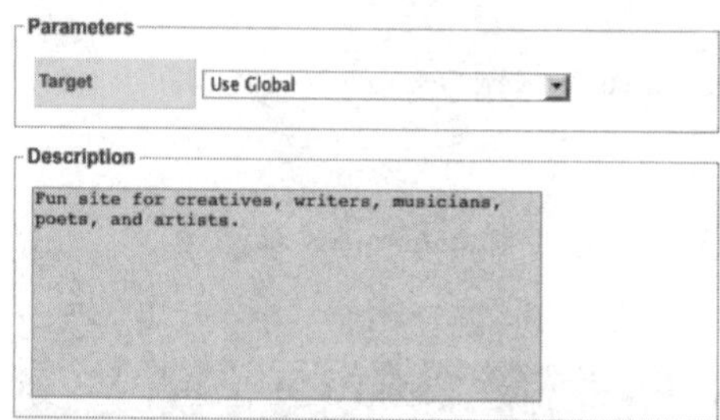

Figure 6.44 The web link parameters and description

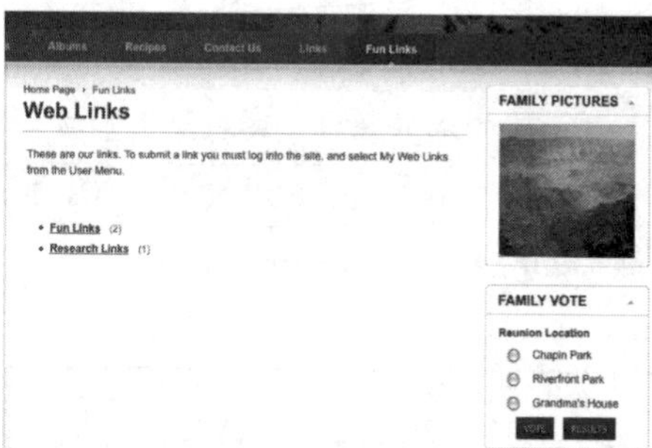

Figure 6.45 The Web Links categories on the web site

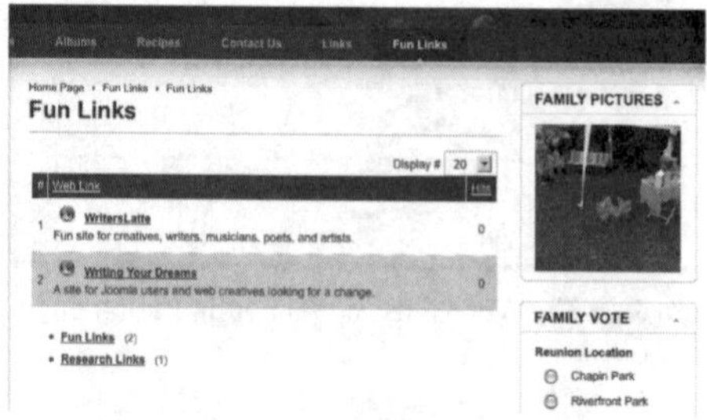

Figure 6.46 The web links displayed after selecting the category link

Using Third-Party Extensions

Joomla currently has the largest extension developer community available for a content management system. Again, with so many extensions available, you can generally find a feature you are looking for, and you still don't need to know any code to use them. The coders have done it all for you. In this section we cover two extensions: a more extendable user registration component and a forum component that uses a bridge created just for Joomla.

Joomla comes with a basic user registration feature, and for most sites this is perfectly adequate. But what if you want a community site, with more than just simple user details? One of the most popular third-party extensions for extending Joomla registration is a component called Community Builder by Joomlapolis.

Community Builder is free to download, but to access user documentation it requires a subscription. Because Community Builder is documented by Joomlapolis, we will not document how to use the component in this book. What we will cover is installing the extension and the added features it provides to a community site.

To download Community Builder:

1. Open a web browser and go to www.joomlapolis.com.

   This is the home of the community builder component extension.

2. Download the files for the suite that is compatible with Joomla 1.5.x natively.

   There are many third-party plugins that work with Community Builder. As with any extension, you may need to register with the site before downloading. One of the business models for current Joomla extensions is a yearly subscription fee for updates, upgrades, and documentation. Check each site carefully for licensing, registration, and subscription information before using an extension (**Figure 6.47**).

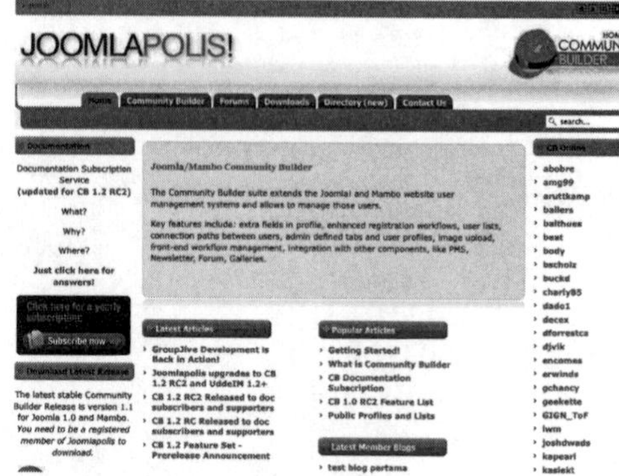

Figure 6.47 The Joomlapolis web site

To install the Community Builder extension:

1. Unzip the file you downloaded from Joomlapolis.

   The folder structure should look similar to **Figure 6.48**.

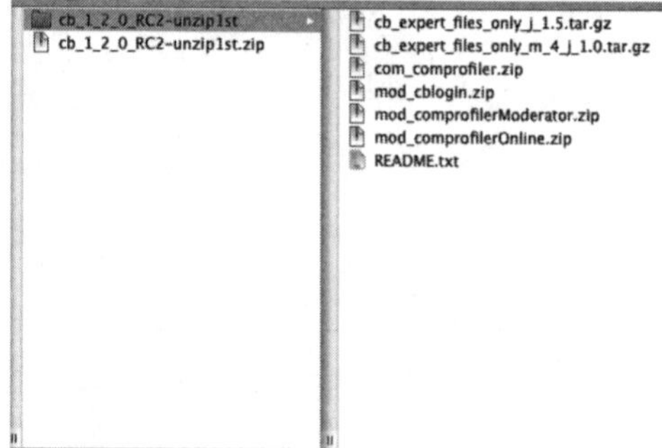

Figure 6.48 The Community Builder files

2. Log in to the back end of your web site as a super administrator.

   Only super administrators can install or uninstall extensions.

3. Choose Extensions > Install/Uninstall.

   The Extension Manager opens.

4. Click the Browse button next to the Package File field, and select com_comprofiler.zip. This is the component for Community Builder.

   All extensions are contained in ZIP files. These files contain everything necessary to install the extension on your site. You install all extensions, components, modules, and plugins from Upload Package File field (**Figure 6.49**).

5. Click the Upload File & Install button.

   Some components can take a few minutes to install. Things that can prevent a successful installation are the FTP layer being disabled on a remote server, or, on a local server, if the size of the scripts allowed to run is set too low. If you have trouble installing an extension, visit the extension's site or the Joomla.org site, or see the extension's documentation.

continues on next page

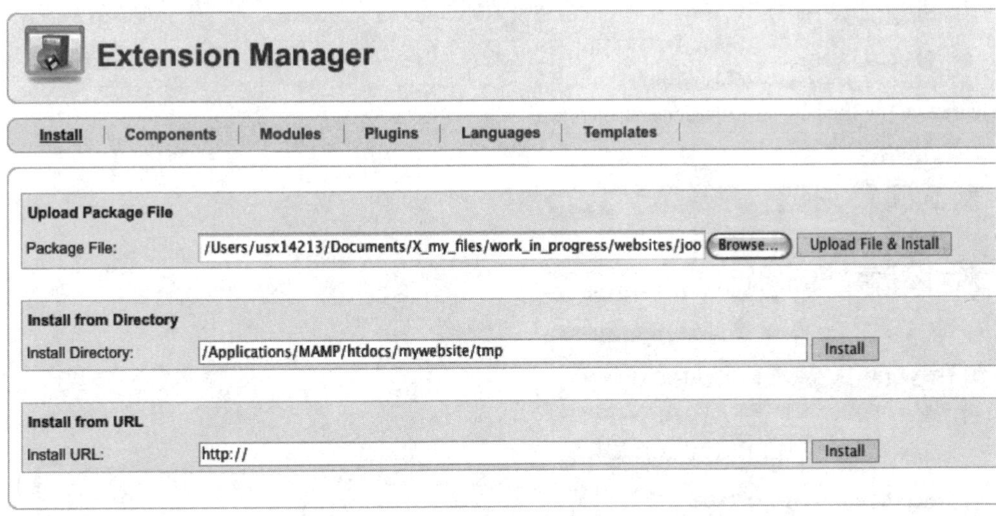

Figure 6.49 The Extension Manager Upload Package page

6. Install the mod_cblogin.zip, mod_comprofilerModerator.zip, and mod_comprofilerOnline.zip files.

7. In the Extension Manager, click the Components link.

   The comprofiler component is installed. Clicking the Modules link shows that the modules associated with Community Builder are also installed (**Figure 6.50**).

8. Choose Components from the back end administrative menu.

   The component appears in the menu, along with all the modules and configuration tools (**Figure 6.51**).

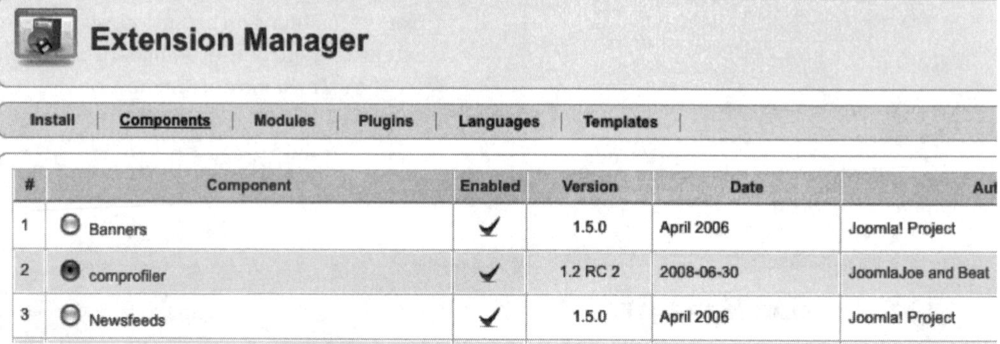

Figure 6.50 The Components Extension Manager

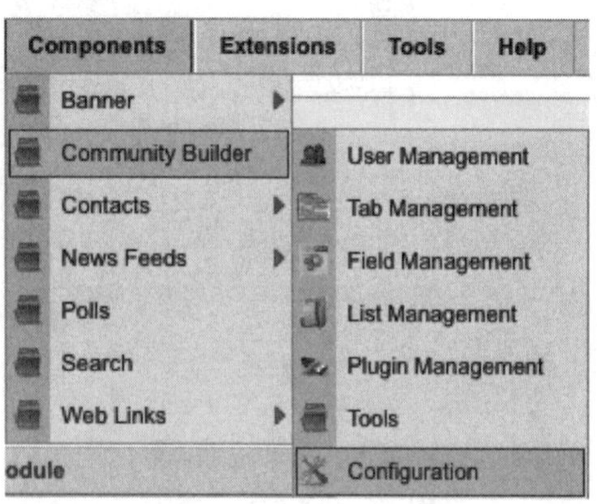

Figure 6.51 The new Community Builder component menu

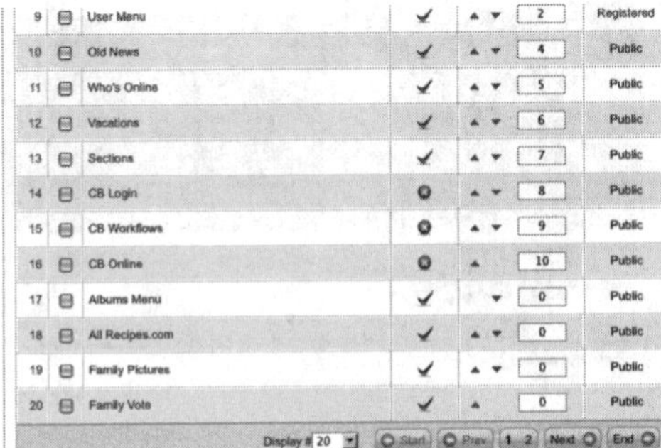

Figure 6.52 Enabling the Community Builder modules

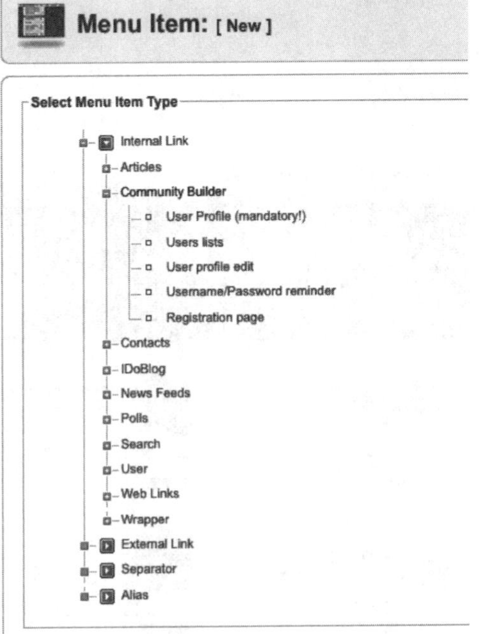

Figure 6.53 The Community Builder menu item types example

To enable the Community Builder component, modules, and plugins:

1. Choose Extensions > Module Manager.

   The CB Login, CB Workflows, and CB Online modules all appear and need to be enabled in order to use (**Figure 6.52**).

2. Click the red circled Xs to enable the modules.

   You can now configure these modules the same as any other module you have used before on the site.

   Community Builder also has specific menu item types that you can now use on your site (**Figure 6.53**).

Adding a Forum

A popular feature on web sites today is forums. Forums allow users to post and comment on a web site. Most forums are used for announcements, troubleshooting, or grouping discussions into a broad range of categories that pertain to the site's products or services.

Several forums are directly integrated into Joomla, including Simplest Forum, Fireboard, and Joo!BB. These forums can be installed through the Extension Manager.

There are also open-source free forums, such as Vanilla, SMF, and phpBB. These forums do not install directly into Joomla but require a bridge to interface with your Joomla web site.

One such interface bridge is RokBridge from RocketWerx. This third-party extension is free and integrates your Joomla user registration directly with phpBB.

Both web sites, phpBB3 and RocketWerx, contain complete instructions for installing both the forum and using the bridge, so we will move quickly through the installation.

To download phpBB:

1. Open a web browser and go to `www.phpbb.com/downloads/`.
2. Download the latest phpBB (**Figure 6.54**).

Figure 6.54 The phpBB web site

To download RokBridge:

1. Open a web browser and go to `www.rocketwerx.com`.
2. Download the RokBridge files (**Figure 6.55**).

Figure 6.55 The RocketWerx web site

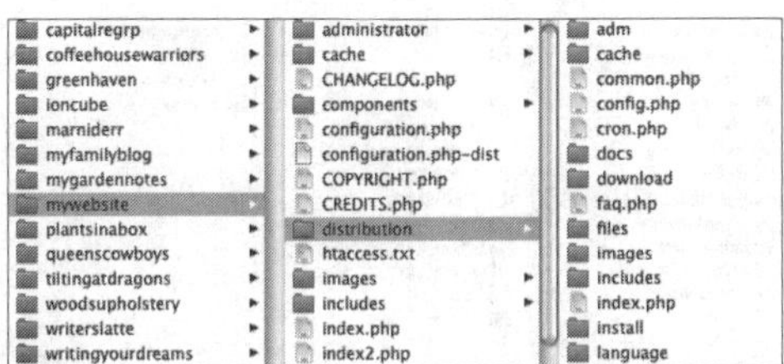

Figure 6.56 The file path to the phpBB distribution folder

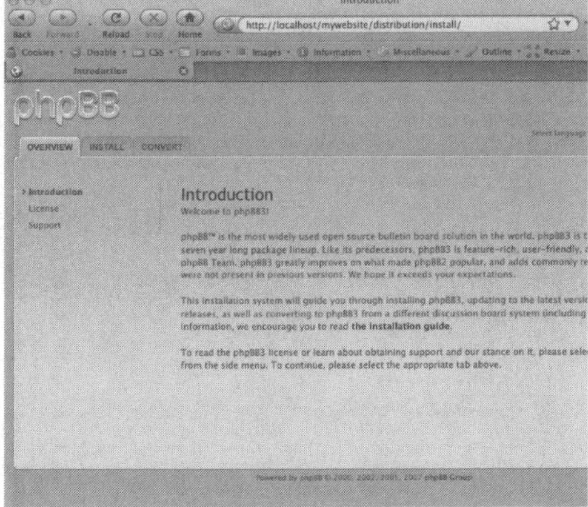

Figure 6.57 The phpBB installation screen

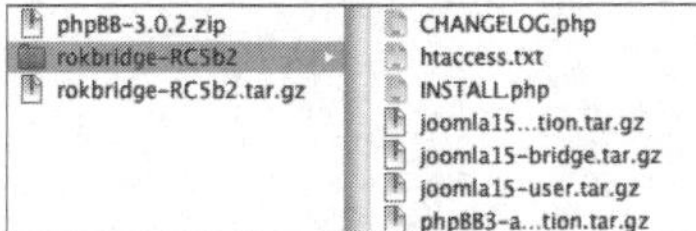

Figure 6.58 The RokBridge folder files

To add the phpBB forum:

1. Unzip the phpbb file into a folder called `distribution`.
2. Place the entire distribution folder in the root directory for your Joomla installation (**Figure 6.56**).
3. Open your web browser and type: `localhost/mywebsite/distribution/install`.

   This installs phpBB. Follow the installation instructions to completion. On its web site, phpBB has documentation and instructions on using the forum if you run into issues (**Figure 6.57**).
4. When you are done, be sure and remove the installation folder from the distribution folder.

To add the RokBridge files:

1. Unzip the RokBridge files. The folder structure should look like **Figure 6.58**.
2. Unzip the phpBB3-authentication.tar.gz folder.
3. Place the auth_joomla.php folder into your distribution/includes/auth/ folder.

   This is the file that allows your web site's registered user to also be logged into the forum. It tells phpBB to authenticate user login using the Joomla user manager (**Figure 6.59**).

continues on next page

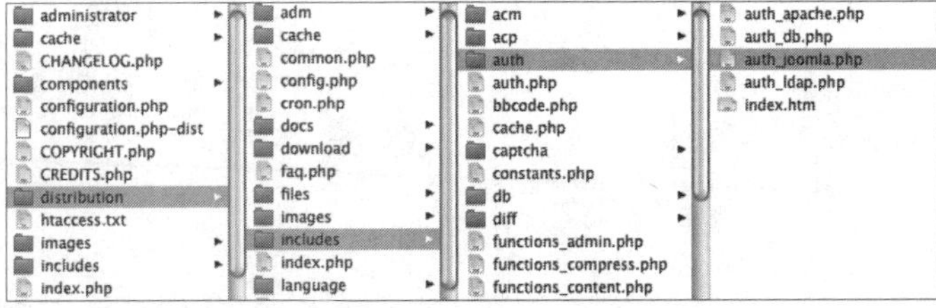

Figure 6.59 The RokBridge auth_joomla.php file path

4. Unzip the joomla15-bridge.tar.gz file.

5. Place the entire forum folder into the root directory of your Joomla installation.

   This is the bridge between Joomla and phpBB3 (**Figure 6.60**).

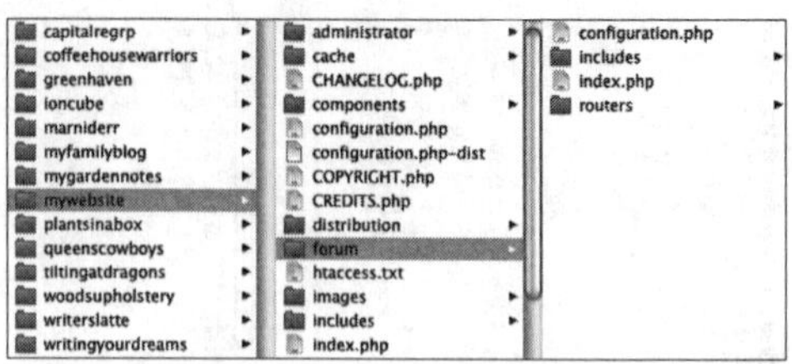

Figure 6.60 The RokBridge forum folder path

6. Log into the back end of your web site and install the joomla15-authentication.tar.gz file and the joomla15-user.tar.gz file.

7. Choose Extensions > Plugin Manager.

8. Enable the User-phpBB3 and Authentication-phpBB3 plugins (**Figure 6.61**).

   These plugins allow phpBB and Joomla to communicate and share logged-in user authentication. This means a user does not have to log in twice when going to the forum.

   You now have all the necessary files to run the forum; next you need to create the menu item to link to it.

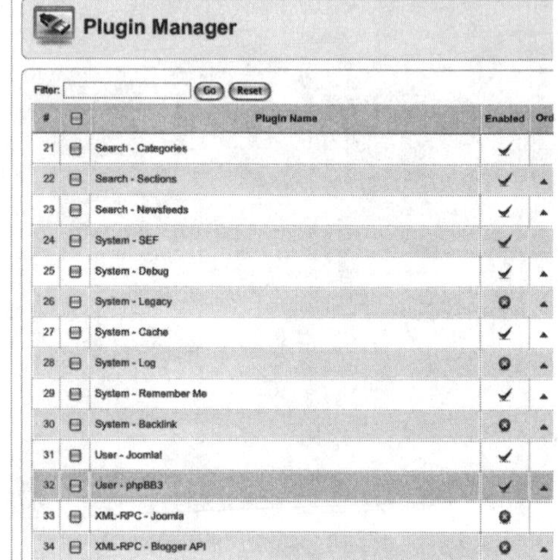

Figure 6.61 Enabling the RokBridge plugins

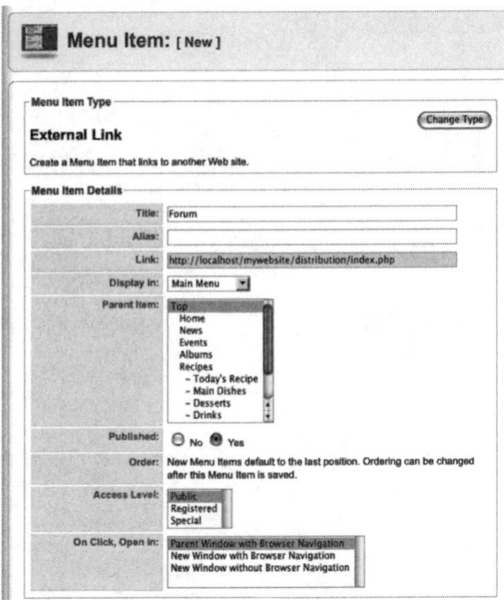

Figure 6.62 Creating an external link

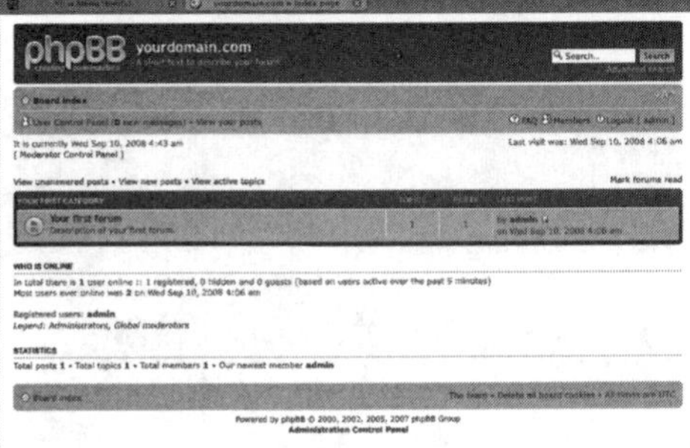

Figure 6.63 The new phpBB forum

To create the external menu item link:

1. Choose Menus > Main Menu.
2. Click New.
3. From the Menu Item Type list, choose External Link.

   This creates a link to the forum as a separate site. Even though the forum is bridged to Joomla, it is a site running almost completely separate.

   You can also select the Wrapper layout. The Wrapper layout places the forum inside your web site's main body. Use this if you want to keep your header and footer information and the look of your web site intact when users are using the forum. To use the Wrapper layout, however, you must be using a template that supports it.
4. In the Title field, type `Forum`.
5. In the Link field, type: `http://localhost/mywebsite/distribution/index.php`

   If the site were on a remote server, you would drop the `localhost/mywebsite` and replace it with your domain name (**Figure 6.62**).
6. Click Save, and then click Preview.
7. From the Main menu, choose Forum.

   The forum opens and is completely integrated with your Joomla web site (**Figure 6.63**).

Plugins

Plugins are the hardest working of the component, module, and plugin types. Plugins are grouped by the feature or function they are related to. Installing third-party extensions can expand this list.

To access the Plugin Manager:

Plugins are also extensions, just like modules and components. Plugins, however, are used to manipulate or transform data. For example, enabling the Authentication OpenID plugin authenticates a user logging in to the site with an OpenID username and password. For more details on the default Joomla plugins, see **Table 6.1**.

- Choose Extensions > Plugin Manager.

  The Plugin Manager opens with a list of every plugin installed on the site (**Figure 6.64**).

#		Plugin Name	Enabled	Order	Access Level	Type	File	ID
1		Authentication - Joomla	✓	1	Public	authentication	joomla	1
2		Authentication - LDAP	✗	2	Public	authentication	ldap	2
3		Authentication - OpenID	✗	3	Public	authentication	openid	4
4		Authentication - GMail	✗	4	Public	authentication	gmail	3
5		Content - Page Navigation	✓	2	Public	content	pagenavigation	17
6		Content - Rating	✓	4	Public	content	vote	13
7		Content - Email Cloaking	✓	5	Public	content	emailcloak	14
8		Content - Code Highlighter (GeSHi)	✗	5	Public	content	geshi	15
9		Content - Load Module	✓	6	Public	content	loadmodule	16
10		Content - Pagebreak	✓	10000	Public	content	pagebreak	12
11		Editor - No Editor	✓	0	Public	editors	none	18
12		Editor - TinyMCE 2.0	✓	0	Public	editors	tinymce	19
13		Editor - XStandard Lite 2.0	✗	0	Public	editors	xstandard	20

Figure 6.64 The Plugin Manager

Table 6.1

Plugins	
PLUGIN	DESCRIPTION
AUTHENTICATION	
Joomla	Allows authentication through Joomla's user registration.
LDAP	Allows authentication through the LDAP authentication method.
OpenID	Allows user to use their OpenID as user authentication in Joomla.
GMail	Allows users to use their GMail account as their user registration authentication.
	You can enable more than one authentication method at a time.
CONTENT	
Page Navigation	Enables or disables the ability to show page navigation in articles.
Rating	Enables or disables the ability to add voting functionality to articles.
Email Cloaking	Enables or disables the ability to cloak emails in content from spambots.
Code Highlighter	Uses the GeSHi highlighting engine to display formatted code in articles.
Load Module	Enables or disables the ability to load modules within content.
Pagebreak	Enables or disables the ability to add the Table of Contents (Article Index) to articles.
EDITOR	
No Editor	Enables or disables the ability to select No Editor as one of the editor options for back end and front end users.
TinyMCE 2.0	Enables or disables the ability to select TinyMCE 2.0 as one of the editor options for back end and front end users.
XStandard Lite 2.0	Enables or disables the ability to select XStandard Lite 2.0 as one of the editor options for back end and front end users.
Button - Image	Enables or disables the Image Button when creating articles.
Button - Pagebreak	Enables or disables the Pagebreak button when creating articles.
Button - Readmore	Enables or disables the Readmore link button when creating articles.
SEARCH	
Content	Enables or disables the ability to search articles.
Weblinks	Enables or disables the ability to search weblinks.
Contacts	Enables or disables the ability to search contacts.
Categories	Enables or disables the ability to search categories.
Sections	Enables or disables the ability to search sections.
Newsfeeds	Enables or disables the ability to search newsfeeds.

continues on next page

Table 6.1 *continued*

Plugins	
PLUGIN	**DESCRIPTION**
SYSTEM	
SEF	Enables or disables the ability to add SEF support.
Debug	Enables or disables debugging Joomla.
Legacy	Enables or disables Legacy mode in Joomla 1.5.x. Some third-party extensions will only work with version 1.5.x in legacy mode.
Cache	Enables or disables page caching.
Log	Enables or disables system logging.
Remember Me	Enables or disables the Remember Me function for User Login forms.
Backlink	Enables or disables support for Joomla 1.0.x links.
USER	
Joomla	Enables or disables the handling of Joomla's user synchronization.
XML-RPC	
Joomla	Enables or disables the Joomla XML-RPC.
Blogger API	Enables or disables the Blogger API remote procedure calls.

7

Modifying Global Settings

In this chapter, you'll learn how to work with the various categories of global settings and some administrative tools, what they can do for you, and when you might need to adjust them. The settings and tools covered are:

- **Global Configuration settings:** These settings include Site settings, System settings, and Server settings. Site settings control site functions; System settings control the Joomla administrative settings; and Server settings enable Joomla to communicate with your database and your web server.
- **User Registration settings:** These settings enable you to specify whether or not you want user accounts, how these accounts are created, and more.
- **Media settings:** These settings control media file sizes, where media is stored, and the types of media that is allowed.
- **Language settings:** These settings determine the languages that users have on the back and front ends of the web site.
- **Administrative tools:** These tools allow the super administrator to send private messages and mass e-mails, check in all items, and clear the web server cache.

Modifying Site Settings

Site settings are *about* your web site. For example, whether the site is online or offline, what information and keywords search engines will use to identify your web site, and whether or not to use search engine–friendly URLs in the user's browser address field.

Note: You must be logged in as a super administrator to change global configurations.

To access the Global Configuration pages:

◆ Choose Site > Global Configuration to open the Global Configuration pages (**Figure 7.1**).

The Global Configuration page contains three links: Site, System, and Server. Here you will be working with the site settings. Clicking any of the three links takes you to that Global Configuration page (**Figure 7.2**).

Figure 7.1 Choosing Global Configuration

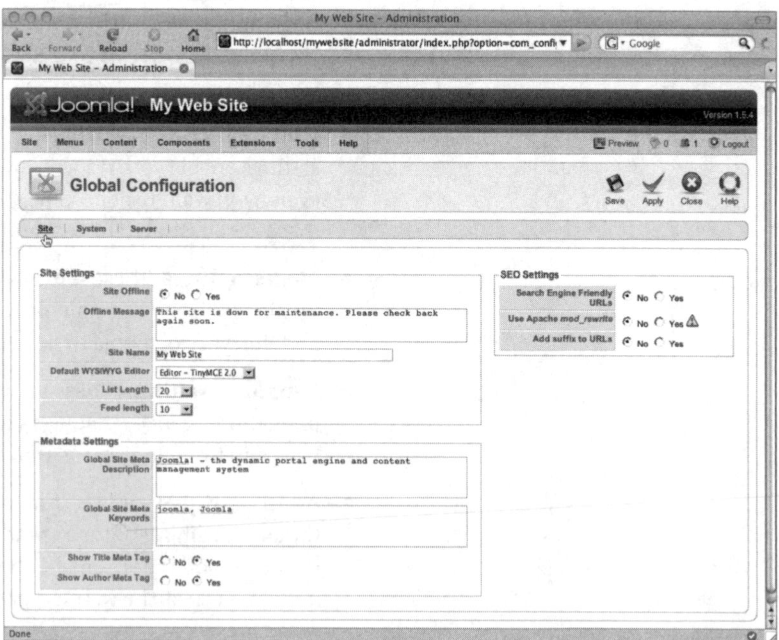

Figure 7.2 The Global Configuration page

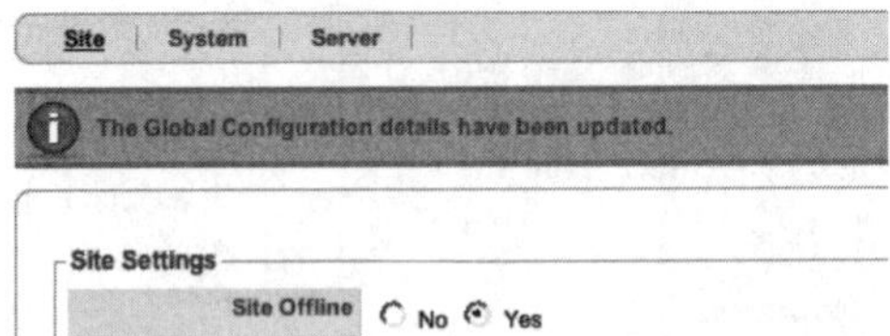

Figure 7.3 The message confirming that you've changed the Global Configuration settings

Figure 7.4 The Welcome page stating the site is offline

To take the site online/offline:

1. Choose Site > Global Configuration.
2. Click the Site link.

   The Site Global Configuration page opens.
3. Click the Yes radio button for Site Offline.
4. In the Offline Message field, type a brief message reflecting why the site is offline, or leave the default message.

   This message will be displayed on your web site's home page, letting users know your site is unavailable. Only administrators are able to see the web site when it is set to offline.
5. Click Apply.

   A message appears confirming changes to your Global Configuration settings (**Figure 7.3**).
6. Click Preview.

   Clicking Preview opens a new browser window and displays any changes made to your site. This comes in handy when you want to see your changes as you are working.

   Your site is now offline, and the message you entered appears as the home page with a login for administrators only (**Figure 7.4**).
7. To bring your site back online, click the No radio button for Site Offline, and then click Apply.

✔ Tip

- Clicking Save after making changes saves your changes but takes you back to the Control Panel page. If you want to preview changes you make, but not leave the page you are working in, click Apply.

To modify the web site name:

1. Choose Site > Global Configuration.
2. Click the Site link to open the Site Global Configuration page.
3. In the Site Name field, type the full name of your web site (**Figure 7.5**).

   The name in this field can be used by Joomla in a variety of places. For example, if you choose to have the name of your web site as text instead of a graphic, Joomla uses the site name from this field and places it in your default template header (see Chapter 9, "Creating Joomla Templates").
4. Click Save.

Figure 7.5 Entering the site name

To select a default editor:

1. Choose Site > Global Configuration.
2. Click the Site link to open the Site Global Configuration page.
3. From the Default WYSIWYG Editor drop-down menu, choose Editor – TinyMCE 2.0 (**Figure 7.6**).

   Joomla comes with two editors: TinyMCE 2.0 and XStandard Lite. The XStandard Lite editor has not been enabled, so it doesn't display yet in the list of options. The editor is used when you are adding or modifying content for your site. The editor looks like any standard word processing application, and it is covered in Chapter 3, "Adding Your Content."
4. Click Apply.

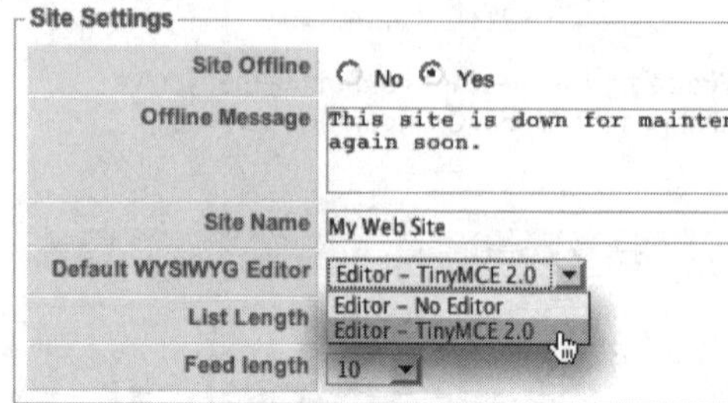

Figure 7.6 Choosing an editor

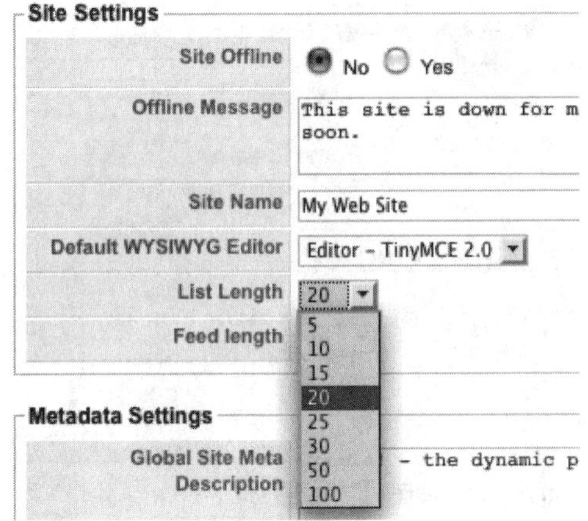

Figure 7.7 Choosing the list length

To set a default list length:

1. Choose Site > Global Configuration.
2. Click the Site link to open the Site Global Configuration page.
3. From the List Length drop-down menu, choose the number of list items you want to be displayed on a given back end page (User Manager, Module Manager, and so on) (**Figure 7.7**).

   List length sets the number of items to be displayed down a page. In addition, you can adjust the list length on the page itself. In **Figure 7.8** the Module Manager displays 20 items in the list. You can change the number of items in the list by changing the number in the Display field (**Figure 7.9**).
4. Click Apply.

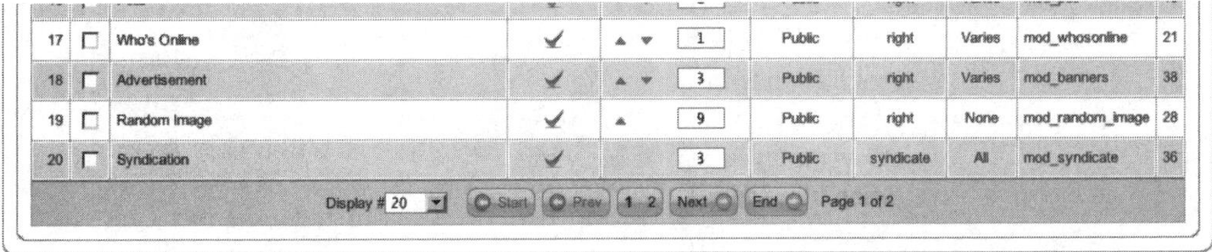

Figure 7.8 The Module Manager lists

Figure 7.9 The Display field

To set a default feed length:

1. Choose Site > Global Configuration.
2. Click the Site link to open the Site Global Configuration page.
3. From the Feed Length drop-down menu, choose the number of feed titles to display (**Figure 7.10**).

   The default feed length sets the number of syndicated feed content items to display on the web site (see Chapter 5, "Working with Modules").
4. Click Apply.

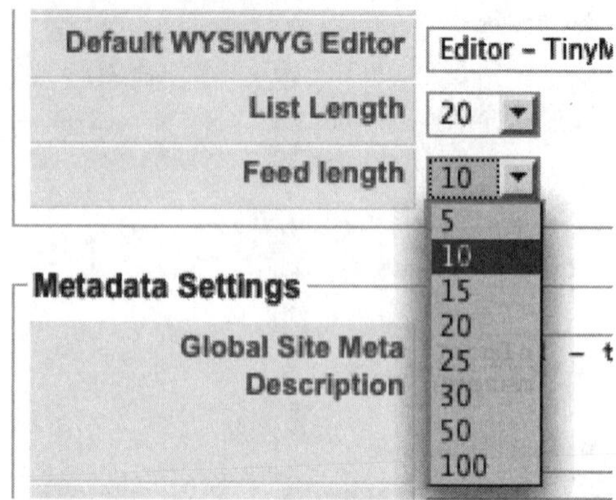

Figure 7.10 The Feed Length field

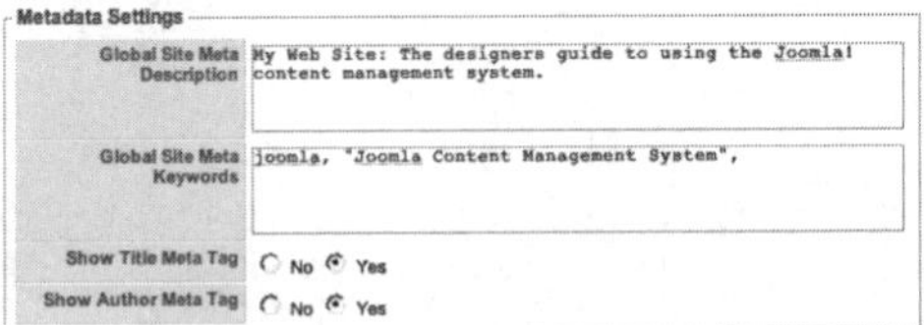

Figure 7.11 The Metadata Settings area of the Site settings

Making the Web Site Search Engine–Friendly

Content management systems, such as Joomla, generate your web site content dynamically from a database. Because content is *responsive* to user interaction and contains hard-to-read database IDs and the like, search engines can have difficulty reading it. Joomla has search engine optimization (SEO) settings to optimize your content and URLs for search engines. Joomla contains a variety of global functions that help make your site search engine–friendly.

To modify metadata settings:

1. Choose Site > Global Configuration.
2. Click the Site link to open the Site Global Configuration page.
3. In the Global Site Meta Description field (located in the Metadata Settings section), type a short sentence that reflects what your web site is about.

   This text generally appears on the search engine results page and is used by the search engines to index your web site.
4. In the Global Site Meta Keywords field, type accurately descriptive keywords or keyword phrases to describe your site. Separate each keyword with a comma. Enclose phrases in quotes (**Figure 7.11**).

   Keywords and phrases are the terms users enter into search engines like Google, Yahoo, and so on. The closer the match to your keywords and phrases, the higher the chance you have of being listed on the first few pages of a user's search.

continues on next page

5. For the Show Title Meta Tag radio buttons, click:
   - ▲ Yes if you want search engines to index the meta tag information you define for every article on your web site.
   - ▲ No if you want to block search engines from indexing meta tag information.
6. For the Show Author Meta Tag radio buttons, click:
   - ▲ Yes if you want to use the author's name as a meta tag in articles.
   - ▲ No if you do not want to use the author's name as a meta tag in articles.
7. Click Apply.

✔ Tip

- A few years ago, keywords and meta tags were very important. As such many site creators would throw any and all keywords they could think of into the meta tag descriptions. Although still relevant, search engines today rank content, how often it is updated, and links to and from the site. Many more factors come into play.

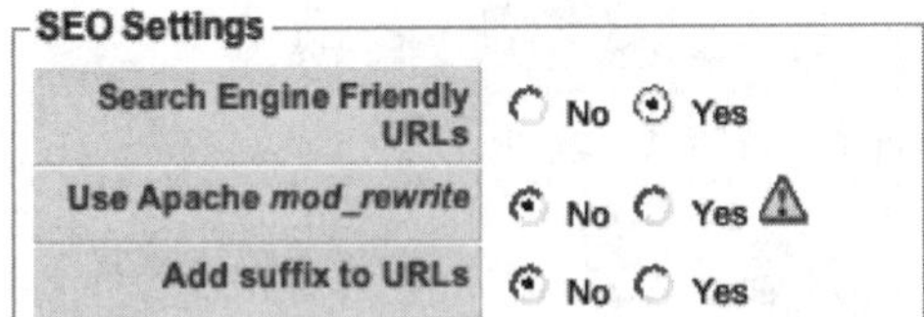

Figure 7.12 The SEO Settings area of Site settings

To create search engine–friendly URLs:

1. Choose Site > Global Configuration.
2. Click the Site link to open the Site Global Configuration page.
3. In the SEO Settings section, click the Yes radio button for Search Engine Friendly URLs (**Figure 7.12**).

   Joomla has the ability to create search engine–friendly URLs (Universal Resource Locators). Because Joomla interacts with a database that assigns an ID number to each section, category, article, link, module, and so on, these titles can get lengthy, hard to read, or hard to understand. When you click a link on a site such as Amazon, the address field displays a cryptic *parameterized* URL similar to the following example:

   `http://www.amazon.com/b/ref=amb_link_1753562_21?ie=UTF8&node=172574&pf_rd_m&pf_rd_i=541966`

   This URL means nothing to you and is virtually useless to search engines. When you set Joomla to use search-friendly URLs, you are asking Joomla to hide the cryptic URL and instead use what is called an *alias*. For instance, when you set Search Engine Friendly URLs to Yes, Joomla converts the example above to display in the browser address field as:

   `http://www.amazon.com/computer-pc-hardware-accessories-add-ons`

   This URL is far more readable by you, me, and the search engine.
4. Leave the radio buttons for "Use Apache mod_rewrite" and "Add suffix to URLs" set to No.
5. Click Apply.

Modifying System Settings

System settings are the *controls* for your web site. They address such questions as:

- Do you want registered users?
- What type of media is allowed on the site?
- Can users upload files to your site?

System settings also control troubleshooting and debugging functions.

✔ Tip

- The secret word listed under System Settings is used by Joomla for security purposes and cannot be changed.

To specify a different log folder:

1. Choose Site > Global Configuration.
2. Click the System link (**Figure 7.13**).
   The System Global Configuration page opens.
3. Under System Settings, in the "Path to Log folder" field, type the full path to the new system log folder (**Figure 7.14**).
   Joomla keeps logs on system information, debugging, and analytics. Changing this path is recommended for experienced users only.
4. Click Apply.

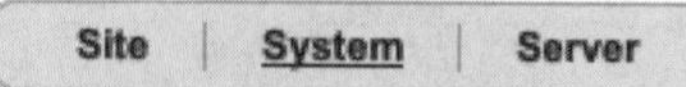

Figure 7.13 The System link

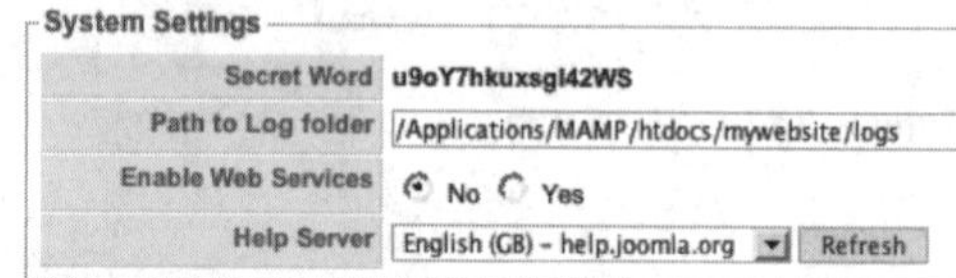

Figure 7.14 The System Settings page

Figure 7.15 The System link

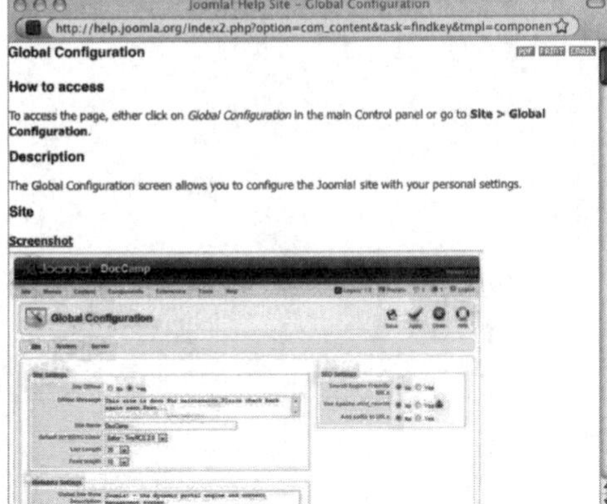

Figure 7.16 The Joomla help documentation page

To enable web services:

1. Choose Site > Global Configuration.
2. Click the System link.

   The System Global Configuration page opens.
3. Click the Yes radio button for Enable Web Services.

   Web services allows Joomla to make RPC (Remote Procedure Calls) using HTTP as the transfer protocol and XML as the encoding language. It is recommended that you enable web services to ensure that third-party extensions work properly.
4. Click Apply.

To select a help server:

1. Choose Site > Global Configuration.
2. Click the System link to open the System Global Configuration page (**Figure 7.15**).
3. Leave the default "[your language] - help.joomla.org" as the help server.

   The internal (local) help system for Joomla 1.5 is no longer supported.

   When users click the Help button, Joomla accesses the help system over the Internet. You are able to print, download a PDF, or e-mail the help information displayed. **Figure 7.16** shows an example of a help page.

Allowing User Registration

The user registration settings tell Joomla whether you want to allow user accounts, how you want new user account creation handled, and which privileges or permissions to assign new users.

Although creating accounts on web sites is becoming more common, and quite often necessary, some users still will leave your site if *forced* to create an account.

When deciding whether to require accounts for your site, consider a few things:

- Do not make users create an account if there is no valid reason to do so.
- Make as much of the site as possible available to nonregistered users before requiring them to create an account. Forcing users to create an account before they are able to make an informed decision may encourage them to leave your site and look elsewhere.
- If possible, list the benefits for creating an account with this web site.
- Always create a privacy notice so users are aware of how their information will be used and protected.
- For community sites (blogs, media sharing sites, or any site where users can participate and add to your web site), it is best practice to have users registered. In the rare case where a person can be abusive, offensive to others, or simply misuse your site, the ability to block a user is often necessary.

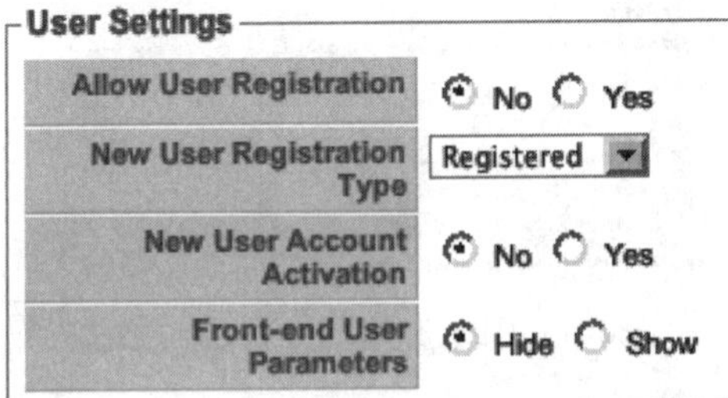

Figure 7.17 The User Settings area of System settings

To allow user registration:

1. Choose Site > Global Configuration.
2. Click the System link.
   The System Global Configuration page opens.
3. Under User Settings, click the Yes radio button for Allow User Registration to allow users to register and create accounts on the web site (**Figure 7.17**).
4. From the New User Registration Type drop-down menu, choose Registered.
   This sets the default access type for a user's newly created account. A registered user can log in and view parts of the web site assigned to registered users only.
5. Click Apply.

Front End User Registration Types

The other access levels are:

- **Author:** An author can contribute content (to locations defined by you) and modify his or her account information on the web site.
- **Editor:** An editor has all author privileges and is able to edit content written by an author user type.
- **Publisher:** A publisher has editor privileges and is able to publish content to the site if you have restricted publishing to publishers only.

For the New User Account Activation radio buttons, click:

- Yes if you want new users to be sent a confirmation e-mail with activation instructions. This ensures that a valid e-mail address has been used and protects against spammers.
- No if you do not require a confirmation e-mail. This will create a new user account as soon as the user clicks the Submit button.

For the Front-end User Parameters radio buttons, click:

- Hide if you want to hide user-defined parameters from logged-in users.
- Show if you want to enable registered users to select their language, help system, and editor from their user details pages.

Defining System Media Settings

In the Media Settings section of the System settings, you define the types of media allowed and not allowed on the site, the maximum file sizes, where the media is to be stored, and what, if any, file types can be uploaded by front end users.

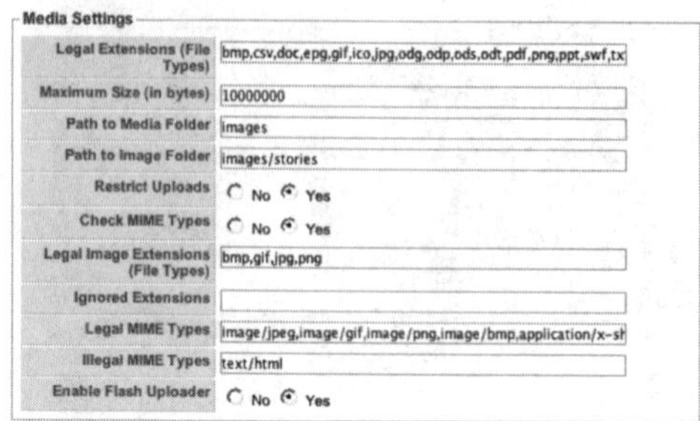

Figure 7.18 The Media Settings area of System settings

To set allowable media file types:

1. Choose Site > Global Configuration.
2. Click the System link.

   The System Global Configuration page opens.
3. Under Media Settings, review the file types in the Legal Extensions (File Types) field (**Figure 7.18**).

   This field lists all media file type extensions you will allow to be uploaded to your web site by users. By default it is prefilled with the image and document file types most commonly used on the web. To limit these, remove extensions from this field. To add additional file types, type their extensions in the field, separating each entry with a comma but using no spaces.
4. In the Maximum Size field, enter the maximum size, in bytes, allowed for media uploads.

   The larger the file size allowed, the slower the upload, and large files stored on your web site will slow it down. The file size maximum is usually no more than 10 MB.

5. Leave the "Path to Media Folder" and "Path to Image Folder" fields at their default settings.

   Leave the defaults because third-party extensions and the Joomla code rely on these paths. For information on creating new folders and uploading media, see Chapter 3, "Adding Your Content."

6. For the Restrict Uploads radio buttons, click:
   - Yes if you want to restrict media uploads to users with manager access levels (and above). With this setting, users can still upload images.
   - No if you want to allow any user to upload media or images to the web site.

7. In the Legal Image Extensions field, enter all the *image* file types you will allow to be uploaded to your web site.

8. In the Ignored Extensions field, enter any file type extensions you do not want uploaded to your web site.

9. For the Check MIME Types radio buttons, click:
   - Yes if you want Joomla to check the MIME information in media files. This helps to ensure users are not uploading malicious or harmful files to the web site.
   - No if you do not want Joomla verify the MIME types of uploaded files.

10. Do not change the Legal MIME Types and Illegal MIME Types fields from their default values unless you understand how MIME types work.

    These options use MIME Magic or Fileinfo to verify files; see the Joomla.org help for more information.

11. Click Apply.

Debugging Joomla

Your web server and Joomla keep what are called debugging, statistical, and analytical logs.

If you enable debugging, Joomla will provide diagnostic, language, and SQL error information on the bottom of each page, front and back end.

To enable debugging:

1. Choose Site > Global Configuration.
2. Click the System link.

   The System Global Configuration page opens.
3. Under Debug Settings, click Yes for Debug System (**Figure 7.19**).

   Joomla displays all debugging information at the bottom of your web site page (**Figure 7.20**).
4. Click Apply.

✔ Tip

- You can change Debug System back to No if the displayed code gets distracting during site creation.

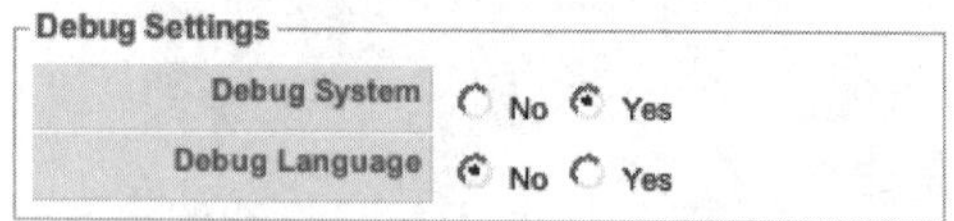

Figure 7.19 The Debug Settings area of System settings

Figure 7.20 Errors reported on the bottom of the page

Debugging Joomla

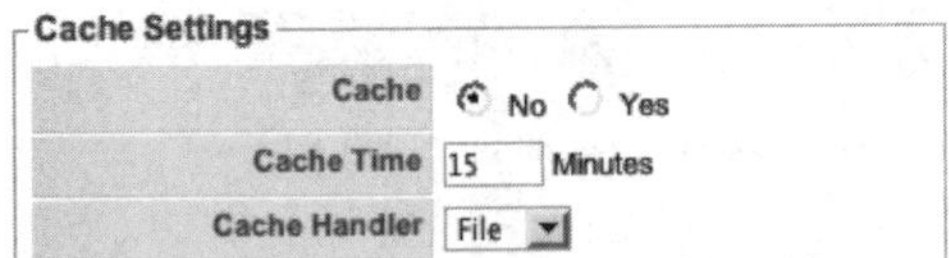

Figure 7.21 The Cache Settings area of System settings

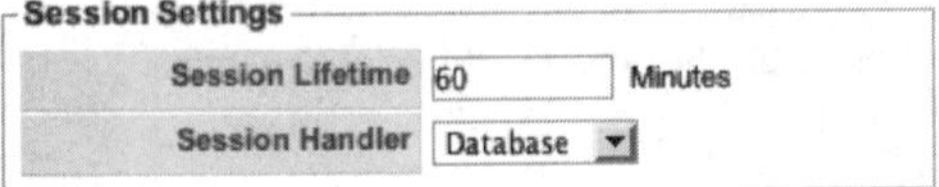

Figure 7.22 The Session Settings area of System settings

To enable cache settings:

1. Choose Site > Global Configuration.
2. Click the System link.

   The System Global Configuration page opens.
3. Under the Cache Settings area, to enable web server caching of files, click the Yes radio button for Cache (**Figure 7.21**).

   Cache settings enable Joomla to keep a local copy of your web site content on the server, which speeds up accessing information and reduces the load on the database.
4. In the Cache Time field, type the amount of time, in minutes, for the cache file to be stored before it is refreshed.
5. From the Cache Handler drop-down menu, leave the default setting of File.
6. Click Apply.

To change the administrator session settings:

1. Choose Site > Global Configuration.
2. Click the System link.

   The System Global Configuration page opens.
3. Under the Session Settings, in the Session Lifetime field, type the time, in minutes, you want the system to keep you logged in to the administrative back end (**Figure 7.22**).
4. Under Session Handler, leave Database as the default.

   Selecting Database lets Joomla track the amount of time a user is logged in.
5. Click Apply.

Configuring Server Settings

Server settings relate directly to communicating with your web server and the database. This section shows you where you can modify your server and database settings originally set up during first installation.

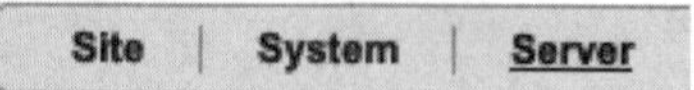

Figure 7.23 The Server link

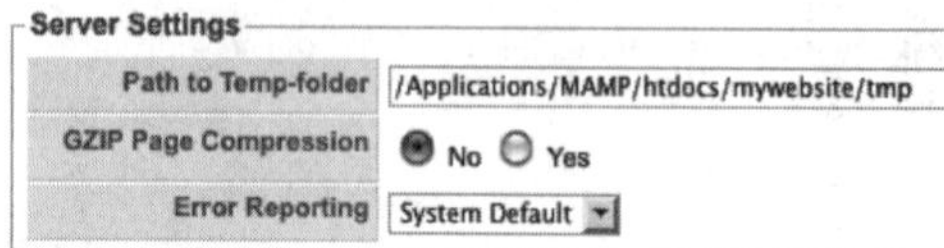

Figure 7.24 The Server Settings area of Server settings

To modify server settings:

1. Choose Site > Global Configuration.
2. Click the Server link (**Figure 7.23**).

   The Server Global Configuration page opens.
3. Under Server Settings, leave the default setting for Path to Temp-folder (**Figure 7.24**).

   Joomla creates this file to store temporary files. Changing this folder can cause errors on the web site.
4. Click the Yes radio button for GZIP Page Compression.

   This option allows Joomla to use compression on files to increase the speed of your web site.
5. From the Error Reporting drop-down menu, choose the type of error reporting for your server.
6. Click Apply.

System Error Reporting

- **System Default:** Basic code error reporting. This is the default.
- **None:** No error reporting.
- **Simple:** A simplified high level of error reporting, generally hard stop errors.
- **Maximum:** All errors are reported, even those that don't affect the functionality of the site.

Figure 7.25 The Locale Settings area of Server settings

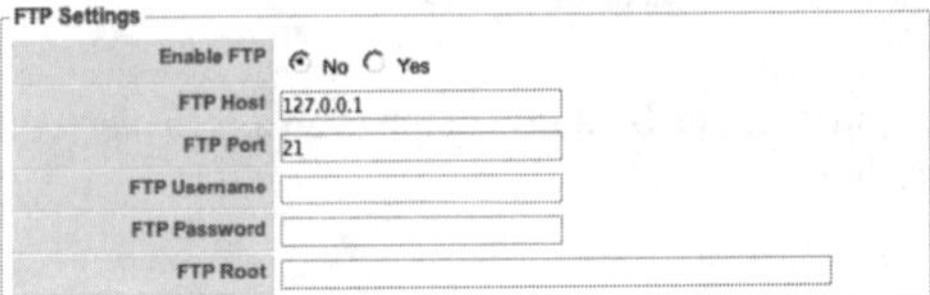

Figure 7.26 The FTP Settings area of Server settings

To modify locale settings:

1. Choose Site > Global Configuration.
2. Click the Server link.

   The Server Global Configuration page opens.
3. Under Locale Settings, from the Time Zone drop-down menu, choose the appropriate time zone for your web server (**Figure 7.25**).
4. Click Apply.

To modify the FTP settings for your server:

1. Choose Site > Global Configuration.
2. Click the Server link to open the Server Global Configuration page.
3. In the FTP Settings section, click the Yes radio button for Enable FTP.
4. Enter the FTP settings for your web server (**Figure 7.26**).

   Enabling FTP (File Transfer Protocol) settings allows Joomla to use the FTP protocol instead of the normal upload process handled by PHP. Some extensions, scripts, and files are too large to be handled by PHP, and on a hosted server, modifying the php.ini file to allow larger uploads is not possible.

✔ Tips

- If you are unsure of the FTP settings for your hosted server, contact your hosting service for assistance.
- FTP settings are not necessary when testing on a local server, but they should be enabled if your remote web server is Linux based.

Database Settings

Database settings were configured during installation, and you should not modify them (**Figure 7.27**). If you do, you will lose your connection to the database, and the web site will not display.

The only time you should modify database settings is when you are ready to upload the site to a hosted server (see Appendix A, "Local and Remote Servers").

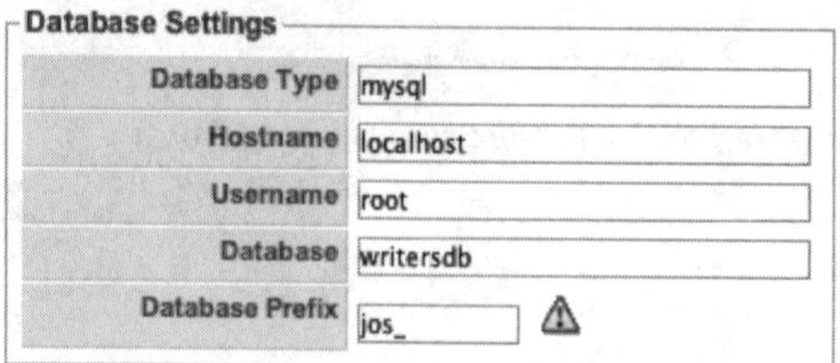

Figure 7.27 The Database Settings area of Server settings

Mail Settings

Mail settings are for the super administrator account. These settings were created during the initial installation, and you should modify them only if you need to change the e-mail accounts and settings, or if you are familiar with your personal e-mail account settings (**Figure 7.28**).

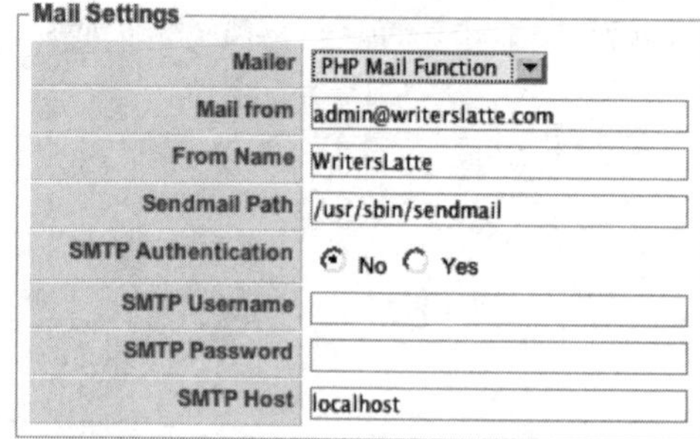

Figure 7.28 The Mail Settings area of Server settings

Using the Language Manager

Joomla supports multiple languages for both the back and front end of your web site. You can specify a language to use, or users can select their own languages in their user details accounts. With language packages installed, you can have the back end or front end display for that user in the user's native language.

You can find many language and translation packages on the Joomla.org web site. These allow your users to see both the front and back ends in their native languages. Basically the plugins translate the English text for your users. These are created and maintained by various third-party developers, however, so we will not cover them here.

To use the Language Manager:

1. Choose Extensions > Language Manager.

   The Language Manager opens, displaying all the language packages installed (**Figure 7.29**).

2. To change the language for the front end of the web site, click the Site link and click the radio button next to the language you need.

3. To change the language for the back end, click the Administrator link and select the language.

4. Click Default to set the chosen language (or languages) as the default.

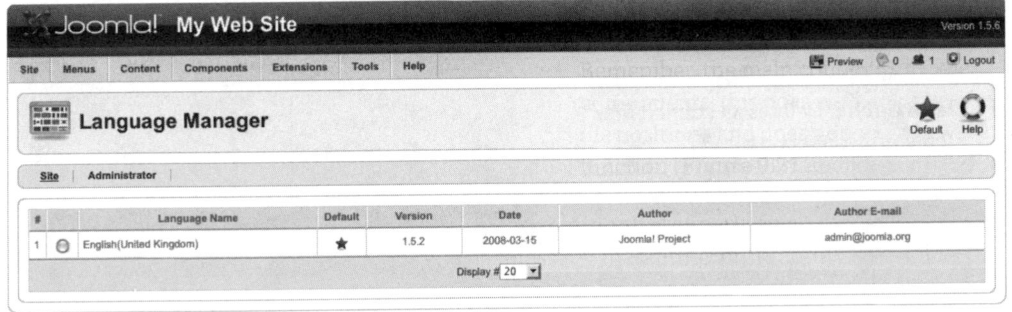

Figure 7.29 The Language Manager

Using the Tools Menu

The Tools menu contains what are called *mass* administrative functions a super administrator can use for reading private messages, sending out mass e-mails to other administrators, checking in content that is pending approval or in use by editors and publishers, and clearing the cache on the web server. (**Figure 7.30**)

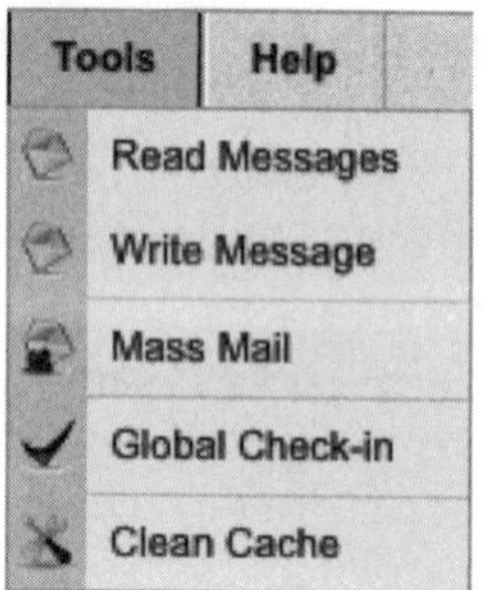

Figure 7.30 The Tools menu

The Tools menu choices are:

- **Read Messages:** Accesses the administrator's private messaging system. Read Messages lists all messages sent to you from other administrators.
- **Write Messages:** Sends private messages to other administrators.
- **Mass Mail:** Creates mass e-mail messages that will go out to user groups you specify.
- **Global Check-in:** Tells Joomla to check in any locked items or content currently checked out for editing.
- **Clean Cache:** Deletes all cached files from your web server.

Using Private Messaging

Joomla comes with an internal private messaging service. Super administrators can use the private messaging feature through the back end to send messages to other super administrators. In addition, Joomla automatically sends private messages to super administrators when content is updated on the site by other users. This provides a way for super administrators to track what others are doing on the web site.

To write messages:

1. Choose Tools > Write Messages.

   The Write Private Message page opens.

2. In the To drop-down menu, choose admin (or if you change your super administrator name, choose it from the drop-down menu instead).

3. In the Subject field, type `Hello Me`.

4. Type a brief message in the Message field (**Figure 7.31**).

5. Click Send.

   You have just sent a private message to the super administrator.

Figure 7.31 Write private messages

To read messages:

1. Choose Tools > Read Messages.

   The Private Messaging Manager opens, displaying a list of your read and unread private messages (**Figure 7.32**).

2. To read your message, click the subject link.

   The message opens. After you have read and closed the message, a green checkmark appears in the Read column of the Private Messaging Manager.

To delete private messages:

1. Choose Tools > Read Messages.

   The Private Messaging Manager opens.

2. Check the box next to the message you want to delete, and then click the Delete button (**Figure 7.33**).

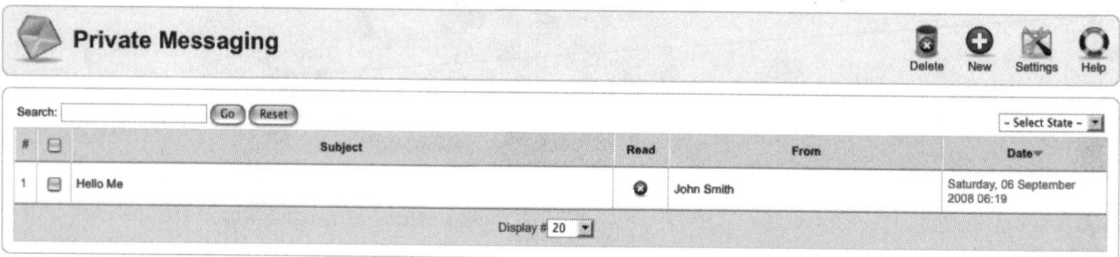

Figure 7.32 Read private messages

Figure 7.33 Delete button

To modify private messaging settings:

1. Choose Tools > Read Messages.

   The Private Messaging Manager opens.

2. Click the Settings icon.

   The Private Messaging Configuration page opens (**Figure 7.34**).

3. Leave Lock Inbox set to No so you can continue to receive messages. Selecting Yes means no private messages can be sent.

4. For the "Mail me on new Message" radio buttons, click:

   - Yes to send an e-mail to the super administrator's e-mail account alerting them they have a private message.
   - No to not send an e-mail message to the super administrator's e-mail account.

5. In the Auto Purge Messages field, type in the number of days you want messages to remain in the Private Messaging Manager.

   This sets the system to remove all private messages over X number of days old.

Figure 7.34 Private messaging configuration

Using Mass Mail

You can use Joomla's mass mail feature to send e-mails to all your registered users. This is handy when you need to alert users to new information on your site; for example, mass mailings can also act as newsletters.

To configure a mass mailing:

1. Choose Tools > Mass Mail.

   The Mass Mail page opens (**Figure 7.35**).

2. In the Details section, select "Mail to Child Groups."

   This enables you to select a top-level group and then send to all users of that group and below. For example, with this option selected, if you select Public Back End as the group, all users below that group (managers, administrators, and super administrators) would receive the e-mail as well.

3. Select "Send in HTML mode."

   This will send the e-mail with HTML elements. However, if a recipient's e-mail client is set to accept only text e-mails, the HTML elements will not show, only the text will.

4. Select "Recipients as BCC" if you want all other user e-mail addresses hidden.

   It is best practice to BCC mass e-mails for public sites. Giving out user e-mails can violate your users' privacy.

5. Enter a subject in the Subject field.

6. Type your message.

7. Click Send Mail.

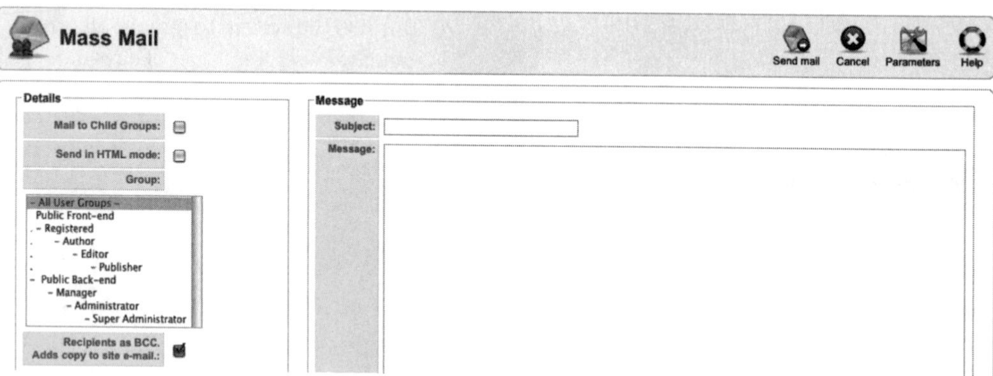

Figure 7.35 The Mass Mail page

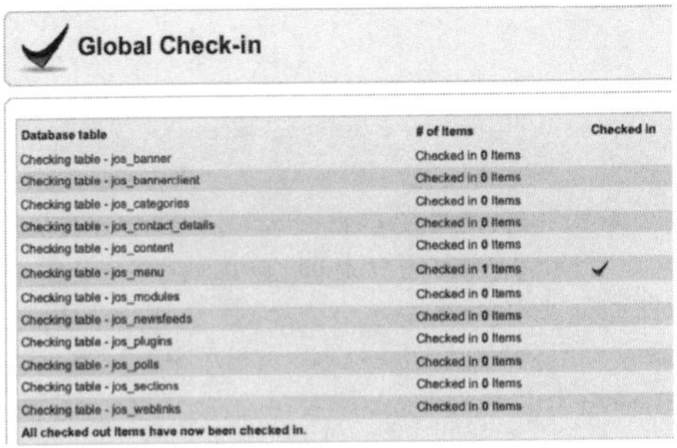

Global Check-in

Database table	# of Items	Checked in
Checking table - jos_banner	Checked in **0** Items	
Checking table - jos_bannerclient	Checked in **0** Items	
Checking table - jos_categories	Checked in **0** Items	
Checking table - jos_contact_details	Checked in **0** Items	
Checking table - jos_content	Checked in **0** Items	
Checking table - jos_menu	Checked in **1** Items	✓
Checking table - jos_modules	Checked in **0** Items	
Checking table - jos_newsfeeds	Checked in **0** Items	
Checking table - jos_plugins	Checked in **0** Items	
Checking table - jos_polls	Checked in **0** Items	
Checking table - jos_sections	Checked in **0** Items	
Checking table - jos_weblinks	Checked in **0** Items	
All checked out Items have now been checked in.		

Figure 7.36 The Global Check-in page

Checking In Content

The global check-in feature is used to check in all content currently in the editing or creation process. This allows a super administrator to unlock content in use by another user.

To check in all checked-out content:

◆ Choose Tools > Global Check-in.

All items will be checked in, and the results page will display (**Figure 7.36**).

Cleaning Your Web Server's Cache

Cache files are temporary files that the web server stores to increase the speed and performance of your site. When you create a web site or add new extensions, the cache files on the server can become out of date. This is a good time to clean the cache.

To clean the web server cache:

1. Choose Tools > Clean Cache.

   The Cache Manager opens, displaying a list of cached groups, the number of files cached in the group, and the total size (**Figure 7.37**).
2. Select each group you want cleaned out of the web server cache.
3. Click Delete.

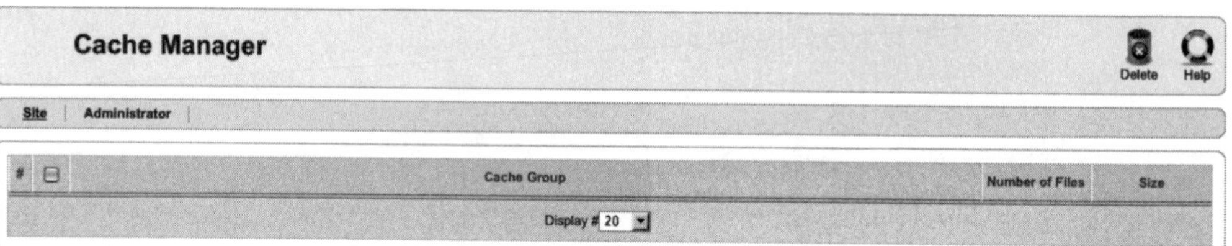

Figure 7.37 The Cache Manager page

8

ENGAGING YOUR USERS

The web site as the public sees it is called the *front end*. One of the benefits of Joomla is that users can edit and add web content from this public view. Even if you create a web site for nontechnical users, Joomla makes it easy for them to add or edit content using the front end of your web site. In order for users to contribute to the site, you need to enable user registration and assign access levels.

This chapter covers creating front-end user accounts, as well as adding, editing, publishing, printing, and emailing content. Finally, you'll learn how you, as the administrator, can manage this content from the *back end*.

Adding Front End Users

Before users have access to the web site, they must have an account with the appropriate access level. You enable user registration in the Global Configuration System settings. You also set the initial access level of a user: registered, author, editor, or publisher (see Chapter 7 "Modifying Global Settings"). Once user registration is enabled, users can create their own accounts from the front end. If you do not enable user registration through the front end, administrators can still create user accounts manually through the User Manager. Either way, front end users cannot access the back end.

Joomla supports several *front end* access levels for users:

- **Guest:** A guest is a visitor without a registered user account.
- **Registered:** A registered user can log in and view parts of the web site assigned to registered users only.
- **Author:** An author can contribute content to locations (defined by you) and modify his or her account information on the web site. An author cannot modify content.
- **Editor:** An editor has all author privileges and is able to edit content written by an author user type.
- **Publisher:** A publisher has editor privileges and is able to publish content to the site if you have restricted publishing to publishers only.

✔ Tip

- All back end users, super administrators, administrators, and managers can modify content through the front end.

To create front end users using the User Manager:

1. Log in to the back end as a super administrator.
2. Choose Site > User Manager.

   The User Manager page opens (**Figure 8.1**).
3. Click New.

   The User Details page opens, where you configure user details and parameters (**Figure 8.2**).
4. In the Name field, type `John Doe`.
5. In the Username field, type `jpublisher`.
6. In the E-mail field, type `jpublisher@mywebsite.com`.

continues on next page

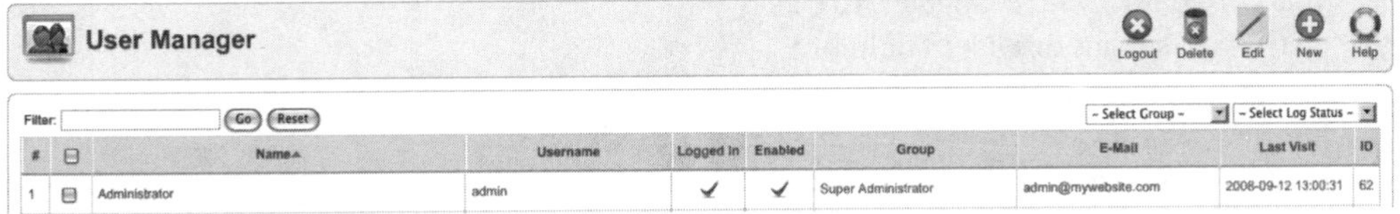

Figure 8.1 The User Manager

Figure 8.2 The User Details page

7. In the New Password field, type `joomla`.
8. Select Publisher from the Group list.
9. For the Block User radio buttons, leave the default of No.

   When set to Yes, this user is blocked from logging in to the web site.
10. For the Receive System E-mails radio buttons, leave the default of No.

    This feature is only for super administrators and administrators.
11. In the Parameters area, leave the Back-end Language drop-down menu on the default Select Language.

    Because you did not set back end access for this user, no language is needed.
12. From the Front-end Language drop-down menu, choose English United Kingdom.

    This tells Joomla which language to use on the web site for this user. For information on additional language packages, go to www.joomla.org and search on the phrase *language extensions*. Most are offered free and are easily installed. Joomla contains only English by default.
13. From the User Editor drop-down menu, choose Editor - TinyMCE 2.0.

    This is the WYSIWYG editor the user will use when adding or editing content from the front end of the web site.
14. Leave the Help Site drop-down menu on the default of Local.

    Previous versions of Joomla had a choice between the local help system (local on your system) and the Joomla.org help documentation out on the web. Joomla 1.5.x now contains only the online help documentation.
15. From the Time Zone drop-down menu, choose the appropriate time zone for your user (**Figure 8.3**).

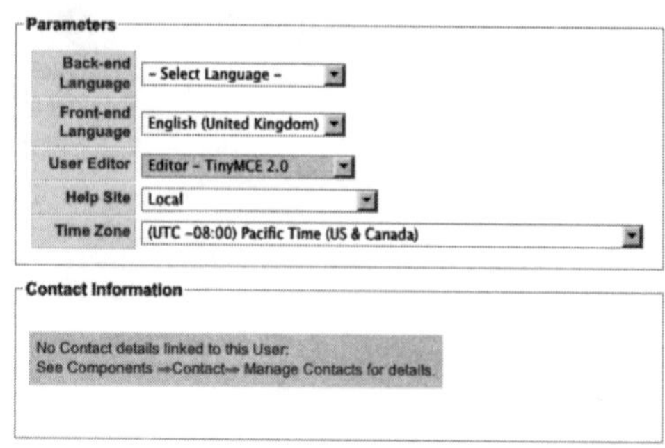

Figure 8.3 The User Details parameters

ADDING FRONT END USERS

16. Click Save.
17. Repeat steps 2 through 16 and create an editor user with the following information:
    - Name: Jane Doe
    - Username: jeditor
    - Password: joomla
    - Group: Editor
18. Repeat steps 2 through 16 and create an author user with the following information:
    - Name: Jack Doe
    - Username: jauthor
    - Password: joomla
    - Group: Author

    You now have four users listed in your User Manager (**Figure 8.4**).

✔ Tip

- Any user contact information created in the Contact component is displayed in the Contact Information area below the Parameters area. Chapter 6, "Extending Your Site" covers using the Contact component.

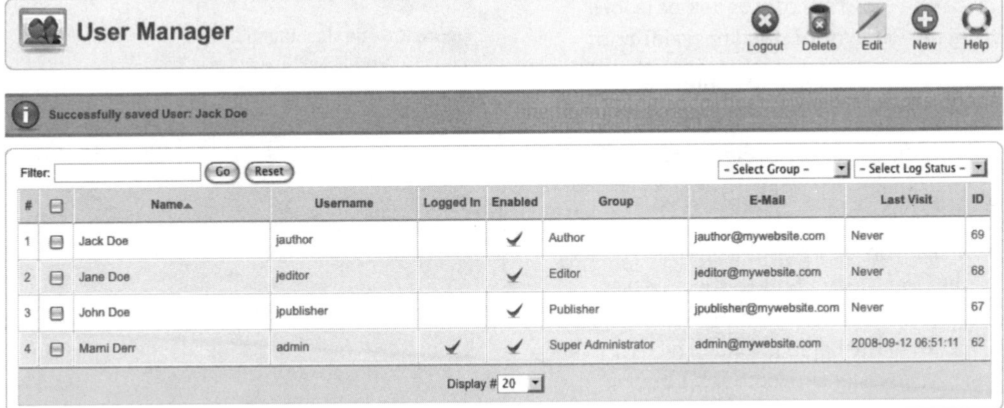

Figure 8.4 The completed User Manager page

Modifying User Content from the Front End

The experience of your users from the front end will depend entirely on the purpose of your web site. Users can not only add content, but interact with your content through blogs, forums, and voting in polls. If enabled, users can also print, create a PDF, or e-mail content from the site.

For this section, you have already created a User Details menu item and a Web Link Submission menu item. In addition you have an "Add a New Recipe" link in the Recipes menu. Because all content (pictures, recipes, events, news, and so on) is created as articles, most content will be edited using the Article Submission form. Exceptions will be feeds and web links, which have their own submission forms. For information on adding menu items, see Chapter 4, "Making Your Site Dynamic with Menus."

To log in to the front end:

1. Open the front end of the web site in a browser window.
2. In the Login Form Username field, type `jauthor`.
3. In the Password field, type `joomla`.
4. Click the Login button (**Figure 8.5**).

   After you log in, Joomla replaces the form with the User Menu (**Figure 8.6**).

✔ Tip

- When you create your site, you can tailor the User Menu items to specific user access levels. If you have the greeting set to Yes in the Login module, the user will see a greeting with a Log Out button.

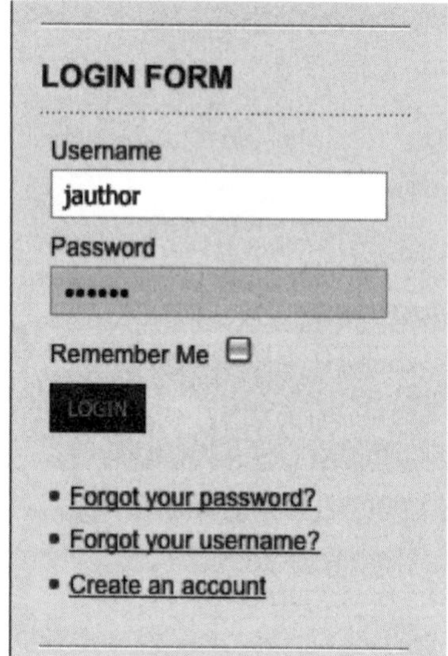

Figure 8.5 The login form

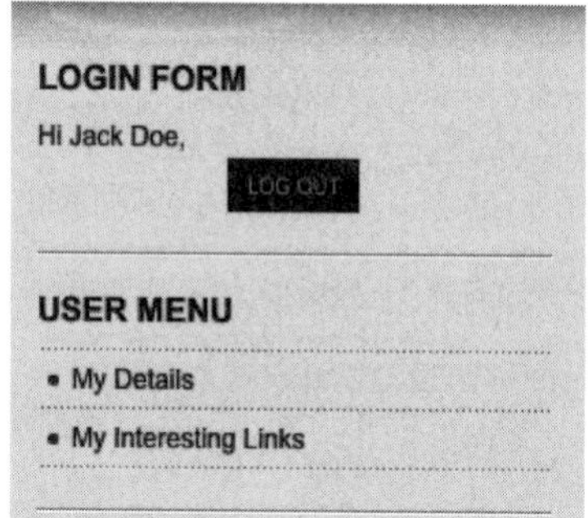

Figure 8.6 The User menu

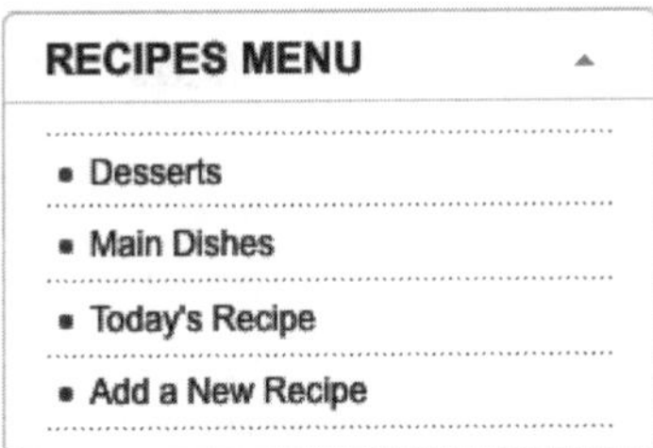

Figure 8.7 The Recipes menu

Figure 8.8 The "Submit an Article" page

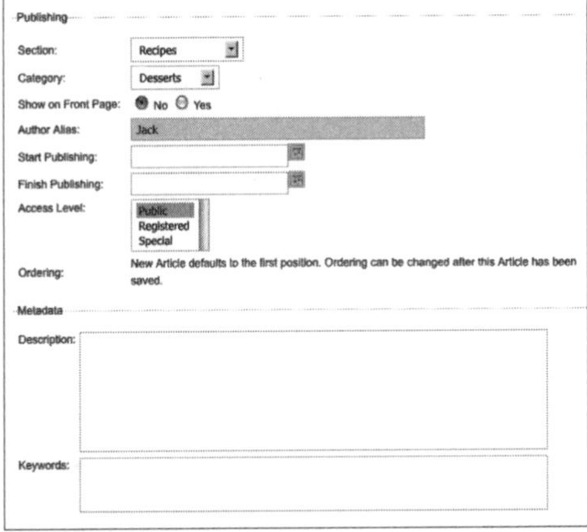

Figure 8.9 The Publishing section of the "Submit an Article" page

To add an article through the front end:

1. Log in to the front end with the username of `jauthor` and the password of `joomla`.

   To add an article, a user must have author level access or higher.

2. Choose Recipes from the Main menu.

3. Click the "Add a New Recipe" link in the Recipes menu (**Figure 8.7**).

   The "Submit an Article" page opens (**Figure 8.8**).

4. In the Title field of the Article Editor, type `Fruit Cream Pops`.

5. In the Editor field, type:

   ```
   Ingredients
   2 quarts any fruit juice
   2 cups vanilla ice cream
   Instructions:
   Blend the fruit juice and ice cream.
   Pour into popsicle containers.
   Freeze at least 8 hours.
   ```

6. From the Publishing area's Section drop-down menu, choose Recipes (**Figure 8.9**).

   This assigns the article to the Recipes section.

   You have the choice of Uncategorized in this menu. If you choose Uncategorized, this article won't appear unless you place it on the front page. It has to be assigned to a section before it can appear on the web site unless it is a front page article.

7. From the Category drop-down menu, choose Desserts.

   This assigns the article to the Desserts category, which is contained in the Recipes section.

continues on next page

You also have the choice of Uncategorized in this field. If you choose Uncategorized, the article won't appear unless you place it on the front page. You can only choose Uncategorized in the Category drop-down menu if you chose Uncategorized in the Section drop-down menu also.

8. For the "Show on Front Page" radio buttons, leave the default of No.

   Clicking the Yes radio button would place this article on the front page.

9. In the Author Alias field, type `Jack`.

   The Author Alias field enables users to specify the name displayed with their articles. For example, an author wants her screen name to show instead of her actual name. You could also use this field if you added the article for someone else and wanted the actual author's name to display instead of the person adding the article.

10. Leave all other fields blank.

    Publishing articles is controlled by the user's access level settings. If the user's access level is set to any level below publisher, this article will not be published until someone with publisher-level access has reviewed it. Authors can only enter Start Publishing and End Publishing dates, but they can't actually publish the article.

    You can enter keywords and descriptions for the article. This allows Joomla to link similar articles when users search the site (see Chapter 3, "Adding Your Content").

11. Click Save.

    A message appears, telling the user about his or her submission. The article does not appear on the web site yet; it still needs to be published by a user with publishing privileges (**Figure 8.10**).

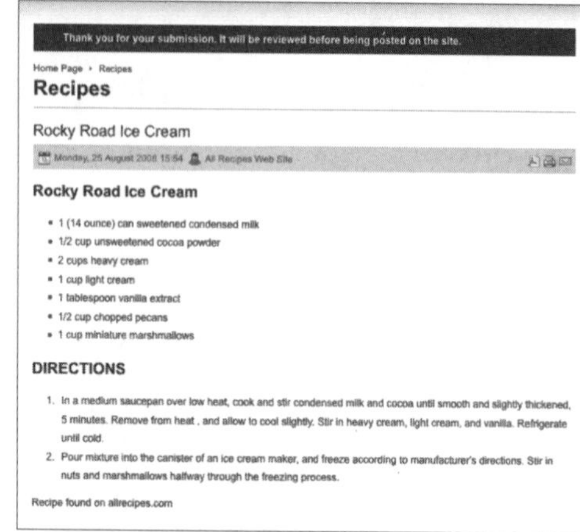

Figure 8.10 The article submission statement

Modifying User Content from the Front End

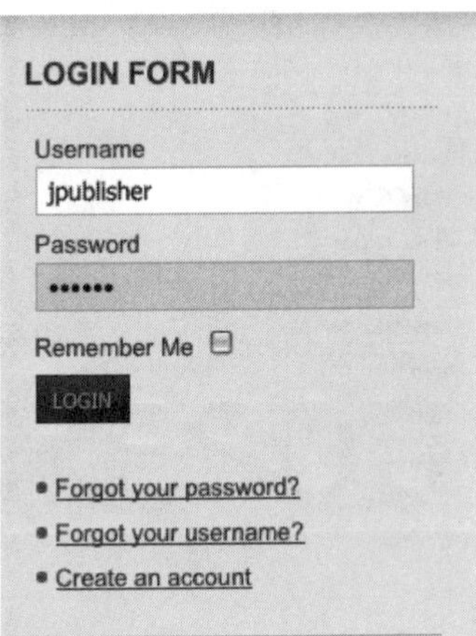

Figure 8.11 The login form

Figure 8.12 The edit icon

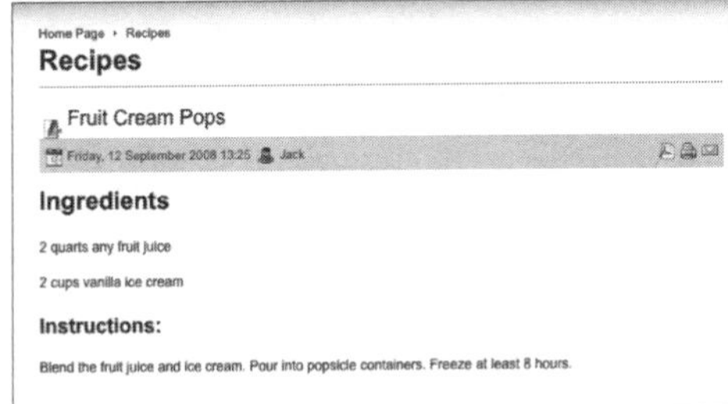

Figure 8.13 An unpublished article

To publish an article from the front end:

1. Log in to the front end with the username of `jpublisher` and the password of `joomla` (**Figure 8.11**).

   To publish an article, you must have publisher access level or higher. Notice when you log in as a publisher that an edit icon (orange pencil) appears over articles (**Figure 8.12**).

2. Choose Recipes from the Main menu.

   The new recipe article is at the top of the Recipes page. The icon is a blue pencil. This alerts a publisher (or higher) that the article has not yet been published to the web site (**Figure 8.13**).

3. Click the edit icon (blue pencil) next icon Fruit Cream Pops article.

   The icon tells the publisher when the article was added, the published state, the access level set, and who submitted the article (**Figure 8.14**).

continues on next page

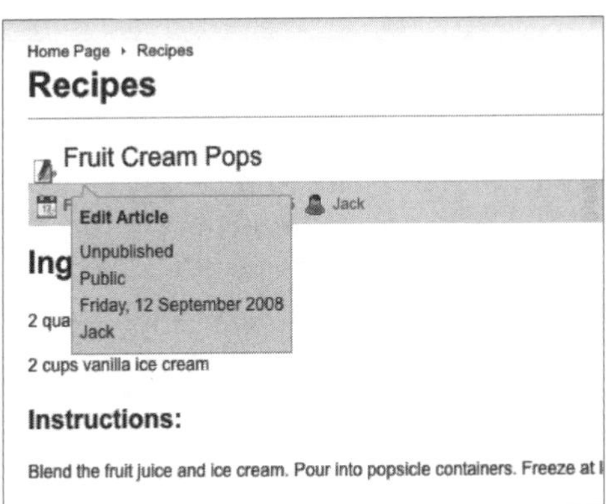

Figure 8.14 Click the edit icon to get more information about the article

4. Click the Yes radio button for Published.

   The form contains all the original information, except now there is a Published choice and the ability to set the Ordering (**Figure 8.15**).

5. From the Finish Publishing drop-down menu, choose Never.

6. Click Save.

   The article has been published and can now be viewed by users (**Figure 8.16**).

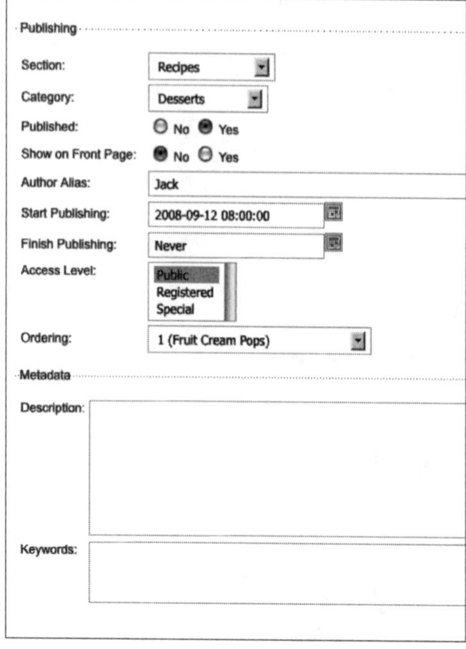

Figure 8.15 Publishing an article from the front end

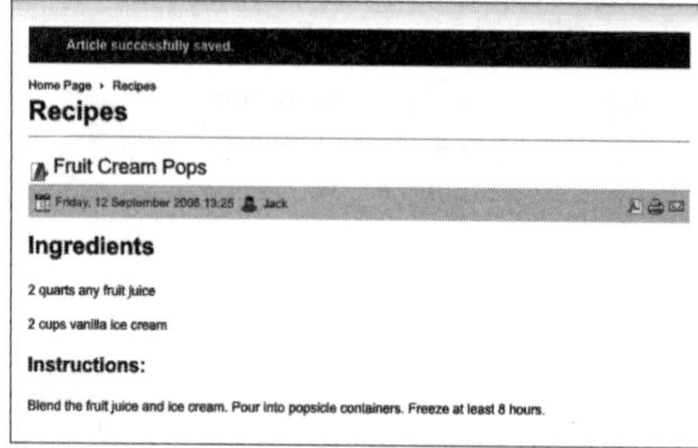

Figure 8.16 The published article

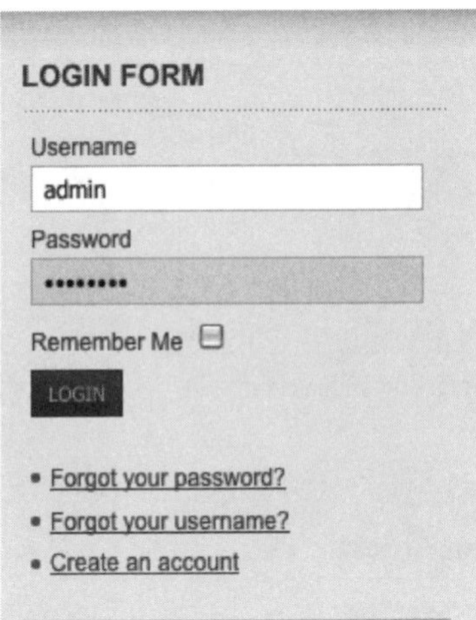

Figure 8.17 Logging in as an administrator

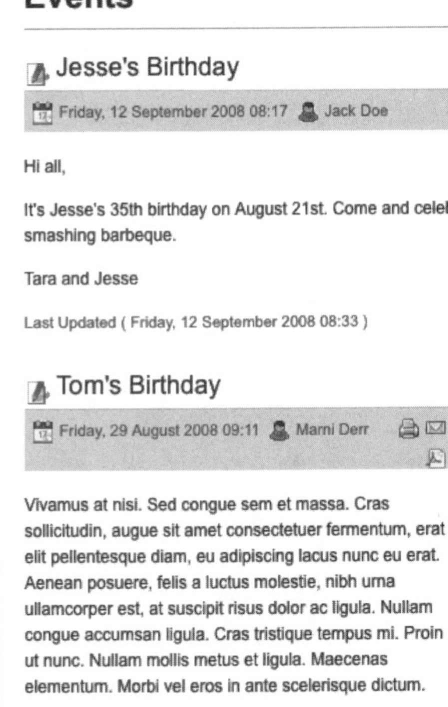

Figure 8.18 Editing an article

To unpublish an article from the front end:

1. Log in to the front end as the super administrator (**Figure 8.17**).

   Any user with a publisher or higher access level can unpublish articles from the front end.

2. Choose Events from the Main menu.
3. Click the edit icon next to the Tom's Birthday article (**Figure 8.18**).
4. Click the No radio button for Published.

   This unpublishes the article from the front end. Or, if a Finish Publishing date had been set to a specific date, the article would automatically be unpublished from the front end on that date. Remember the article is not removed from the site. You can delete the article from the back end or set it to archive. See Chapter 3, "Adding Your Content" for more information (**Figure 8.19**).

5. Click Save.

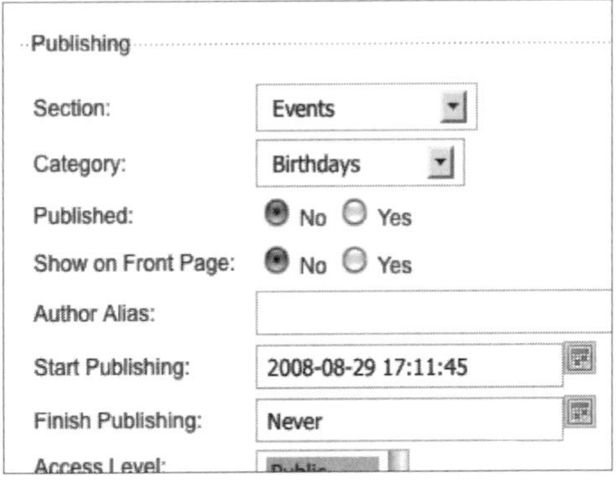

Figure 8.19 Unpublishing an article

To edit an article:

1. Log in to the front end with the username of `jeditor` and the password of `joomla`.

   To edit an article, you must have a user with an editor or higher access level.

2. Click the edit icon next to the article "Welcome to our Family Web Site" (**Figure 8.20**).

3. Make any edits, and then click Save.

   Each time you edit an article, it has to be published again so it will not display on the web site until it has been reviewed and republished (**Figure 8.21**).

✔ Tip

- If you want users to have the ability to publish articles immediately, set the default User Registration type to Publisher. See Chapter 7, "Modifying Global Settings."

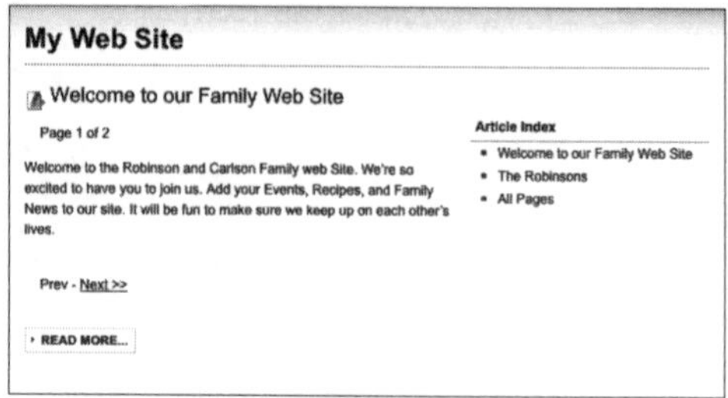

Figure 8.20 Selecting an article to edit

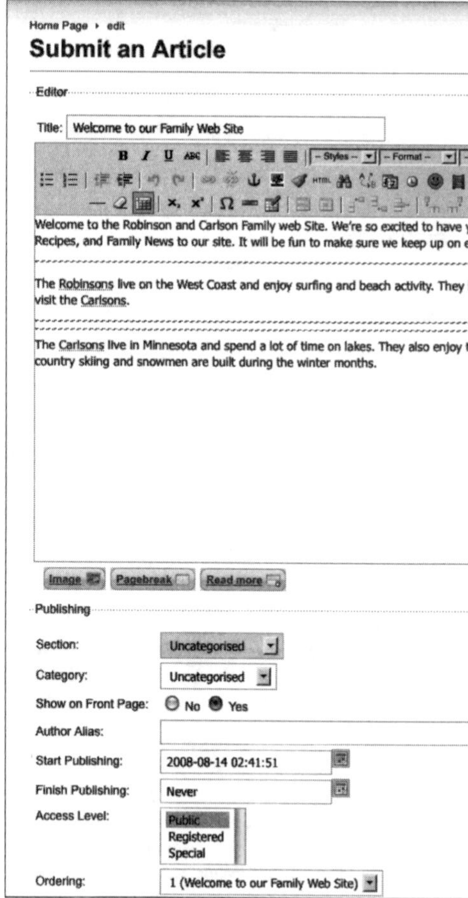

Figure 8.21 Republishing an article after editing

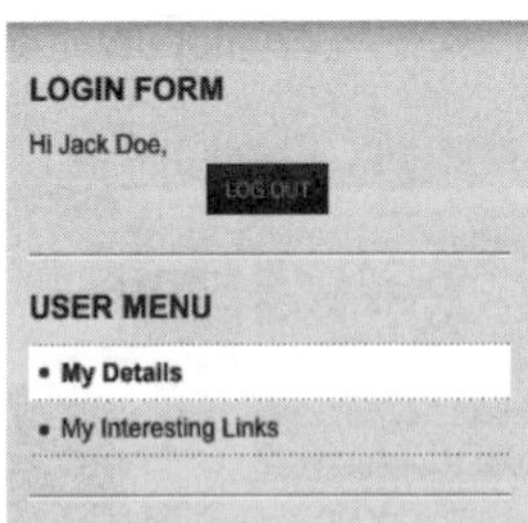

Figure 8.22 The My Details link

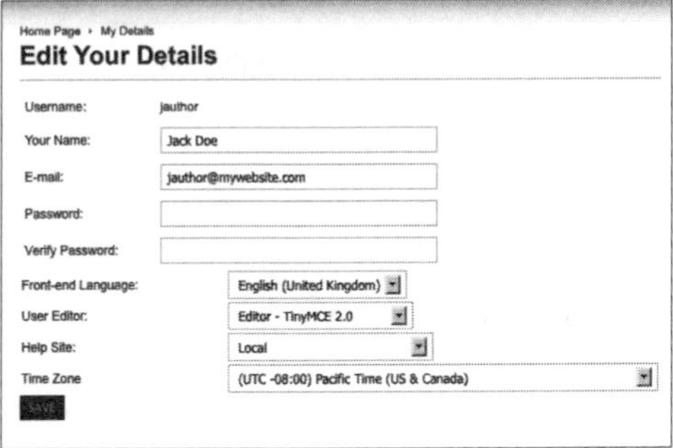

Figure 8.23 The Edit Your Details page

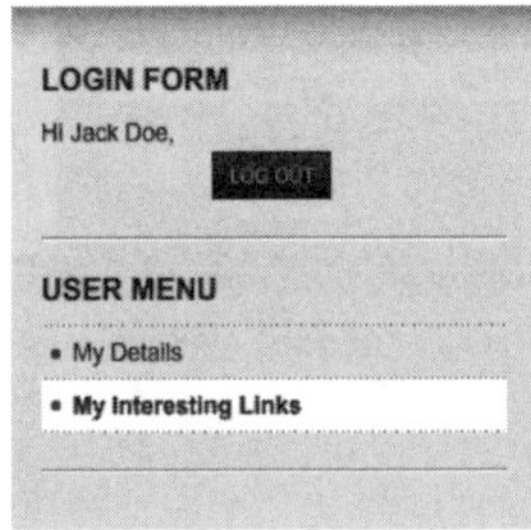

Figure 8.24 My Interesting Links on the User menu

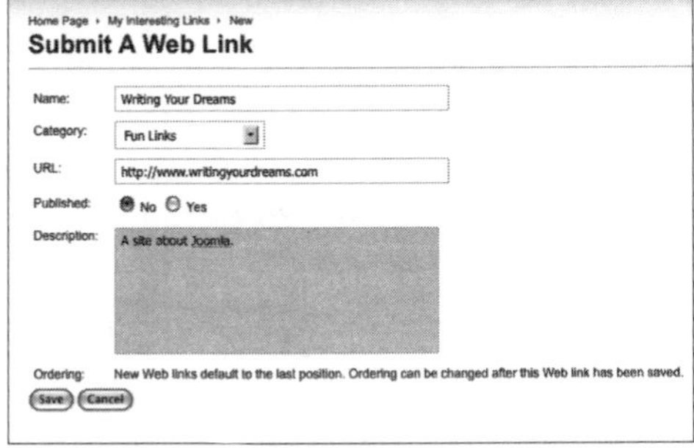

Figure 8.25 The "Submit a Web Link" page

To edit user details:

1. Log in to the front end with the username of `jauthor` and the password of `joomla`.

   Each user can access and modify his or her user information.

2. In the User menu, click the My Details link (**Figure 8.22**).

   The Edit Your Details page opens (**Figure 8.23**).

3. Modify any user details, and then click Save.

✔ Tip

- The standard user details form in Joomla is very basic. Installing a third-party extension, such as JUser or Community Builder, can extend user information (see Chapter 6, "Extending Your Site").

To submit a web link:

1. Log in to the front end with the username of `jauthor` and the password of `joomla`.

   To submit a web link, you must have a user with an author or higher access level.

2. In the User menu, click My Interesting Links (**Figure 8.24**).

3. In the Name field, type `Writing Your Dreams`.

4 From the Category drop-down menu, choose Fun Links.

5. In the URL field, type `http://www.writingyourdreams.com`.

6. Click Save (**Figure 8.25**).

Using the PDF, E-mail, and Print Icons

1. Open the web site in a browser.
2. Choose Events from the Main menu.

   The global settings for each of these articles is set to show the Print, E-mail, and PDF icons (**Figure 8.26**).
3. Click the PDF icon next to the Tom's Birthday article.

   This opens a download dialog box, where users can save the content of this article as a PDF.
4. Click the Print icon next to the Tom's Birthday article.

   This opens a separate browser window, where users can print this article.
5. Click the E-mail icon next to the Tom's Birthday article.

   This opens a dialog box, where users can send this article to friends (**Figure 8.27**).

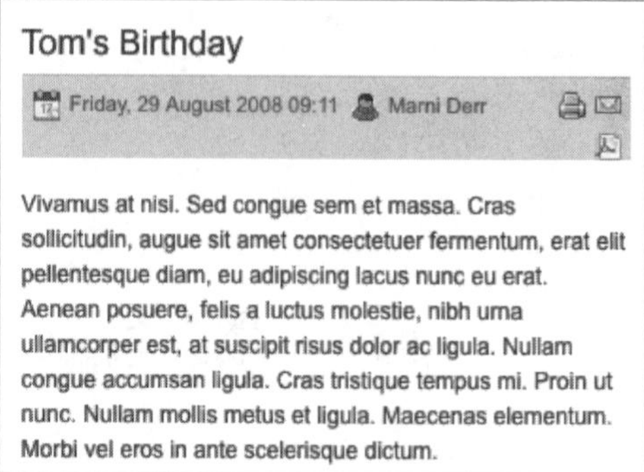

Figure 8.26 The Print, E-mail, and PDF icons

Figure 8.27 "Email this link to a friend" page

9 Creating Joomla Templates

The template system in Joomla is one of the main reasons, we believe, that Joomla is gaining so rapidly in popularity. If you are not comfortable with HTML and CSS, there are hundreds of free and commercial templates available for download. For those knowledgeable about HTML and CSS, this chapter shows you how to use a standard web site design and change it into a Joomla template.

The Joomla template system is self-contained in its own folder structure, which keeps presentation and content separate. You don't need to alter the content in any way to make the new template work; simply change a few position settings, and the site is ready for the public.

This chapter shows you what a Joomla template requires to function, what the positions mean and how they are used, and how to create the XML file required by Joomla. Before you delve into this chapter, be aware that we assume you already know CSS layout and XHTML. If you are not familiar with these concepts, you might want to get an XHTML/CSS book, such as *HTML, XHTML, and CSS, Sixth Edition: Visual QuickStart Guide*, before reading this chapter.

✔ **Tip**

- It's becoming common among Joomla template designers to create CSS styles for components and modules by tying into the core Joomla framework. This is the only way to get a pure CSS "table-less" layout.

Joomla Template Requirements

Joomla allows developers and designers to keep content and presentation separate, so it is easy to update the look of your web site without having to change any of the content. You only need a text editor, such as Notepad, Text Edit, or BBEdit, and an application capable of creating web graphics, such as Adobe Fireworks or Photoshop to create a template.

You need the following files and folder structures for a Joomla template to function properly:

- **index.php file:** This file contains all the XHTML information. It tells Joomla where the components, modules, and content are on the web page. This file must be a PHP file, with the .php extension. Joomla uses the PHP scripting language to communicate with a MySQL database. If you use any other file type (.htm or .html, for example), the template won't work.
- **templateDetails.xml file:** The XML file lists all files contained in the template in order for Joomla to render the template correctly. Every template filename, each image name, and position used must be listed in this file. Only the images used by the template are contained in this file, however; it does *not* contain the media files located in the site content (articles).
- **CSS folder:** This folder contains all the CSS styles used by the template. You can have a single template.css file or any number of CSS files according to personal design preferences.
- **Images folder:** This folder contains all the images used by the template.

In addition to the minimum requirements, most templates contain the following, though they aren't required by Joomla to operate:

- **favicon.ico:** This is the icon used in the browser's address bar to identify the site. This icon is generally a small version of the site's logo or brand.
- **template_thumbnail.png:** This is a small .png thumbnail image of the site design, generally 150 x 150 pixels. This is used in the template manager to display a small image of the site design.
- **Misc. folders and files:** You can have a js (JavaScript, or JavaScript libraries such as jquery or mootool) folder, PHP include folder, a file for parameters, and so on.

Can I Use a WYSIWYG?

One of the main questions we get when discussing Joomla templates is, "Can I use a WYSIWYG editor like Adobe Dreamweaver?" Yes, you can. Although WYSIWYG editors cannot display live data without the use of a web browser, there are some really handy extensions that allow you to use such applications as Dreamweaver to create a Joomla template. These extensions enable you to see the design and accurately preview that design. We currently use the following Dreamweaver extensions, both of which speed up the template creation process and are written for Joomla 1.5.x:

- **Joomla Template Kit 3.x:** This commercial extension comes from www.m65.net.
- **Joomla 1.5 Template Builder:** This is from www.webmasterschool.biz and is free with registration.

To create the base template files:

1. Open your Joomla folder and locate the templates folder.

   Joomla has a templates folder, where all the templates used for the site are contained. The template folder can contain as many templates as you want (**Figure 9.1**).

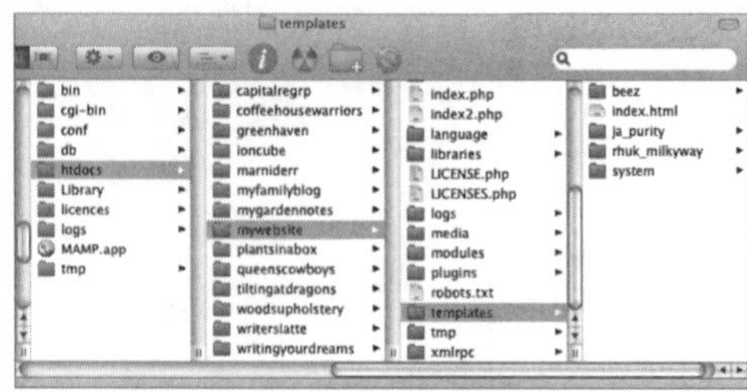

Figure 9.1 Joomla template folder

2. Create a new folder called `myTemplate`.

   This folder will contain all the template files needed for your design.

3. Inside the myTemplate folder, create two new folders: `css` and `images`.

   You can also have a js folder for JavaScript, and an include folder for includes if your design will incorporate custom JavaScript or PHP. These are not required.

4. Open any text editor and create a file named `index.php` and a file named `templateDetails.xml`.

   Your myTemplate folder should now look like **Figure 9.2**. Don't worry about the thumbnail or favicon yet. You can create them later.

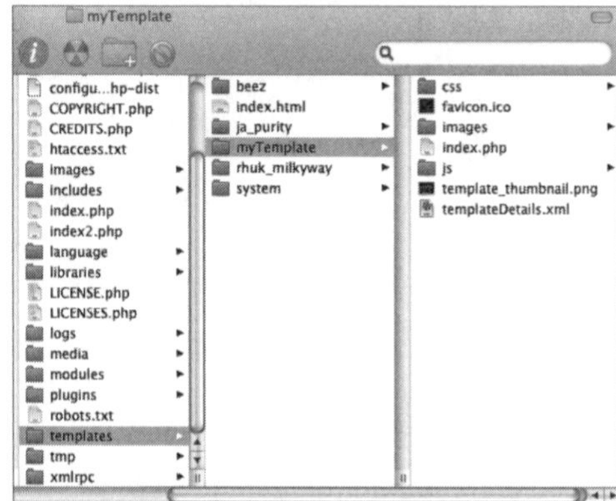

Figure 9.2 MyTemplate structure

✔ Tip

- If you are using a WYSIWYG editor, rather than a plain text editor, be sure to create an index.php page. For example, if you created a new index page in Dreamweaver, with an .html extension, and then saved that file with a .php extension, the file will not work. It must be created by the application as a PHP file.

Creating the index.php File

In this section, you will add the basic XHTML tags needed to define your template structure. You will be using the `<div>` tag to create containers. Although there are no hard and fast rules to creating the `divs`, it is recommended to keep the following best practice guidelines in mind.

Best Practices

- **Do not place any standard XHTML tags (h1, h2, p, and so on) in the index.php file.** Everything will be styled using a CSS stylesheet. It is a pure CSS layout. To help you style your content, you will find a list of the Joomla core class styles at the end of this chapter. These classes must be styled in your CSS, or they will use a browser's default styling.
- **When creating your index.php file, organize your div containers in a logical order.** Remember that a browser reads from top to bottom. To a browser, you are just creating a large stack of boxes, one on top of another. Keep in mind where you want things to be placed on the web page and create the `div` containers accordingly. This makes it easier to read the code in the template and make changes later.
- **Give similar descriptive names to your divs and positions.** For example, a left column `div` should have a name such as left_col. It will make it easier when you are assigning positions to your content and adding code.
- **Although you can give positions any name, it is best practice to use common Joomla names.** Most template designers use the standard Joomla positions, such as top, mainnav, footer, user1 through user9, and so on. This also helps when your site already contains content and modules. If the positions in the new template vary a great deal, you will need to go back and reassign all those modules to new positions. User1 may not seem to be very descriptive, but it is a standard used throughout the Joomla community.

When you first design a web site, you usually create some kind of sketch or wireframe that indicates where your content will be. **Figure 9.3** displays a wireframe layout with boxes that will become your `divs`.

Figure 9.3 Wireframe with containers

To create the index.php file:

1. From the myTemplate folder, open the index.php file in any text editor.

   All of the examples in this section can be copied from our website www.writingyourdreams.com/JoomlaVQS, or you can type the code in yourself.

2. Type the following code into the index.php file, starting with lines 1 through 10:

```
<?php
/**
 * @copyright Copyright (C) 2005 -
 →2007 Open Source Matters. All
 →rights reserved.
 * @license  GNU/GPL, see LICENSE.
 php
 * Joomla! is free software. This
 →version may have been modified
 →pursuant
 * to the GNU General Public License,
 →and as distributed it includes or
 * is derivative of works licensed
 →under the GNU General Public
 →License or
 * other free or open source software
 →licenses.
 * See COPYRIGHT.php for copyright
 →notices and details.  */
```

   The index page begins immediately with a PHP function that calls the Joomla copyright and details the GNU/GPL licensing.

continues on next page

3. Starting on line 11, type the following:

```
// no direct access
defined( '_JEXEC' ) or die
→( 'Restricted access' );
?>
```

This ends the first PHP function. The _JEXEC function replaces the Joomla 1.0.x version _VALID_MOS. The page should look like **Figure 9.4**. This ensures that the index.php file is not being accessed directly, and is used for security purposes.

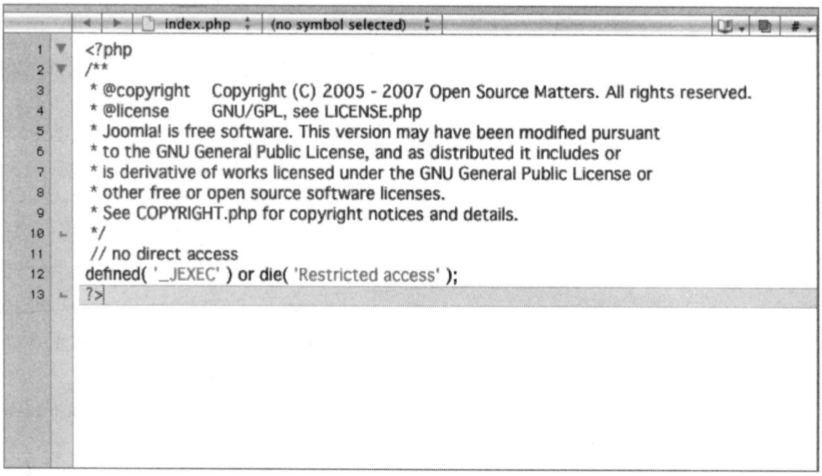

```
index.php   (no symbol selected)
1  <?php
2  /**
3   * @copyright   Copyright (C) 2005 - 2007 Open Source Matters. All rights reserved.
4   * @license     GNU/GPL, see LICENSE.php
5   * Joomla! is free software. This version may have been modified pursuant
6   * to the GNU General Public License, and as distributed it includes or
7   * is derivative of works licensed under the GNU General Public License or
8   * other free or open source software licenses.
9   * See COPYRIGHT.php for copyright notices and details.
10  */
11  // no direct access
12 defined( '_JEXEC' ) or die( 'Restricted access' );
13 ?>
```

Figure 9.4 The first PHP statement for the index.php file

4. Press Enter twice to create a blank line, and then type the following:

```
<!DOCTYPE html PUBLIC "-//W3C
→//DTD XHTML 1.0 Transitional//EN"
→"http://www.w3.org/TR/xhtml1/DTD/
→xhtml1-transitional.dtd">
<html xmlns="http://www.w3.org/1999/
→xhtml" xml:lang="<?php echo
→$this->language; ?>" lang=
→"<?php echo $this->language; ?>">
```

Line 15 is the !DOCTYPE declaration required by all sites, to tell the browser what DOCTYPE is being used for the XHTML in this document. You can also use the XHTML 1.0 Strict DOCTYPE. Using the strict DOCTYPE helps your code to work across most browsers with minimal hacks to the code. It will not, however, resolve CSS issues with Internet Explorer 6 and lower browser versions.

Line 17 contains the PHP function used by Joomla to identify what language to use on this site. This is pulled from the global configuration page in Joomla (**Figure 9.5**).

Lines 1 through 17 all come before the <head> tag.

continues on next page

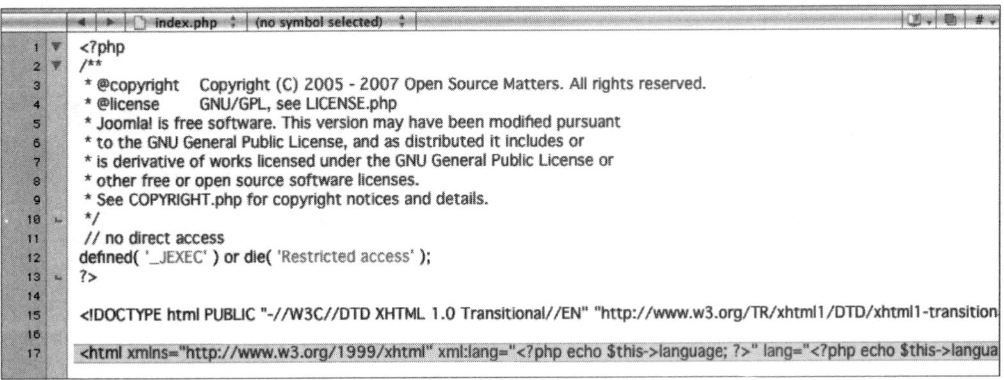

Figure 9.5 Adding the !DOCTYPE declaration

5. Type <head>, add a few blank lines, and close the head of the document with </head>.

   Included in the head of the index page are the paths to the CSS files, any custom PHP files, and JavaScript files or libraries being used by this template.

6. Between the <head> </head> tags, type `<jdoc:include type="head" />`.

   The `jdoc:include` (object:method) is the primary method you will use to call all the objects used in Joomla.

   The line `<jdoc:include type="head" />` replaces the <meta> tags on a standard web page. This tells Joomla to use the meta tag information entered in the back end administrative global configuration pages. So there is no need to title the page or add metadata as you would on a standard web page (**Figure 9.6**).

7. To call the CSS files, type the following directly below the `jdoc`, but before the </head> closing tag:

```
<link rel="stylesheet" href=
→ "<?php echo $this->baseurl;?>
→ /templates/<?php echo $this->
→ template;?>/css/layout.css"
→ media="screen" type="text/css" />
<link rel="stylesheet" href=
→ "<?php echo $this->baseurl;?>
→ /templates/<?php echo
→ $this->template;?>/css/
→ template.css" media="screen"
→ type="text/css" />
```

   If your template contains more than one stylesheet, repeat this line and replace the `/template.css` filename with the name of the other CSS file.

   If you have PHP includes, special parameter files, or JavaScript files, the paths to these files also need to be contained in the <head> </head> tags of the index page.

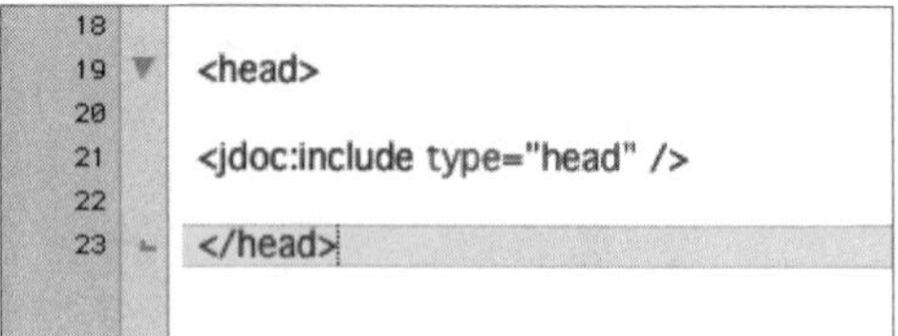

Figure 9.6 The head of the index.php file

8. To tell the browser the character set, type the following:

```
<meta http-equiv="Content-Type"
→ content="text/html;
→ charset=UTF-8" />
```

Joomla 1.5.x is UTF-8 compliant, meaning it uses the Unicode character set.

9. To display your favicon in the browser address bar, add the line:

```
<link rel="shortcut icon"
→ href="<?php echo "$GLOBALS
→ [mosConfig_live_site]/templates/
→ $GLOBALS[cur_template]/
→ favicon.ico"; ?>" />
```

10. If you want to use Dreamweaver to create your templates, you can add the following line of code:

```
<link href="css/layout.css"
→ rel="stylesheet"
→ type="text/css" media="all" />
```

This code allows Dreamweaver to link to your CSS stylesheet and display it in design view. Once your template is complete, you can delete this line.

It is best practice to add comments to your code. Your index.php file should now look like **Figure 9.7**.

11. To finish the base XHTML needed for the index.php file, add the following tags:

```
<body>
</body>
</html>
```

The remaining tags and functions will all go inside the `<body> </body>` tags (**Figure 9.8**).

12. Save the file.

```
<?php
/**
 * @copyright   Copyright (C) 2005 - 2007 Open Source Matters. All rights reserved.
 * @license     GNU/GPL, see LICENSE.php
 * Joomla! is free software. This version may have been modified pursuant
 * to the GNU General Public License, and as distributed it includes or
 * is derivative of works licensed under the GNU General Public License or
 * other free or open source software licenses.
 * See COPYRIGHT.php for copyright notices and details.
 */
// no direct access
defined( '_JEXEC' ) or die( 'Restricted access' );
?>

<!DOCTYPE html PUBLIC "-//W3C//DTD XHTML 1.0 Transitional//EN" "http://www.w3.org/TR/xhtml1/DTD/xhtml1-transitional.dtd">

<html xmlns="http://www.w3.org/1999/xhtml" xml:lang="<?php echo $this->language; ?>" lang="<?php echo $this->language; ?>">

<head>
<jdoc:include type="head" />
<meta http-equiv="Content-Type" content="text/html; charset=UTF-8" />

<!-- This links to the main layout css stylesheet. The layout css file calls all of your other stylesheets -->
<link href="templates/<?php echo $this->template ?>/css/layout.css" rel="stylesheet" type="text/css" media="all" />
<link href="templates/<?php echo $this->template ?>/css/template.css" rel="stylesheet" type="text/css" media="all" />
<!-- This so you can see the css styles in Dreamweaver,  you can delete this link once editing your template is complete, or leave in-->
<link href="css/layout.css" rel="stylesheet" type="text/css" media="all" />

<!-- These links will call in javascript files being used in your template -->
<script>
</script>

</head>
```

Figure 9.7 The links to your stylesheets

```

</head>

<body>



</body>
</html>
```

37 76 HTML Unicode™ (UTF-8, no BOM) Unix (LF)

Figure 9.8 The basic XHTML tags

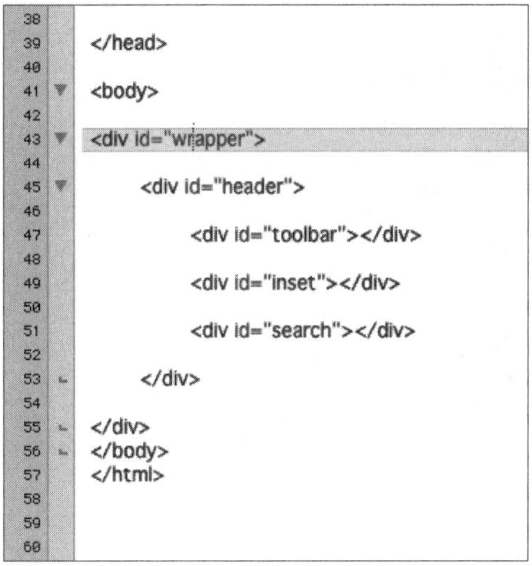

```
</head>

<body>

<div id="wrapper">

    <div id="header">

        <div id="toolbar"></div>

        <div id="inset"></div>

        <div id="search"></div>

    </div>

</div>
</body>
</html>
```

Figure 9.9 The first container divs

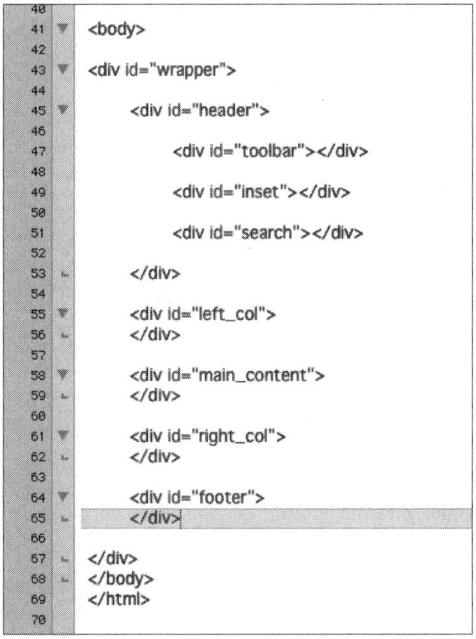

```
<body>

<div id="wrapper">

    <div id="header">

        <div id="toolbar"></div>

        <div id="inset"></div>

        <div id="search"></div>

    </div>

    <div id="left_col">
    </div>

    <div id="main_content">
    </div>

    <div id="right_col">
    </div>

    <div id="footer">
    </div>

</div>
</body>
</html>
```

Figure 9.10 The basic structure divs

To add the XHTML/CSS base structure:

1. Open the index.php file in any text editor.
2. Type the following lines of code between the body tags:

```
<div id="wrapper">
<div id="header">
<div id="toolbar"></div>
<div id="inset"></div>
<div id="search"></div>
</div>
</div>
```

   These lines add a wrapper that will enclose the entire design. They place a header container inside the wrapper that contains positions for a toolbar, an inset, and a search box (**Figure 9.9**).

3. After the closing `</div>` for the header, but before the closing `</div>` for the wrapper, type the following:

```
<div id="left_col">
</div>
<div id="main_content">
</div>
<div id="right_col">
</div>
<div id="footer">
</div>
```

   Containers for the left column position, main body (for components), right column position, and the footer position are added and contained within the main wrapper. Creating a Joomla template is not so different from creating any standard web design; the only difference will be in where and how to use the PHP functions so Joomla can render your site correctly (**Figure 9.10**).

continues on next page

4. Add the rest of the code, as shown in **Figure 9.11**, or download the completed index.php file from the companion web site.

5. Save the file.

✔ Tip

- What you currently have is no different than any standard CSS laid out web page. At this point, it is a good idea to create a separate layout.css file and get the page working correctly. The template at this stage cannot communicate directly with Joomla, but you don't want to be fighting with the layout when troubleshooting the PHP functions. Don't panic, they are very easy, basic functions at this point. If you already have a working design, continue with adding the j:doc include statements. You can tweak the layout at any time.

```
<body>
<?php echo $mainframe->getCfg('sitename');?><br />

<div id="wrapper">

    <div id="header">

        <div id="toolbar">
        </div>
        <div id="inset">
        </div>
        <div id="search">
        </div>

    </div>

    <div id="mainnav">
    </div>

    <div id="breadcrumbs">
    </div>

    <div id="top">
            <div id="user1"></div>
            <div id="user2"></div>
            <div id="user3"></div>
    </div>

    <div id="maincontentwrap">

        <div id="left_col">
        </div>

        <div id="main_content">
            <div id="user4"></div>
            <div id="user5"></div>
            <div id="user6"></div>
        </div>

        <div id="right_col">
        </div>

    </div>

    <div id="bottom">
        <div id="user7"></div>
        <div id="user8"></div>
        <div id="user9"></div>
    </div>

    <div id="footer">
    </div>

</div>
</body>
</html>
```

Figure 9.11 The remaining div containers for a Joomla template

Adding the jdoc:include Statements to the index.php File

Without jdoc:includes, the template will not work. The jdoc method tells Joomla what to place in the positions used by your template. **Figure 9.12** shows you an example of the positions being used. As you can see, there should be a one-to-one correlation between divs and positions. It is best practice to give your positions and your div ids the same name. Then, when you are choosing the position for your menus and modules, you will find it easy to choose the right position.

continues on next page

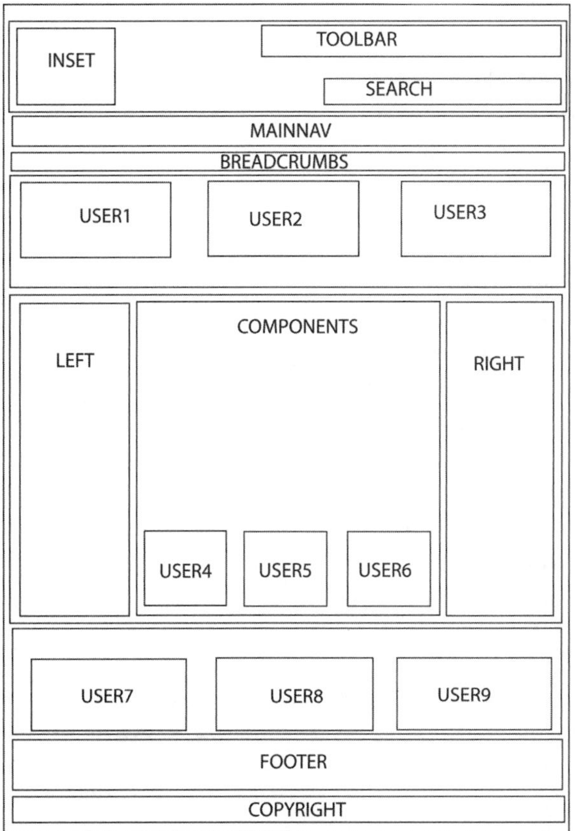

Figure 9.12 The wireframe showing positions of a Joomla template

The jdoc:include module statement contains four parts:

- `jdoc:include`: The object:method function that tells Joomla to display the type being called.
- `type="modules"`: This tells Joomla the type of object to include. There are three types: head, module, and component.
- `name="location"`: The head and component do not have a location, as this is defined by the system. The head is the metadata to be displayed dynamically on each page. A component can only be called into the main body of the page. A module can be placed into any location you specify. For example, left, right, top, bottom, user1, and so on.
- `style="optional"`: The style is optional, and it applies only to modules. The choices for style are:
  - `table`: Displays modules using a table layout; this is the default display, if you don't declare a style.
  - `horz`: Displays the module horizontally using a table format.
  - `xhtml`: Displays a module using a simple div element, and not a table.
  - `rounded`: Allows a module to use the rounded-corner CSS styling with nested divs. This is covered later in the CSS portion of this chapter.
  - `outline`: Wraps the module in a border.
  - `none`: Displays a module as pure content, without styling. The text will still use the template.css styles.

Most templates use the xhtml and rounded styling options. This produces cleaner code and a table-less layout for the modules. This also allows for more advanced CSS layout techniques. **Figure 9.13** shows a wireframe detailing where the jdoc statements will go.

✔ Tip

- The `jdoc:include type="component"` and `jdoc:include type="head"` are the only two include statements that do not have a name or type.

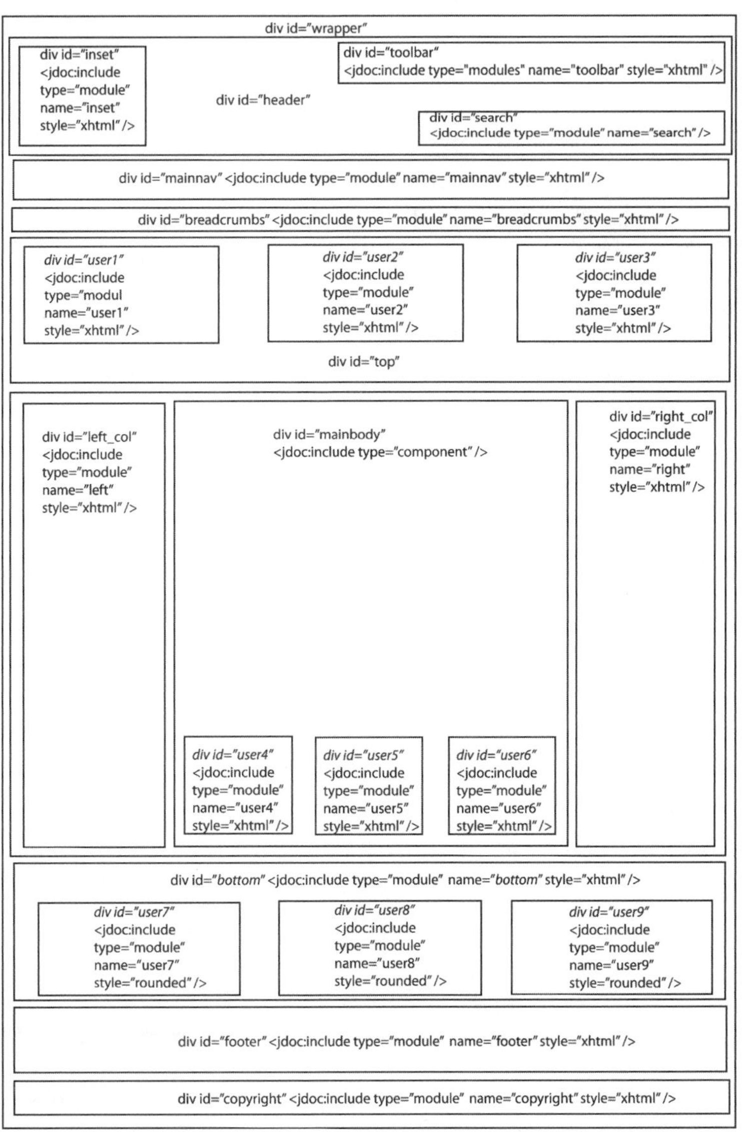

Figure 9.13 The wireframe displaying the jdoc statements

To add the required jdoc:includes:

1. Open the index.php file in any text editor.
2. Add a blank line between `<div id="toolbar">` and its closing `</div>`, and then type the following:

   ```
   <jdoc:include type="modules"
   name="toolbar" style="xhtml" />
   ```

3. Add a blank line between `<div id="main_content">` and its closing `</div>`, and then type the following:

   ```
   <jdoc:include type="component" />
   ```

   Because components can only be used in the main body of the page, this statement does not include `style=` or `name=`. To make components "table-less" or to style components, you need to override the core Joomla output. This is addressed at the end of this chapter.

4. To add the rest of the `jdoc:include` statements, use **Figure 9.14** and **Figure 9.15** as a guide. Remember the statements must be inside the opening and closing `<div>` tags for that element.

✔ Tip

- Watch out for typos; they're the number one reason code fails to work properly.

```
<body>

<div id="wrapper">
	<div id="toolbar">
		<jdoc:include type="modules" name="toolbar" style="rounded" />
	</div>

	<div id="header">
		<div id="inset">
			<jdoc:include type="modules" name="inset" style="xhtml" />
		</div>

		<div id="search">
			<jdoc:include type="modules" name="search" style="xhtml" />
		</div>

	</div>

	<div id="mainnav">
		<jdoc:include type="modules" name="mainnav" style="xhtml" />
	</div>

	<div id="breadcrumbs" class="clearfix">
		<jdoc:include type="modules" name="breadcrumbs" style="xhtml" />
	</div>

	<div id="top" class="clearfix">
			<div id="user1">
				<jdoc:include type="modules" name="user1" style="rounded" />
			</div>

			<div id="user2">
				<jdoc:include type="modules" name="user2" style="rounded" />
			</div>

			<div id="user3">
				<jdoc:include type="modules" name="user3" style="rounded" />
			</div>

	</div>
```

Figure 9.14 Adding the jdoc:include statements to the div containers

```
    <div id="maincontentwrap">

        <div id="left_col" class="clearfix">
            <jdoc:include type="modules" name="left" style="xhtml" />
        </div>

            <div id="main_content" class="clearfix">
                <jdoc:include type="component" />
            </div>

            <div id="user4">
                <jdoc:include type="modules" name="user4" style="xhtml" />
            </div>

            <div id="user5">
                <jdoc:include type="modules" name="user5" style="xhtml" />
            </div>

            <div id="user6">
                <jdoc:include type="modules" name="user6" style="xhtml" />
            </div>

        <div id="right_col" class="clearfix">
            <jdoc:include type="modules" name="right" style="xhtml" />
        </div>
    </div>

    <div id="bottom">

        <div id="user7">
            <jdoc:include type="modules" name="user7" style="rounded" />
        </div>

        <div id="user8">
            <jdoc:include type="modules" name="user8" style="rounded" />
        </div>

        <div id="user9">
            <jdoc:include type="modules" name="user9" style="rounded" />
        </div>
    </div>

    <div id="footer">
        <jdoc:include type="modules" name="footer" style="xhtml" />
    </div>

<br clear="all" />
</div>
</body>
</html>
```

Figure 9.15 Adding the remaining jdoc:include statements

Creating the templateDetails.xml File

The index.php page now has the fundamental pieces of information it needs to function as a Joomla template. Without the templateDetails.xml file, however, the template will not work. The templateDetails.xml file lists everything the template contains so Joomla can render it properly. Creating the XML file can be a bit tedious, but it's not difficult. The main rule to keep in mind is if it exists in your template folder, it must be in the XML file.

The templateDetails.xml file is broken down into six areas:

- Joomla version
- Template and designer details
- List of files
- List of positions
- List of images
- List of parameters (optional)

✔ Tip

- XML and XHTML files are case-sensitive. It is best practice to only use lowercase when naming images and files. The one exception is the templateDetails.xml file, as this is the required filename used by Joomla.

To create the templateDetails.xml file:

1. Open the templateDetails.xml file in a text editor.
2. At the top of the page, type

   ```
   <?xml version="1.0" encoding="utf-8"?>
   ```

   This identifies the type of document (XML), the version of XML (1.0), and the encoding type (UTF-8).
3. On the next line, type

   ```
   <install version="1.5"
   type="template">.
   ```

   This tells Joomla this is for version 1.5 and this is an XML file for a template.
4. For lines 3 through 8, enter the following:

   ```
   <name>myTemplate</name>
   <creationDate>2008</creationDate>
   <author>Your Name</author>
   <copyright>Your Company</copyright>
   <authorEmail>youremail</authorEmail>
   <authorUrl>www.mydomain.com
   → </authorUrl>
   <version>1.0</version>
   <description> This is my first
   → Joomla template</description>
   ```

   Each item needs to be on its own line. These are the details for your template; they will display in the Template Manager fields. When finished, your file will look like **Figure 9.16**.

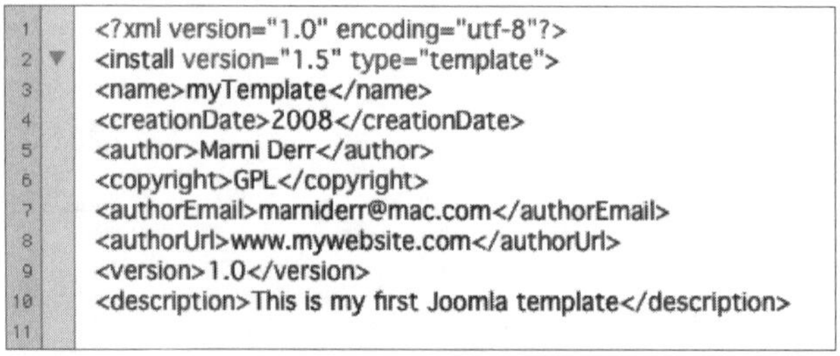

```
1  <?xml version="1.0" encoding="utf-8"?>
2  <install version="1.5" type="template">
3  <name>myTemplate</name>
4  <creationDate>2008</creationDate>
5  <author>Marni Derr</author>
6  <copyright>GPL</copyright>
7  <authorEmail>marniderr@mac.com</authorEmail>
8  <authorUrl>www.mywebsite.com</authorUrl>
9  <version>1.0</version>
10 <description>This is my first Joomla template</description>
11
```

Figure 9.16 The templateDetails.xml metadata file

5. Save the file.
6. On line 11, type `<files>` and close the file tag, `</files>`.

   Every file the template uses must be listed with the correct path between the opening and closing tags.
7. Between the opening and closing `<file>` tags, type:

   ```
   <filename>index.php</filename>
   <filename>templateDetails.xml
   → </filename>
   <filename>params.ini</filename>
   ```

   Currently, these are all the files used for the template. As you add more files, JavaScript, and so on, they will need to be added here (**Figure 9.17**).
8. Add the following lines directly below the closing `</files>` tag:

   ```
   <css>
   <filename>css/template.css
   → </filename>
   <filename>css/layout.css
   → </filename>
   </css>
   ```

continues on next page

```
1  <?xml version="1.0" encoding="utf-8"?>
2  <install version="1.5" type="template">
3  <name>myTemplate</name>
4  <creationDate>2008</creationDate>
5  <author>Marni Derr</author>
6  <copyright>GPL</copyright>
7  <authorEmail>marniderr@mac.com</authorEmail>
8  <authorUrl>www.mywebsite.com</authorUrl>
9  <version>1.0</version>
10 <description>This is my first Joomla template</description>
11
12 <files>
13         <filename>index.php</filename>
14         <filename>templateDetails.xml</filename>
15         <filename>params.ini</filename>
16 </files>
```

Figure 9.17 The files added to the templateDetails.xml file

You can add the CSS files in the `<files>` section; this is a matter of personal preference. But for easier editing later, we recommend grouping your files by type. Notice the path `css/` is included. Joomla needs to know where the file is located within the template folder.

9. Add the following lines directly below the `</css>` closing tag:

```
<positions>
   <position>toolbar</position>
   <position>inset</position>
   <position>search</position>
   <position>mainnav</position>
   <position>breadcrumbs</position>
   <position>left</position>
   <position>right</position>
   <position>user1</position>
   <position>user2</position>
   <position>user3</position>
   <position>user4</position>
   <position>user5</position>
   <position>user6</position>
   <position>user7</position>
   <position>user8</position>
   <position>user9</position>
   <position>footer</position>
   <position>debug</position>
</positions>
```

These are all the positions currently created in the template. These are all based on personal design preference. The only requirement is if it is a position called by the `jdoc:include`, then it needs to be listed here in the XML file as a position. Notice that in the example index.php file, header, top, bottom, and the wrappers are not listed. These are not positions in this template; they are simply layout containers (**Figure 9.18**).

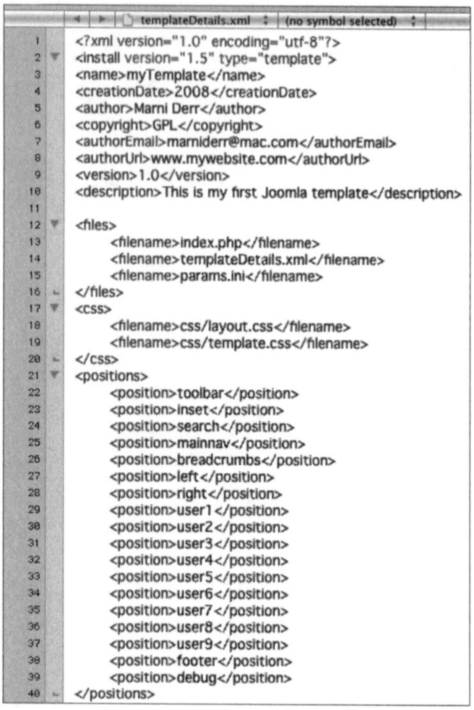

```
templateDetails.xml    (no symbol selected)
<?xml version="1.0" encoding="utf-8"?>
<install version="1.5" type="template">
<name>myTemplate</name>
<creationDate>2008</creationDate>
<author>Marni Derr</author>
<copyright>GPL</copyright>
<authorEmail>marniderr@mac.com</authorEmail>
<authorUrl>www.mywebsite.com</authorUrl>
<version>1.0</version>
<description>This is my first Joomla template</description>

<files>
      <filename>index.php</filename>
      <filename>templateDetails.xml</filename>
      <filename>params.ini</filename>
</files>
<css>
      <filename>css/layout.css</filename>
      <filename>css/template.css</filename>
</css>
<positions>
      <position>toolbar</position>
      <position>inset</position>
      <position>search</position>
      <position>mainnav</position>
      <position>breadcrumbs</position>
      <position>left</position>
      <position>right</position>
      <position>user1</position>
      <position>user2</position>
      <position>user3</position>
      <position>user4</position>
      <position>user5</position>
      <position>user6</position>
      <position>user7</position>
      <position>user8</position>
      <position>user9</position>
      <position>footer</position>
      <position>debug</position>
</positions>
```

Figure 9.18 The positions in the templateDetails.xml file

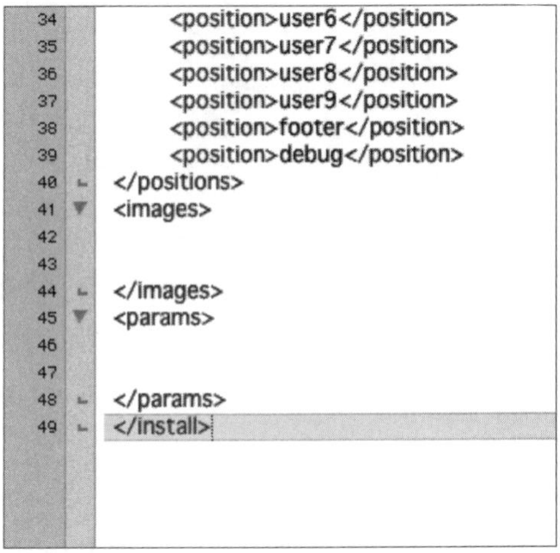

```
        <position>user6</position>
        <position>user7</position>
        <position>user8</position>
        <position>user9</position>
        <position>footer</position>
        <position>debug</position>
    </positions>
    <images>


    </images>
    <params>


    </params>
</install>
```

Figure 9.19 The remaining structure for a templateDetails.xml file

10. Add the following directly after the closing `</position>` tag:

```
<images>
</images>
<params>
</params>
</install>
```

Currently, the file references no images or parameters. You can add them later as the template is finalized. The closing `</install>` tag closes the opening `<install>`. All XML elements must be between the opening `<install version ="1.5" type="template">` and closing `</install>` tags (**Figure 9.19**).

11. Save the file.

Adding the PHP Functions

The basic index.php file along with a layout CSS stylesheet and the templateDetails.xml file can now render your Joomla template. However, without PHP functions, every position will appear, with or without content. This would leave large areas of blank space all over your web site. Even if you place as many usable positions in the template as possible, that does not mean a user is going to use all of them.

The basic PHP `if` functions covered in this section tell Joomla to either hide or to display modules based on whether or not there are module(s) assigned to this specific position. Assigning the modules to positions is done through the Joomla administrative back end.

To add the basic PHP functions:

1. Open the index.php file in any text editor.
2. Locate the first div after the header div container.

   In the sample, this is the mainnav. The header should always display, so we do not add a PHP `if` statement to the header div container.
3. Right above the `<div id="mainnav">`, type `<?php if ($this->countModules ➝ ('mainnav')): ?>`.

   Joomla reads the PHP `if` function, and if a module is assigned to this position, Joomla renders the module. If there are no modules assigned to this position, Joomla renders nothing in this position and moves on to the next position.

4. Right after the closing `</div>` for the mainnav, type `<?php endif; ?>`.

   This ends the PHP function. You can place any other `if`, or `else if`, statements between these functions. Your code now looks like **Figure 9.20**.

5. The following div containers are all positions we want available to display modules, so each needs the appropriate PHP `if` statements:

   - `insert`
   - `toolbar`
   - `search`
   - `mainnav`
   - `breadcrumbs`
   - `user1`, `user2`, and `user3`
   - `left_col` (this is position left)
   - `right_col` (this is position right)
   - `user4`, `user5`, and `user6`
   - `user7`, `user8`, and `user9`
   - `footer`

   Remember, the main content is for the components; this does not have any module positions and does not need the PHP function (**Figure 9.21** and **Figure 9.22**).

```
<?php if ($this->countModules('mainnav')): ?>
<div id="mainnav">
    <jdoc:include type="modules" name="mainnav" style="xhtml" />
</div>
<?php endif; ?>
```

Figure 9.20 Adding your first PHP function

```
<div id="wrapper">

      <div id="toolbar">
      <?php if ($this->countModules('toolbar')): ?>
            <jdoc:include type="modules" name="toolbar" style="rounded" />
      </div>
      <?php endif; ?>

      <div id="header">
            <?php if ($this->countModules('insert')): ?>
            <div id="inset">
                  <jdoc:include type="modules" name="inset" style="xhtml" />
            </div>
            <?php endif; ?>

            <?php if ($this->countModules('search')): ?>
            <div id="search">
                  <jdoc:include type="modules" name="search" style="xhtml" />
            </div>
            <?php endif; ?>

      </div>

      <?php if ($this->countModules('mainnav')): ?>
      <div id="mainnav">
            <jdoc:include type="modules" name="mainnav" style="xhtml" />
      </div>
      <?php endif; ?>

      <?php if ($this->countModules('breadcrumbs')): ?>
      <div id="breadcrumbs" class="clearfix">
            <jdoc:include type="modules" name="breadcrumbs" style="xhtml" />
      </div>
      <?php endif; ?>

      <div id="top" class="clearfix">
                  <?php if ($this->countModules('user1')): ?>
                  <div id="user1">
                        <jdoc:include type="modules" name="user1" style="rounded" />
                  </div>
                  <?php endif; ?>

                  <?php if ($this->countModules('user2')): ?>
                  <div id="user2">
                        <jdoc:include type="modules" name="user2" style="rounded" />
                  </div>
                  <?php endif; ?>

                  <?php if ($this->countModules('user3')): ?>
                  <div id="user3">
                        <jdoc:include type="modules" name="user3" style="rounded" />
                  </div>
                  <?php endif; ?>
```

Figure 9.21 More PHP functions added to the index.php file

```
	<div id="maincontentwrap">

	<?php if ($this->countModules('left')): ?>
		<div id="left_col" class="clearfix">
			<jdoc:include type="modules" name="left" style="xhtml" />
		</div>
		<?php endif; ?>

		<div id="innerwrap">

			<div id="main_content" class="clearfix">
				<jdoc:include type="component" />
			</div>

			<?php if ($this->countModules('user4')): ?>
			<div id="user4">
				<jdoc:include type="modules" name="user4" style="xhtml" />
			</div>
			<?php endif; ?>

			<?php if ($this->countModules('user5')): ?>
			<div id="user5">
				<jdoc:include type="modules" name="user5" style="xhtml" />
			</div>
			<?php endif; ?>

			<?php if ($this->countModules('user6')): ?>
			<div id="user6">
				<jdoc:include type="modules" name="user6" style="xhtml" />
			</div>
			<?php endif; ?>

		</div>

		<?php if ($this->countModules('right')): ?>
		<div id="right_col" class="clearfix">
			<jdoc:include type="modules" name="right" style="xhtml" />
		</div>
		<?php endif; ?>
	</div>

	<div id="bottom">

		<?php if ($this->countModules('user7')): ?>
		<div id="user7">
			<jdoc:include type="modules" name="user7" style="rounded" />
		</div>
		<?php endif; ?>

		<?php if ($this->countModules('user8')): ?>
		<div id="user8">
			<jdoc:include type="modules" name="user8" style="rounded" />
		</div>
```

Figure 9.22 The remaining PHP functions added to the index.php file

Creating the Stylesheets

You can start with any standards-based CSS design and make it work with Joomla. As long as your index.php page has the correct `jdoc` commands and the templateDetails.xml file lists all template files and folders, your design will work.

Most Joomla template designers like to keep the layout separate from the core Joomla CSS styles. To do this, you need to create a separate layout.css file. This makes adjusting the layout of the template easier.

To create the layout.css stylesheet:

1. Create a CSS stylesheet named `layout.css` and save it to the css folder in your myTemplate folder.
2. Style the layout CSS.

   It is up to you whether you want a fixed or fluid layout, and whether you want three columns or two. The example in **Figures 9.23** and **9.24** set up a three-column layout with no images. It is a good idea to create your CSS anticipating the site will expand and change.

   Make sure the layout.css stylesheet is linked in your index.php page.
3. Log in to the back end of the site as a super administrator.

   As long as the entire myTemplate folder is in the Joomla template folder, your template should appear in the administrative back end.

```
/* CSS Document */

*{
margin: 0px;
padding: 0px;
}
body {
    background-color: #333333;
}
.clearfix {
    padding: 7px;
}
#wrapper {
    min-width: 800px;
    max-width: 980px;
    margin-right: auto;
    margin-left: auto;
}
#header {
    height: 150px;
    background-color: #CCCCCC;
    clear: both;
    width: 100%;
}
#toolbar {
    height: 30px;
    float: right;
    clear: both;
    background-color: #999999;
}
#inset {
    width: auto;
    height: auto;
    background-color: #8F8890;
}
#search {
    float: right;
    background-color: #999999;
}
#mainnav {
    background-color: #333333;
    height: 40px;
    clear: both;
}
```

Figure 9.23 The basic CSS layout file

```
#breadcrumbs {
    background-color: #CCCCCC;
    clear: both;
}
#top {
    clear: both;
    background-color: #999999;
}
#maincontentwrap {
    width: 100%;
    margin-right: auto;
    margin-left: auto;
}
#left_col {
    float: left;
    width: 20%;
    overflow: hidden;
    background-color: #CCCCCC;
}
#main_content {
    float: left;
    width: 55%;
    background-color: #999999;
}
#right_col {
    float: left;
    width: 20%;
    overflow: hidden;
    background-color: #CCCCCC;
}
#bottom {
    clear: both;
    background-color: #CCCCCC;
}
#footer {
    clear: both;
    background-color: #999999;
}
```

Figure 9.24 The basic CSS layout file

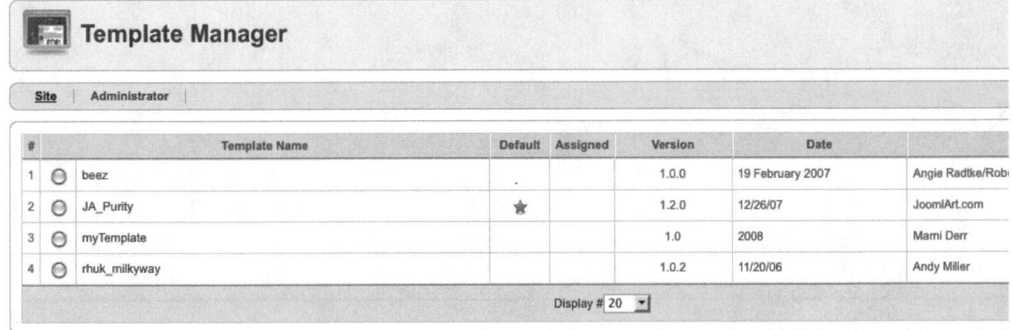

Figure 9.25 The Template Manager

4. Choose Extensions > Template Manager.

   The Template Manager opens. Notice that the myTemplate template was added to the list of templates for the web site (**Figure 9.25**).

5. Click the radio button next to myTemplate, and then click the Default icon to set myTemplate as the default for the site's front end.

continues on next page

6. Click Preview.

   Not very pretty, no, but you get the point. The site displays, and everything that has a position assigned to it that exists in the template is displayed (**Figure 9.26**).

   You have yet to style the Joomla core CSS, and the positions in your new template vary from those in the JA_Purity template used originally to assign positions.

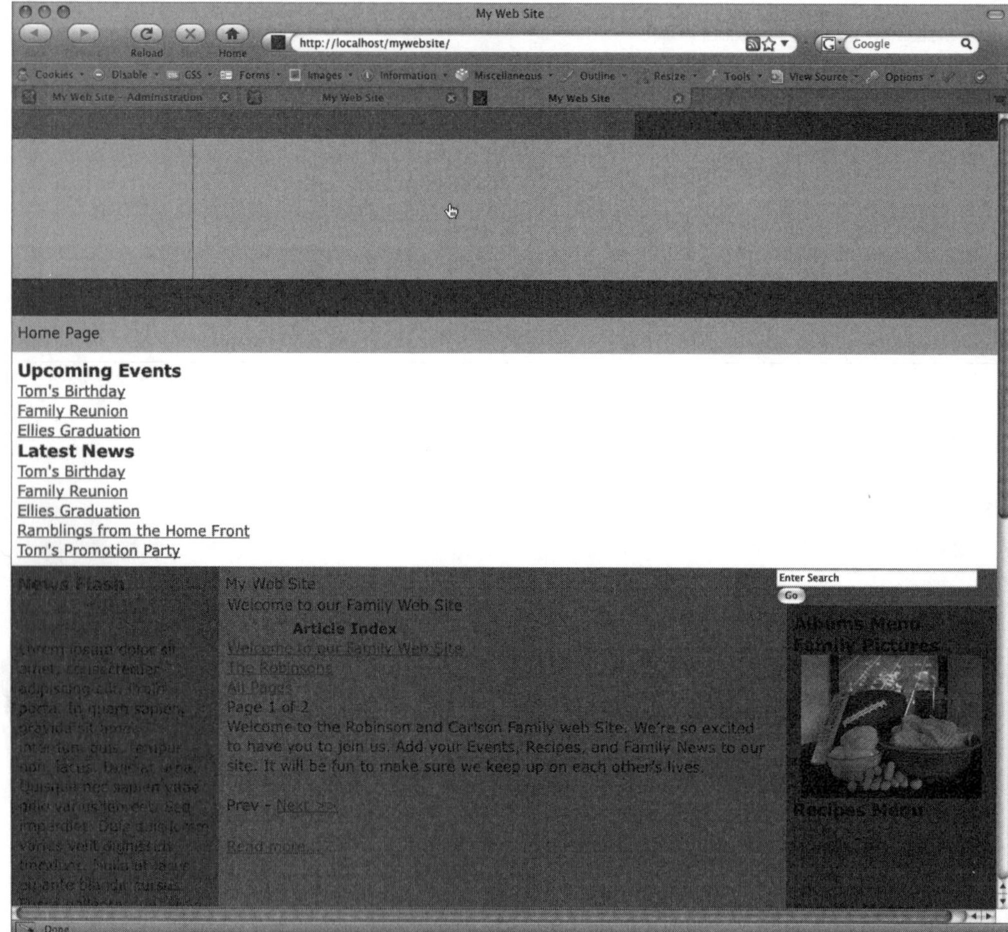

Figure 9.26 The results of the MyTemplate applied to the web site

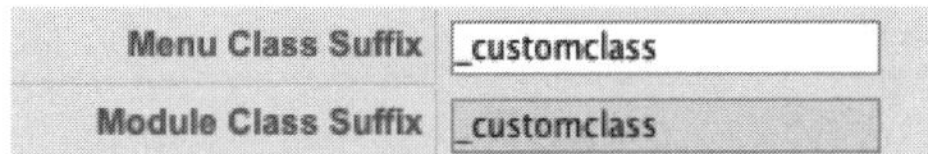

Figure 9.27 An example of where to add the custom CSS class suffixes

Joomla Base CSS Style Tables

We cannot walk you through creating each style; those depend entirely on your particular design. To show you what tools are at your disposal, however, we list all the Joomla core classes and what they are applied to. In addition, you can find a list of where the classes are used on the Joomla.org documentation site at:

```
http://docs.joomla.org/List_of_Joomla!_
→ generated_core_CSS_classes
```

To override Joomla classes:

1. Choose Extensions > Module Manager.
2. Choose the module you want to style.
3. In the Parameters area, enter the class name in the Module Class Suffix field to style the module.
4. To override menu items, enter the class name in the Menu Class Suffix field (**Figure 9.27**).

The following tables give a basic overview of the core CSS classes used by default in Joomla. The descriptions are generalizations to give you an idea of where to style default classes; they are by no means exclusive.

✔ Tips

- To view the styles being used, you can open your web browser, navigate to the front end of your web site, and select view source. You will see the classes in the source pages.
- In Joomla 1.5, you can also override the core Joomla styles by using the component's or module's own templates. These are located in their respective folders called tmpl. For more information on overriding Joomla core styles and creating templates, visit our web site www.writingyourdreams.com.

Table 9.1

Global CSS Styles	
CLASS NAME	DESCRIPTION
a	Global styles to be used unless a more specific style is specified.
a:hover	
a:active	
a:visited	
a.image	
a.image:hover	
h1	
h2	
h3	
h4	
h5	
li	
p	
td	
th	
ul	

Table 9.2

Articles = Content Styles	
CLASS NAME	DESCRIPTION
SECTION	
.sections	Styles used for a section layout.
.sectiontableentry	
.sectiontablefooter	
.sectiontableheader	
CATEGORY	
.category	Styles used for category list and links.
a.category	
ARTICLES	
.article_separator	Styles used in article layouts.
.author	
.blog	
.blogsection	
.blog_more	
.blog_heading	
.content_rating	
.content_vote	
.contentdescription	
.contentheading	
.contentpagetitle	
.contentpane	
.contentpaneopen	
.contenttoc	
.createdate	
.created-date	
.date	
.hastip	
.highlight	
.intro	
.title	
.modifydate	
.mosimage	
.mosimagecaption	
.readon	
.small	
.smalldark	
.wrapper	Style used when selecting the wrapper layout.

Table 9.3

Banners	
CLASS NAME	DESCRIPTION
.bannerfooter .bannergroup .bannerheader .banneritem	Styles used when creating the banner component and module.

Table 9.4

Breadcrumbs Styles	
CLASS NAME	DESCRIPTION
.pathway a.pathway:link a.pathway:visited a.pathway:active a.pathway:hover	Styles used with the breadcrumb navigation.

Table 9.5

Components	
CLASS NAME	DESCRIPTION
.componentheading	Style used for the main component heading.

Table 9.6

Forms and Input Boxes	
CLASS NAME	DESCRIPTION
.button .buttonheading .contact_email .fieldset .input .inputbox .search .searchintro .selectbox .text_area	Styles used for all buttons and form fields unless otherwise specified.

Table 9.7

Main Menu Navigation Styles	
CLASS NAME	DESCRIPTION
MAIN MENU	
.mainlevel a.mainlevel a.mainlevel:visited a.mainlevel:hover a.mainlevel:active	Styles used by the main menu.
SUBMENU	
a.sublevel a.sublevel:visited a.sublevel:active a.sublevel:hover	Styles for submenus under the main menu.

Table 9.8

Modules – General	
CLASS NAME	DESCRIPTION
.latestnews .mostread .newsfeed .pollstableborder	Styles for individual modules.

Table 9.9

Modules – Table Styles	
CLASS NAME	DESCRIPTION
table.moduletable table.moduletable th	Styles used for modules that use a table layout.

Table 9.10

Modules – XHTML or Rounded Styles	
CLASS NAME	**DESCRIPTION**
div.module	Use these styles to create rounded or pure table-less modules.
div.module h3	
.module li	
.module ul	
.module a:link	
.module a:visited	
.module a:hover	
.module a:active	
ROUNDED CORNERS	
.module	
.module div	
.module div div	
.module div div div	
.module div div div div	

Table 9.11

Page Navigation	
CLASS NAME	**DESCRIPTION**
a.pagenav	Styles for the page navigation, previous, next, page count, and so on.
a.pagenav:hover	
.back_button	
.pagenav	
.pagebar	
.pagenav_prev	
.pagenav_next	
.pagenavcounter	

Table 9.12

Tabbed Edits	
CLASS NAME	**DESCRIPTION**
.adminform	Styles used to override the background styling.
.code	
.edit-tabs	
.message	
.moscode	
.pagetext	
.ontab	
.offtab	
.tabheading	
.tabpadding	

A

Local and Remote Servers

It is best practice to use a local server, running on your computer, when first creating a Joomla web site. If you do not already have a local server installed on your computer, the easiest way to install a web server is to use such prepackaged software as MAMP for the Mac or XAMPP for Windows.

The benefits to working on a local web server are:

- Faster to create and test the site
- Reduces the risk of bringing down your live "production" site
- Allows you to test third-party extensions, before deployment on a live site

This appendix describes two local server environments, and it shows you a simple method to upload your entire site to a remote (hosted) server.

Installing a Local Server (Windows)

To install a local server for a Windows operating system, such as Windows XP or Vista, you must have a version that supports Windows Internet Information Services (IIS). If IIS is not enabled or not available, a web server will not run on your computer.

To install XAMPP on a Windows computer:

1. In a web browser, type `www.apachefriends.org`.

   The Apache Friends web site opens.

2. Scroll down until you see the XAMPP icon right underneath the heading "Our most important project," and click the XAMPP icon (**Figure A.1**).

3. Scroll down, and then click XAMPP for Windows (**Figure A.2**).

4. Under Download, click XAMPP.

5. Under Basic Package, click Installer.

6. Download the installer file and double-click the file that you downloaded.

Our most important project

XAMPP

Many people know from their own experience that it's not easy to install an Apache web server and it gets harder if you want to add MySQL, PHP and Perl. XAMPP is an easy to install Apache distribution containing MySQL, PHP and Perl. XAMPP is really very easy to install and to use - just download, extract and start.

At the moment there are four XAMPP versions:

- a version for Linux systems (tested for Ubuntu, SuSE, RedHat, Mandrake and Debian),
- a version for Windows 98, NT, 2000, 2003, XP and Vista,
- a beta version for Solaris SPARC (developed and tested under Solaris 8),
- and a beta version for Mac OS X.

These Mac OS X and Solaris versions of XAMPP are still in the first steps of development. Use at you own risk!

Want more?

Look at our projects page to find out more about our other projects.

Figure A.1 The XAMPP web site

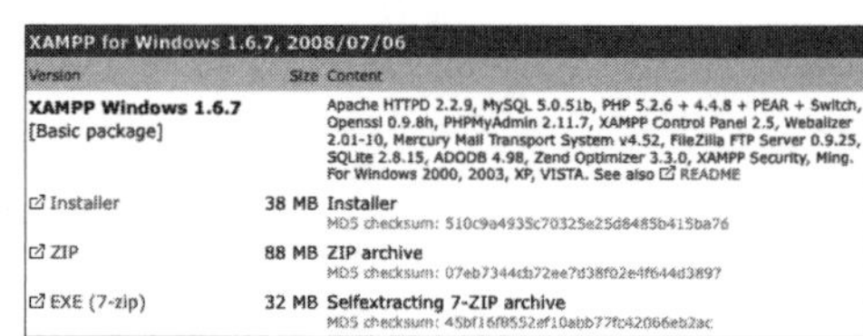

XAMPP for Windows 1.6.7, 2008/07/06

Version	Size	Content
XAMPP Windows 1.6.7 [Basic package]		Apache HTTPD 2.2.9, MySQL 5.0.51b, PHP 5.2.6 + 4.4.8 + PEAR + Switch, Openssl 0.9.8h, PHPMyAdmin 2.11.7, XAMPP Control Panel 2.5, Webalizer 2.01-10, Mercury Mail Transport System v4.52, FileZilla FTP Server 0.9.25, SQLite 2.8.15, ADODB 4.98, Zend Optimizer 3.3.0, XAMPP Security, Ming. For Windows 2000, 2003, XP, VISTA. See also README
Installer	38 MB	**Installer** MD5 checksum: 510c9a4935c70325e25d8485b415ba76
ZIP	88 MB	**ZIP archive** MD5 checksum: 07eb7344cb72ee7d38f02e4f644d3897
EXE (7-zip)	32 MB	**Selfextracting 7-ZIP archive** MD5 checksum: 45bf16f8552ef10abb77fc42066eb2ac

Figure A.2 Downloading XAMPP

Figure A.3 The installer wizard

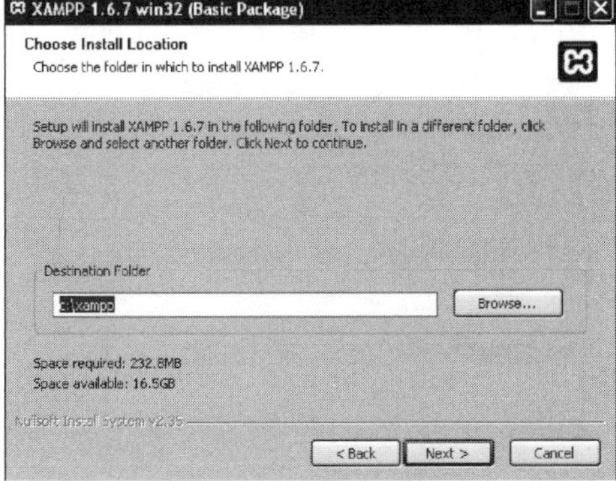

Figure A.4 XAMPP install location

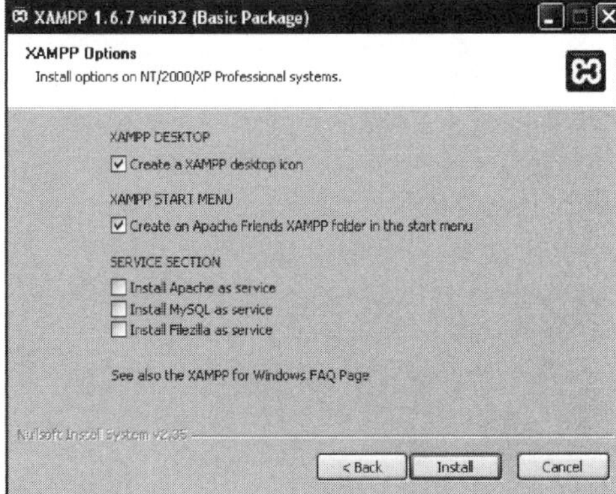

Figure A.5 The install selection screen

7. Choose your language, and then click OK (**Figure A.3**).

   The installer wizard starts.

8. Click Next.

9. Select the location where you want to install XAMPP, and then click Next (**Figure A.4**).

10. Click Install, and then click Finish.

    You can choose to install Apache, MySQL, and FileZilla as a service. This starts Apache, MySQL, and FileZilla automatically. If you don't want the services to start automatically, do not select these options (**Figure A.5**).

To start your local server:

1. Ensure Windows IIS services are enabled. See your operating system documentation for how to do this.

2. Open XAMPP, and start Apache and MySQL server.

3. In a web browser, type `http://localhost`.

   This gives you access to all the files located at the root of your web server. All the web sites created and tested on a local server go into the htdocs directory. This is the web root folder. Typing `localhost` takes you to the server root. Typing `localhost/mywebsitename` opens the web site.

Installing a Local Server (Macintosh)

The Apple operating system, 10.4 and higher, comes with Apache and PHP preinstalled. This leaves only the installation of the MySQL database. Because installation and enabling varies, we recommend installing the MAMP package for those not already familiar with web servers, databases, and how to configure them manually.

To install MAMP:

1. In a web browser, type `www.mamp.info/en/mamp.html`.
2. Click Download (**Figure A.6**).
3. Click the appropriate MAMP file for your Mac platform (**Figure A.7**).
4. Double-click the .dmg package, and then drag the MAMP folder into your applications folder.
5. Choose Applications > MAMP, and start MAMP.

   This opens the MAMP start page in a web browser, and the Start Servers dialog appears (**Figure A.8**).
6. Make sure Apache and MySQL are started.
7. In your browser window, type `localhost`.

   This gives you access to all the files located at the root of your web server. All the web sites created and tested on a local server go into the htdocs directory, the web root folder. Typing `localhost` takes you to the server root. Typing `localhost/mywebsitename` opens the web site.

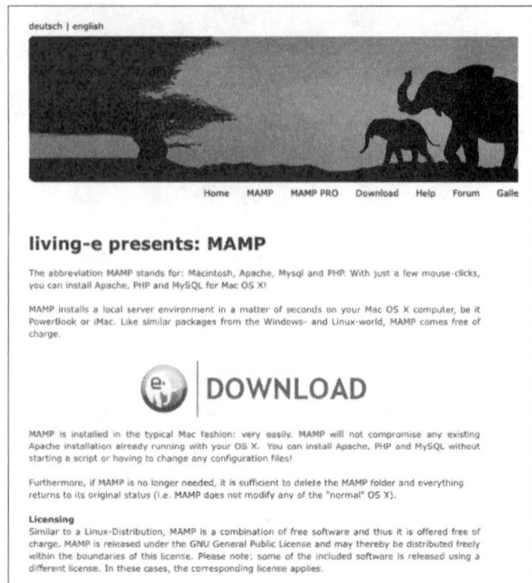

Figure A.6 The MAMP download page

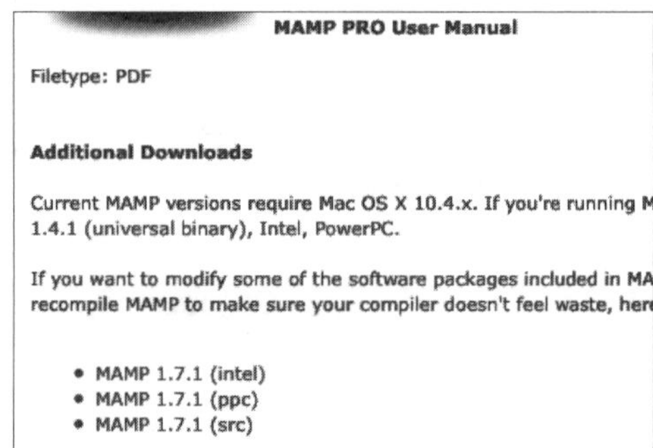

Figure A.7 Selecting your MAMP package.

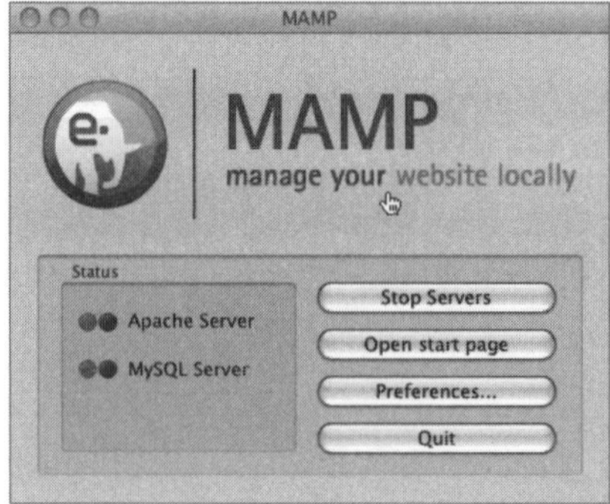

Figure A.8 The MAMP dialog box, showing the servers running

Uploading the Test Site to a Remote Host

One of the main themes in the questions we find on the forums is people struggling with uploading a Joomla site to a hosted server. Hosting companies vary, and so do the processes by which you can place your Joomla site on a remote server. However, we have come up with a simple way that should work for most hosting companies. We have tested this process on a virtual dedicated server and a standard shared hosting account.

Before you begin you need to:

- Know the location and name of your web server's root folder.
- Have PHP and MySQL installed and enabled on your hosted server.
- Create a MySQL database for your Joomla site on the hosted server.
- Know the database name, user name, and password on the hosted server.
- Have FTP privileges to the hosted server.

To install Joomla on a hosted server:

1. FTP the entire Joomla package to the root folder of your hosted server.

   This is a clean package installation and will run through your browser.

2. On your local server, open phpMyadmin, and then export the database for your local Joomla web site to a .sql file.

3. In a browser window, enter your domain name to open your web site. If you uploaded the Joomla files, the installation process will begin.

4. Follow the Joomla installation to completion, adding your hosted server information.

5. Once complete, remove the install.php file and installation folder from the hosted server.

6. Using phpMyadmin, log in to your MySQL database, and import the MySQL database you exported from your local site.

   Your web site should be completely installed and working on the hosted server.

   If you experience problems, generally it is due to Joomla being unable to communicate with the database. To fix this issue, you can modify the configuration.php file. The database hostname, username, and password must match your hosted database.

The configuration.php File

The configuration.php file keeps your web site global configuration settings, passwords, and user names to communicate with your database. It looks like this:

```
<?php
class JConfig {
/* Site Settings */
var $offline = '0';
var $offline_message = 'This site is
→ down for maintenance.<br /> Please
→ check back again soon.';
var $sitename = 'WritersLatte';
var $editor = 'tinymce';
var $list_limit = '20';
var $legacy = '0';
/* Debug Settings */
var $debug = '0';
var $debug_lang = '0';
/* Database Settings */
var $dbtype = 'mysql';
var $host = 'localhost';
var $user = 'root';
var $password = 'root';
var $db = 'mywebsitedb';
var $dbprefix = 'jos_';
/* Server Settings */
var $live_site = '';
var $secret = 'fKyJPY3X3PsZ3kOm';
var $gzip = '0';
var $error_reporting = '-1';
var $helpurl = 'http://help.joomla.org';
var $xmlrpc_server = '0';
var $ftp_host = '127.0.0.1';
var $ftp_port = '21';
var $ftp_user = '';
var $ftp_pass = '';
var $ftp_root = '';
var $ftp_enable = '0';
/* Locale Settings */
var $offset = '0';
var $offset_user = '0';
/* Mail Settings */
var $mailer = 'mail';
var $mailfrom = 'admin@mywebsite.com';
var $fromname = 'My Web Site';
var $sendmail = '/usr/sbin/sendmail';
var $smtpauth = '0';
var $smtpuser = '';
var $smtppass = '';
var $smtphost = 'localhost';
/* Cache Settings */
var $caching = '0';
var $cachetime = '15';
var $cache_handler = 'file';
/* Meta Settings */
var $MetaDesc = 'Joomla! - the dynamic
→ portal engine and content management
→ system';
var $MetaKeys = 'joomla, Joomla';
var $MetaTitle = '1';
var $MetaAuthor = '1';
/* SEO Settings */
var $sef           = '0';
var $sef_rewrite    = '0';
var $sef_suffix     = '0';
/* Feed Settings */
var $feed_limit    = 10;
var $log_path = '/Applications/MAMP/
→ htdocs/writerslatte/logs';
var $tmp_path = '/Applications/MAMP/
→ htdocs/writerslatte/tmp';
/* Session Setting */
var $lifetime = '15';
var $session_handler = 'database';
}
?>
```

B

RESOURCES

As with all open source applications, Joomla's supporting communities—from developers, to extension creators and template designers, from personal blogs to tutorials—is vast.

This appendix gives you a brief overview of the major improvements of Joomla 1.5.x over 1.0.x, examples of sites currently using Joomla, and a few links for more information, templates, and extensions.

What's New in Joomla 1.5.x

An overview of the improvements of Joomla 1.5.x over Joomla 1.0.x follows (to get a full list of differences, visit www.joomla.org):

- Completely reworked administrative interface
- Improved template preview
- Better program logic separated from design logic; easier for designers to truly customize every detail of a Joomla template
- New plugin manager
- One place to install/uninstall everything
- Multi-CSS file editing
- Full support for Atom 1.0 and RSS 2.0 feeds
- Improved accessibility and SEF options
- Improved URL generation
- Increased focus on internationalization, including full UTF-8 support, RTL support, and translation using INI files
- Native LDAP support
- XML-RPC support
- A streamlined component call interface that allows easy implementation of Ajax applications
- Completely overhauled Joomla core programming framework

Web Links for Joomla Resources

It would be impossible to list all the resources available for Joomla. Here is a very brief list of sites that have impressed and helped us in our Joomla travels.

Application and Information Links

`www.joomla.org`

`www.phpbb.com`

`www.compassdesigns.com`

Joomla Template Links

`www.rocketThemes.com`

`www.joomla-templates.com`

`www.yootheme.com`

`www.JoomlArt.com`

`www.joomlashack.com`

Joomla Extensions Links

`http://extensions/joomla.org`

`www.m65.net`

`www.joomlapolis.com`

`www.ijoomla.com`

`www.ninjoomla.com`

`www.rocketwerx.com`

`www.ijoomla.com`

Web Sites Using Joomla

The following web sites all use the Joomla CMS. These examples show just how diverse and flexible Joomla is.

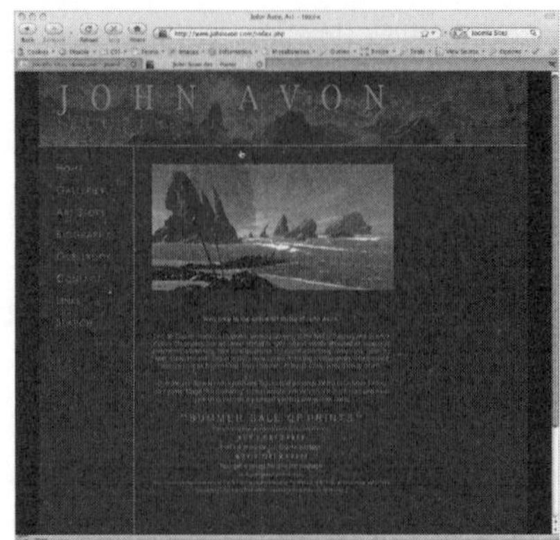

Creative artist John Avon's gallery site, at www.johnavon.com

Fantasy and Science Fiction Publishing House, Tor, at www.tor.com

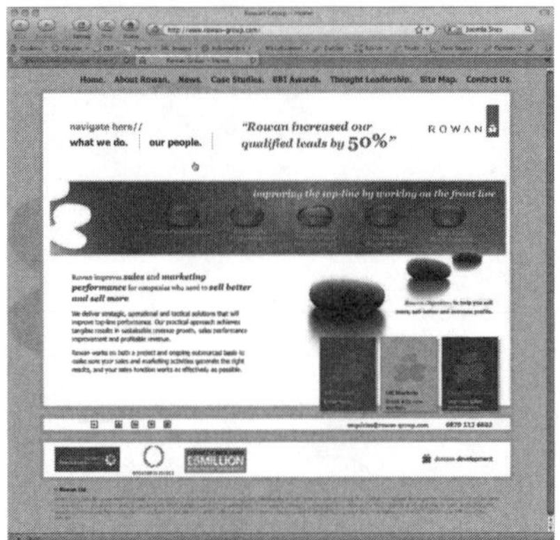

Consulting firm, Rowan, at www.rowan-group.com

Italian hotel and resort site, Grande Real Villa, at www.grandrealvillaitaliahotel.com

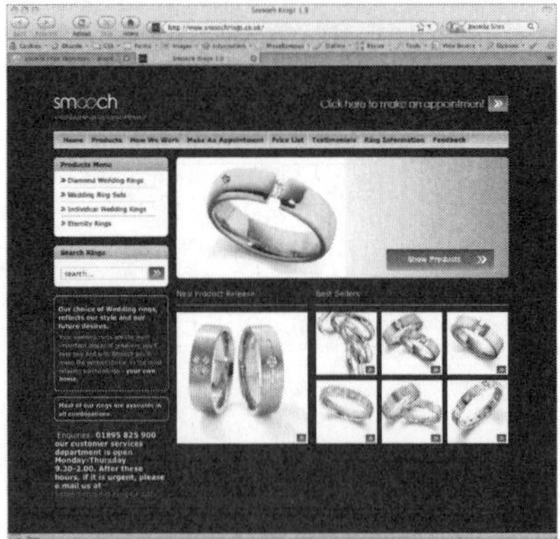

E-commerce jewelry site, Smooch Rings, at www.smoochrings.co.uk

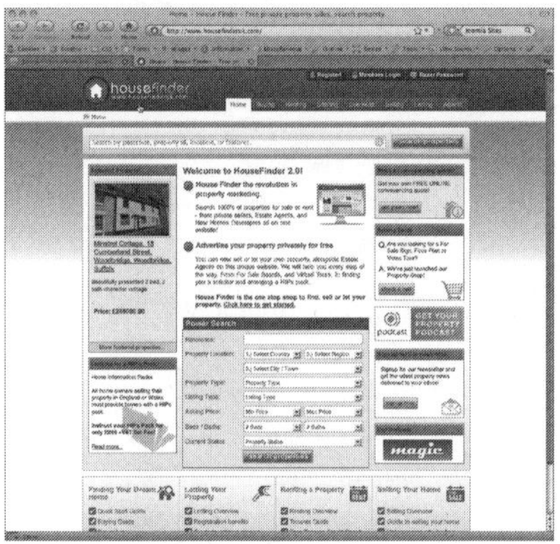

Real Estate locators, Housefinder, at www.housefinderuk.com

A personal blog on Joomla and the web, My Way to Success, at www.mywaytosucess.com

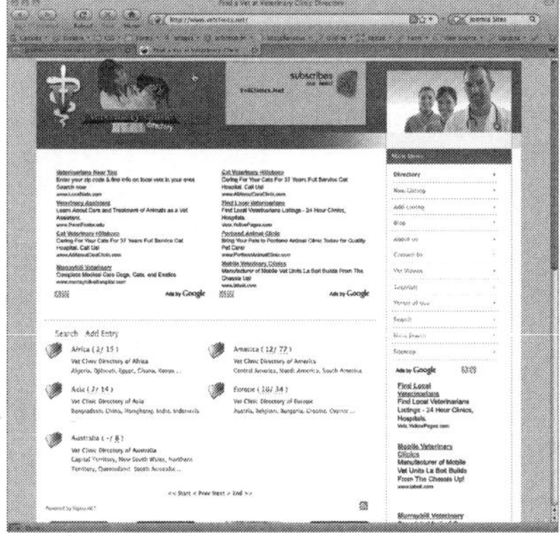

A portal for Veterinary Clinics directory at www.vetclinics.com

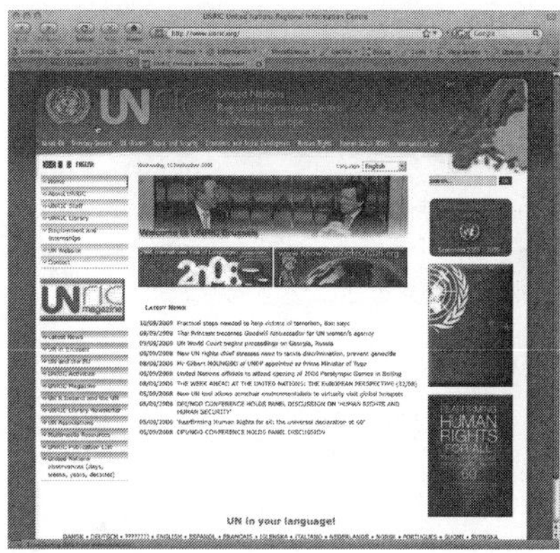

Government agency, The United Nations Regional Information Centre for Western Europe, at www.unric.org

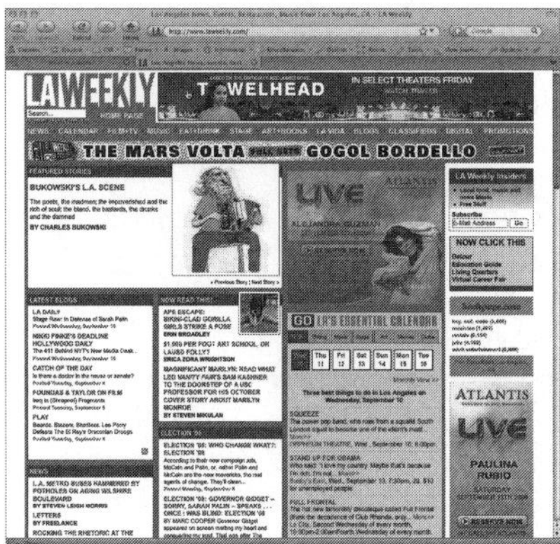

An online magazine by LA Weekly, at www.laweekly.com

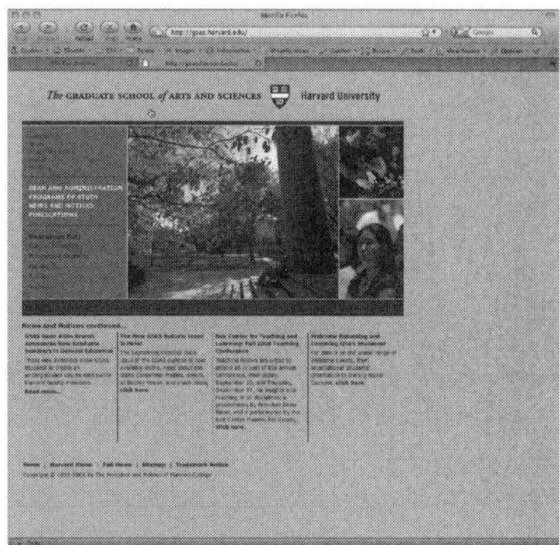

Academic institution, Harvard University, at www.gsas.harvard.edu

INDEX

B

C

D

E

F

G

H

I

INDEX

N

INDEX

O

P

R

S

T

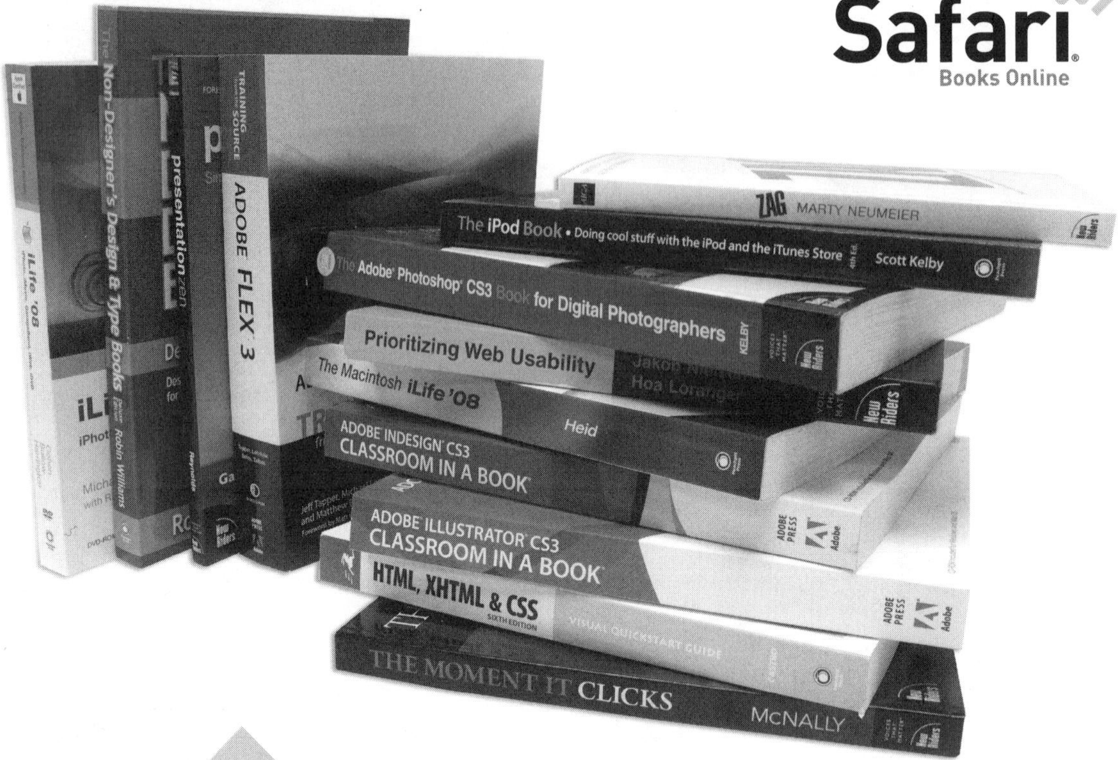
The Non-Designer's Design & Type Books
Robin Williams
presentationzen
ADOBE FLEX 3
ZAG
MARTY NEUMEIER
The iPod Book • Doing cool stuff with the iPod and the iTunes Store
Scott Kelby
The Adobe Photoshop CS3 Book for Digital Photographers
KELBY
Prioritizing Web Usability
Hoa Loranger
The Macintosh iLife '08
Heid
ADOBE INDESIGN CS3 CLASSROOM IN A BOOK
ADOBE ILLUSTRATOR CS3 CLASSROOM IN A BOOK
HTML, XHTML & CSS
SIXTH EDITION
VISUAL QUICKSTART GUIDE
THE MOMENT IT CLICKS
McNALLY
New Riders
ADOBE PRESS
Adobe